'This A–Z is a superlative, incisive update of books navigating the forever rapidly changing South African political landscape. It is essential reading, a reference work for all who need swift and accurate insights into South Africa's roller-coaster politics. It is entertaining. It captures the present, offers glimpses of the future, and remains historically anchored. It is an authoritative roadmap to South African politics, 25 years into democracy.'

– Prof. Susan Booysen, author and political analyst

'This book is one of the most valuable and timely contributions in understanding our complex expansive political landscape of a noisy, argumentative and robust young democracy. This is an easy, accessible and detailed guide to our various role players.'

– Dr Somadoda Fikeni, academic, community development activist and political analyst

First published by Jacana Media (Pty) Ltd in 2019

10 Orange Street
Sunnyside
Auckland Park 2092
South Africa
+2711 628 3200
www.jacana.co.za

ISBN 978-1-4314-2841-0

Cover design by Maggie Davey and Shawn Paikin
Editing by Lara Jacob
Design and layout by Alexandra Turner
Proofreading by Megan Mance
Set in Stempel Garamond 9/12pt
Printed and bound by ABC Press, Cape Town
Job no. 003384

See a complete list of Jacana titles at www.jacana.co.za

The A–Z of South African Politics

People, parties and players

Written and compiled by
Kashiefa Ajam, Kevin Ritchie, Lebogang Seale,
Janet Smith & Thabiso Thakali

For Michael Komape (6) and Lumka Mketwa (5),
innocents who lost their lives in school pit latrines because of dangerous politics.
And to all the children whose human rights are denied by politicians.

You are not forgotten.

Foreword

Professor Thuli Madonsela

A PARADOX OF OUR TIME IS THAT we now live in a world of enormous access to information, yet actual knowledge eludes many, if not most of us, often at our peril. This book is a collection of issues and people that shape our modern country, yet one of its unusual features is that it shows how its subject matter in fact transcends what we think of as 'politics'. And that is because gaining knowledge about our political parties, political events, key political actors and social movements gives us access to uniquely South African phenomena.

Books can inspire us to love or hate. Books can influence who and what we admire or despise. Our perspective on what's important and what isn't is also greatly influenced by what we read. Books are generally an important socialising agent which impacts on our values and perspectives of what is normal and aberrant.

Books have been stepping stones, clues and triggers for me in my line of work as a lawyer and investigator. Books heighten our interest in people, things, places, ideas and values, leading us to do more searching on our own. During my term as Public Protector, my team and I often relied on books to get leads on what to look for and where to look.

The book you're reading now does all these good – and not so good – things. Traversing various subjects, its main contribution is as an introduction to the most prominent South Africans and events that have shaped our recent history.

When I was growing up, teachers used to give us lessons in general knowledge at school as a way of developing our understanding of the who-is-who in contemporary political and social history. It seems this doesn't happen in classrooms anymore.

Recently I noted a tweet referring to Cyril Ramaphosa's wife's surname as 'Moloi'. That is in fact the surname of Dr Precious Moloi-Motsepe, who is married to Patrice Motsepe, who is the president's brother-in-law as the president is married to Dr Tshepo Motsepe, Patrice's sister. Complicated for sure, but I figured that at least the tweeter knew *something*.

Many of the good people who approach me with great admiration on the streets are like that too. They refer to me as 'minister', 'Parliamentarian' or 'the woman on TV'. But that saddens me because knowing the powers of the Public Protector and using its services promptly may save a job, a business or a long wait for a pension payout from government. The same applies to knowing as much as possible about all the other institutions, processes and individuals mentioned in this book.

If your interest is in 'democracy literacy', a pursuit we encourage at the Thuma Foundation, it may offer a place from which to start navigating. It also provides ideas on dominant trends and figures in democracy leadership. It helps to know where to go for what, and what to expect from whom. I also believe the book can be a useful introductory text to the forever-changing political landscape in South Africa.

This cross between a Little Black Book and a history narrative gives you a sense of who or what is likely to move the needle – whether forwards or backwards – thus giving you a measuring instrument if you want to do some analysis of your own.

This may give you some idea of how much the people and things in it will really influence the course of history.

The book provides some insights into ideologies and the trajectory of important yet thorny issues such as land redistribution, corruption and ethics. I'd recommend it to young people like those we train on epic leadership in the Thuma Foundation, because their ability to be able to identify themes in society and develop opinions about those will be critical for them. I'm also convinced lawyers will find this a useful guide to recent watershed jurisprudence on various matters, particularly on government procurement, and areas of administrative and constitutional law. Some of the cases also touch on human rights and related dimensions of social justice.

In this regard, the book is likely to be a useful starting point for the national brigade of ambassadors such as those we are grooming at Stellenbosch University to lead the nation on an 'M-Plan', which is an ambitious project that seeks to awaken and leverage civic input towards ending poverty and reducing structural inequality by 2030. This is as envisaged by the United Nations Sustainable Development Goals and in our own National Development Plan.

Through this book, business leaders, investors and start-up entrepreneurs may gain a greater appreciation for environmental contours in a volatile, ambiguous, complex and ambivalent operations sector. It could provide them with better navigational preparedness and be a source of hope as its subject matter often reminds us how much this country is, indeed, an 'overcomer'.

I must point out that the authors naturally have their own take on people, events and ideas, which you may agree or disagree with. You might even find some of those opinions and perspectives offensive. But one thing is clear – this is a book whose ideas are worth examining, even if you regard the authors as proffering 'alternative' views. Understanding how a range of influences – such as those in this book – can affect our own take on people and events is priceless for those who believe we don't have to buy into the so-called 'dominant' view. We are free to engage and, like the authors here, offer our opinions in an impactful way.

The commentary flows easily as it looks at seemingly innocuous issues and then moves into some of South Africa's toughest recent challenges to democracy, including state capture and the grip that at least two families appear to have had on government's human machinery.

The book has its unique interpretation of the events and personalities, and I certainly didn't give all of these the thumbs-up, but it's a vital and useful compact reference resource – even for foreigners, comedians and scriptwriters. Those are, of course, among our most penetrating commentators.

I hope *The A–Z of South African Politics* sparks interesting conversations, even if only about its authors' observations. But I particularly hope its contents will get people talking about the business ahead of us in terms of rebooting our democracy while addressing our unfinished business. It highlights our vulnerability as much as it exposes how much our hard-earned Constitution should eventually result in a sustainable peace.

Stellenbosch, January 2019

Introduction

It wasn't deliberate, but it is notable that this political reference book recounting events of the last 10 years begins with the shack-dwellers' movement Abahlali baseMjondolo and ends with Jacob Zuma. To organise the book with this start and end was not a considered plan but, once done, should be seen as capturing the essence of the past decade. This 2019 guide describes a new era of both activism and post-liberation politics – a time of fighting against corruption as the political elites cement their power a quarter-century on. As it crosses from left to right, the book captures the polar opposite nature of our national psyche.

If this book, *The A–Z of South African Politics*, was a narrative, it would have started on 6 April 2009 when Advocate Mokotedi 'Cocky' Mpshe cut a forlorn figure at the National Prosecuting Authority (NPA) headquarters in Pretoria as he stepped up to the mic to address a press conference. The acting head of the NPA was about to make an announcement that would change South Africa's course. Mpshe drew an emotional silence out of those gathered in front of him and then stated that he would be dropping charges against the new ANC president Jacob Zuma, thus opening the doors to the Union Buildings to a man who had faced more than a dozen charges of racketeering, corruption, money laundering and fraud. A total of 783 incidents had been described in the court papers.

Mpshe could blame Scorpions head Leonard McCarthy. He could blame his predecessor at the NPA Advocate Bulelani Ngcuka, who had worked behind Mpshe's back with McCarthy. He could have wondered why his life had taken such a turn. He may have looked back fondly at his comparatively quiet life as a judge of the Land Claims Court, having previously led evidence at the Truth and Reconciliation Commission after working his way up the ranks from being prosecutor and magistrate in the bantustan of Bophuthatswana. But Mpshe couldn't get around the McCarthy-Ngcuka 'spy tapes', in which those two men discussed a way forward to see Zuma prosecuted.

And indeed, on 7 April 2009, the case against the most powerful man in the ANC – and, soon, the nation – was withdrawn in the High Court in Durban. A month later, Zuma was sworn in as president, and so began a 10-year period of considerable descent for South Africa. The darkest and most dirty deeds would multiply into the state capture in this decade. Billions have been stolen, wasted and diverted while parastatals, the security infrastructure and our moral stature have crumbled to nothing.

One could say that Mpshe's unforgettable press conference provided the optics for the moment at which the last edition in 2009 of *The Mail & Guardian A–Z of SA Politics* ended. This new edition, the sixth, takes off as the advocate reckoned with history. Containing more than 300 entries, the book catalogues the Guptas via the Saxonwold Shebeen, documents the rise of the Red Berets, tracks the re-emergence of investigative journalism and much more. We hope it provides a unique means of understanding the who, the what and the why of the nation once optimistically dubbed a 'rainbow'.

Although it uses the A–Z convention to map people, parties and the major players, it also allows you, the reader, to extract the change agents, the power brokers, those suspected of capture and the captured, using a separate navigation tool for quick reference for each. Some entries include two of these sub-titles, as it is of course possible to be both a power broker and suspected of capture. Change agents are those people and entities who and which have the skills and power to articulate a vision and are then most likely to facilitate and steer it into reality. Generally, they are portrayed as having a positive effect, and working towards the social good. Power brokers are those with the greatest influence on decisions. With an expansive base of useful connections and experience, these are people and players with the real reach. Power brokers may have either a positive or a negative image attached to them, and may be working for social good or for narrow gains. Those suspected of capture are the ones who have not been nailed yet, but where the cloud over them is so thick with suspicion that it has cast a shadow from which they can't yet emerge. The captured are those who have already been named and affirmatively linked to the corruption that has brought South Africa down, and who, in most cases, now await the legal processes that may well see them jailed or rendered outcasts for long periods to come. In addition, most of the entries allow you to quickly see where each is positioned in terms of party allegiance and, where it comes to actual political parties, their latest documented support. That scope is common to all, unless we are referring to a concept like 'coalitions', or a basic model of governance, like a commission of inquiry.

We had to exercise version control of this map at the end of January 2019 – before President Cyril Ramaphosa announced the final date of the election set for May – as we had to meet publishing deadlines. But the fluidity of South African politics is such that, by the time this book is on the shelves, it is likely some of the captured may be in the process of prosecution, some of those suspected of capture may have dug themselves an even deeper hole, some of the power brokers may have extended their sphere of influence to the good or the bad of the nation, and some of the change agents may have further climbed or taken a step down in our estimation.

We hope that you will be reminded of incidents and individuals you may have forgotten when you use this book, and that there will be as much entertainment as there are revelations. Our intention is that you will be able to use it to tie the loose ends and make essential connections in your head, while also being introduced to facts not widely known.

2019 promises to be a tipping point – an election year in an alarming and uncertain economic and political climate, in a country in which the numbers of the poor are rapidly rising while the cabal of the super-rich embraces a few more with every deal struck.

We hope you enjoy it.

Kashiefa Ajam, Kevin Ritchie, Lebogang Seale, Janet Smith, Thabiso Thakali
Johannesburg, January 2019

Abahlahi baseMjondolo (also known as AbM or the red shirts)

Activist | Non-aligned

Change Agents

AbM is a landless people's movement, which mobilises those living in informal settlements, many of whom endured evictions and forced removals.

The AbM became prominent among growing numbers of similar organisations protesting deficiencies in the democratic state. It was formed after the eThekwini municipality took a decision in 2001 to clear shack settlements, leaving large numbers of people marginalised from society.

Its message first took political hold in the troubled Clare Estate ghetto, after which it also attracted members in KwaZulu-Natal's provincial capital Pietermaritzburg, Marikana in the North West province and in Cape Town. But AbM's activism was often met with a harsh response from government, which included police harassment and torture.

Several of its members have been assassinated, including S'fiso Ngcobo, its chairperson in eKukhayeni in Marianhill outside Durban, who was gunned down at his home. On the same day that Ngcobo lost his life, AbM member Ndumiso Mnguni was shot by the security detail for the Anti-Land Invasion Unit, a paramilitary organisation, in the Foreman Road settlement.

AbM's greatest success was a Constitutional Court ruling that declared the KwaZulu-Natal Slums Act, which had allowed the city's government to stage unlawful evictions in settlements in 2001, unconstitutional.

One of its other goals has been to push government to deliver sanitation and other services to informal settlements.

AbM's call for the public expropriation of urban land for housing, rather than for its commercial value, played out dominantly in 2018 after President Cyril Ramaphosa announced in Parliament that there would be expropriation of land without compensation. It does not link itself organisationally with any political party.

In late 2018, AbM's president, S'bu Zikode, had been in hiding for three months after threats on his life. The movement had meanwhile distanced itself from those within its structures who were believed to be assisting the ANC to 'capture' it with its 55,000 members.

Abrahams, Advocate Shaun

AKA: Shaun The Sheep; Nobody's man | Former National Director of Public Prosecutions (NDPP)

Suspected of capture

The advocate, who has B Iuris, B Proc and LLB degrees from the University of

Natal in Pietermaritzburg, was the NDPP in the National Prosecuting Authority (NPA) before he retired at the end of August 2018.

His retirement from the NPA was preceded by a Constitutional Court ruling that his appointment was unconstitutional as Jacob Zuma's decision to terminate Abraham's predecessor Mxolisi Nxasana as the NDPP had been an abuse of power. Abrahams – who many times denied he was Zuma's lackey – was thus a beneficiary of Zuma's unconstitutional conduct, and the court declared the post of NDPP vacant.

In December 2017, Judge President of the Gauteng Division of the High Court Dunstan Mlambo ordered then deputy president Cyril Ramaphosa to appoint a new director as Zuma, still the president, had a corruption case pending against him, rendering him conflicted. The president would, under normal circumstances, appoint the NDPP.

Abrahams drew attention after his appointment in 2015 when he was politically linked to former acting NDPP, advocate Nomgcobo Jiba, whom he elevated to the key position of head of National Prosecution Services (NPS) – the most senior post at the NPA after that of national director. It could be said that being the head of prosecutions was more important than being the boss who could, if a president so wanted, simply be a figurehead.

Abrahams withdrew charges of fraud and perjury which Nxasana had laid against Jiba in relation to her unlawful decision to prosecute General Johan Booysen – the former head of the KwaZulu-Natal Directorate for Priority Crime Investigation (the Hawks) – for racketeering.

Advocate Silas Ramaite, who was effectively demoted by Abrahams to head corporate services and the witness protection unit of the NPA, was previously the deputy NDPP. Upon Abrahams's retirement, Ramaphosa, by then the president, appointed Ramaite as acting head of the NPA until Advocate Shamila Batohi was awarded the post in December 2018.

African Christian Democratic Party (ACDP)

Political Party | Conservative | Number of seats in Parliament in 2018: 3

On the way down

The ninth-largest party in Parliament, the ACDP opposes abortion, safe sex campaigns, homosexuality and pornography. Its philosophy is based on what it said was the Biblical standard: reconciliation, justice, compassion, tolerance, peace and 'general Christian values'.

With three seats in Parliament and one in the Western Cape legislature, the party, founded in 1993, is expected to lose support in the 2019 elections.

The African Content Movement (see Motsoeneng, Hlaudi)

African Global Operations (see Bosasa)

African National Congress (ANC)

Ruling party | Partner of the South African Communist Party (SACP) and the Congress of South African Trade Unions (Cosatu) in the Tripartite Alliance | Neoliberal & Nationalist | Number of seats in Parliament in 2018: 249

Some members suspected of state capture | Power brokers | Change agents

The governing party since the country's first democratic elections in 1994, it has triumphed at the ballot for nearly 25 years. It took 81 years for the party, founded on 8 January 1912 in Bloemfontein as the South African Native National Congress (SANNC), to take power.

At first, the SANNC was an anti-colonial organisation, its leadership comprising mostly black intellectuals, some of whom had been educated abroad. With great names like educator and writer John L. Dube, lawyers Alfred Mangena, Pixley ka Isaka Seme and George Montsioa, and journalist and writer Sol Plaatje in its political gallery, it demanded voting rights for all.

It went through a period of dormancy while South Africa was a dominion of the British Empire and then a self-governing nation state still within the British Empire. Then it changed its policies to build a mass, non-racial movement after the supremacist National Party came into power in 1948.

The ANC's Defiance Campaign of the 1950s initiated a powerful period of boycotts, strikes and community action, punctuated by the adoption of the Freedom Charter by the Congress of the People in 1955. This was an alliance formed of the ANC, the South African Communist Party (SACP), the South African Indian Congress, the South African Congress of Democrats (COD) and the Coloured People's Congress.

It launched its military wing, Umkhonto we Sizwe (MK), the Spear of the Nation, in 1960 – the year it and other liberation organisations were banned by the state. MK's aim was to utilise guerrilla war tactics to fight apartheid.

By the 1970s, state-sanctioned violence had intensified, using the security forces of police and army, and death squads kidnapped, tortured and assassinated ANC activists, while many went into exile to join MK in its camps in southern Africa or to be trained in the Soviet Union and other countries that supported the liberation movements.

After two states of emergency, massacres by the South African Defence Force (SADF) inside South Africa and in its neighbouring states, and a hard-won sanctions and divestment campaign against the racist regime, the last apartheid state president, F.W. de Klerk, unbanned the ANC on 2 February 1990.

This was followed by the release of Nelson Mandela, from Victor Verster Prison in Cape Town on 11 February 1990. Mandela would become the democratic state's first president in 1994.

The ANC won the national elections in 1999, 2004, 2009 and 2014. It is expected to do the same in 2019, although its majorities of the past are no longer assured.

Corruption, state capture, scandals, fierce factional divisions and a lack of delivery to the masses have discredited it, and there is pressure to reform or face ever-greater pushback from voters.

There has been competition from the Democratic Alliance at the liberal centre and the Economic Freedom Fighters on a hybrid nationalist-socialist ticket to the right of centre to gain the support of traditionally ANC supporters at the polls. But there were adjacent threats too, including the possibility of a pro-Jacob Zuma movement that could play off traditional and religious leadership – two areas of massive influence in South Africa.

African National Congress Women's League (ANCWL)

THE PRECURSOR TO THE ANCWL, the Bantu Women's League (BWL), was founded in 1918 with Charlotte Maxeke as its first president, but as the African National Congress (ANC) did not admit women until 1943, the BWL operated independently of its structures. Thereafter, it became part of the ANC and the ANCWL was founded in 1948.

The BWL was formed largely in response to the reintroduction of pass laws for women in 1918. It fought against this discrimination mostly through passive resistance campaigns.

The first official president of the ANCWL was Ida Mtwa, following a short introductory period in which Madie Hall-Xuma was at the helm.

The ANCWL joined forces with the Federation of South African Women (Fedsaw) in the 1952 Defiance Campaign and the Women's March of 9 August 1956. That was also the year when the ANC leadership finally accepted a woman into its ranks. That woman was Lilian Ngoyi, who was elected onto the ANC National Executive Committee (NEC).

Discredited in recent years for a lack of common purpose around societal issues centred on women and for its failure to properly promote women's leadership within the ANC, its lowest point was supporting Jacob Zuma in his rape trial in 2006. Since then, it has been accused of falling prey to male-led factions within the party and losing its character.

Its president in 2018, Bathabile Dlamini, was criticised not only for failing to promote women's issues in South African society as a custodian of the liberation movement, but was also personally disgraced when she was held partly liable for the near collapse of the South Africa Social Security Agency (Sassa) – which issues social grants – in 2017.

Also under fire in 2018 was the ANCWL deputy president, Sisi Ntombela, who offered the League's public support for Zuma, again, including at his court appearances on fraud and related charges. Ntombela said the ANCWL had 'long taken a decision that we are going to support him'.

Further, in 2018, ANCWL secretary general Meokgo Matuba apologised to *Sunday Times* journalist Qaanitah Hunter for reportedly sending her threatening messages and a picture of a gun in an apparent attempt to intimidate her. This was after Hunter claimed Zuma and his allies had met in a hotel in Durban allegedly to discuss the ousting of Cyril Ramaphosa.

The organisation's relevance is maintained through evoking the memory of the mighty women who were once part of it in decades gone by, including Ngoyi, Mtwa, Helen Joseph, Dorothy Nyembe, Sophie du Bruyn, Ray Alexander, Frances Baard, Rahima Moosa, Winnie Madikizela-Mandela and Ruth Mompati.

African National Congress Youth League (ANCYL)

ESTABLISHED IN 1944 BY ANTON LAMBEDE, who became the ANCYL's first president, Nelson Mandela, Ashby Mda, Walter Sisulu and Oliver Tambo, they were joined by Duma Nokwe, Ida Mtwa, Lillian Ngoyi, Dan Tloome, Charlotte Maxexe and others in their vision to mobilise young people to fight segregation. Its manifesto was launched at the Bantu Social Centre in Johannesburg, stating that Africanism should be promoted and African youth united, under the motto 'Africa's cause must triumph'.

The ANCYL developed a programme that included boycotts, strikes and a range of defiance tactics, which the ANC adopted in 1949 to transform itself into a revolutionary mass movement. But the League went into decline, partly over a split in its ranks because of the ANC's adoption of the Freedom Charter in 1955, leaving the League without substantial leadership.

The ANCYL was re-established after the apartheid regime unbanned the ANC in 1990, with Peter Mokaba as president. Mokaba was succeeded in turn by Lulu Johnson, Malusi Gigaba, Fikile Mbalula and Julius Malema. Following the democratic elections in 1994, the League aimed to mobilise young people. It played a pivotal role in the campaigns of would-be ANC leaders of its choosing. There was no more powerful an example of this than in 2007, when the ANCYL under Malema backed Jacob Zuma. In later years, Malema expressed his regret over that decision.

The ANCYL in 2018, under Collen Maine as the president, was a shadow of its former self, and had not been able to claim back the influence it once had – not only within the ANC, but also among the youth and in the broader South African politic – since the expulsion of the Malema generation in 2012.

A National Task Team (NTT) under the leadership of party apparatchik Mzwandile Masina was set up by the ANC in 2013 to investigate the Youth League. Its work saw it disband its Limpopo, Northern Cape, Free State, North West, Gauteng and Eastern Cape provincial executive committees (PECs).

Ronald Lamola, formerly deputy to Malema, was the acting ANCYL president when the ANC's National Executive Committee (NEC) dissolved the Youth League's NEC. Lamola protested that action as well as those of the NTT.

He believed the dissolving and disbandings were designed to erase the ANCYL's achievements under Malema. That said, the distance between Malema and Lamola was only to grow as the years went on.

By late 2018, ahead of the ANCYL's elective conference, #FeesMustFall activist Mcebo Dlamini – who was facing charges of public violence, theft, assault and violating a court order related to 2016 protests at the University of the Witwatersrand (Wits)

– indicated he may contest the position of ANCYL president. Others considered for the position included ANCYL KwaZulu-Natal secretary-general Thanduxolo Sabelo and ANCYL treasurer Reggie Nkabinde.

ANC Veterans League

OPEN TO ALL ANC MEMBERS AGED 60 or older who have served the ANC and the movement over an unbroken period of 40 years, the League was designed to operate on a national, provincial and branch basis. Its objectives were to ensure that veterans made 'a full and rich contribution to the work of the ANC, the movement and the life of the nation'. The Veteran's League functions as an autonomous body within the overall structure of the ANC, of which it is 'an integral part', but with its own constitution.

In 2018, Snuki Zikalala – best known for once being a controversial head of news at the South African Broadcasting Corporation (SABC) – was its president.

The League is not the same organisation as the 101 Stalwarts, which was a grouping of concerned former Robben Islanders, former Umkhonto we Sizwe (MK) operatives and other veterans formed in 2016, who railed against the disintegration of the ANC. But there were common members between the two.

The African People's Convention (APC)

Political party | Black Consciousness (BC) in origin | Centrist | Number of seats in Parliament in 2018: 1

On the way down

LEADER THEMBA GODI HELD ONTO the only APC seat in Parliament even as questions lingered about how the party came into existence. Godi, who was also the chairperson of the Standing Committee on Public Accounts (Scopa), defected from the Pan-Africanist Congress (PAC) in September 2007 to form the APC under the floor-crossing system which was introduced in 2002. Floor-crossing was no longer allowed after 2009.

Godi 'defected' with two other PAC MPs, Eastern Cape MPL Zingisa Mkabile and Gauteng Member of the Provincial Legislature (MPL) Malesela Ledwaba. At the APC launch event, Godi described the PAC as 'a weak vehicle carrying a strong message' and said he was launching the APC because 'there was no viable, credible, progressive political party'.

The party declared on its website that it offered an 'alternative voice of the voiceless ... that will never betray the revolution'.

The party retained its seat in the 2009 and 2014 general elections. But some APC members approached the South Gauteng High Court in Johannesburg in 2015, accusing Godi of accepting cash from the ANC in return for leniency towards the party's members involved in corrupt activities.

That the APC, a tiny party, had itself succumbed to factionalism was perhaps indicative of the dire straits in which any offshoot of the former liberation movements seems to have found itself.

Godi denied the charges against him and survived. But, barring a miracle, the 2019 election is expected to sound the death knell of the party he founded.

African Freedom Revolution (AFR)

Splinter party

Jacob Zuma defender Bishop Timothy Ngcobo, the KwaZulu-Natal secretary of the National Interfaith Council of South Africa, became known as the leader of the Friends of Jacob Zuma campaign.

His lobby group, the AFR, announced its intention to contest the 2019 elections on consumer issues in 2018, but some commentators said it was part of a deliberate 'fracturing' campaign within the ANC to see Zuma's faction back in power after the poll.

African Transformation Congress (ATC) (also known as the Mazibuye African Congress or MAC)

New party established ostensibly to support Jacob Zuma

Former Economic Freedom Fighters (EFF) KwaZulu-Natal regional chairperson Reggie Ngcobo was a co-ordinator for this initiative, originally known as Mazibuyele Emasisweni, which also had former EFF provincial co-ordinator Nathi Phewa.

Mazibuyele Emasisweni was seen to be a primary driver behind speculation in early 2018 that supporters of Jacob Zuma were marshalling a campaign to target the ANC. Supporters included the controversial Durban-based Delangokubona Business Forum (DBF), business owners from the taxi and funeral services sectors, and traditional leaders and religious bodies which can muster support of 'millions' behind it.

Among the religious leaders was 'chief apostle' and Zuma confidante Bishop Caesar Nongqunga of the Twelve Apostles Church in Christ, which was reported to have more than 4 million members.

There were rumours in mid-2018 that the ATC planned to rope in Black First Land First (BLF) and other extra-parliamentary political groupings with the ultimate aim of forcing out the ANC, or, if not the entire party, the Ramphosa government.

Commentators were concerned that the ATC planned to split the ANC and weaken the ruling party as much as possible in order to create conditions for coalitions between the ANC and itself.

African Transformation Movement (ATM) (see Manyi, Mzwanele)

Africa Check

Research organisation | Non-aligned

Change agents

A non-profit organisation set up in 2012 to promote accuracy in public debate and the media in Africa, Africa Check was devised by the non-profit media development arm of the international news agency Agence-France Presse (AFP). It was established as an independent organisation with offices in Johannesburg, Nairobi, Lagos, Dakar and London, producing reports in English and French, testing claims made by public figures, institutions and the media against the best available evidence.

AfriForum

Minority rights lobby group | Conservative, Afrikaner nationalist

Non-aligned

A focus on the white Afrikaner community saw AfriForum established in 2006. It regularly challenged government in court and Parliament around subjects like farm murders, racial quotas in sport and for the maintenance of language policies that benefit Afrikaans-speaking students.

Its dramatic press conference announcing an intention to stage a private prosecution against Economic Freedom Fighters (EFF) leader Julius Malema earned headlines in 2018. It wished to litigate against Malema on charges of money laundering, racketeering and corruption. AfriForum had previously taken Malema to the Equality Court.

Its CEO Kallie Kriel attracted adverse attention for his opinion expressed on The Eusebius McKaiser Show on Talk Radio 702 in May 2018 that apartheid was not a crime against humanity as there were no 'mass killings'. This attracted public fury. AfriForum deputy president Ernst Roets said the organisation 'could not comment' on Kriel's remarks, but 'our view as AfriForum,' he told *The Citizen* newspaper, 'is that the law around crime against humanity is not applied consistently because you have systems in countries where millions of people were murdered, but those systems were never considered crimes against humanity'.

Challenged previously as to why AfriForum did not seek to prosecute apartheid leaders, Kriel said it had 'closed the book on the past', viewing the end of apartheid as 'a negotiated settlement'.

Much like its political opposite, the EFF, AfriForum focused on land retention, but lost its urgent application in the Western Cape High Court in November 2018 to have MPs interdicted from amending Section 25 of the Constitution to allow land expropriation without compensation.

AfriForum organised on the ground and had branches throughout South Africa, but would not be on the ballot sheet in 2019.

AgangSA

Political party | Centrist | Number of seats in Parliament in 2018: 2

On the way down

Former Black Consciousness Movement (BCM) leader Mamphela Ramphele earned her credentials as a medical doctor, academic, business person and former managing director of the World Bank before she went into active politics.

Ramphele believed her public profile was strong enough a gauge of her popularity to take on the ANC in the 2014 elections. And so, she launched AgangSA in June 2013 in Pretoria with a strategy to 'unlock' the development potential of South Africa through a programme called the Smart 5Es (empowerment, education, entrepreneurship, effective government and employment).

Agang largely targeted the black middle class, who were disgruntled with the ANC but didn't trust the official opposition, the Democratic Alliance (DA), or any other political party. Yet for all the promise Agang may have had as an alternative party led by a black woman with struggle credentials, it failed spectacularly at the polls.

While there were concerns that the party lacked a clear political policy, the fatal blow for Agang was when Ramphele's flirtation with the DA collapsed. Agang failed dismally to achieve its 5% election target in 2014.

It only earned one seat in Parliament, and Ramphele's political career was wrecked. She soon left her limping party and it took about four years after she quit politics, with Ramphele nursing a bruised reputation, for her to begin appearing on public forums again, commentating on various social issues.

Agrizzi, Angelo (see Bosasa)

The amaBhungane Centre for Investigative Journalism

Research and publication organisation | Non-aligned

Change agents

A NON-PROFIT COMPANY FOUNDED TO DEVELOP investigative journalism in the public interest, its aim is to promote a free media and an open democracy. amaBhungane means 'the dung beetles' in isiZulu.

Veteran investigative journalists Sam Sole and Stefaans Brümmer were amaBhungane's joint managing partners. Its board of directors included Sole and Brümmer, as well as: Chairperson Professor Tawana Kupe, who is the vice chancellor of the University of Pretoria; human rights and gender activist, and writer, Sisonke Msimang; Angela Quintal, Africa programme co-ordinator at the Committee to Protect Journalists in New York; Nic Dawes, deputy executive director for media at Human Rights Watch; University of Pretoria Politics lecturer, Sithembile Mbete, and amaBhungane investigator, Tabelo Timse.

Among amaBhungane's high-profile investigations have been: various aspects of state capture in the era of Jacob Zuma and the Gupta brothers, and the release of the explosive #GuptaLeaks emails; alleged payments from a fleet firm which earned a mega-deal from the City of Joburg to a company whose account was reported to have been used to benefit the Economic Freedom Fighters (EFF); revelations that Nhlanhla Nene's son Siyabonga Nene asked the Public Investment Corporation (PIC) to fund part of a deal between a company he ran with a business partner to acquire 50% of a refinery in Mozambique, while Nhlanhla Nene was the chairperson of the PIC; the case of Texan-Nigerian Kase Lawal, who appropriated discount Nigerian crude meant to benefit South Africa with the assistance of leading

ANC figures and then donated millions to Zuma's education trust; and the callous disregard for poor black farmworkers' family graves by private property developers who own Dainfern golfing estate in Johannesburg.

Its advocacy work became increasingly important. Among its successes were: keeping open the Department of Energy's briefing on the procurement of nuclear power stations to Parliament's Energy Portfolio Committee in November 2016, as those power stations, if they were to be built, would cost R1 trillion; its determination to see the selection of a new Inspector-General of Intelligence (IGI) restarted after Parliament's Joint Standing Committee on Intelligence (JSCI) was believed to have accepted none of the eight short-listed candidates; and joining investigative journalists from 20 countries in a campaign asking MPs to disclose their tax returns.

The 'arms deal'

Instituted by government

Many individuals involved captured

Politician Patricia de Lille first led a call for an investigation into alleged corruption into government's purchase of weapons to modernise the South African National Defence Force (SANDF) in 1999, the same year in which the deal was signed off.

By today's prices, this procurement of small warships, submarines, helicopters and military aircraft from British, French and other foreign manufacturers would be worth about R50 billion, although some investigations have shown the true cost could have been closer to R72 billion.

But it wasn't only the cost, which seemed to escalate without explanation from about R3 billion to R5 billion at the time, which raised alarm from 1999 onwards. The arms deal – formally, the Strategic Defence Package – was believed to have benefitted certain key individuals within the ANC through bribery and corruption.

Prominent among these were late former defence minister Joe Modise and his 'special advisor', Advocate Fana Hlongwane, and Jacob Zuma and his associate, public servant Chippy Shaik.

A R140-million inquiry instituted by Zuma while he was president concluded its business in 2015 under Judge Willie Seriti, clearing most parties who or which had been identified by whistleblowers. In October 2018, Corruption Watch and Right2Know filed a supplementary affidavit based in part on a record of the inquiry's work, which took the Seriti Commission's findings on review.

De Lille and other whistleblowers – including senior ANC MP Andrew Feinstein, who resigned from Parliament when government moved to curtail an investigation – believed 'ANC crooks' were being 'let off the hook' and that this would send the wrong message to South Africans.

Apart from a shocking cover-up of massive corruption – which saw another Zuma associate, Schabir Shaik, and ANC Parliamentary chief whip Tony Yengeni briefly jailed, but not many others affected – there were also failed promises which compromised the economy. For example, offset agreements which claimed 65,000 jobs would be created and a R104- to R110-billion investment did not substantially materialise, as was revealed in a 2014 review report.

The arms deal – which, at the time, cost more than what was spent on HIV/AIDS treatment, bursaries for tertiary education and low-cost housing combined – was also regarded as a supreme catalyst for the ANC factionalism that has deepened over the past two decades.

Armaments Corporation of South Africa (Armscor)

The arms procurement agency of the Department of Defence

ARMSCOR WAS FOUNDED IN 1968 out of the need for apartheid South Africa to deal with the effects of sanctions agreed to by the United Nations in 1963, formalised in 1967 and made mandatory in 1977. Ultimately, the regime would spend billions of rand buying on the black market and through covert arms deals, particularly with Israel, while also increasingly producing weapons on home soil.

The 'border war' between the South African Defence Force and the People's Movement for the Liberation of Angola (Movimento Popular de Libertação de Angola, MPLA) and its allies, the Cubans, from 1975 to 1989, saw a hike in defence expenditure against the backdrop of the international arms embargo. But this built an arms infrastructure with a global reputation, despite its very dark side, as the weapons were often turned on South Africans inside the country itself.

Two years before the first democratic elections, Denel was established as South Africa's arms manufacturing company and split off from Armscor, which then engaged only in procurement for the united South African National Defence Force.

Armscor's apartheid-era sanctions-busting came back to haunt it in January 2019 when the *Daily Maverick* revealed that the auditor-general faced a High Court application to produce records relating to the purchase of 50 Puma helicopters through a French connection in the late 1980s.

This was not a new civil claim, having been scrupulously researched for investigative journalist Hennie van Vuuren's best-selling book, *Apartheid Guns and Money: A Tale of Profit* (Jacana, 2017) – but it was an expensive one at R8 billion.

The protagonist was identified as Portuguese arms trader Jorge Pinhol, who said he was never paid his agreed commission, and now sought access to top secret records via the auditor-general to support his case.

That was not the only controversy Armscor faced in January 2019. Its CEO Kevin Wakeford was granted special leave after his name came up at the Zondo Commission (into state capture) as an alleged beneficiary of bribes by security and catering company Bosasa.

Asset Forfeiture Unit (AFU)

Prosecutorial responsibilities | Government body

ESTABLISHED IN 1999 IN THE OFFICE of the National Director of Public Prosecutions (NDPP), the unit's focus was on the prevention of organised crime and to ensure powers to seize criminal assets would be used to the maximum effect.

Its strategic objectives were to develop the law by taking test cases to court and creating precedents necessary to allow the effective use of the law, and to build capacity to ensure asset forfeiture was used as widely as possible. Its key partners were the South African Police Service (SAPS) and the South African Revenue Service (SARS).

When the AFU was set up, international experts warned it should expect litigation from rich and powerful criminals desperate to hang on to ill-gotten gains, who could afford to employ the best legal brains to find any possible weakness or lack of clarity in the law or exploit technicalities in existing civil procedure.

This indeed proved to be the case and the AFU was involved in intensive litigation since inception. But by 2018, it seemed it was in trouble, and this had been growing as a problem for years. The essential unity that should have existed between it and the Hawks, the SAPS, the Financial Intelligence Centre (FIC), the National Prosecuting Authority (NPA) and SARS was in jeopardy.

Analysts identified a primary reason as the loss – or deliberate dampening – of forensic audit skills during the Jacob Zuma administration. The removal of Advocate Willie Hofmeyr as the head of the AFU by controversial NDPP Shaun Abrahams was believed to have contributed markedly to this. For example, the AFU's urgent preservation order in March 2018 to attach rehabilitation funds from mines belonging to the disgraced Gupta family demonstrated it had not paid attention to a line of legal actions. As these monies were not the proceeds of crime, the Organisation Undoing Tax Abuse (OUTA) had already filed a strong application to prevent those funds from being tampered with by the Guptas in 2017 already. The AFU's seemingly contrary application caused confusion as to what should happen to the funds and was an unnecessary move that jeopardised the earlier case which had already frozen the money.

Meanwhile, hundreds of AFU cases have piled up over the years.

Auditor-General of South Africa (AG)

Chapter 9 institution | Government body

Change agent

The AG annually produces audit reports on government departments, public entities, municipalities and public institutions. The outcomes are analysed in general reports that cover the Public Finance Management Act (PFMA) and the Municipal Finance Management Act (MFMA). Reports on discretionary audits, performance audits and other special audits are also produced.

The AG's powers were significantly extended in November 2018 when the Public Audit Bill was signed into law, coming into force in April 2019. The AG is now able to refer cases of irregular and unjustified spending by public servants – including the CEOs of state-owned enterprises (SOEs) – to the Hawks and the SAPS.

Previously, the AG could only go so far as to table its reports to Parliament, provincial legislatures and municipal councils, leaving those bodies to decide on remedial action.

As irregular government spending tilted towards R80 billion in 2018, the new legislation was preceded by the AG being given a permanent bodyguard amid increasing instances of intimidation and even violent acts against government auditors.

As a Chapter 9 institution, the Constitution guarantees its independence. It does not focus on inefficient or improper bureaucratic conduct but on the proper use and management of public money.

The AG in 2018 was Thembekile 'Kimi' Makwetu, who was appointed by former president Jacob Zuma in December 2013 for a constitutionally mandated period of seven years. Makwetu earned a BCompt Hons from the University of Natal and is a chartered accountant. He was previously a director in Deloitte's forensic unit before he was appointed Deputy AG to the erstwhile AG, Terence Nombembe.

Azanian People's Organisation (Azapo)

Extra-parliamentary political party | Black Consciousness | Leftwing

After the state-sanctioned murder of Steve Biko in detention in 1977, Azapo emerged out of the ashes of the Black People's Convention (BPC), the South African Students' Organisation (SASO) and the Black Community Programmes (BCP) – some of the key organisations forming the Black Consciousness Movement (BCM). Azapo escalated the mission of the BCM by propagating Black Consciousness and organising black people to be a fighting force for their liberation.

Azapo pursued co-operation between at least 200 ideologically similar groups, which led to the launch of the National Forum (NF) in 1983 at a conference.

Azapo did not participate in the Convention for a Democratic South Africa (Codesa) negotiations between 1990 and 1993, and decided in 1993 not to participate in the 1994 elections.

Following the adoption of the 1996 Constitution, Azapo entered formal politics in the 1999 elections, allowing its president, Mosibudi Mangena, to serve in government as Deputy Minister of Education and as Minister of Science and Technology.

After Azapo withdrew Mangena from government in 2008 at the same time as a number of other senior members of government resigned, Mangena became Azapo's honorary president. The resignations and Mangena's withdrawal were prompted by Thabo Mbeki being recalled by the ANC in order to make way for Jacob Zuma.

The national president is former Maths teacher, political detainee, SASO and BCM leader and founding member of the Azanian National Liberation Army, Strike Thokoane, who was Azapo's secretary-general from 2006 to 2010, when he was elected its deputy president.

Azapo is today an extra-parliamentary fringe party which, by retaining its BC ethos, associates itself with activists on the left working on land campaigns, specifically black human rights issues and broader continental African topics.

Its slogan is 'One Azania, One Nation'.

B

Bapela, Obed

Deputy Minister of Co-operative Governance and Traditional Affairs | ANC politician | Former political prisoner | Former ANC international relations committee head

Power broker

BAPELA WAS A DEPUTY MINISTER THREE TIMES – first in communications, then in the Presidency for performance monitoring and evaluation and, in 2018, in co-operative governance and traditional affairs. His vast experience in political office in central and provincial (Gauteng) government gave him a strong platform to also serve the ANC National Executive Committee (NEC) in the North West, a troubled province that witnessed the first post-1994 election revolt against the government, owing to poor service delivery and corruption.

Bapela took centre-stage in that province's party politics during 2018's fiery protests for and against the resignation of premier Supra Mahumapelo. Mahumapelo did later resign, but the ANC's North West Provincial Executive Committee (PEC) was disbanded and a Provincial Task Team (PTT) set up under new premier Job Mokgoro. That PTT, which initially included Mahumapelo, was reinforced by NEC members.

Thus, Bapela was expected to continue to play a role there ahead of the 2019 elections to work at restoring the trust of ANC supporters and others in North West against the backdrop of the party's political rivals, the Democratic Alliance and the Economic Freedom Fighters, having set their sights on deposing the ruling party there.

Bapela came in 10th on the 80-member list of the party's NEC during its December 2017 elective conference at Nasrec, Johannesburg, which saw Cyril Ramaphosa elected president.

He gained attention beyond mainstream politics for repeatedly crossing swords with the Jewish community in South Africa for his stance against Israel in his capacity as the ANC's international relations committee head. Bapela threatened to punish South African students who visited Israel under the auspices of the South African-Israel Forum, saying the move was aimed at 'embarrassing' the ANC, which was opposed to the 'imperialist agenda' of the United States and its allies, including Israel. Bapela also raised the ire of the Jewish community for criticising the dual citizenship with Israel that some of them held.

Bapela had backed Ramaphosa's opponent, Nkosazana Dlamini-Zuma at the ANC's Nasrec conference.

Batohi, Advocate Shamila

National Director of Public Prosecutions (NDPP) | Former senior legal advisor at the International Criminal Court (ICC) | Non-aligned

On the way up

President Cyril Ramaphosa appointed Batohi to the biggest job in crime-fighting in December 2018, following the order of the Constitutional Court (ConCourt) made on 13 August 2018 that he appoint an NDPP within 90 days. This was in the wake of former NDPP Advocate Shaun Abrahams resigning from office in August 2018 after it was found that Jacob Zuma should not have appointed him.

Batohi was given the massive challenge of heading up a National Prosecuting Authority (NPA) that had experienced high levels of leadership instability and a major decline in public confidence amid rumours of corruption, actual corruption and political interference which had developed over the previous 10 years.

The ConCourt had dictated in its order that the office of the NDPP should 'be cleansed of all the ills that have plagued it for the past few years ... as, with a malleable, corrupt or dysfunctional prosecuting authority, many criminals – especially those holding positions of influence – will rarely, if ever, answer for their criminal deeds'.

Ramaphosa said that Batohi would have to address 'the state of dysfunctionality and deficiencies in the NPA that were identified by the court'. He gave her the task of 'ensuring the efficiency and integrity of law enforcement', sketching a backdrop of state capture, corruption and widespread crime.

Ramaphosa has departed from the usual protocol in appointing the new NDPP. As the head of the national executive, the President can appoint without consultation, as Zuma appeared to have done. But Ramaphosa sought the assistance of a panel from the legal fraternity and Chapter 9 institutions in recommending suitable candidates. The panel included chairperson of the panel and Minister of Energy Jeff Radebe, Auditor-General Thembekile Kimi Makwetu, South African Human Rights Commission chairperson Bongani Majola, Jaap Cilliers from the General Council of the Bar of South Africa, Richard Scott from the Law Society, Lutendo Sigogo from the Black Lawyers Association, Lawrence Manye from the Advocates for Transformation and Mvuzo Nyotesi from the National Association of Democratic Lawyers.

A process of nominations, shortlisting and interviews open to the media followed before the advisory panel proposed five candidates. Batohi was selected on the basis of an extensive and distinguished career which began when she was appointed as a junior prosecutor in the Chatsworth magistrates' court in 1986, finally becoming the Director of Public Prosecutions in KwaZulu-Natal in 2009. During that time, Batohi was part of the Investigation Task Unit established by Nelson Mandela in 1995, which examined options in how to set up a new prosecutions directorate.

One of her most famous prosecutions when she was with the NPA was being the evidence leader during the King Commission that investigated disgraced Proteas captain Hansie Cronje for match-fixing.

In 2011, Batohi moved to the Netherlands as a senior legal advisor to the prosecutor of the ICC at The Hague. She was scheduled to start work as the NDPP in February 2019 after serving her notice at the ICC, and one of her first major challenges would be to ensure that Zuma faced justice. Zuma was expected to appear in court on charges of corruption in May 2019.

Bell Pottinger

Disgraced British reputation management company, now closed

Allegedly involved in corruption in South Africa

WHEN BELL POTTINGER WAS FINALLY EXPELLED from the prestigious Public Relations and Communications Association in the UK in September 2017, it was a pyrrhic victory for those who had been its victims in South Africa.

The company – which had operated for 30 years as premium spin doctors representing clients as diverse as the Bahrain and Egyptian governments and murderer Oscar Pistorius – was hired by Ajay, Tony and Atul Gupta, the notorious brothers whose Johannesburg-based empire was alleged to be at the core of state capture.

Bell Pottinger's job may not have been to stoke hate, but that was the result as it drew up a campaign to fight the suspicion and then anger that had started to grow around the power of the Guptas. That their power had apparently been amassed via their close friend Jacob Zuma only strengthened the arrogance of the assignment, as, for the better part of seven to eight years while he was in power from 2009 to 2018, Zuma was virtually untouchable.

Bell Pottinger developed and then pushed a dangerous race-based narrative centred on 'white monopoly capital'. But the 'spin' went out of control and ended up being one of the many levers of endemic corruption that would pull the country apart in a fever of racism and political factionalism.

Black Economic Empowerment (BEE)

Government programme

Change agent

THE FIRST DEMOCRATIC GOVERNMENT SET OUT to fix the inequalities of the past and central to that was a legislative framework. In 2003, the Broad-Based Black Economic Empowerment (BBBEE) Strategy was published as a precursor to the BBBEE Act, designed to advance economic transformation and comprehensively bring black people into the economy.

Codes of Good Practice and Transformation Charters were published in 2007 and a BBBEE Advisory Council was finally set up in 2009.

Companies were to use the services of accredited verification agencies (VAs) after widespread and fraudulent 'fronting', window-dressing, benefit diversion or tokenism looked to destabilise BEE entirely.

'BEE' has become a metonym for racists who use it to describe successful black people. This was partly also based on ignorance around who 'benefitted' from BEE as legislated by government, rather than black people who had legitimately gained wealth as 'economic deployees', entering the economy with political credibility but on their own terms.

Examples of the latter would include President Cyril Ramaphosa and former Gauteng premier and Cabinet minister Tokyo Sexwale who left politics to join business before BEE was created as a legal entity. Both rejoined the ANC's political leadership in government once they had created their economic empires, although Sexwale would leave, seemingly for good, after the ANC's 2012 elective conference in Mangaung, Free State.

The major criticism of the 'economic deployees' was that not many other black people benefitted from what were rewards for a limited number. Another downside of that deployment was that many 'white' companies made use of the same people over and again on their boards to appear transformed. This unfortunate situation somewhat stabilised once BEE and BBBEE were normalised into the economy from 2007 onwards.

Black industrialist businesses and black entrepreneurs could gain funding through programmes offered by the private sector interests, Business Unity South Africa and the Black Business Council, while government developed the Black Industrialists Scheme (BIS) and stated its aim would be to buy 75% of all industrial goods and services from black-owned businesses.

Black First Land First (BLF)

Extra-parliamentary political party | Black Consciousness (BC) in origin | Leftwing, Socialist in aspiration

Captured | Potential power brokers

CHAMPIONS OF THE BLF ASPIRE TO PAN-AFRICANISM and 'revolutionary socialism', two ideological persuasions that should have easy traction in South Africa, but neither has played out. The BLF, founded in 2015 by academic and writer Andile Mngxitama after he was expelled from the Economic Freedom Fighters (EFF), has battled with its image, direction and purpose, particularly since it was exposed in 2017 as being an ally of the notorious Gupta family.

Although Mngxitama represented the EFF as an MP after it entered Parliament in 2014, relationships between him and the party's leadership are now hostile. He has been the focus of the BLF's adversarial approach – including physically attacking journalists, issuing death threats, threatening 'house negroes' ('sell-outs') and loud-hailing against whites.

The organisation has been lampooned and litigated against. However, rumours that Jacob Zuma supporters would rope in BLF to work at unseating the Ramaphosa government put it back on the national agenda.

Ostensibly, the BLF fights for the restoration of land to black South Africans. The BLF's 'revolutionary call' identified land as 'the basis of our freedom, our identity, our spiritual well-being, our economic development and culture', and said that, since the land had been stolen, it would get it back 'by any means necessary'. Among the BLF's most prominent actions against the colonial and apartheid land theft have been participating in land occupations in Gauteng and Limpopo, and protesting against 'white monopoly capital'.

BLF claims it has 100,000 members and believes it will be a part of the National Assembly after the 2019 general elections by way of supporters of Zuma. Mngxitama shared a stage with Zuma and addressed thousands of Zuma supporters during the former president's court appearance on corruption charges in early 2018.

Mngxitama told the Mail & Guardian newspaper that the BLF is 'a recognisable brand … bigger than (the) UDM (United Democratic Movement) ... bigger than Agang, and electorally ... bigger than the PAC (Pan Africanist Congress)'.

The BLF registered as a political party with the Electoral Commission of South Africa (IEC) in 2018, relying on crowdfunding for the R600,000 deposit required by the IEC for it to contest elections in 2019. Mngxitama said the BLF would not accept funding from white monopoly capital or white people, or from black people who 'attached conditions'.

The BLF had been cited as the respondent in several hate-speech incidents reported to the South African Human Rights Commission by the end of 2018. The IEC warned the party in December 2018 against making such statements which were against the Constitution.

Black Industrialists Scheme (BIS)

Government programme

THE DEPARTMENT OF TRADE AND INDUSTRY launched this incentive scheme to unlock the potential of black industrialists in the economy through financial interventions.

The BIS offered a cost-sharing grant ranging from 30% to 50% to approved entities to a maximum of R50 million. The quantum of the grant would depend on the level of real black ownership and black management control, the economic benefits of the project and the value of the project itself.

The scheme was introduced in 2014, but government started to take some flak around it in 2018 when its unashamed efforts to create capitalists were weighed up against its comparatively paltry attempts to reform its land policies and provide the poor with homes and services.

Black Twitter

Social media phenomenon

Change agents

BLACK TWITTER IS A SOCIAL MEDIA CULTURAL IDENTITY focusing on issues of interest to the black community, particularly in the United States but more prevalent in South Africa since 2012. Its best-known global protagonist was Feminista Jones, the online pseudonym of Michelle Taylor, an activist and writer whose blogs on black feminism earned her attention.

Jones described Black Twitter as a virtual community of primarily African-American users who aimed at bringing about socio-political changes.

Taylor's goal was to get people to accept that Black Lives Matter – a theme summed up in her often-repeated tweet: 'Even if you don't experience something, it doesn't mean it didn't happen.'

Rebone Masemola, a young strategist with a Master's in Anthropology from the University of the Witwatersrand (Wits), wrote on www.bizcommunity.com in 2015 that 'in the South African context, Black Twitter seems to carry a different tone because it appears to be intended for a niche market of black young middle-class twelebs (twitter celebs)'.

'In comparison to their US counterpart, the movement here is not just for any black person with something to say, but for a few intellectuals who are very equipped and versed when it comes to issues of culture, current affairs and politics. Thus it's known to be an exclusive community that proves difficult to break into.'

Masemola observed that Black Twitter users in South Africa 'not only hold white people to account, but also other black people whom are regarded as not being "black enough", hence there are "levels of blackness" observed which are used to criticise behaviour regarded as below par'.

Among prominent white South Africans who had no comeback to the acerbic and often hilarious socio-political commentary on Black Twitter, were Western Cape Premier Helen Zille, billionaire businesswoman Magda Wierzycka and former Bafana Bafana (national football team) star Mark Fish. In Zille's case, the response was to her tweets praising colonialism, while Wierzycka missed the point around job creation and published an incorrect image to mark the anniversary of the Sharpeville Massacre. Fish also got an image wrong and was pilloried for weeks through the hashtag #MarkFishChallenge, which went viral.

Not just a community of young influencers, Black Twitter also delivered pointed political barbs, consciousness and analysis from individuals like writer Khaya Dlanga and musician Simphiwe Dana.

Those examining the future ANC have paid note to Black Twitter where traditional support for the liberation movement was shown to be waning, and where Jacob Zuma's alleged corruption and links with state capture had had a marked effect.

Bloom, Jack

Shadow member of the Executive Council on Health in the Gauteng legislature | Former Gauteng Democratic Alliance (DA) caucus leader and leader of the official opposition in Gauteng

Change agent | Star

THE DA'S LONGEST-SERVING MEMBER in the Gauteng legislature, Bloom kept a hawk's eye on the state of health services in the country's richest province. He had had two decades of experience in democratic politics at the provincial level, having been the youngest member of the then Democratic Party (DP) caucus in Gauteng, when he eventually served as leader of the official opposition from 2007–09 and again from 2011–14.

Bloom's relentless auditing of and reporting on healthcare facilities throughout the province became legendary across political divides. He was, for instance, one of the first and most vocal critics of the Life Esidimeni tragedy, in which nearly 150 mentally challenged patients under state care died in 2016/17 after being transferred from private healthcare to NGO facilities selected by government. Bloom had warned that the transfer would be a 'disaster'. But the Health Member of the Executive Council (MEC), Qedani Mahlangu, who initiated the transfer, was one of many officials who were held responsible for the deaths – some even through starvation – of at least 144 people.

Bloom also criticised Gauteng's ANC Premier David Makhura, who claimed ignorance at an inquiry into the tragedy chaired by Deputy Chief Justice Emeritus Dikgang Moseneke.

Bobani, Mongameli

Executive mayor of the Nelson Mandela Bay (NMB) metro | Leader of the United Democratic Movement (UDM) caucus in the NMB council

Power broker | Suspected of corruption

BOBANI, A LAWYER, CAME TO PROMINENCE after the UDM beat the ANC in a by-election in the Port Elizabeth townships of Veeplaas and KwaMagxaki on his watch in 2015. His party lost that ward in the 2016 local government elections, but the UDM selected him as its mayoral candidate for Nelson Mandela Bay.

No party won an outright majority in the council and so the UDM initially went into a coalition with the Democratic Alliance (DA), which was the largest party with 57 seats, four short of a necessary majority of 61. Other parties involved were the Congress of the People (COPE) and the African Christian Democratic Party (ACDP).

The UDM withdrew its membership of the coalition in 2017 over Bobani when he was removed as member of the mayoral committee (MMC) for public health and then dismissed as deputy mayor. The executive mayor, the DA's Athol Trollip, alleged maladministration and impropriety in the public health directorate, and called Bobani's conduct unacceptable.

Bobani was installed as mayor after a DA councillor abstained from supporting his party's Speaker in August 2018, leading to the Speaker being removed, and a walkout by the DA. When Bobani was declared mayor, he appointed a mayoral committee dominated by the ANC in a multi-party coalition which also included minnows the African Independent Congress (AIC) and the United Front (UF).

Allegations of impropriety continued to dog Bobani into 2019.

Bongo, Advocate Bongani

Former State Security minister | ANC MP

Suspected of capture

FORMER PRESIDENT JACOB ZUMA TOOK MANY parliamentarians by surprise when he appointed the virtually unknown Bongo, an MP drawn from the national ANC caucus, to the key position of State Security Minister in 2017. This post is especially important as the person who occupies it is also the political head of the

State Security Agency (SSA). Bongo was promoted during Zuma's second Cabinet reshuffle in seven months.

A former Provincial Executive Committee (PEC) member of the party in Mpumalanga, he was said to have had a 'long-standing relationship' with former Mpumalanga Premier David Mabuza, but later, rumour had it that the two men were 'not as close' as before. (Mabuza became the deputy president of South Africa in 2018.)

Bongo was believed to have been a supporter of Nkosazana Dlamini-Zuma for ANC president at the party's elective conference at Nasrec in Johannesburg in December 2017.

An ANC MP by 2014, Bongo sat on the portfolio committees on Defence and Military Veterans, and Justice. But by 2017, having been promoted by Zuma, he was in the crosshairs of Democratic Alliance (DA) chief whip John Steenhuisen, who laid corruption charges against him relating to allegations that he offered to bribe Advocate Ntuthuzelo Vanara, the evidence leader in the Parliamentary Inquiry into State Capture at Eskom.

Media reports claimed Vanara had filed an affidavit and submitted it to the Speaker of the National Assembly, Baleka Mbete, in which he claimed Bongo had offered him a 'blank cheque' to step down. Mbete referred the matter to Parliament's Joint Committee on Ethics and Members' Interests which, in May 2018, had decided to institute disciplinary proceedings against him.

And this was not the only accusation made against Bongo. A forensic report of the Special Investigating Unit (SIU), which appeared to have been leaked, was believed to show that Bongo may have been linked to the inflated purchase of farmland in Mpumalanga in 2011. Bongo was the head of legal services in the Mpumalanga Department of Human Settlements at the time. Contracts for such purchases would likely have been drafted through his unit.

In the case of Naauwpoort Farm in Emalahleni, the land was allegedly purchased by the department for millions more than it was worth. The 'balance' after the farmer selling the land was paid its sale amount was then spuriously handled by lawyers and 'land developers'. Bongo's brother was cited as a possible beneficiary, in that one of the 'developers' apparently bought him a luxury vehicle which then appeared to have been used by Bongani Bongo.

Booysen, Major-General Johan

Former state operative

Non-aligned

THE FORMER HEAD OF THE HAWKS in KwaZulu-Natal sued government in 2015 after he was held in 2012 on claims that he was involved in operating a 'death squad' as part of the organised crime unit's activities in Cato Manor outside Durban. Booysen's unlawful arrest led to charges of fraud and perjury against then acting National Director of Public Prosecutions (NDPP) Nomgcobo Jiba, who tried but was unable to prosecute him.

Booysen – who was appointed Hawks head in 2010 by Bheki Cele, then the

National Commissioner of Police – believed he had been charged to stop him pursuing specific cases of corruption, some involving members of Jacob Zuma's family and friends. Booysen and his co-accused were originally charged with 116 counts, including racketeering, murder and attempted murder. In 2018, Booysen was tipped to become a special adviser to Cele.

In October 2018, the *Sunday Times* – whose investigations unit had originally written stories that were published about Booysen and the 'Cato Manor death squads' – retracted those stories with apologies from its editor. Awards given to journalists involved in the fake news were returned, along with money given as prizes.

Private anti-corruption organisation Forensics for Justice had first made the claim about the fake news back in 2016, in a report on state capture titled 'Joining the dots'.

Agrizzi admitted at the conclusion of his testimony at the state capture commission that he was racist after being caught on tape using racial slurs. The South African Human Rights Commission then announced it would be pursuing charges of hate speech against Agrizzi at the Equality Court.

Bosasa (African Global Operations)

Controversial group of companies based in Mogale City, outside Johannesburg | Have scored major government tenders | Work with departments of Correctional Services, Justice and Home Affairs | Run the Lindela Repatriation Centre, South Africa's deportation centre for illegal immigrants | Provide food services to prisons across the country | Provide prison and airport security

Linked to corruption

South Africans became fixated with Bosasa in January 2019 when its former COO, Angelo Agrizzi, gave bombshell testimony to the Zondo Commission, alleging that the company had paid millions in bribes to government officials to secure tenders.

Investigative journalists Adriaan Basson and others first exposed Bosasa in 2006 when Basson, who was then working for the *Mail & Guardian*, noticed the-then little-known company was getting multi-million-Rand tenders. Thereafter, the National Prosecuting Authority began an investigation which had gone on for more than a decade by the time Agrizzi gave testimony.

But a possible role in corruption had only gained the attention of many South Africans in 2015, when the media obtained a secret recording of a meeting between Bosasa CEO Gavin Watson, Agrizzi and then prisons boss Linda Mti, on which Watson spoke about his 'friendship' with and seeming influence over Jacob Zuma.

Those recordings reveal Watson planned to discuss the appointment of a new National Director of Public Prosecutions (NDPP) with Zuma. The Special Investigations Unit (SIU) had earlier investigated Bosasa upon allegations that it had paid bribes to Mti and Correctional Services Chief Financial Officer Patrick Gillingham in exchange for a range of government tenders for prison catering and fencing worth more than R1.5 billion.

All sorts of 'coincidences' followed, among them the appointment of Advocate Shaun Abrahams as NDPP in June 2015, preceded by a visit by Zuma – accompanied Dudu Myeni, who would become the SAA chairperson and was also the executive chairperson of the JG Zuma Foundation, and Bheki Cele – to Bosasa's offices in April 2015. The day after that visit, Zuma celebrated his birthday with a party sponsored by Bosasa, which did the same thing the following year, spending an estimated R3.5 million. Meanwhile, the tenders in Bosasa's favour mounted up.

In late 2018, the company was exposed for having given money to ANC MP Vincent Smith in 2015. This appeared to be as a result of Smith having 'assisted' Agrizzi's son, Giancarlo Agrizzi, to get a job as a researcher at the ANC in Gauteng. Smith was the chair of the Portfolio Committee on Correctional Services.

Disgraced former SABC boss Hlaudi Motsoeneng admitted in January 2019 that he had been bailed out by Bosasa on a legal bill amounting to R1.1 million.

In November 2018, President Cyril Ramaphosa backtracked on a reply he made to the Democratic Alliance (DA) in Parliament regarding an amount of R500,000 which had been deposited into his son, Andile Ramaphosa's, trust account by Bosasa in 2017. At first, the president said this had been for 'a business service' involving his son, but soon corrected himself, saying he had found out that the money supported his ANC presidential campaign, but that this was done without his knowledge. In January 2019, Ramaphosa asked Public Protector Busisiwe Mkhwebane to investigate the matter.

Breytenbach, Advocate Glynnis

Democratic Alliance (DA) MP | Former state prosecutor

Breytenbach was a senior prosecutor with the National Prosecuting Authority (NPA) before she became a DA MP in 2014. Her decision to join formal politics may have been a reaction to being forced out of her job for having investigated the politically connected Richard Mdluli who was the police crime intelligence head.

Mdluli was charged, then those charges were withdrawn, then he was charged again for fraud, theft, corruption, kidnapping and murder. Intense political interference was believed to have been at play throughout.

Breytenbach was first suspended from her job in 2012 with the NPA saying she had 'mishandled' criminal fraud and forgery complaints laid by Imperial Crown Trading 289 (ICT) in its dispute with Kumba Iron Ore over lucrative mineral rights to Kumba's subsidiary, the Sishen mine, in the Northern Cape. ICT was a shelf company with big names behind it, including former president Kgalema Motlanthe's partner Gugu Mtshali and, later, an associate within the notorious Gupta empire, Jagdish Parekh, who would be linked with another stakeholder, Jacob Zuma's son Duduzane. (The Constitutional Court would later restore full rights to Kumba.)

At the time of Breytenbach's suspension, Menzi Simelane – who was appointed

National Director of Public Prosecutions (NDPP) by Zuma in 2009 – was being investigated for his fitness to hold office, and Nomgcobo Jiba was the acting NDPP. Simelane was then removed from the NPA and his appointment as NDPP declared invalid by the Constitutional Court in 2012. (Zuma was believed to have appointed Simelane without considering any other CVs, and despite Simelane's own CV being less than adequate to the position.)

Charges would be laid against Jiba for fraud and perjury in 2013, before the NDPP who laid those charges, Advocate Mxolisi Nxasana, agreed to step down while an inquiry into his fitness to hold office was underway.

That was the environment under which Breytenbach was working when she was suspended while her colleague Lawrence Mrwebi, head of the Specialised Commercial Crimes Unit, demanded that charges against Mdluli be withdrawn.

In February 2018, she was acquitted of charges laid by the NPA that she had modified the contents on her official laptop while she was still in its employ. This related specifically to documents about the mining rights case involving ICT and Sishen. But it turned out Breytenbach was not only authorised to delete personal information from the work laptop. She could also make a mirror image of all its contents, as per an agreement with the NPA, in the presence of NPA officials.

In the end, she was found not to have deleted the files with the intention to conceal any aspect of these.

Breytenbach was included in a list of 12 candidates shortlisted by a panel assisting President Cyril Ramaphosa in appointing a new NDPP in November 2018 in the wake of Advocate Shaun Abrahams, who retired under a cloud in August 2018. Breytenbach said her decision was based on the needs of the NPA which, she believed, should be free of party-political influence.

BRICS

Programme of government

An association of five major emerging national economies – Brazil, Russia, India, China and South Africa – South Africa joined the formation in 2011, becoming the fifth member of the group. There have been trade and diplomatic benefits regionally and internationally through this association, but the multilateral platform needs to find responses to challenges including unemployment, poverty and inequality.

BRICS launched its first institution – the New Development Bank – in 2014 to fund developmental projects in the BRICS countries. It intends to establish its own credit rating agency that would serve the needs of the global south and other emerging economies as a way to challenge the three Western-dominant credit rating agencies of Fitch; Moody's and S&P.

The Brown Umbrella

Collective of small political parties contesting the 2019 elections

In January 2019, five parties – the Khai-ma Independent Candidates Coalition

(Koko), the Khoisan Revolution, the Tsantsabane Coalition, Die Forum and the Khoisan Defiance Campaign – announced they would be collaborating on providing a new platform for voters under the moniker The Brown Umbrella.

Their focus would be on alleviating poverty, and while they aimed to attract Khoi voters, the group said their campaign would be non-racial. Among its leaders were Stanley Petersen of the Khoisan Revolution and Erick Strauss of Die Forum, and among its members were existing councillors in municipalities who intended to fight to keep their seats.

Analysts showed interest in The Brown Umbrella, acknowledging the global shift towards identity politics of the kind espoused by the group.

Buthelezi, Prince Mangosuthu

AKA: Gatsha; Shenge | Founder of the Inkatha Freedom Party | IFP MP

Captured by the apartheid government

After four decades of leading the Inkatha Freedom Party (IFP), the party he founded, Buthelezi retired as its president at the age of 89 in 2017. Or, so it was thought. By 2019, he was still at the helm. It was believed that the KwaZulu-Natal IFP secretary, Velenkosini Hlabisi, would take over, but the party had not yet held an election to choose a successor.

Although there have been very deep troughs in the influence or impact Buthelezi has had on South African politics, he has certainly played an historic role.

There were indications in the late 1940s, when the number of black African intellectuals was growing significantly, that he would lead in some way. He studied at the University of Fort Hare from 1948 to 1950, where he came into contact with outstanding African minds, including future Zimbabwe president Robert Mugabe and the founder of the Pan-Africanist Congress (PAC) Robert Sobukwe.

Buthelezi was expelled after student boycotts and was compelled to complete his degree at the University of Natal. Then a member of the ANC and its Youth League, he founded the IFP with the 'blessing' of the ANC in 1975. But thereafter, Buthelezi was increasingly regarded as a sell-out, particularly by the Black Consciousness Movement (BCM), and especially when he agreed to run the KwaZulu-Natal bantustan as a chief minister on behalf of the apartheid regime. He continued in that position until 1994, presenting as a 'benign' face of a 'moderate' black South African leader successfully marketed to whites.

Yet, Buthelezi cannot be separated from the bloodshed that happened mostly in the Transvaal during the 1980s and early 1990s as his party's militia fought not only the ANC but entire communities. He allowed those militia to be trained by apartheid's security forces in the interests of creating violent divisions that were to the benefit of the IFP and the National Party (NP).

Nonetheless, in an act of 'reconciliation', Nelson Mandela made Buthelezi not only a deputy in the Government of National Unity (GNU) after 1994, but also home affairs minister.

Buthelezi, Sfiso

Deputy Minister of Agriculture, Forestry and Fisheries | Former Deputy Minister of Finance | Former chairperson of the Public Investment Corporation (PIC) | Former chairperson of the Passenger Rail Agency of South Africa (Prasa) | ANC politician | Former political prisoner

Suspected of corruption

A UNIVERSITY OF CAPE TOWN (UCT)-TRAINED ECONOMIST, the Deputy Minister of Agriculture, Forestry and Fisheries previously served as the Deputy Minister of Finance when appointed by Jacob Zuma in 2017. Buthelezi, who is a member of the ANC's National Executive Committee (NEC), has been a member of the party for more than 30 years, eight of which were spent on Robben Island, during which time he got close to Zuma, who was also a prisoner on the island.

Buthelezi was employed as a consultant to Zuma in 1994.

Previously the chairperson of the Passenger Rail Agency of South Africa (Prasa) board, and a businessman, Buthelezi – together with former Prasa chief executive Lucky Montana – was a target of the Democratic Alliance (DA), which opened a case against them for financial mismanagement with the Cape Town police in December 2017. Buthelezi denied all allegations of corruption during his 10 years as Prasa chairperson. But allegations were that he and his brother, Nkanyiso, had benefitted from contracts worth R150 million.

Swifambo Rail Leasing, a supplier of locomotives to Prasa, had appointed Inala Shipping to manage the shipping of trains. Inala was apparently owned by Nkanyiso Buthelezi.

Treasury's investigation concluded that 'crippling mismanagement and criminality' at Prasa had reached 'systemic proportions' while Buthelezi was on the board. It calculated that of the 216 contracts with a combined value of about R19 billion, only 13 were 'above board'. It found that 'crucial and confidential documents were lost, stolen and destroyed'.

In his capacity as Deputy Finance Minister, Buthelezi automatically assumed the position of Public Investment Corporation (PIC) board chairperson.

C

Cachalia, Ghaleb

Shadow Minister of Trade and Industry | Democratic Alliance (DA) politician | Unsuccessfully campaigned for the provincial leadership of the DA in Gauteng in 2017

Change agent | On the way up

THE SCION OF ONE OF THE ANC's most important struggle families surprised – even shocked – many when he joined the DA just ahead of the 2014 local government elections. He stood as the party's mayoral candidate in Ekurhuleni, outside Johannesburg, where the ANC's comfortable majority had dropped from 62% to 48%. Then elected as a DA MP, Cachalia was believed to be playing a critical role in the rethinking of the liberal party, which underwent a serious reputational, moral and political crisis in 2018.

The son of anti-apartheid activists Yusuf and Amina Cachalia, he was a campaigner for the Anti-Apartheid Movement (AAM) in London where he studied history at the School of Oriental and African Studies. Upon his return, he attended the University of the Witwatersrand to study law, a degree which he did not complete. While at the university, he joined the Black Students Society (BSS) and became its vice president.

Cachalia, who worked in management consultancy, served as the DA's Deputy Shadow Minister of Trade and Industry in 2018.

He attracted the ire of the Economic Freedom Fighters (EFF) in October 2018 when he claimed EFF leader Julius Malema had owned shares in a company called Dyambeu Investments which fell under Vele Investments, a business intricately involved in the R2-billion looting of the Venda Building Society (VBS Bank). Cachalia made an official apology, saying his information was incorrect.

Cameron, Justice Edwin

Former Constitutional Court (ConCourt) Justice | Former Supreme Court of Appeal (SCA) judge | First director of the Aids Law Project

Change agent | Star

ACADEMIC, ACTIVIST, ADVOCATE AND AUTHOR Edwin Cameron became one of the most high-profile gay judges in the world. Born in 1953 and educated at Pretoria Boys High, Cameron did his BA (Law) at Stellenbosch and lectured there before winning a Rhodes Scholarship to Oxford University where he obtained a Bachelor of Civil Law.

Returning to South Africa, Cameron obtained his LLB through Unisa, graduating as the best student. He practised as an advocate at the Johannesburg Bar from 1983 to 1994, working mainly in the field of human rights. He was the first director of the

Aids Law Project and played a critical role in ensuring the Constitution understood and protected gay rights.

Cameron was diagnosed as HIV positive in 1986 and voluntarily disclosed his status in 1999 after the 1998 murder of Gugu Dlamini, who was stoned to death when she told her community in KwaMashu township near Durban her status.

Nelson Mandela appointed Cameron a judge in 1995, a year after Cameron took silk. He was elected to the Supreme Court of Appeal (SCA) in 2000 and from there to the Constitutional Court in 2008.

Widely recognised as being one of the most progressive judges on the bench in the history of the South African judicial system, Cameron made seminal contributions to both the law of defamation and advancing media freedom.

Cardo, Dr Michael

Shadow Minister of Economic Development | Democratic Alliance (DA) politician

ON THE ONE HAND DESCRIBED AS A RISING STAR, Cardo is, on the other, identified as a 'neocon'.

At issue for the DA MP, who has an MPhil and PhD in History from Cambridge, is the debate of diversity versus progressive black advancement within his own party. In this, he was linked to other DA MPs and apparatchiks who were unimpressed with party leader Mmusi Maimane's speech on Freedom Day 2018 in which he decried white privilege. Cardo entered a controversial space in early 2018 when he penned a letter with the DA's former policy chief Gavin Davis around racial transformation in the party. It appeared he and Davis were against quotas being imposed on the DA's representation.

Cardo joined the political staff of the DA in 2003 and became the party's National Director of Research in 2004.

He was awarded a Visiting Research Fellowship at the Helen Suzman Foundation in 2006, during which time he wrote a biography of the former South African Liberal Party leader Peter Brown.

Cardo returned to the DA as party leader Helen Zille's speechwriter for the 2009 national and provincial elections campaign. Between 2011 and 2014, he worked in the policy and strategy unit at the office of the premier in the Western Cape.

Cardo was elected an MP in 2014 and became the Shadow Minister of Economic Development.

Cele, 'General' Bheki

Minister of Police | Former National Police Commissioner (NPC) | Former Deputy Minister of Agriculture, Forestry and Fisheries | ANC politician

Fired for corruption, then rehired

CELE HAD AN EVENTFUL POLITICAL LIFE EVEN BEFORE he appeared, as if out of nowhere for many South Africans, when Jacob Zuma appointed him National

Police Commissioner (NPC) in July 2009. Cele was, however, no stranger within top ANC circles, particularly in KwaZulu-Natal where he had once worked closely with Zuma. Cele was a member of the Executive Council for Transport, Safety and Security in the province from 2004.

Arriving in the national spotlight offered the fedora-wearing Cele an opportunity to take control of rampant crime. He portrayed himself as a no-nonsense, gun-friendly, cop-protecting leader who was as tired of being under threat from criminals as every other ordinary person.

Zuma was compelled to fire him as NPC in 2012 when he failed to disclose a relationship with property mogul Roux Shabangu over a dubious R1.6-billion, 10-year lease of buildings for SAPS use in Pretoria and Durban. Then Public Protector Thuli Madonsela issued two reports concerning the matter, describing Cele's conduct as 'improper, unlawful and (amounting) to maladministration'. As NPC, Cele was the SAPS's accounting officer.

Cele left the limelight a villain, but rebuilt himself politically as he withdrew his support for Zuma. He was never at a loss for power in his own party structures, elected onto its National Executive Committee (NEC) at its elective conference in Mangaung, Free State, the same year he was fired.

By the time President Cyril Ramaphosa made him police minister in 2018, Cele had re-entered the stage in the anti-Zuma chorus. He brought as much of KwaZulu-Natal – Zuma's stronghold – into Ramaphosa's camp as he could ahead of the elective conference at Nasrec, Johannesburg, where Ramaphosa narrowly won the position of president of the ANC over Nkosazana Dlamini-Zuma.

The Chamber of Mines

Private sector | Traditionally, 'white monopoly capital' | Mining lobby group

Formalised in 1889 as the Witwatersrand Chamber of Mines by three founding members – Corner House, Consolidated Gold Fields and the Robinson Group – its aims were to promote and protect mining interests, lobby government and stimulate debate about mining in the public sphere.

By 1896, it was refashioned as the Chamber of Mines of the South African Republic, then, after the Anglo Boer War, as the Chamber of Mines of the Transvaal and the Free State until, in 1968, it became the Chamber of Mines of South Africa, which it remains to this day.

Largely moribund and parochial in recent times, mirroring the general state of decay of the mining industry in South Africa, it has been pressured by ever-dwindling reserves and rising costs. Although the Chamber rediscovered its voice in fighting the appointment of Gupta family acolyte Mosibenzi Zwane as the mining minister by Jacob Zuma, it would not necessarily find President Cyril Ramaphosa's replacement choice of former ANC secretary-general Gwede Mantashe an easy partner in its revival.

The Chamber would be challenged by a landmark judgment in the Gauteng High Court in late 2018 that gave any community the right to refuse mining under customary law. This followed a 15-year battle by the Eastern Cape community of Xolobeni, through the activist organisation the Amadiba Crisis Committee, over the mining of titanium-rich dunes in the Wild Coast.

The ruling stated that Mantashe had no lawful authority to grant a mining right unless full and informed consent had been obtained from the affected community. This was in terms of the Interim Protection of Informal Land Rights Act which protects customary communities.

Also in 2018, the Chamber did not support the government appealing a judgment that year which said that if mining companies had complied with the Charter's minimum requirement of a black shareholding of 26 per cent, as per the 2004 and 2010 iterations, those companies would not have to 'top up' if they lost black partners who later sold their shares.

Chapter 9 institutions

Government bodies

ESTABLISHED IN TERMS OF THE CONSTITUTION to guard democracy, the Chapter 9 institutions are: the Public Protector (PP), the South African Human Rights Commission (SAHRC), the Commission for the Promotion and Protection of the Rights of Cultural, Religious and Linguistic Communities (CRL Rights Commission), the Commission for Gender Equality (CGE), the Auditor-General (AG), the Electoral Commission of South Africa (IEC) and 'an independent authority to regulate broadcasting' (the Act does not specifically name the current institution, the Independent Communications Authority of South Africa, ICASA).

The power of the Chapter 9 institutions was confirmed in March 2016 when the Constitutional Court (ConCourt) found that then president Jacob Zuma had failed to uphold, defend and respect the Constitution as the supreme law of the land. This was in regard to his inactivity upon the release of 'Secure in Comfort', the PP's report critical of his handling of the cost of non-security upgrades to his private residence in Nkandla, KwaZulu-Natal.

Although the PP, the AG and the IEC have been praised for their achievements, not all the Chapter 9 institutions have been as effective. The CRL Rights Commission was little known in the country until its investigation into religious practices, which ran through 2016 and 2017, while the CGE has been criticised for failing to extend an understanding of its mandate. The SAHRC performed well under Judge Jody Kollapen, but seemingly withdrew from the national picture under former PP, Advocate Lawrence Mushwana. It is expected to regain prominence under Professor Bongani Majola, previously with the United Nations.

Chester Missing

Satirical puppet

Non-aligned

VENTRILOQUIST CONRAD KOCH WAS STUDYING anthropology at the University of Cape Town (UCT) when he decided comedy was his favoured route to dealing with his privileged, liberal upbringing and the effects of racism that he saw everywhere around him.

Chester Missing started out as coloured, but in an interview with Radio 702, Koch explained how that changed as Koch's understanding of his craft developed. 'I reinvented him and he became the sort of latex dude that didn't look like any race,' said Koch. 'Is he black? Is he Mediterranean? He could be black, but maybe he is coloured? He could be Zulu or Moroccan. Chester specifically makes claims to confuse your idea of race. It gets quite complex in my head. I have my critics though, which I'm fine with.'

Through Chester Missing, Koch has interviewed most of South Africa's politicians, often with hilarious and sometimes ironic results. The puppet was a key figure at the ANC's December 2017 elective conference at Nasrec, and was then invited to cover the ANC's annual 8 January speech as a political commentator for independent 24-hour TV news channel, eNCA.

Chester Missing got his own weekly show called *Almost News* on the channel in November 2018.

Coalitions

In use throughout governing structures in South Africa

A COALITION IS SIMPLY AN AGREEMENt for co-operation on common political agendas, usually to clear election thresholds.

The Democratic Alliance (DA) and the Inkatha Freedom Party (IFP) are particularly well known for forming coalitions, for example in the Johannesburg metropolitan municipality, to win votes on particular issues.

Coalitions expert Leon Schreiber, a South African-born senior research specialist at Princeton University, wrote in his book *Coalition Country*, that 'with 226 local municipalities, 44 district municipalities, eight metropolitan municipalities and nine provinces, it is likely that there will soon be dozens of different political combinations in charge of local, municipal and national governments (in South Africa)'.

Schreiber noted that the country had 288 different elected governments (278 municipalities, nine provinces and one national). He also concluded that, 'as politics becomes more competitive, the influence of independent candidates, especially in municipalities, will become yet another important factor that introduces even more uncertainty'.

Confidence-and-supply model

In use in Johannesburg, Tshwane and Nelson Mandela Bay metropolitan municipalities, in addition to more conventional coalitions

THE ECONOMIC FREEDOM FIGHTERS (EFF) is not in coalitions with the Democratic Alliance (DA) and other parties in the Johannesburg, Tshwane and Nelson Mandela Bay metros. Rather, the DA (and others) observed the EFF's choice of the 'confidence-and-supply' model after it, the EFF, held the keys to power in what were hung councils after the 2016 local government elections.

The confidence-and-supply model allows the EFF to vote with or against the DA or other parties in coalition with the DA, depending on the issue, thereby determining the outcome of a council event.

This gave the EFF more power than it might have had in a conventional coalition as it was not bound by a particular course of action, unlike, say, the Inkatha Freedom Party (IFP) and the DA which had an agreement that they would vote together in certain councils on certain issues at local government level.

Confidence-and-supply has been widely used in politics in the United Kingdom, India, Canada, Malaysia, Ireland and New Zealand, and is mostly linked to the British Westminster system as it has successfully propped up a number of minority governments in the UK.

The Johannesburg, Tshwane and Nelson Mandela Bay metros were run by minority governments or multiparty councils from 2016. In the case of Johannesburg, the ANC won 45%, which was not enough to lead the city, allowing the EFF to add its 11% to the DA's 38% to out-vote the ANC. The DA beat the ANC in Tshwane with its 43% which, together with the EFF's 12%, took it over 50% against the ANC's 41%.

EFF leader Julius Malema explained the party's stance after the 2016 local government elections at a press conference famously held on an open field in Alexandra, a Johannesburg township, saying the ANC would be punished 'collectively' for refusing to get rid of Jacob Zuma. The EFF negotiated with both the ANC and the DA after the local government polls, as both parties needed its support. But it put pressure on the ANC to win its support by removing Zuma, agreeing to the expropriation of land without compensation and the nationalisation of banks, and other conditions.

In the end, due to the ANC's refusal to accede to most of its demands, the EFF chose what it called 'the better devil', the DA, and said it was prepared to vote with the DA in those hung metros to bring down the ANC.

Commission for the Promotion and Protection of the Rights of Cultural, Religious and Linguistic Communities (CLR Rights Commission)

Chapter 9 institution

Responsible for 'deepening the appreciation of South Africans for the wide array of cultures, religions and languages found in the country', the Commission is tasked with social transformation. Little was known about it, or that it even existed, until it embarked on a long-running investigation into the commercialisation of religion and the abuse of people's belief systems in 2015.

This investigation followed reports that some religious leaders were putting the lives of their congregants in danger. Among the most notorious examples were pastors feeding worshippers grass and snakes, spraying pesticides in their faces and giving them paraffin to drink.

While the CLR Rights Commission's report to Parliament after it had concluded its investigation in 2017 made recommendations to curb the activities of such religious leaders, there was pushback from some religious communities. Most often, rejection of the findings was based on claims about free speech and freedom of association.

The CLR Rights Commission proposed an extensive national structure to licence every 'religious practitioner' and 'place of worship'. But Parliament's view was that a call for 'religious regulation', 'demonstrated poor understanding of the constitutional mandate of Parliament and its relations with the commission'.

The commission's chairperson, Thoko Nonhle Mkhwanazi-Xaluva, said it was 'unfortunate' that Parliament doubted 'the constitutionality of religious regulation' and said the Commission may have to go to the Constitutional Court to obtain a declaratory order.

Parliament's Co-operative Governance and Traditional Affairs Portfolio Committee said the 'constitutional provisions of freedom of religion (mean) that the state cannot prescribe when it comes to people's beliefs and religious conviction'.

This series of defensive rebuttals between commissioners, politicians and communities became more hostile after a tragedy befell the village of Ngcobo, between the towns of Mthatha and Queenstown in the Eastern Cape, in February 2018. Attackers entered the Ngcobo police station and five policemen and a retired soldier were killed. Two days later, seven suspects were shot dead and 10 others arrested at the Seven Angels Ministry church after a shootout with police. Three brothers from the local Mancoba family, who were the 'church' leaders, were among those killed.

A war of words ensued, with the commission and Parliament effectively blaming each other for inaction in Ngcobo. Residents there had warned such an event was possible at the church, whose activities it had reported out of concern before. Mkhwanazi-Xaluva had interviewed the Seven Angels church leaders in 2016 as part of the CLR Rights Commission's investigation and said she had made the Parliamentary committee aware of underlying dangers in Ngcobo in June 2017. Her contention was that Parliament had 'only dealt with our recommendations' (regarding Seven Angels) in February 2018.

Drawing its mandate from the Constitution, the CLR Rights Commission's new commissioners were inaugurated in 2014 for a period of five years.

Commission for Gender Equality

Chapter 9 institution

The Commission for Gender Equality (CGE)'s role is to 'advance, promote and protect gender equality in South Africa through undertaking research, public education, policy development, legislative initiatives, effective monitoring and litigation'. But what it really does or how it executes its important mandate, was not clear. Neither were its specific achievements.

Its chairperson in 2018, Lulama Nare, was previously with the National Economic Development and Labour Council (Nedlac) and the gender unit of the South African Democratic Teachers Union. Deputy chairperson Tamara Mathebula had a clinical background.

There were several men in the management of the CGE, with the most prominent being Mbuyiselo Botha, who was well known for his pioneering work at Sonke Gender Justice. The mandate given to the commissioners who were men was to mobilise other men to 'fully embrace gender equality'.

Commissions of Inquiry

Government-appointed probes

THERE HAVE BEEN MULTIPLE COMMISSIONS of inquiry established by the executive and national, provincial and municipal departments since 1994. Although the Constitution only gives the president and premiers the authority to appoint these, there is a facility for delegation of such executive power.

Government still operates off the pre-apartheid Commissions Act of 1947, which states that commissions must report their findings to the president before their finds are made public, but there is no legal obligation for these to ever be made fully available to the public.

Commissions are believed to have cost more than R300 million in public funds since the start of democracy.

Commission on Restitution of Land Rights

Government body

LAND RESTITUTION WAS THE MOST IMPORTANT, and incendiary, issue in South African politics ahead of the 2019 elections – and it had a powerful basis in law.

The 1993 Interim Constitution provided that legal basis, followed by the Restitution of Land Rights Act in 1994. Section 25 of the 1996 Constitution finally stated that people whose families, and communities whose earlier iterations, had been dispossessed after the Natives Land Act was passed on 19 June 1913, had the right to have their property restored or to claim compensation.

The Natives Land Act of 1913 had allocated a mere 7% of arable land to black South Africans, while white South Africans could settle on and farm more than 90% of the fertile land. That Act effectively set aside reserves for black people.

A Land Claims Commission was established in 1995 under a chief land claims commissioner. Regional land claims commissioners represented the nine provinces. A Land Claims Court was simultaneously established to handle disputes that could not be solved by the commission, whose primary role was to screen claims and attempt to solve these through administrative or mediation procedures.

Initially, land claims had to be lodged by 31 December 1998, but the Restitution of Land Rights Amendment Act passed in 2017 gave new land claimants an opportunity until 30 June 2019 to lodge claims.

Nomfundo Ntloko-Gobodo was Land Claims Commissioner in 2019. She was previously a director at the Legal Resources Centre in Johannesburg where she focused on land law, housing law, children's rights, access to justice, and customary law, among other related areas. Gobodo also worked at the South African Human Rights Commission (SAHRC) and the Community Law Centre.

The commission – which fell under the Department of Rural Development –

had to fall in line with amendments to Section 25 of the Constitution as decided by Parliament's Joint Constitutional Review Committee in 2018, relating to land expropriation without compensation.

Congress of the People (COPE)

ANC breakaway party | Centrist | Number of seats in Parliament in 2018: 3

On the way down

IN DECEMBER 2008, THE COUNTRY WAS in the grip of a festive season in which the name COPE was a buzzword. The new party was a brazen breakaway by some ANC leaders ahead of the 2009 election.

Its raison d'etre was the party's recall of Thabo Mbeki as president in September 2008 – a decision which would allow Jacob Zuma, already the ANC president, to lead the country instead. Popular stalwart, the party's deputy president, Kgalema Motlanthe, was installed as caretaker president of the country in the wake of Mbeki, whose recall had seen numbers of his senior supporters resign as ministers and MPs amid the growing power of the incumbent Zuma.

Some Mbeki supporters left the ANC entirely to establish or join COPE.

At that moment, it was unpopular to suggest COPE could disintegrate as quickly as it did. After all, its unleashing was not devoid of fanfare. But scarcely had the elections come in April 2009 when a power struggle ensued between founding leaders Mosiuoa Lekota, the minister of defence in Mbeki's cabinet, and Mbhazima Shilowa, the former premier of Gauteng.

Such was the damage that COPE could not even depose the Democratic Alliance (DA) as the Official Opposition, obtaining just over 1.3 million votes and less than half of the DA's 67 seats. When the elections were over, the power struggle intensified into a tedious feud that eventually took the courts to declare Lekota as leader.

Shilowa, a former general secretary of the Congress of South African Trade Unions (Cosatu), gave up a prime position in the ANC when he resigned as Gauteng premier, and was regarded as a significant loss to COPE. He had vast political experience, having played a vital part in the formation of the National Economic Development and Labour Council and was on the ANC's negotiating team at the Convention for a Democratic South Africa (Codesa). When Shilowa finally lost his court battle with his former comrade, who had expelled him from the party after an internal hearing found Shilowa guilty of 'mismanaging parliamentary funds', Shilowa decided to step away from politics, but has remained an active political commentator on Twitter.

As COPE lurched from one crisis to another, the effects were felt – especially in the 2014 national elections, when it could only muster three seats, down by 27 from 2009.

Lekota – who had a public argument with Economic Freedom Fighters (EFF) Commander-in-Chief Julius Malema on the first day of key hearings into land reform in mid-2018 – remained a visible and outspoken figure, but the party faces possible extinction in the 2019 elections.

It would not have helped its potential for attracting more black voters when it went into a partnership with conservative minority rights advocacy organisation Afriforum in September 2018 to fight proposed amendments to Section 25 of the Constitution. The proposed amendments – which were endorsed by the ANC before these went before Parliament – were designed to facilitate the expropriation of land without compensation.

But it was becoming clear by the end of 2018 that COPE had refined its political strategy to attract more conservative white voters, particularly around the land expropriation issue. Apart from its partnerships with AfriForum, it also teamed up in December 2018 with rightwing leader Steve Hofmeyr of Afrikaner/Boer lobby group ToekomsVonk when Hofmeyr laid charges against Black First Land First (BLF) leader Andile Mngxitama for his threats against white people.

COPE had earlier laid charges itself against Mngxitama.

Congress of South African Trade Unions (Cosatu)

Partner of the ANC and SACP in the Tripartite Alliance | Essentially leftwing, but ideologically mixed | Some in leadership suspected of corruption, others guilty of corruption

Change agent

OFFICIALLY ESTABLISHED IN DECEMBER 1985 after four years of unity talks between unions and federations, Congress of South African Trade Unions (Cosatu) was at the forefront of the political struggle against apartheid. Together with the South African Communist Party (SACP), it became a pillar of the ANC-led Tripartite Alliance.

The overwhelming nature of the continuing political struggle in South Africa has, however, dogged Cosatu's compliance with the more conventional approach of trade union federations: class struggle. Although it has driven new labour legislation and campaigned for a national living wage since inception, Cosatu's involvement in the ANC's internal strife has led to schisms.

The most dramatic of these was the expulsion of its second-biggest affiliate, the National Union of Metalworkers (Numsa) in 2014, followed by the departure of a further nine affiliates. This rattled the wider labour movement. Cosatu's public stance was that Numsa was expelled because it would not give its public support to the ANC under Jacob Zuma in the 2014 elections.

Cosatu, which was in turn criticised for following government's neo-liberal policy trajectory, said this rebellion transgressed the federation's constitution.

A circuitous route united Numsa, the Food and Allied Workers Union (FAWU) and others as the South African Federation of Trade Unions (Saftu) in 2017, affecting Cosatu's finances as the rebel unions' members no longer paid fees to it. Since that cataclysm, Cosatu has tried to restore cohesion under its flag whose familiar wheel (representing the economy), workers and woman with a baby (the triple challenge of economic, racial and gender oppression) in red (for the working class), black (the struggle against racial oppression) and gold (the wealth of South Africa) had started to lose their revolutionary symbolism.

Cosatu issued a statement upon the election of Cyril Ramaphosa as ANC president in December 2017, saying it expected 'the new leadership to revive our revolutionary alliance and the mass democratic movement at large'. Its biggest affiliates, the National Union of Mineworkers (NUM), the National Education, Health and Allied Workers' Union (Nehawu), the Police and Prison Civil Rights Union (Popcru) and the South African Democratic Teachers Union (Sadtu) all stood behind the ANC.

Cosatu's slogan, 'An injury to one is an injury to all', was invoked as a means of reinvigorating their purpose. But much had been lost.

A decade ago, the federation was a mighty political force, with labour in its thrall and big business a reasonably deferential adversary. With its emphasis on worker control, Cosatu within a Zuma-led administration was still fit to carry the description, 'giant', given by its first president, Elijah Barayi.

Although the ANC's alliance partner had stepped away from the non-partisan role it adopted upon its launch in 1985, the federation had continued aligning itself with progressive community movements and grassroots campaigns. But the Zuma years saw a dramatic plunge in membership and an ideological crisis which detracted from Cosatu's authenticity. This was largely due to its leadership conflating political power with class struggle, which culminated in the schism with Numsa, and with its charismatic general-secretary, Zwelinzima Vavi.

Numsa and Vavi were eventually expelled in 2014 due to factionalism and infighting reflective of the ANC's own internal battles over Zuma's legitimacy. But the loss of Numsa challenged Cosatu to regain its radical reputation to lure back affiliates representing the worker world in big business, and to stay financially afloat.

Meanwhile, the federation's political alliance with the ANC and the SACP was still shaky on the inside. There was no real unity within its membership around class and ideological positioning.

With leaders Bheki Ntshalintshali, Sdumo Dlamini and Zingiswa Losi failing to harness a singular position on many pressing bread-and-butter issues, it was uncertain how much political power Cosatu would finally hold during the ANC's 2019 election campaign. But when Losi was elected in September 2018 as the first woman to head the federation, it felt like it might be possible to seize a political moment, as Losi also occupied a role in national government.

The Congress of South African Students (Cosas)

Youth formation | ANC-aligned

From the 1980s, the Congress of South African Students (Cosas) has led the mobilisation of black youth. Formed in 1979 after the South African Student Movement (SASM) was banned, along with other Black Consciousness (BC)-supporting organisations and individuals in 1977, it remained the student movement with the most authentic liberation history.

Like its predecessor, SASM, it emerged out of the fiery courage of the 1976 uprisings led by school children. Driven by the memory of BC leader Steve Biko, murdered by the apartheid state in 1977, it set out to organise young people, not only at school level but also tertiary institutions, and those who were unemployed.

Along with this, Cosas supported worker struggles – a feature also evident in the #FeesMustFall (Fallist) student movement, where students and workers fought the system that oppressed them together.

Cosas started out with BC as its basis, but as BC itself was gradually politically outmanoeuvred by the United Democratic Front (UDF) in the early 1980s, so too did Cosas declare its allegiance to the Freedom Charter and the ANC underground.

Its internecine fighting with the rival, BC-aligned Azanian Students Movement in the bloody 1980s, remained a blight on its history, although both contributed significantly to conscientising and leading young black people.

It had extraordinary success at grassroots level, quickly establishing branches all over the country and remaining undaunted even as its first president, Ephrahim Mogale, was convicted of furthering the aims of the ANC. Its slogan – Liberation Now, Education Later – remained one of the most resonant of the struggle and the many Cosas members who were part of the organisation when it was banned by the regime in 1985 were regarded as revolutionaries by many young South Africans. Their heroes of the time were other young people, like Solomon Mahlangu and Emma Sathekge, both killed by the apartheid state.

Cosas was estimated to have a membership of about 3 million young people at its height at the end of the 1980s. It was revived in 1990 and continues to play a role predominantly in protest politics involving students, but mostly as a partner to the ANC. Economic Freedom Fighters (EFF) leader Julius Malema was among its post-democratic leaders. In 2019, the president-general of Cosas was John Macheke, while Nkhabo Khomongoe was secretary general.

The Constitutional Court (ConCourt)

South Africa's apex court

Sitting at Constitution Hill next to the historic Old Fort prison in Johannesburg, the ConCourt may only hear constitutional matters. But enthusiastic amateur jurists like former president Jacob Zuma and convicted fraudster and Zuma associate Schabir Shaik have found ways to test the apparent constitutionality of often the most banal legal issues.

The ConCourt's findings are binding on all lower courts. It has proved its worth throughout South Africa's young democracy, starting with the abolition of capital punishment in 1995.

Its guiding document is the Constitution, to which its 11 justices, led by the chief justice and assisted by the deputy chief justice, must abide. The entire bench sits in judgment for each case, and judgment is by simple majority – although there is space for disagreement. That disagreement is sometimes profound but always collegial among the justices – an example being in December 2017 when Chief Justice Mogoeng Mogoeng differed from the majority of his bench.

Judges, known as justices, are shortlisted by the Judicial Service Commission and appointed by the president for a non-renewable term of between 12 and 15 years, depending on the age of the justice upon appointment.

Contralesa (the Congress of Traditional Leaders of South Africa)

Conservative lobby group

Power brokers

THIS ORGANISATION HAS ITS ROOTS in an anti-apartheid project that started in the late 1980s in bantustans, which would be dismantled within the following five years.

Traditional leaders in kwaNdebele were the first to work with the ANC's then proxy, the United Democratic Front, but as democracy drew nearer, more and more traditional leaders joined the congress. It remained closest, politically, to the ANC, but has not supported many of the tenets of the Constitution, particularly LGBTQ rights, which it rejects.

Contralesa was a loud voice against the award-winning 2018 film, *Inxeba*, which, among other issues, exposed traditional circumcision in South Africa.

Its president in 2019 was Kgoshi (Chief) Lameck Mathibela Mokoena, the leader of the Mathibela Tribal Authority of the Mpumalanga House of Traditional Leaders.

Corruption Watch

Activists | Non-aligned

Change agents | Stars

THE AIM OF THE ADVOCACY ORGANISATION, which was accredited as the South African chapter of Transparency International, was to expose rampant abuse in business and government. It had many successes, including a 2018 High Court win against Cash Paymaster Services (CPS), the company involved in disputable dealings with the Department of Social Services to distribute and process social grants. CPS was ordered to repay some R316 million plus interest to the South African Social Security Agency.

As political parties made anti-corruption a 2019 election priority, the organisation kept a close eye on particularly the ANC as it campaigned to stem its decline in power.

The chairperson of Corruption Watch in 2019 was Mavuso Msimang, ANC veteran, former director-general of Home Affairs and the CEO of the Oliver and Adelaide Tambo Foundation. Former Competition Tribunal chairperson David Lewis was its executive director. Others on its board included top human rights lawyer Adila Hassim, former Constitutional Court (ConCourt) judge, Kate O'Regan, and the former head of the National Prosecuting Authority, Advocate Vusi Pikoli.

Creecy, Barbara

Gauteng MEC for Finance | ANC politician | Member of the ANC's National Working Committee (NWC)

On the way up

AN ACTIVIST IN THE UNDERGROUND STRUCTURES of the ANC while a politics student at the University of the Witwatersrand (Wits) in the 1970s, Creecy went on to serve in the United Democratic Front and later in training and organisational development support to trade unions.

She was elected as a member of the Gauteng Provincial Executive Committee (PEC) of the ANC in 2004. A former Member of the Executive Committee (MEC) for Sports, Recreation, Arts and Culture, and then for Education, Creecy received an award from the South African Institute for Government Auditors for the best financial statements in Gauteng while leading the Education portfolio. She was also a high achiever in the Education portfolio, where a strategy to improve matric results in underperforming township schools won her department a United Nations prize.

Gauteng's MEC for Finance in 2019, Creecy's announcement during her Budget speech for 2018/2019 of a process to design the province's first new highway since the 1970s was well received as Gauteng is one of the most congested cities in the country.

Crucial Information Regulator

Government-appointed body

Jacob Zuma appointed the regulator in late 2016 as an independent governing body responsible for regulating the use of consumer data and holding companies to account for that data's safe storage and protection. Its mandate was to promote access to information in line with the Promotion of Access to Information Act of 2000 (PAIA) and monitor and enforce compliance by public and private bodies of the Protection of Personal Information Act of 2013 (POPI).

But the chairperson, Advocate Pansy Tlakula, was somewhat paralysed in setting up the regulator as she had not been able to hire key staff 18 months after its establishment due to an administrative impasse in its legislative framework.

The regulator is classified as a national public entity, meaning that its board has to be the accounting authority. Treasury argued that the Public Finance Management Act (PFMA) required that the chairperson of the board, in this case Tlakula, was the accounting officer.

But this is in conflict with POPI, which allows only for a CEO to be the accounting officer. Finally, after Tlakula took the matter to Parliament, the country's executive agreed that a CEO had to be appointed, as agreed, and that this person would be the accounting officer. The debacle was a poor reflection on Parliament, drawing attention to its tendency for passing weak, or flawed, legislation.

Under POPI, businesses and organisations are not allowed to sell consumer data without consent and can be fined up to R10 million. Directors of offending companies can also face prosecution as concern around breaches of personal data has grown substantially.

As the 2019 election approached, there was significant concern that a hack could occur in the voting system, or that a third party – as, allegedly, happened with Russia in the American presidential election in 2017 – could interfere if the regulator was not in place.

Cwele, Dr Siyabonga

Minister of Home Affairs | Former minister of Telecommunications and Postal Services | Former minister of Intelligence | Former State Security Minister | ANC politician

CWELE REGAINED SOME POLITICAL MOMENTUM in November 2018 when Cyril Ramaphosa saw fit to appoint him minister of home affairs in the wake of the disgraced Malusi Gigaba, who resigned before he was likely to be fired.

Cwele was minister of telecommunications and postal services before he was moved to home affairs. That shift happened at the same time as Ramaphosa merged the department of communications and the department of telecommunications and postal services into one ministry, of telecommunications.

Cwele's reputation had been affected during his tenure in State Security, which started to implode in 2010 when he appointed a team to investigate the Principal Agent Network (PAN) – a unit overseen by controversial spy boss Arthur Fraser, who was then Deputy Director-General (DG) of the National Intelligence Agency. Fraser resigned during Cwele's investigation, which found that he, Fraser, had tried to establish what amounted to a parallel intelligence network and defied organisational security procedures.

Jacob Zuma then gave Cwele the task of restructuring what was previously one government entity, the department of communications, into two departments in 2014. Thereafter, Zuma appointed Cwele to run telecommunications, with some analysts speculating Zuma had split the two so as to have control over communications in order to create propaganda that suited his faction of the ANC.

At the height of the crippling South African Post Office (SAPO) strike in 2014, which lasted for almost four months and was a crisis that required definitive action, Cwele – as Minister of Telecommunications and Postal Services – seemed conspicuous by his absence. When he eventually broke his silence, he offered a timid intervention, calling on the unions and the SAPO board to 'speed up' negotiations".

Cwele, who was a long-standing member of the ANC Provincial Executive Committee (PEC) in KwaZulu-Natal, was appointed an ANC MP in 1994. He served as chairperson of the Joint Standing Committee on Intelligence and prior to his appointment as Minister of State Security, as Minister of Intelligence from 2008 to 2009.

Despite his position, Cwele claimed to have been wholly unaware of his then wife Sheryl trafficking cocaine. Sheryl Cwele was originally sentenced to 12 years in prison. The couple divorced in 2011.

Siyabonga Cwele holds an MBchB from the University of KwaZulu-Natal and an MPhil in economic policy from the University of Stellenbosch.

D

Davies, Dr Rob

Minister of Trade and Industry | ANC politician | South African Communist Party (SACP) Politburo member

AN ANTI-APARTHEID EXILE FROM 1979 to 1990, Davies lived mostly in Mozambique where he worked at the Centre for African Studies at Eduardo Mondlane University with Ruth First, an SACP activist and academic who was murdered by the apartheid regime in Maputo in 1982. Davies became an economics researcher for the ANC and the Southern African Development Community (SADC) when the ANC was unbanned in 1990, working at the Centre for Southern African Studies, University of the Western Cape.

Although Davies – a member of the central committee and politburo of the SACP – had been an ANC MP since the first democratic Parliament in 1994, he was promoted in 2005 to the position of Deputy Minister of Trade and Industry. Former president Jacob Zuma then promoted him to Minister of Trade and Industry in 2009 and re-appointed him in 2014.

Davies played a significant role in formulating and building the tripartite SADC-COMESA-EAC Free Trade Area. (COMESA or the Common Market for Eastern and Southern Africa is a free trade area with 19 member states stretching from Libya to eSwatini formed in December 1994; the EAC is the East African Community, an intergovernmental organisations comprising Burundi, Kenya, Rwanda, South Sudan, Tanzania and Uganda.)

Davies was also active within BRICS (Brazil, Russia, India, China and South Africa), the Economic Partnership Agreement with the European Union (EU), the United States' Africa Growth and Opportunity Act (AGOA), and the World Trade Organisation's (WTO) 2013 Bali package, which sought to lower import tariffs and agricultural subsidies to improve trade opportunities between the developed and developing world.

Davis, Dr Gavin

Political consultant | Former shadow minister of Energy | Former special advisor to the premier of the Western Cape | Former Democratic Alliance (DA) politician

Power broker

STRONG AT BRIDGING THE GAP BETWEEN TRADITIONAL and new, or digital, propaganda, Davis joined the DA in 2004 as a researcher and was later appointed as the party's executive director of communications. But the DA former policy chief had a tendency for run-ins with the media and rival politicians.

Davis wrote several key speeches for the DA's leadership, most notably party leader Mmusi Maimane's memorable Broken Man speech, which Maimane delivered to great effect during a ferocious debate on former president Jacob Zuma's 2015 State of the Nation address.

Davis proved highly capable of polemic, one of his most debatable acts taking a reactionary stance on racial transformation in his party, and doing so with a fellow DA MP, Dr Michael Cardo, in 2018. This followed Maimane's stated intention to see the party reconfigure itself to better reflect the country's demographics, to more seamlessly be able to attract more black supporters. Davis and Cardo were portrayed in some circles as leading a 'white cabal' within the DA, which was against the kind of quota system Maimane was envisaging, and rather promoting its political staff according to liberal loyalty.

De Lille, Patricia

Leader of Good, a new political party | Former Cape Town mayor | Former leader of the Independent Democrats | Former PAC negotiator at Codesa | Former trade unionist

Whistleblower

De Lille spent her life fighting political battles, first as a trade unionist in the South African Chemical Workers Union where she was a shop steward, then a regional secretary, then a national executive member, and finally the national vice-president of the National Council of Trade Unions.

A talented if tough negotiator, she worked on behalf of the Pan-Africanist Congress (PAC) delegation during the Convention for a Democratic South Africa (Codesa) which led to the first democratic elections.

During nearly a decade of government work representing the PAC, De Lille served as chairperson of the Parliamentary Committee on Transport, on other portfolio committees including those for health, minerals and energy, trade and industry, communications and on the Rules committee where she engaged directly with the Code of Ethics.

De Lille is remembered for her powerful role as a whistleblower on the 'arms deal', the weapons procurement programme costing billions, which was signed off during the administration of Nelson Mandela. The 'arms deal' is regarded as one of the primary reasons why South African politics descended into corruption over 25 years of democracy.

De Lille left the PAC to found the Independent Democrats (ID) in 2003 during a floor-crossing window. (Floor-crossing was abolished after a Constitutional amendment in January 2009, as it was regarded as contrary to the party-list proportional representation system.) Seven years later, De Lille merged the ID into the Democratic Alliance (DA), which was then the Official Opposition, although the ID was only officially dissolved in 2014.

There were benefits that came with the merger, including De Lille ascending to Cape Town's mayoral seat when she defeated the expected winner, the DA's Dan Plato, in 2011. Ironically, Plato would replace her in 2018. But she was long at odds with the ideological direction of the liberal DA, and clashed with the party's more conservative cabal before she finally left the mayoral office and the party, at war with the DA, in October 2018.

In December 2018, she announced the formation of her new political organisation, simply called Good, and said while it would contest the 2019 elections, its leadership and premier candidates would only be elected after the poll. Thus, an interim leadership would helm its election campaign.

Democratic Alliance (DA)

Official Opposition | Centrist, liberal | Number of seats in Parliament in 2018: 89

THE SECOND-LARGEST PARTY IN SOUTH AFRICA, the DA has consistently increased its margins over a series of elections. It received 22.2% of the votes in the National Assembly elections in 2014 and 26.9% in the 2016 local government elections. The 2014 poll gave it 89 seats in Parliament, and it intended to mount a strong campaign in 2019 around ending corruption – the ANC's greatest obstacle to decisive victory.

The DA has, however, not been free of controversy and reputational damage.

The Nelson Mandela Bay (NMB) metro in Port Elizabeth, Eastern Cape, was the site of ongoing and even violent conflict between the DA and other parties, particularly the Economic Freedom Fighters (EFF) and the United Democratic Movement (UDM). That conflict eventually unseated DA mayor Athol Trollip, who was replaced by the UDM's Mongameli Bobani, Trollip's previous deputy.

The DA was the biggest party in NMB after the 2016 municipal ballot with 57 seats but, because this was four seats short of a majority, it went into a coalition with the African Christian Democratic Party (ACDP), the Congress of the People (COPE) and the UDM. The UDM later withdrew from the coalition.

The house of cards collapsed in August 2018 when a DA councillor abstained from supporting his party's Speaker, meaning the Speaker had to be removed. When the DA contingent left the council in disgust after that happened, the UDM's candidate, Bobani, was elected mayor. He went on to appoint a committee that consisted largely of ANC members.

Problems were raised around the DA in Tshwane in May 2018 while its then mayor, Solly Msimanga, was embarrassed by revelations that his chief of staff, Marietha Aucamp, faked her qualifications. Msimanga was faced with whistleblowers' questions around tender irregularities involving a R12-billion deal with a project management company employed by the city and resigned in January 2019 to concentrate on his bid to become Gauteng premier.

The party lost the mayoral seat in Mogale City municipality in Gauteng – a province that still tended to favour the ANC – while claims were building that the DA's Johannesburg mayor, Herman Mashaba, was too soft on the EFF as it needed the Fighters' support to pass budgets in the council. The EFF had helped the DA govern Johannesburg over the ANC when the ANC won the 2016 polls. It was clear that if the EFF and the DA joined forces, they would have the numbers to run the city – which is what they did.

Meanwhile, the fallout within the DA's own ranks in Cape Town over the future of Patricia de Lille, as well as contradictory statements made by leader Mmusi Maimane about black representation in the party, did not assist the party's image-building ahead of the 2019 polls.

Neither did its disappointing and confusing first response to the water crisis, dubbed Day Zero, in Cape Town in 2018, which earned it negative headlines around the world. Nonetheless, the DA was expected to perform in its traditional constituencies in 2019, especially if it could show it was capable of overcoming difficulties around race and gender.

The liberals entered the first post-1994 Parliament as the Democratic Party, but won a mere 1.7% of the national vote under the leadership of Tony Leon. By the 2004 general elections, the DA was on track, gaining 12.3% of the vote, and a remarkable 50 seats in the National Assembly. It went on to win the Western Cape and the City of Cape Town by 2006, when Leon stepped down and Helen Zille – in 2018, the Premier of the Western Cape and former Cape Town mayor – was elected leader.

Maimane, who would be 39 in 2019, was elected DA leader in May 2015. But he was to face a number of unexpected challenges as his party approached the 2019 elections, not the least of which was the fury of the families of mental health patients who died in the Esidimeni tragedy. This was because the DA used the patients' names on an electioneering billboard in which it cited the ANC as being responsible for their deaths.

The DA's Jack Bloom, a long-time health activist in Gauteng, had helped to drive an investigation into the tragedy that saw former Gauteng Health MEC Qedani Mahlangu, an ANC deployee, and other government officials move the patients from a private facility owned by Life Healthcare, to a number of unsuitable and even dangerous NGOs.

Denel

State-owned defence conglomerate | Arms manufacturer

Some managers alleged to be corrupt

Concerns about Denel came under the spotlight when President Cyril Ramaphosa appointed Pravin Gordhan as Minister of Public Enterprises in February 2018. Responsible for state-owned enterprises (SOEs) such as Denel, Gordhan appointed a new board in May 2018, chaired by former Airports Company South Africa chief executive and chairperson of Royal Bafokeng Holdings, Monhla Hlahla. Other appointments to the board included: General Siphiwe Nyanda, who previously served as Chief of Defence Force Staff, General Officer Commanding (Gauteng) and Minister of Communications; Nonzukiso Zukie Siyotula, who served as the CEO of Thebe Capital (of Thebe Investment Corporation); Professor Tshilidzi Marwala, the vice chancellor and principal at the University of Johannesburg, and General Temba Templeton Matanzima, a retired South African army officer and the first South African Military Ombudsman.

Chief Financial Officer Odwa Mhlwana was placed on special leave in June 2018 amid allegations of irregular expenditure which led to a disciplinary process.

In November, he was found guilty of all charges and fired with immediate effect. Mhlwana was a chartered accountant who had been in the CFO's seat since 2017 after being the CFO for Denel Vehicle Systems and the finance director for BAE Land Systems before that.

Denel's CEO Zwelakhe Ntshepe and its board chairperson Daniel Mantsha resigned in May 2018. The #Guptaleaks emails revealed how Mantsha – an attorney who was struck off the roll in 2007 after multiple client complaints, and readmitted in 2011 – leaked confidential Denel documents and information to the Guptas and their business partners.

A special adviser to former minister of Communications Faith Muthambi in 2011, Mantsha was then appointed as a non-executive director and the chairperson of Denel for a three-year period by public enterprises minister Lynne Brown. Brown did not disclose Mantsha's chequered past at the time of his appointment.

Mantsha – who was by late 2018 on Jacob Zuma's defence team, after Zuma fired his long-time attorney, Michael Hulley – was believed to have known about the spurious awarding of a R1-million bursary to the son of the North West province's former premier, Supra Mahumapelo, as well as the allocation of a tender to his brother. In December 2018, Denel found the bursary award to have been illegal, and referred the matter to the SAPS as a crime. It requested the Special Investigating Unit (SIU) to recover the money spent on the bursary allocated to Oarabile Mahumapelo to become a pilot.

Denel was shown to have serious 'liquidity challenges' in 2018, and it was noted by Solidarity (the trade union that represents a majority white worker base) that the SOE had offered a 4% salary increase for the year for staff, while its executive management had accepted 'salary adjustments of 47% and more' in the previous year.

In January 2018, a new controversy blew up around Denel when Cabinet approved the appointment of Danie du Toit as CEO. The Cosatu-affiliated trade union, the Liberated Metalworkers Union of South Africa, had complained about the appointment of a 'white male' to the post, but Denel's chairperson Hlahla said the former managing director at German company SAAB Meday Technologies was the best person for the job. Du Toit replaced Ntshepe, with the task of dealing with the 2018 loss of R1.7 billion by the arms manufacturer.

Development Bank of South Africa (DBSA)

Finance institution wholly owned by the state

After a period of instability, the restructuring of the state bank reached a new high in June 2018 with the signing of an MoU with the New Development Bank (NDB) in Shanghai, China. This marked the formalisation of a framework of co-operation between the NDB, the multilateral development bank established by Brazil, Russia, India, China and South Africa (BRICS) in 2014, and the DBSA.

The DBSA's chief executive Patrick Dlamini and NDB president K.V. Kamath said the banks would look at investing and co-financing projects, and leverage the strengths of multilateral development finance institutions around the world, to develop Africa, especially the Southern African Development Community (SADC).

The DBSA supported regional integration through participating in programmes such as the South African Renewable Energy Independent Power Producer Procurement Programme (REIPPPP) and the Programme for Infrastructure Development in Africa (PIDA) Priority Action Plan.

Global and regional institutions on board included SADC's Development Finance Resource Centre, the Association of African Development Finance Institutions and the World Economic Forum's Sustainable Development Investment Partnership.

The DBSA also managed the Infrastructure Investment Programme for South Africa on behalf of the European Union (EU).

The DBSA's former CFO Kameshni Naidoo and group executive for international financing Rieaz Shaik resigned during the review of the bank's operating model. Chartered Accountant Boitumelo Mosako then took over as CFO, having previously been at the South African Bureau of Standards (SABS). She had worked at the DBSA before as its general manager for finance.

Didiza, Thoko

National Assembly house chairperson for internal arrangements | ANC politician | Member of the Pan-African Parliament (PAP) | Member of the ANC's National Working Committee (NWC)

On the way up

SOME THOUGHT DIDIZA WOULD NOT SURVIVE politically having been the ANC's divisive choice for mayoral candidate opposite the Democratic Alliance's Solly Msimang in Tshwane for the local government elections in 2016. Putting Didiza up for power was a major blunder by the ruling party and led to often-violent protests in the executive capital. Some felt it was not only aan unfortunate political move but also unfair to a politician who had once been a favourite of the ANC – a likeable young leader who had earned her stripes under former president Thabo Mbeki.

Didiza joined the exodus of ministers out of Mbeki's administration after he was recalled by the ANC in 2008. She'd been his Minister of Public Works, and it took another four years for her to make a comeback in 2012 when she was elected to the NEC at the ANC's Mangaung elective conference in Mangaung.

Yet, Didiza did survive Tshwane. She went on to serve as the National Assembly house chairperson for internal arrangements and was growing her popularity again to the point where she was being touted as a possible ANC chief whip or even the speaker. Generally, she is considered a top parliamentary presiding officer.

Didiza, who earned an Honours degree in politics, but also has experience in civil society, looked like a strong figure in the 2019 elections for an ANC desperate to present its best face.

Diko, Khusela

President's spokesperson | ANC communications expert

On the way up

THE FORMER ANC NATIONAL COMMUNICATIONS manager and chief director of communications in the Gauteng Provincial Government, Diko was announced as President Cyril Ramaphosa's spokesperson in March 2018.

A marketing professional, Diko – who had a BCom degree and was completing her Bachelor of Law – previously served as the spokesperson for the ANC Youth League and for ANC Treasurer General, Paul Mashatile.

Khusela (previously Sangoni), an AbaThembu princess of the Nobetha royal clan from Qokolweni near Mthatha, Eastern Cape, drew headlines in December 2018 when she married AmaBhaca King Madzikane ka Zulu Thandisizwe Diko. The king occupies the Elundzini Great Place at Ncutheni village in KwaBhaca, Eastern Cape. His mother is Queen Nosizwe Diko, and Khusela's mother is Queen Nolwandle Sangoni.

Dintwe, Professor (Dr) Setlhomamaru

Inspector General of Intelligence (IGI) | Government-appointed

DINTWE WAS THRUST INTO PUBLIC VIEW in April 2018 when he brought a matter before the North Gauteng High Court in Pretoria about the State Security Agency's director-general, Arthur Fraser. Dintwe wanted Fraser barred from 'interfering with his (Dintwe's) duties'.

His case was initiated by an urgent court application after Fraser apparently tried to revoke his security clearance and interfere with his functions while Dintwe was investigating a complaint lodged by the Democratic Alliance (DA) over Fraser's involvement in an alleged parallel intelligence network. Fraser was said to have improperly awarded tenders and contracts to people associated with his family, and other individuals, through that network. In turn, Fraser said he had withdrawn Dintwe's security clearance 'because the IGI could not be trusted with State secrets', claiming Dintwe had disclosed classified information to representatives of political parties in Parliament, specifically the DA.

State Security Minister Dipuo Letsatsi-Duba quickly restored full security clearance to Dintwe and committed to co-operate with his investigations, while Fraser was moved to the Correctional Services.

Dintwe was appointed as IGI in 2017 after a hiatus of two years following a vacancy in the post at the end of March 2015. Dintwe was awarded a doctorate in police science, with specialisation in forensic investigation, from the University of South Africa (Unisa) where he was the head of the department of police practice in the School of Criminal Justice.

Dlakude, Doris

ANC deputy chief whip in Parliament

On the way up

NOTORIOUS FOR A PHOTOGRAPH OF HER and fellow ANC MP Mamoloko Kubayi-Ngubane painting their nails during Parliament's ad hoc committee session probing the R240-million spend on then president Zuma's Nkandla homestead, Dlakude did not improve the ANC's image.

She was, however, given substantial power as the deputy chief whip of the ANC in Parliament, having been an active member of the party for more than 20 years and an MP since 2010. As second-in-command of all the ANC's MPs, Dlakude enjoyed the trust of the ruling party and, by extension, served as the link between the party and its deployees in government and in the National Assembly. Dlakude was previously a treasurer of the ANC Youth League in the Ehlanzeni region of Mpumalanga, as well as its ANC branch secretary for six terms and a member of the party's Regional Executive Committee.

Dlakude's husband, Vusi Dlakude, would bring her adverse headlines in January 2018 when it was alleged he had faked a hijacking. Vusi Dlakude appeared in court on a charge of perjury.

Dlamini, Bathabile

Minister of Women in the Presidency | Former minister of Social Development | ANC Women's League president | Member of the ANC's National Working Committee (NWC)

Suspected of corruption

DLAMINI APPEARED TO BE AS ENTRENCHED within the ANC as she was embattled outside it in 2018. Given the post of Minister of Women in the Presidency by Cyril Ramaphosa in early 2018, she was voted back onto the party's National Executive Committee (NEC) at its elective conference at Nasrec the previous December. Her new government appointment happened despite a range of voices across society calling for her to be fired.

Dlamini was Minister of Social Development at the time of being voted onto the NEC – a position that made her effectively responsible for the South Africa Social Security Agency (Sassa), which paid out the grants to about 17 million people. But her role was highly controversial.

In 2018, the Constitutional Court revoked the contract of Cash Paymaster Services (CPS), which administered the grants, with Dlamini accused of failing to ensure Sassa was equipped to handle the bureaucracy after the contract with CPS was due to expire. The court was then forced to temporarily extend the CPS contract, even though it had been found illegal.

A few months later, the court ordered Dlamini to pay back 20% of Sassa's legal costs accrued during the ensuing judicial processes. Her acerbic persona saw her draw acrimony when she appeared before retired Judge Bernard Ngoepe at an inquiry into that personal liability. Dlamini claimed the Constitution did not confer powers to a court to hold a Cabinet member to account in their personal capacity, and that only the National Assembly could do this.

But the Constitutional Court was undaunted. It further instructed the National Director of Public Prosecutions to decide whether Dlamini should be prosecuted and charged with perjury. The Democratic Alliance (DA), among others, also called for her to face criminal charges.

Dlamini went viral in 2017 when she told an SABC interviewer that 'all of us in the (ANC) NEC have our smallanyana skeletons, and we don't want to take all skeletons out or all hell will break loose'. That statement seemed to indicate not only that Dlamini herself had 'skeletons', but that she also had knowledge of others' misdeeds which she might make public if she was punished.

Among other concerns about Dlamini was her tendency for excess, including unnecessarily luxurious official car purchases for her and her deputy, and the hiring of bodyguards paid by the state to shield her children.

Dlamini supported Nkosazana Dlamini-Zuma's bid for the ANC presidency at Nasrec and was visibly shaken when Dlamini-Zuma came second, within days calling a press conference at which she said the ANCWL felt the party had 'failed the women of South Africa'. Journalists questioned her on why the League had not stood with Dlamini-Zuma in 2007 when she previously ran for party president, and why it had not supported ANC veteran Lindiwe Sisulu for the position of deputy president to Ramaphosa at Nasrec, instead of David Mabuza, who was appointed to the post, but Dlamini did not provide an answer.

A former activist in the South African Student Congress (Sasco), Dlamini was in the interim leadership to rebuild the ANC Women's League in the KwaZulu-Natal region in 1991. She became deputy secretary-general of the League in 1993 and was elected as its president in 2016.

Dlamini, Cathy

Former mayor of several Mpumalanga municipalities, including the provincial capital, Mbombela | National Council of Provinces (NCOP) member

Linked to corruption

REGARDED AS HAVING SIGNIFICANT INFLUENCE WITHIN THE ANC in terms of her achievements as a woman in the party, she was mayor of the Greater Malalale Local Municipality overseeing the towns of Malelane and Hectorspruit, and KaMhlushwa village, in Mpumalanga before she was appointed as the monitoring and evaluation director in the office of the Mpumalanga premier, and finally made mayor of the province's capital city, Mbombela.

Dlamini promised she would be a transparent public figure, noting that after Parliament passed the Political Party Funding Bill, she planned to reveal the sources of the funding behind her own campaigns. She remarked that the funds were 'not innocent ... they come with conditions'. But Dlamini had not been 'transparent' in every respect, taking a suspicious and unbudgeted, taxpayer-funded, R250,000 trip to Disney World and other tourist sites in the United States and the UK in 2011 with her bodyguard, five councillors and municipal managers.

She was appointed as an ANC member of the NCOP in 2014, drawing surprise in Mbombela where some officials said at the time that they did not know she was no longer mayor.

Dlamini, Sdumo

Former Congress of South African Trade Unions (Cosatu) leader | ANC-aligned

Suspected of corruption

SEVERAL HUNDRED WORKERS WALKED OUT on the then Cosatu president when he delivered his Workers' Day speech on the National Minimum Wage in May 2018. But this didn't seem to affect Dlamini as he continued giving his keynote address in Kwazakhele, near Port Elizabeth, in spite of the drama.

Still, the backdrop was fierce. Dlamini had become increasingly unpopular. There was a major threat to him keeping his position at Cosatu at that time. But more than that, Dlamini – who had veered between supporting Jacob Zuma and then joining the Cosatu throng towards the end of Zuma's time in office condemning him – appeared to have succumbed to corruption.

There were allegations that he had received a R300,000 bribe from Western Cape abalone dealer Deon Larry – a shady figure to whom Zuma was also linked, being investigated by the State's elite unit, the Hawks, for allegedly accepting a R1-million-cash bribe from Larry in exchange for keeping then minister of Agriculture, Forestry and Fisheries Senzeni Zokwana in his Cabinet.

This unfolded when businessman Chaile Seretse deposed an affidavit at the Lyttelton Police Station in Centurion, outside Pretoria, in December 2017, claiming that Zokwana, Dlamini and deputy director-general of the Department of Agriculture, Siphokazi Ndudane, had each received a R300,000 bribe from Larry. (Seretse was the chief operating officer at abalone processing company Willjarro in Gansbaai outside Cape Town.)

Hawks spokesperson Hangwani Mulaudzi confirmed that the Hawks were investigating bribery claims against Zuma, Zokwana, Dlamini and Ndudane.

Swaziland-born Dlamini – who was a nurse before he became a trade unionist – lost his key position as Cosatu president at its congress in September 2018 to his deputy, Zingiswa Losi, who became the first woman at the helm of the federation.

Dlamini-Zuma, Dr Nkosazana

Minister in the Presidency | Former minister of Health | Former minister of Home Affairs | Former minister of (then) Foreign Affairs | Former African Unions (AU) Commission chairperson | ANC politician | Member of the ANC's National Working Committee (NWC)

DLAMINI-ZUMA WAS APPOINTED MINISTER IN THE PRESIDENCY in 2018 at the age of 69 under Cyril Ramaphosa, bringing a measure of political wisdom and experience to government.

She had served in Cabinet after 1994 before she became head of the AU Commission in 2012. Ironically, it was believed Dlamini-Zuma was 'exiled' to its headquarters in Addis Ababa, Ethiopia, so that she wouldn't be a political threat to Jacob Zuma (who happened to be her ex-husband) at the time. By 2017, she was Zuma's choice to succeed him as ANC president, but she lost that bid to Ramaphosa.

That was the second time Dlamini-Zuma lost a vote for high office in the ANC, with Kgalema Motlanthe receiving more support than she did to become the deputy president of the party at the explosive Polokwane conference in Limpopo in 2007. That was the conference at which Jacob Zuma was elected ANC president.

Previously having held the portfolios of Minister of Health and Foreign Affairs (now International Relations), Dlamini-Zuma was praised when she was at Home Affairs, credited with turning around a department mired in mismanagement to achieve clean audits for the first time in 16 years in 2011. There were those who believed her director-general, ANC veteran Mavuso Msimang, was, however, the one ultimately responsible for the turnaround. Msimang was at the department from 2007 to 2010.

During her time at Foreign Affairs, she was noted as having played a role in the brief end to the civil war in the Democratic Republic of Congo.

Honoured with the Order of Luthuli in Gold in 2013 for her contribution to the struggle, Dlamini-Zuma was, however, stained by the revelation that she had accepted a R250,000 'prize' from the controversial Gupta family after being named South African of the Year. Leaked emails showed that her 'prize' money was among a large sum that had allegedly been laundered by the Guptas through corrupt cronies in government.

Dlamini-Zuma was also not universally praised for her work at the AU and left without much fanfare to return to treatment from the ANC more suited to a president than a former Cabinet minister. Until the complaints grew too loud and too obvious, Dlamini-Zuma had been afforded bodyguards, vehicles and other privileges by the ANC to campaign for president of the party.

She has, however, been noted for her quiet but efficient handling of her new position in Ramaphosa's administration, and the pair seem to work well together.

Dlamini-Zuma was honoured with the Order of Luthuli in Gold, the highest South African honour granted by the president, in 2013. Jacob Zuma was president at the time.

Dlodlo, Ayanda

Minister of Public Service and Administration | Former minister of Home Affairs | Former minister of Communications | Former adviser to President Jacob Zuma | ANC politician

On the way up | Linked to corruption | Star

DLODLO'S RISE TO POWER IN THE ANC came as no surprise. Likeable, competent, young enough and with struggle credentials as a former Umkhonto we Sizwe (MK) operative, the Minister of Public Service and Administration emerged as an influential candidate for future leadership within the party hierarchy in 2007, shortly before its bruising elective conference in Polokwane.

Dlodlo, who was then secretary-general of the MK Military Veterans' Association (MKMVA), campaigned for Zuma's success at that conference. She also led a meeting with the National Prosecuting Authority (NPA) to urge it to drop corruption charges against Zuma before his election, having previously worked as a director of the now-defunct corruption-busting unit, the Scorpions.

Dlodlo didn't end her association with Zuma there. She went on to serve as his adviser in 2009 and 2010, and then to lead the departments of Home Affairs and Communications.

Dlodlo joined MK at just 18 after she fled South Africa. She received military intelligence training in Moscow in 1984 and 1985.

In 2017, she admitted to not declaring a trip to Dubai in which a Gupta company paid for her accommodation while she was deputy minister of Public Service and Administration in 2015.

Dlodlo was also named in an article in the Sunday Times in January 2019 about a 'botched broadband project' for the City of Johannesburg. The newspaper alleged affidavits by city officials claimed 'mismanagement' in contracts involving telecomms giant Ericsson. Dlodlo was a director of CitiConnect Communications (CCC), the BEE company attached to the contracts. She told the Sunday Times the directors may have been 'a bit naïve ... at the time'.

Dlodlo joined CCC in 2008 and resigned in 2010. The city bought the broadband project in 2015. A case of fraud and corruption was being investigated in January 2019.

Dodovu, China

North West ANC deputy provincial chairperson | Former chairperson of the agriculture and rural development executive committee in the North West Provincial Legislature | Former Member of the Executive Council (MEC) for Co-Operative Governance and Traditional Affairs in the North West Provincial Legislature

Power-broker

A CONTENDER FOR POLITICAL POWER amid ANC factionalism in North West province, Dodovu gained attention for standing up to his former friend Supra Mahumapelo, who was compelled to step down as North West Premier in early 2018, amidst allegations of corruption. Dodovu and Mahumapelo had been roommates at the Technikon Northern Transvaal.

Following a period of relative political obscurity after he was sidelined by Mahumapelo, Dodovu drew attention when he appeared to defy the Jacob Zuma faction of the ANC, of which Mahumapelo was part, in February 2017. Dodovu refused to agree that disgraced former Eskom CEO Brian Molefe was either a resident of North West, or a branch member within the province. The ANC sought to see Molefe made an MP in 2017, possibly with an eye to ultimately replace then finance minister Pravin Gordhan, and it needed the nomination of a branch to do that.

Identified as being within the Cyril Ramaphosa faction, Dodovu was in conflict with Dakota Legoete, a long-time rival, over this, as Legoete insisted Molefe was indeed a branch member of good standing in the Hartbeespoortdam ANC in North West.

The divide between Dodovu and Legoete was at its most extreme in 2013, when Dodovu – who was an MEC at the time – was arrested and charged for the murder of Oubuti Chika, the regional secretary of the Dr Kenneth Kaunda district in North West, during the run-up to the ANC's Mangaung conference in 2012. Dodovu was found not guilty and discharged.

Dodovu appeared to have the last laugh when Mahumapelo – who he said had turned North West into 'a pure kleptocratic state' – stepped down.

Dramat, Anwa

Former head of the Hawks | Historically, ANC-aligned

Forced out of his job by corrupt officials

DRAMAT'S SUSPENSION IN 2014 as the head of Hawks was a dramatic moment in the bloody fight for state capture in the era of Jacob Zuma. Manufactured charges that said he had been involved in the renditions of four Zimbabweans in 2010 showed how determined a certain faction within the ANC was to protect high-profile individuals from being investigated.

Dramat – a former Umkhonto we Sizwe (MK) operative and Western Cape deputy police commissioner – resigned rather than fight, having effectively been forced out of his job, seemingly for conducting probes into 'very influential people'. He was not alone in his explosive claims. Among others, he had an ally in Robert McBride, head of the Independent Police Investigations Directorate (IPID), who said there was a growing political conspiracy aimed at blocking the fight against crime – and it was coming from the top.

The flurry around the 'renditions' led to McBride's suspension too, as he was accused of altering a draft report into the events. Although that draft report recommended Dramat and his colleague, former Gauteng Hawks head General Shadrack Sibiya, be charged, the final report exonerated them.

Formerly holding the rank of Lieutenant General, Dramat reached a settlement with the police, but the *Mail & Guardian* newspaper claimed this was not executed under ordinary circumstances. It was believed the settlement was simply a means of getting Dramat out of the way to see Mthandazo 'Berning' Ntlemeza, an ally of Jacob Zuma, appointed.

Then National Police Commissioner Riah Phiyega – who was later also suspended – was rumoured to have offered Dramat a R3-million severance, in addition to R60,000 per month until he turned 60, in return for his voluntary departure. Phiyega was believed to have been acting on behalf of then police minister, Nathi Nhleko, also a Zuma ally.

Even when the North Gauteng High Court in Pretoria ruled Dramat's suspension unconstitutional and said he should be reinstated, Dramat declined. He was replaced in June 2018 by former deputy national police commissioner, Advocate Seswantsho Godfrey Lebeya, who took over from Lieutenant-General Yolisa Matakata.

In late 2018, criminal charges were first provisionally withdrawn by the North Gauteng High Court against Dramat and Sibiya. The state said it would reconsider its position once the trial of the men's former colleague, Lesley Maluleke, had been completed. Then it withdrew its charges unconditionally, opening the way for Dramat, if he so desired, to join the State Security Agency.

Dramat, Sibiya and Maluleke faced charges of organised crime, kidnapping, violations of the Immigration Act and obstruction of justice in 2016, following trumped-up charges related to the 'rendition'.

Duarte, Jessie

ANC deputy secretary-general | Former high commissioner to Mozambique | Former national spokesperson of the ANC | Former chief operations officer in the Presidency | Former Gauteng MEC for Safety and Security

Suspected of being linked to corrupt individuals

An activist dominant in the Federation of Transvaal Women (FEDSAW), a vital United Democratic Front (UDF) affiliate during apartheid, Duarte – who was detained without trial and placed under restrictions during the 1980s – is known as one of the ANC's most abrasive yet powerful protagonists.

Although she seemingly endeared herself to two of the struggle's most enduring individuals – Reverend Beyers Naude and Nelson Mandela – working closely with both, Duarte would in later years become embroiled in controversies.

These date back to 1998 when she was Gauteng MEC for Safety and Security, having risen through the party's ranks and been elected to the Gauteng Provincial Executive Committee (PEC), chaired by Tokyo Sexwale, in 1990. This was a time of deep and widening divisions within the ANC, which had only been in power for about 40 months.

Duarte believed a commission of inquiry, appointed by then Gauteng Premier Mathole Motshekga to investigate allegations of mismanagement and corruption against her, was a front to get rid of her. The commission comprised Advocate

Marumo Moerane and then chair of the National Public Service Commission, Professor Stan Sangweni. Mathole was believed to be under pressure to sack Duarte from some within the ANC, with rumours of 'old scores' needing to be settled. Among those alleged to have been among her detractors were senior Gauteng leaders like then Health MEC, Amos Masondo, then Transport MEC, Paul Mashatile, and Obed Bapela, chair of the provincial standing committee on safety and security.

Motshekga, who was understood to have battled to promote transparent government within the party after the premiership of Tokyo Sexwale, was himself facing an inquiry into allegations of the misuse of donor funds.

More recently, in 2017, Duarte – seen as a Zuma ally – came under fire when it was revealed that her son-in-law, Ian Whitley, had accepted a job as the chief of staff in the office of Des van Rooyen. Van Rooyen occupied the job of finance minister for four days in December 2015.

In 2018, Duarte said she was 'keen' to testify before the Zondo Commission of Inquiry into State Capture, especially after ANC chairperson Gwede Mantashe testified in November that year. Duarte wished to answer former minister Barbara Hogan's allegations that Duarte had been central to the state capture project in her role as deputy ANC secretary-general.

During her political career, Duarte was deployed into Foreign Affairs as the High Commissioner to Mozambique, as the national spokesperson of the ANC and as Chief Operations Officer in the Presidency until 2010.

She was first elected deputy secretary-general of the ANC in 2012.

Duba, Dipuo Letsatsi

Minister of State Security | Former deputy minister of Public Service and Administration | Former media liaison officer for the ANC

On the way up

Educated in Zambia, Zimbabwe and Cuba, Dube left South Africa to join the ANC and Umkhonto we Sizwe (MK) in exile when she was a teenager. Something of an all-rounder, she was editor-in-chief of the *ANC Voice of Women* – good training for her later role as media liaison officer at the party's first headquarters, Shell House, in Johannesburg after the liberation movements were unbanned in 1990. She remained in that structure until 1994.

Although Dube grew up in Gauteng, she was deployed to Limpopo where she was an MEC for Agriculture and served on the Provincial Executive Committee (PEC) as treasurer.

A member of the ANC's National Executive Committee (NEC) and a former acting ANC Western Cape chairperson, Dube was at the helm of Parliament's Portfolio Committee on Public Enterprises and was Deputy Minister of Public Service and Administration before being appointed to the role of State Security Minister.

Dudley, Cheryllyn

African Christian Democratic Party (ACDP) MP

An ACDP MP for 17 years, Dudley served on various Parliamentary portfolio committees including trade and industry, health, higher and basic education.

She made history in Parliament when her private member's bill resulted in same-sex couples and adoptive and surrogate parents being able to take parental leave, and fathers getting at least 10 days' paternity leave. It was passed as a Labour Laws Amendment Bill in 2017, and regarded as a landmark for LGBTQI (lesbian, gay, bisexual, transsexual, queer and intersex) rights.

E

Economic Freedom Fighters (EFF)

ANC breakaway party | Socialist-Nationalist hybrid | Number of seats in Parliament in 2018: 25

Commander-in-Chief (CIC) Julius Malema reported corrupt by the Public Protector in 2012 relating to activities when he was the ANC Youth League president | Deputy CIC Floyd Shivambu denied links to corruption related to party funding, tenders and the VBS Bank

When expelled ANC Youth League (ANCYL) president, Julius Malema, and expelled ANCYL spokesperson, Floyd Shivambu, led a group gathered at Uncle Tom's Hall in Soweto for a two-day 'Economic Freedom Fighters (EFF) national assembly' in July 2013, it looked like a stunt to deflect attention from Malema's criminal charges on tax evasion.

But the EFF quickly became a phenomenon. A brilliant orator, Malema swept anew onto the political stage, and by the time his party officially launched that October, it was wooing workers, the poor, unemployed people, young black people, rural people and the politically disenchanted. Never one to miss an opportunity to rile adversaries, Malema chose Marikana, the site of the state-sanctioned massacre of Lonmin miners in 2012 in Rustenburg, to unveil itself.

Thousands again packed Mehlareng Stadium in Tembisa outside Johannesburg in 2014 for its election manifesto launch. Then came the election, and the EFF tapped a zeitgeist in its aspirational militant rhetoric to garner 6% of the vote, securing 25 seats in its debut season.

Using robust political tactics, the party all but transformed Parliament. The ANC – which, for the first time in its 20 years of rule, had a potential political rival – responded with strong-arm tactics.

After the 2016 local elections, Malema's party grew in public perception as the DA was forced to accept its sway in governing structures in the Tshwane, Nelson

Mandela Bay and Johannesburg metros, as well as in some smaller municipalities. In his previous incarnation as ANCYL president, Malema had been Zuma's kingmaker at the ANC's tough elective conference in Polokwane, Limpopo, in 2007. Having exceeded the backseat position of 'kingmaker', the EFF would by 2016 be running its own political race for power in hung municipalities.

Meanwhile, the party's leadership embraced higher education, with its national spokesperson and MP Mbuyiseni Ndlozi acquiring a doctorate, Malema earning a degree and Shivambu a Master's. Yet, there were caveats to the EFF's rise, with former public protector Thuli Madonsela's report about Malema's tender scandals during his time with the ANC, remaining unresolved.

The party's reputation faced a challenge in October 2018 when Shivambu's younger brother Brian Shivambu was named in the South African Reserve Bank's report, *The Great Bank Heist*, which detailed how R2 billion was illegally paid out to 53 individuals between 2015 and 2018 by the failed Venda Building Society (VBS). VBS catered primarily to poorer communities, and a large proportion of its deposits were made in Limpopo, a province central to the EFF's success at the polls in 2019.

Although the EFF and Shivambu immediately denied Brian had given part of a R16-million payment he had received from the bank to the EFF, or that he had parted with any of it via any bank account linked in any way to the party or his brother, the story gained traction among the EFF's detractors and 2019 elections rivals.

In November 2018, Parliament said its joint committee on ethics and members' interests would launch a probe into Shivambu over payments he allegedly received via his brother.

It was later exposed that Malema's wife and children were living in a guarded estate mansion in Hyde Park, Johannesburg, which was owned by Adriano Mazzotti, allegedly a cigarette smuggler but officially a cigarette 'manufacturer'. Mazzotti paid the EFF's fees to register as a political party in 2011. Some journalists made a link between that and the EFF's rather surprising support of disgraced former SARS commissioner Tom Moyane, who – best-selling author and award-winning investigative journalist Jacques Pauw claimed in his 2018 book, *The President's Keepers* – had allegedly come to an 'arrangement' with Mazzoti around his tax.

Speculation that the EFF leadership was linked to corruption saw its political enemies baying for its blood but it was moot as to whether that would cost it at the 2019 polls.

Electoral Commission of South Africa (IEC)

Chapter 9 institution | Accountable to Parliament but independent of government | Previously known as the Independent Electoral Commission

A NEPOTISM WRANGLE AROUND A LEASE on the IEC's new headquarters in Centurion outside Pretoria in 2013 would lead to the resignation in 2014 of its CEO, Advocate Pansy Tlakula. But that was the biggest controversy it had faced by 2018. That the fallout around the lease scandal was well managed allowed the IEC to dodge the cloud of corruption that has hovered over many other state bodies.

Even a 2014 vote-rigging campaign in Tlokwe, North West, in which the IEC was inevitably embroiled, had a positive outcome in that the Constitutional Court (ConCourt) ordered the commission to verify all addresses on the voters roll by mid-2018 to avoid fraud, 'miscounts', 'disappearing' ballot sheets and the bussing-in of people from one district to swell another.

The man charged with that responsibility, IEC chairperson Vuma Mashinini, was determined to run a clean operation as he had been scrutinised when he returned to the commission that he had helped develop at its beginning. The fact that he had worked closely with Zuma in the president's office before he went back to the IEC left him open to scrutiny. But there was no valid reason for concern as all was well at the commission three years later.

That didn't mean the IEC would be able to meet the ConCourt's deadline, however. When the ruling was made, only about 32% of addresses had been verified, and by November 2018, this had improved to 82%.

The IEC is a permanent body created by the Constitution to manage free and fair elections at all levels of government. Although publicly funded and accountable to Parliament, it is independent of government. It must declare the results of all elections and compile and maintain a voters' roll as well as a register of parties. It must continuously review electoral laws and proposed electoral laws and make recommendations.

Set up by the interim Constitution of South Africa in 1993 to oversee the landmark 1994 general elections, it ran an exemplary first poll. The IEC was officially established in 1996 by President Nelson Mandela and has since successfully run four general and four municipal elections and more than a thousand by-elections.

Its biggest test yet would be the 2019 general elections – expected to cost R1.3 billion to host. It was up to the IEC to reassure the nation that it would not buckle under any pressure to 'fudge' the results as expectations mounted that the once-monolithic ANC could be voted out in some towns, cities and even provinces. Such concerns were exacerbated by the fact that up to three of the five IEC commissioners' terms of office expired in 2018, raising the spectre of the polls being overseen by inexperienced newcomers.

Mashinini announced in November that the elections would be held in May, with candidate nominations from political parties to be received by March. A major drive was around getting young South Africans to vote as they had been traditionally under-represented on the roll.

Equal Education

Activist organisation | Non-Aligned | Change agents

Power brokers | Stars

A MOVEMENT OF LEARNERS, PARENTS AND TEACHERS striving for quality and equality in education, it identified systemic and localised problems and used mass mobilisation to build public pressure on government.

Policy engagement was a significant aspect of its work. Legal interventions happened through its strategic partner, the Equal Education Law Centre.

Fighting for better – or any – school infrastructure was a major aspect of Equal Education's work, particularly as government had cut the budgets of its Education Infrastructure Grant and the Accelerated Schools Infrastructure Delivery Initiative (also known as the Schools Infrastructure Backlog Grant).

Basic Education Minister Angie Motshekga and President Cyril Ramaphosa were, however, given no further chances to neglect infrastructure that had resulted in the deaths or injuries, and impairment to the dignity of millions of children. In November 2018 Equal Education's campaigns – often together with social justice law NGO SECTION27 – resulted in the Constitutional Court dismissing the department's appeal against a judgment that compelled it to provide timely infrastructure to schools. Government had missed several deadlines to provide proper sanitation and electricity.

Equal Education was a regular attendee at the department and at various portfolio committees in Parliament to assist in setting best practice models and to track education policy changes and budgets. It also lobbied MPs to garner support for its campaigns and research, to hold the executive branch of government to account.

By 2018, the organisation was growing its focus on provincial legislatures.

Esidimeni (see Bloom, Jack and Democratic Alliance and Health Ombudsman)

Eskom

Electricity public utility | State-owned enterprise (SOE)

The crown jewel of the state capture project

ESTABLISHED IN 1923 AS THE ELECTRICITY Supply Commission (ESCOM) by the government of the Union of South Africa, it was also known by its Afrikaans name, the Elektrisiteitsvoorsieningskommissie (EVKOM). The acronyms were combined in 1986 and the company became known as Eskom.

It was identified as one of the state institutions that supported the notorious Gupta brothers who received lucrative contracts at the parastatal.

The largest producer of electricity on the African continent, Eskom was also one of the top such utilities in the world in terms of generation capacity and sales. The Kendal Power Station and the Koeberg nuclear power station, the only nuclear power plant in Africa, were among its major assets. Close to all of South Africa's electricity is supplied by Eskom, with nearly 17 million people, or one-third of the population, used its services. But it had a chequered history that began before the crooked intervention of the Guptas.

There was a determined bid to privatise it before the 1994 elections, and had that happened, say some analysts, new power stations might have been built. Instead, it remained in the hands of the state and the existing infrastructure went into decline.

Prior to the state capture scandal, Eskom experienced an inordinate lack of credibility during 2007 and 2008, and again in 2014 and 2015, when there was countrywide 'load shedding'. This returned in mid-2018 when the National Union of Mineworkers (NUM) and the National Union of Metalworkers (Numsa) joined forces to pressurise the utility for higher wages, leading to an inability on Eskom's part to keep the lights on at that time. (NUM, for instance, had a contract for a wage increase of 23% over three years, and a bonus.)

Then deputy president Cyril Ramaphosa was tasked by then president Jacob Zuma with the turnaround of Eskom (along with that of South African Airways and the South African Post Office). Eskom's Chief Executive Officer (CEO) at the time was Tshediso Matona.

In late 2016, global rating agency Standard & Poor's downgraded Eskom's credit rating further into sub-investment, cutting its long-term credit rating to BB, which is two levels below the investment threshold. In 2018 it had R399 billion in total debt, costing it $2 billion in interest payments in 2017. The Goldman Sachs Group called Eskom the single biggest risk to the country's economy.

Matona was suspended in 2016 along with several other employees while infighting over procurement all but paralysed the Board, led by then chairperson Zola Tsotsi.

The National Energy Regulator of South Africa (Nersa) stepped in in 2017 to deny yet another application by Eskom to increase electricity tariffs to the consumer. That was for the financial year 2018/19 – around the same time as Eskom was found to have thousands of extraneous employees who cost it billions every year, and the year in which it had to suspend its chief financial officer, Anoj Singh. This was because the Development Bank of South Africa (DBSA) threatened to recall its R15 billion loan to Eskom if immediate action was not taken against corrupt officials linked to the Guptas.

Then minister for Public Enterprises, Lynne Brown, at last instructed Eskom to take legal action against firms and individuals involved. That cast a particular spotlight on the Gupta-owned consultancy firm, Trillian Capital Partners Ltd, and consultancy firm McKinsey, which were intertwined through corruption with Singh and former acting CEO Matshela Koko. Brown effectively protected most of the guilty parties through subterfuge, double-speak, lack of accountability, likely corruption and turning a blind eye, and had a possibly fatal inability to properly understand the numbers and what was really at stake for South Africa's long-term economic stability.

About a dozen criminal cases had been opened by 2018, and there had been nearly 250 whistleblowing complaints of graft.

It took rigorous work by the amaBhungane Centre for Investigative Journalism to reveal that the Guptas, in particular, had received contracts worth R11.7 billion from Eskom to supply coal between 2014 and 2017. The parastatal was simultaneously left with its massive debt – R218.2 billion of which was in government guarantees – and was estimated to require another R340 billion just to stay in business by 2022.

Former Telkom chair Jabu Mabuza was installed as chair at Eskom in 2018, with Phakamani Hadebe, a former National Treasury official, the CEO.

In November 2018, a 142-page inquiry report into state capture at Eskom, which was conducted by Parliament's Public Enterprises committee from June 2017 to June 2018, was unanimously adopted. It found there was a corrupt relationship between the Gupta family, their associates and key state functionaries, and that Eskom board members and some members of staff had been induced to act unlawfully. The report was praised for its accountability and oversight.

Among those named in the report as having acted against the best interests of the enterprise were: former public enterprises ministers Malusi Gigaba and Brown, who were described as having been 'grossly negligent'; former Eskom board chairpersons Zola Tsotsi, Ben Ngubane and Zethembe Khoza; former board directors Viroshini Nairoo and Pat Naidoo; former CEO Brian Molefe; former chief financial officer Anoj Singh, and former acting CEOs Sean Maritz and Matshela Koko.

Ensuing criminal and civil matters that were expected to result out of the probe, whose report was submitted to the Zondo Commission of Inquiry into State Capture, were left to regulatory and law enforcement agencies. Meanwhile, the power utility's integrated interim results in late 2018 showed growing debt and the prospect of another consecutive year of above-inflation tariff hikes amid rapidly failing infrastructure.

Expropriation of land without compensation (amendment to Section 25 of the Constitution)

Government policy

Both Houses of Parliament considered the Joint Constitutional Review Committee's (CRC) report, which recommended that Section 25 of the Constitution be amended to allow land expropriation without compensation, in December 2018.

This happened in the days after the Western Cape High Court dismissed minority rights advocacy organisation AfriForum's urgent interdict application, which sought to prevent MPs from voting on the report. The ANC, Economic Freedom Fighters (EFF), National Freedom Party (NFP) and United Democratic Movement (UDM) supported the adoption of the report, while the Democratic Alliance (DA), the Inkatha Freedom Party (IFP), Freedom Front Plus (FFP), the Congress of the People (Cope) and the African Christian Democratic Party (ACDP) opposed it.

Expropriation without compensation was likely the ANC's most important resolution out of its national elective conference held at Nasrec, Johannesburg, in December 2017. Addressing the subject in March 2018, the party's head of policy, Jeff Radebe, said land expropriation would be 'rolled out with urgency'. He promised 'steps would be taken before the party's national general council' in 2019, with the goal being to 'strengthen the agricultural sector' in the interests of economic growth, improving prospects for employment and continuing the fight against inequality.

Primary concerns were that expropriation should not endanger food security, despite political and economic objectives.

The ANC, and later President Cyril Ramaphosa and his government, emphasised that the initial focus would be on state-owned land that was either vacant or underutilised, but not subject to a land claim. Some of these were to be transferred back to traditional communities, but there was a significant dispute over who would control this transfer and what could follow that handover. There was no consensus among parliamentarians that this should be the role of traditional leaders, despite the ANC having proposed this.

Estimates suggested that state-owned land accounted for 13% of the land in South Africa, which would not be enough to repair landlessness. Thus, the ANC and government indicated there would also have to be expropriation of private land that had left its owners in debt that could not be repaid, or which was lying fallow for no reason other than speculation.

The ruling party's first elective manifesto in 1994 endorsed land reform, but after nearly 25 years in power, it was way off its own targets. The pressure had intensified greatly on the ANC to match its intentions with action, the former Constitutional Court Justice Albie Sachs having explained that there was no 'willing buyer, willing seller' provision in relation to land redistribution in the Constitution.

Sachs, selected as one of the architects of the Constitution, said in a discussion to mark the late ANC leader Oliver Tambo's centenary in 2017 that there was 'no defence of existing property rights' in the document. Perhaps one of the most fundamental problems surrounding land and land claims lay, however, in abiding confusion around the wording of the Constitution and a belief that property rights dominate.

Expropriation and the redistribution of land were critical to that. People were angry about the other 87% of land owned residentially or by commerce. Most often, it was this land that was being targeted in land invasions, spurred on by the EFF and, to a lesser extent, Black First Land First.

The EFF was under its own pressure not to see the ANC steal a march on the land expropriation issue which it, the EFF, had brought to the fore and wanted to maximise to improve its own support in the 2019 election. The issue had been one of the party's most important pillars for total emancipation. The party believes all land should be owned by the state with people able to apply for 'land-use' licences, which could only be granted if the purpose for which the land was intended was deemed feasible.

The DA does not support land redistribution without compensation, except state-owned, fallow farmland or so-called 'tribal land'. It does, however, want those who had been, or were, living in state-subsidised housing to be given the title deeds of those properties.

As it stands, there are other difficulties that government faces. It had to bear in mind criminality coming along with demands for expropriation. It heightened attention on by-laws. But long-won amendments to the Prevention of Illegal Eviction (PIE) Act could also affect the way in which expropriation was done. Those amendments – including the provision of alternative accommodation for evictees – were designed to protect the constitutional rights of people threatened with eviction.

The EFF was praised and criticised for its policies on land expropriation, which were, at times, confused. But at the core of its support for a land review was equal redistribution. Its MP Mbuyiseni Ndlozi said in May 2018 that it was an 'historic duty for white people to realise that nobody punished them for apartheid colonisation. No one is even calling for punishment. People are calling for equality'.

R10.4 billion was the total amount allocated to land reform by the Department of Rural Development in the 2018/19 financial year, according to budget data from the National Treasury. Of that, the land reform programme was allocated only R2.7 billion, although land restitution had separately been allocated R3.4 billion. A month before a constitutional review committee was due to close the period for submissions around land in June 2018, it already had about 150,000 submissions.

Meanwhile, the Security of Land Tenure Amendment Bill, intended to legislate against farm evictions, was signed into law in November 2018. The ANC planned to expedite thousands of restitution claims by farmworkers as part of its election strategy for 2019.

Former president Thabo Mbeki alienated his own party, the ANC, when he took aim at expropriation without compensation in a 30-page document leaked in September 2018. His view was that the policy could be a deviation from non-racialism, which is an ANC pillar, as it could be read as being against white ownership.

F

The Federation of Unions of South Africa (Fedusa)

Trade union

Non-aligned | Power broker

By advertising its 'strategic partners', Sanlam, Momentum and Cell C, on its website, Fedusa situated itself in a different union space to that of Cosatu and Saftu. Sanlam and Momentum offered 'preferred' financial services to Fedusa members, while Cell C offered 'customised' packages.

But with 20 affiliates – including the South African Typographical Union, the Hospitality Industries and Allied Workers Union and, critically, the Public Service Association (PSA) – Fedusa, which claimed 700,000 total membership, is not a minnow.

More than two decades in, union organisation had assisted its coup in getting the PSA, with its 230,000-member base, back under its banner as the Cosatu–Saftu divide widened in 2017. Having the PSA under its umbrella meant Fedusa had greater power in the powerful Public Service Co-Ordinated Bargaining Council (PSCBC), where all government employees' pay increases and working conditions are negotiated. Cosatu's public sector union membership, which had supported the ANC through its federation's alliance with the ruling party, had once dominated there, but the positioning of the PSA under Fedusa – which does not give its support to the ANC – meant that the ANC's dominance in PSCBC might not continue. Agreements are most often for three years, so the PSA offered Fedusa a lever within high-level negotiations, which could affect the wider political outcome in the country.

#FeesMustFall

AKA: FMF; Fallists | Student protest movement | Ideologically diverse

Change agents | Power brokers | Some leaders linked to corruption | Some members facing trial or imprisonment

When Jacob Zuma made a sudden announcement on free education at the end of 2017, it seemed the raison détre of the existence of #FeesMustFall, or the Fallist movement, was gone.

As if out of the blue, Zuma said government would subsidise free higher education for poor and working-class students from households with a combined annual income of up to R350,000, starting in 2018 for students in their first year of study. The subsidies would be government grants, not loans, and existing loans out of the National Student Financial Aid Scheme (NSFAS) affecting students in their final year, would be converted to grants immediately.

Few had been expecting this, but those who note political advantage were quick to point out Zuma made the announcement on the morning the ANC's elective conference at Nasrec, Johannesburg, began. His favoured candidate to succeed him as ANC president, Nkosazana Dlamini-Zuma, would be facing down rival Cyril Ramaphosa.

There were, however, highly questionable aspects.

Zuma had effectively overruled the recommendations of his own Heher Commission into the Feasibility of Fee-Free Higher Education and Training, which had found there was no way, at that time, for government to be able to fund free tertiary, and it had recommended funding should rather happen through a cost-sharing model of government-guaranteed loans involving commercial banks.

But there was no return once he'd backed up his announcement with research from Mukovhe Morris Masutha, his former advisor and ex-Fallist, who proposed budgets across government departments be cut to make R40 billion available to fund fees. Likely the most important consequence of FMF then, was that VAT would have to go up by 1 percentage point in part to fund further higher education.

Quick as wildfire, however, a scandal flared around Masutha, centred on two claims: that he had dated Zuma's daughter Thuthukile (also known as Thuthu; her mother is Dlamini-Zuma, Minister in the Presidency and former ANC presidential hopeful); that he had been an agent of the State while Student Representative Council (SRC) president at the University of the Witwatersrand (Wits), along with other spies who may have infiltrated the FMF movement.

Journalist Jacques Pauw asserted in his best-seller, *The President's Keepers*, that intelligence agents could have been involved in the 2015 and 2016 Fallist movement. Meanwhile, the Inspector General of Intelligence (IGI) and the Independent Police Investigative Directorate (IPID) were thought to be investigating whether Secret Service account money was indeed used to fund aspects of the FMF movement.

But whatever the purpose could have been for Masutha to spy, if indeed he did, and whatever the purpose could have been for Zuma's own foundation to fund Masutha's Thusanani Foundation, which worked at youth upliftment, if indeed he did, neither provided a guide as to how to fund needy students without taking from budget government had allocated to deal with massive need in especially basic education.

The impasse was purported to have led to the resignation of Michael Sachs, veteran deputy director-general in the National Treasury and an expert in the budget process.

Meanwhile, the fight for no fees had taken a significant personal toll on student activists who faced criminal charges for public violence. Court interdicts and the use of heavy-handed private security had been tactics of some university vice-chancellors in attempts to maintain 'law and order'.

Freedom Front Plus (FF+)

Afrikaans: Vryheidsfront Plus | Conservative; Nationalist | Number of seats in Parliament in 2018: 4

Led by Pieter Groenewald, a conservative Afrikaner politician and MP who sat on Parliament's Public Administration and Defence Portfolio committees in 2018, the FF+ held true to its commitment to minority rights and 'self-determination'.

But it was only governing agreements, first with the Inkatha Freedom Party (IFP) in the early post-democratic period, and then with the Democratic Alliance (DA) after the key 2016 local government elections to govern Johannesburg, Tshwane and other municipalities that kept it alive as a political entity. That would likely be true after the 2019 elections too, as this party looked to remain a minnow representing even a minority viewpoint within a small white population. Then came January 2019, and the party made a startling announcement. It had been joined by Peter Marais, former premier of the Western Cape, and former member of the National Party, the New National Party, the Democratic Alliance, the New Labour Party and the Congress of the People. Marais was the leader of the lobby group the Bruin Bemagtiging Beweging (Brown Empowerment Movement) at the time he joined the FF+, and said at a press conference that his desire was to fight for Afrikaans, minorities' self-determination and Christian values.

The FF+ announced Marais as its candidate for Western Cape premier. At the time, the party did not yet have a seat in the provincial legislature.

It was likely Marais and the FF+ would be remembered for Marais's words at the press conference: 'All people are brown people. Black people are just darker brown people, and white people are just lighter brown people'.

Pieter Mulder, a former MP for the Conservative Party – the reactionary official opposition during the last years of apartheid – was the FF+'s national chairperson and later party leader. Former president Jacob Zuma appointed Mulder as Deputy Minister of Agriculture, Forestry and Fisheries in 2009.

The FF+ had its roots in the Afrikanervolksunie (AVU), established during the last years of apartheid. The AVU bonded with the Conservative Party and bantustan leaders Lucas Mangope of Bophuthatswana, Oupa Gqozo of Ciskei and Mangosuthu Buthelezi of KwaZulu-Natal to form an alliance called the Concerned South Africans Group (Cosag). Its aim was to hold back democracy to ensure homelands for its constituencies.

Cosag morphed into the Freedom Alliance in 1993, with some of its representatives participating in the Convention for a Democratic South Africa (Codesa) negotiations.

Freedom Under Law (FUL)

Activist | Non-Aligned

Change agents

CREATED AS A NOT-FOR-PROFIT ORGANISATION to promote democracy under law and to advance understanding of and respect for the rule of law and the principle of legality in southern Africa, it institutes or joins in litigation from time to time to combat and correct institutional conduct in conflict with the rule of law.

Its board includes some of South Africa's greatest legal names, including George Bizos SC, Judge Johann Kriegler (chairperson) and former Constitutional Court justice Zac Yacoob. The current executive officer is Nicole Fritz, the founding executive director of the Southern Africa Litigation Centre (SALC).

Among FUL's cases have been: a review of former National Director of Public Prosecutions (NDPP) Shaun Abrahams's withdrawal of charges against his former deputy, Nomgcobo Jiba; a review of the settlement granted former NDPP Mxolisi Nxasana upon termination of Nxasana's appointment; and an inquiry into what has happened to a case relating to fraud and perjury concerning the retired head of police crime intelligence, Richard Mdluli.

Free State

Province | Run by the ANC since 1994

Mired in allegations of corruption in its provincial leadership

SOME OF THE FIERCEST POLITICAL WRANGLING has taken place in this province, which was deeply affected by the manipulation of ANC branch membership audits over a number of years.

In January 2018, the party's provincial leadership was instructed to convene a fresh elective conference supervised by a task team to be appointed by the new National Executive Committee elected at Nasrec in December 2017.

This followed successful litigation after prominent ANC member and former MP Sello Dithebe and others described what had ensued at the conference in 2017 as a 'shameless charade'. The courts agreed and declared the 2017 gathering null and void.

This echoed events in 2012 when the Constitutional Court (ConCourt) declared the province's elective conference that year unlawful too after allegations of the manipulation of branch membership numbers and the establishment of parallel structures. Among those named as being in the thick of factionalism was senior party member Mpho Ramakatsa, who would go on to join the Economic Freedom Fighters (EFF) and become an EFF MP. That party would, however, expel him in 2015.

The factionalism in the 2017 conference had centred on Ace Magashule, the long-serving Free State ANC chairperson and also premier before he was elected party secretary-general at Nasrec.

Following the elective conference in May 2018, ex-trade unionist and former MEC for police Sam Mashinini was elected unopposed as chairperson, with William Bulwane – party secretary under Magashule – as deputy chair. Sisi Ntombela, deputy president of the ANC Women's League, was elected treasurer and then premier, but she was not expected to retain that position after the 2019 elections. Mashinini was believed to be a likely new premier.

The new top five were all former members of the provincial task team (PTT) established to run Free State after the courts declared the 2017 conference illegal. But their election would not be the end of the conflict. A group of aggrieved party members then wrote to the PTT through a lawyer demanding an explanation of how the conference had been arranged and inquiring as to the credibility of delegates.

The Democratic Alliance (DA) in the Free State had also tried to block the ANC from appointing some leaders charged with corruption. Among those were then MEC for Sports, Arts and Culture and former mayor, Mmathabo Leeto, and then MEC for Environmental Affairs, Tourism and Economic Affairs and former municipal manager, Dr Benny Malakoane. Charges of corruption, fraud and racketeering would be laid again Leeto, Malakoane and seven others in the Free State High Court, but the National Prosecuting Authority (NPA) withdrew the charges in July 2018.

The charges related to alleged tender fraud of R2 billion. The NPA said a new indictment was possible.

Frolick, Cedric

ANC's National Assembly Chairperson of Committees

An MP since 1999, Frolick joined the National Assembly as a representative of the United Democratic Movement (UDM), for which he also acted as chief whip. But by the time of the scandal around Nkandla, former president Jacob Zuma's private homestead in KwaZulu-Natal, Frolick was back in his old fold – the ANC.

In 2015, at the height of the Nkandla debacle, there was a plethora of Zuma-related memes, quotes and memorable outbursts. So when Frolick, as head of Parliament's ad hoc committee probe into that public spend, held a press conference and conceded that the swimming pool at Zuma's home – which then police minister Nathi Nhleko had infamously claimed was a 'fire pool' – was, in fact, a recreational facility, he, too, went viral.

'What we saw in front of us is a pool ... a pool is a pool,' he told journalists after the committee had done an inspection. But Frolick had the seniority to make such a declaration, irrespective of party allegiances, as he was the National Assembly chairperson of committees – a position to which he was appointed by the ANC in 2010.

Froneman, Justice Johan

Constitutional Court (ConCourt) Justice | Former Deputy Judge President of the Labour and Labour Appeal Courts

Born on a farm in the Eastern Cape, Froneman earned his law degree at Stellenbosch University, practised as an advocate in Grahamstown before being appointed to the Eastern Cape High Court. He then accepted an appointment as Deputy Judge President of the Labour and Labour Appeal Courts, acted at the Supreme Court of Appeal (SCA), and then put himself into the line of fire as a justice of the Constitutional Court (ConCourt) in 2009.

Froneman was one of former president Jacob Zuma's first appointments to the apex court. He is now best known for delivering its damning judgment on former social development minister Bathabile Dlamini during the 2017 South African Social Grants Agency (SASSA) scandal, which caused concern among recipients. Froneman ordered there be further investigation into Dlamini's personal liability, a decision with which she was still grappling in anger a year later, but which eventually led to the apex court finding her indeed personally liable, for 20% of costs. The court also found that the National Prosecuting Authority should determine whether Dlamini should be prosecuted for perjury.

Meanwhile, there were two minority judgments from Froneman which also drew attention: Chief Justice Mogoeng Mogoeng's dissent over the ConCourt's seeming 'judicial over-reach' in Parliament's presidential impeachment question, and Froneman's own dissent over the majority judgment dismissing Afrikaner lobby group AfriForum's bid to appeal the SCA's ruling, downgrading Afrikaans as a medium of instruction at the University of the Free State.

Gana, Makashule

Member of the Gauteng Provincial Legislature (MPL) | Former shadow minister of Human Settlements | Former Democratic Alliance (DA) National Youth leader | Former DA deputy federal chairperson

On the way up | Change agent

A BSc graduate and business analyst by training, Gana entered politics by joining the DA in 2002, serving as its youth and deputy federal chairperson in 2012 while he was also a councillor in the Johannesburg metropolitan municipality.

By mid-2018, Gana – a member of the provincial legislature (MPL) in Gauteng – was a firm favourite for the position of Gauteng premier, in a province his party believed it could win in the 2019 elections. It had secured Gauteng's key Tshwane and Johannesburg metros in the 2016 local government elections. But that was not to be as Gana was outrun as candidate by Tshwane mayor, Solly Msimanga.

The 2014 general elections saw Gana promoted to MP in the National Assembly and elevated to DA shadow minister of Human Settlements. Gana had been an alternate party choice for mayor of Johannesburg in 2016, but the DA then touted billionaire businessman Herman Mashaba, who indeed wore the chain in 2018.

Gana was among DA senior officials – including Western Cape leader Bonginkosi Madikizela, MP Zakhele Mbhele and Gauteng MPL Khume Ramulifho – who raised objections about internal party processes when MP Natasha Mazzone was elected second deputy federal chairperson. Their objections were seen as symptomatic of deeper rifts in the DA.

Gardee, Godrich

EFF Parliamentary whip | Member of the EFF's Central Command Team (CCT) | EFF Commissar for Mobilisation, Campaigns and Special Projects | EFF Secretary

A young recruit of the ANC underground in the 1980s, Gardee was a matriculant when he joined the liberation movement in Botswana. He never then considered he would eventually leave the beloved party of his youth, as even on his return to South Africa, he was determined to make a contribution and worked in finance for the ANC's departments of Sports and Public Works in Mpumalanga.

Gardee has, however, described how the high levels of ANC corruption which he saw in local government and in the Mpumalanga legislature, affected his loyalty, telling a Sunday newspaper in 2015 how he once refused to sign off on 'a dodgy R300 million contract', but claimed 'those above him approved it'. Gardee even went as far as to complain to the ANC's then premier, David 'DD' Mabuza, that the provincial government had been captured, but Mabuza was himself part of the shadowy politics which had gripped Mpumalanga.

In 2018, he was the EFF Commissar for Mobilisation, Campaigns and Special Projects, having joined the party in 2013.

Gigaba, Malusi

Former minister of Home Affairs | Former minister of Finance | Former minister of Public Enterprises | Former ANC Youth League (ANCYL) president

Suspected of being captured | Found to have lied under oath

2018 was a tough year for one of Jacob Zuma's acolytes. Gigaba spent it fighting for a continued role in government, but resigned in November 2018, after it appeared President Cyril Ramaphosa would bow to escalating calls to dismiss him.

Although Zuma had made him Minister of Finance in 2017, Ramaphosa undercut that power by putting Gigaba back in his old job as the Minister of Home Affairs in February 2018. He had previously held from 2014–17. Since home affairs has the capacity to interfere with state and judicial processes, as its extended powers could see its political head allowing even corrupt individuals to acquire travelling and residence documents, Gigaba's was not a minor influence.

The unpacking of the massive Gupta naturalisation controversy happened at last in late 2018, when Gigaba testified before Parliament's Home Affairs Committee. He rubbished accusations that he had had a corrupt relationship with the Guptas, some of whom were given citizenships to which they were not entitled. But Gigaba was shown to be lying after he brazenly announced in April 2018 that brothers Ajay and Atul Gupta had never been South African citizens. His statement led to Business Leadership SA CEO Bonang Mohale describing him as 'the biggest enabler of state capture'. The department was then placed in the extraordinary position of having to correct its own minister, as Atul Gupta – believed to have fled South Africa ahead of arrest in early 2018 – was indeed given citizenship, a fact proven by him having participated as a voter in elections.

Many suggested governance had been a problem wherever Gigaba had been installed. To this end, he was shown by the North Gauteng High Court to have lied under oath during court action involving private landing and departure arrangement for the super-rich Oppenheimer family's planes through its company, Fireblade Auto. His appeals to the Supreme Court of Appeal and the Constitutional Court to have that judgment overturned were dismissed.

Yet history may show that Gigaba's most rankerous contribution to South Africa's plummeting fortunes by 2017 and 2018 was made during his time as the minister of public enterprises when he restructured the boards of a number of state-owned enterprises (SOEs), seemingly to facilitate ever-greater corruption to benefit the Guptas and their associates.

Gigaba had the tools to make a contribution to nation-building with a Master's in social policy and the political experience of serving his party since a young age. He had risen to become president of the ANC Youth League (ANCYL) by 1996 and an ANC MP by 1999. His champions looked forward to him being promoted to ANC national chairperson or secretary general.

As a final blow, the Zondo Commission of Inquiry into State Capture further exposed the lies Gigaba told the National Assembly Speaker in 2012 when he claimed the South African Airways (SAA) board chaired by Cheryl Carolus had not yet submitted audited financial statements in 2012, which was not the case. He was believed to have done this in order to frustrate a process for the board to gain finance from banks to renew its fleet.

Gigaba would likely be remembered not only for his appalling state of personal capture, but also for a homemade solo sex video which went viral in late 2018. At that point, he stopped tweeting – an activity that had once been one of his favourites.

Godi, Themba

Founding president of the African People's Convention (APC) party | Former deputy leader of the Pan-Africanist Congress (PAC) | Chairperson of Parliament's Standing Committee on Public Accounts (Scopa)

THE APC'S SOLE MP IN PARLIAMENT, Godi began his post-democratic political career with the Pan-Africanist Congress (PAC), but was later suspended as infighting grew in the party which had been founded by the great Robert Sobukwe in the 1950s.

Godi continued to serve as deputy leader of the PAC until the floor-crossing period of 2007, when he left the party with the PAC seat and formed his own party. He was joined by Mofihli Dikotsi, the PAC's chief whip in Parliament and two MPLs – Zingisa Mkabile from the Eastern Cape and Gauteng's Malesela Ledwaba.

Despite representing what was a minuscule political entity in 2018, Godi played an important watchdog role himself as chairperson of Parliament's key Standing Committee on Public Accounts (Scopa).

Godongwana, Enoch

Head of the ANC's Economic Transformation Sub-Committee | Former Deputy Minister of Public Enterprises | Former general secretary of the National Union of Metalworkers (Numsa)

On the way up | Resigned from government linked to fraud and theft

AN ANC VETERAN, GODONGWANA REVEALED himself to be a challenging moral arbiter for a party in decline. This, despite his own slide into corruption.

He spoke out early on against former president Jacob Zuma when it seemed clear the country's leader was trying to shield himself, members of his family and nefarious associates from legal redress in what would then spin out as devastating state capture. Godongwana was one of the few party leaders willing to publicly say that Zuma appeared to have concocted information that facilitated his firing of finance minister Nhlanhla Nene to briefly replace him with a lackey, the Parliamentary backbencher, Des van Rooyen.

Godongwana not only survived that but recovered from voluntary resignation from his post as Deputy Minister of Economic Development in 2012 after he and his wife were named in an inquiry into the disappearance of millions of rands from the South African Clothing and Textile Workers' Union (SACTWU) pension fund. This was especially disappointing as Godongwana had been a worker himself who had toiled through the ranks of the National Union of Metalworkers (NUM) until he became its general secretary in 1994. A talented negotiator, he was appointed by the Congress of South African Trade unions (Cosatu) to be an executive and management board member of the National Economic Development and Labour Council (Nedlac), before he moved into government.

Gondongwana, a member of the ANC's National Executive Committee (NEC), however, continued to see his political fortunes rise in 2018 when international relations minister Lindiwe Sisulu recruited him onto a review panel to steer a new direction for the country's foreign policy.

Godongwana was the CEO of the Financial Sector Charter Council and a member of the Policy Board for Financial Services and Regulation. He served as a director of Denel and as the MEC for Economic Affairs, Environment and Tourism in the Eastern Cape government.

He holds a Master's degree in finance and economics from the University of London.

Gordhan, Pravin

Minister of Public Enterprises | Former minister of Finance (twice) | Former minister of Co-Operative Governance and Traditional Affairs | Former South African Revenue Service (SARS) Commissioner | A former chairperson of the Convention for a Democratic South Africa (Codesa) | Former political prisoner

Retiring in 2019

It could be argued that Gordhan went to hell and back in his various roles in public service between 2015 and 2018, as if he hadn't been there before as a young activist during apartheid as a member of the United Democratic Front (UDF) and the Transvaal Indian Congress (TIC), and an underground leader of the South African Communist Party (SACP).

But out of the drama that beset his later political career, being hounded by the Hawks elite investigations unit as it probed allegations that he had set up a 'rogue unit' that spied on politicians while he was South African Revenue Service (SARS) commissioner, was likely the most stressful.

That would not be the only way in which the Hawks tried to suppress Gordhan as a guardian of democracy during the administration of Jacob Zuma. Another probe, into the payment of retirement benefits to former SARS deputy commissioner Ivan Pillay, was designed to destabilise Gordhan's authority while he was actively undermined in public by the ANC's youth and women's wings.

Gordhan was driven to tears in an open forum in 2017 when he spoke of his pain at being targeted with state resources for political reasons.

Reappointed finance minister in 2015 after Zuma's decision to fire Gordhan's predecessor Nhlanhla Nene (who had succeeded him, Gordhan, in his first tenure as finance minister) and put ANC backbencher Des van Rooyen in the job, wiping billions off the Johannesburg Stock Exchange (JSE), Gordhan would actively agitate for the president's demise.

He courageously spoke out against corruption in government and took aim at Zuma's associates, the nefarious Gupta brothers. As his relationship with Zuma, and Zuma's faction within the ANC, crumbled, Gordhan's popularity outside the ANC grew. As an ANC MP, he remained on Parliament's Public Enterprises Portfolio Committee while Zuma was still in power, and, using that as a platform, vocally urged an investigation into state capture.

President Cyril Ramaphosa appointed Gordhan as Minister for Public Enterprises with command of SOEs in his first Cabinet reshuffle after Zuma resigned.

Gordhan immediately set about installing interim and new boards, and identifying those who were responsible for bringing many of the parastatals to their knees. For this, he attracted the ire of especially the Economic Freedom Fighters (EFF), which went on an extended campaign to discredit him, finally walking out of the National Assembly in the last week of November as Gordhan was about to deliver the closing remarks on a debate on the report of Parliament's own inquiry into state capture at Eskom. The EFF laid charges of money laundering, corruption, racketeering, fraud, contravention of the Intelligence Act and the Prevention and Combating of Corrupt Activities Act, and perjury against Gordhan in November, and also claimed his daughter Anisha had been an unlawful beneficiary of lucrative state tenders. (Anisha Gordhan had, in fact, been a director at Investec, which had earned tenders to which she had not been privy nor gained from in her personal capacity.)

Gordhan had earlier filed a complaint of crimen injuria and criminal defamation against the EFF, and wanted an investigation into incitement to violence against EFF leader Julius Malema after Malema made a public speech against Gordhan in the grounds of the building where the Zondo Commission of Inquiry into State Capture was being held, at the time when Gordhan was testifying. Gordhan further laid a complaint at the Equality Court, seeking an apology and damages.

Gungubele, Mondli

Deputy Minister of Finance | Former mayor of the Ekurhuleni Metropolitan Municipality | Resigned as chairperson of the Public Investment Corporation (PIC), an executive designation, in February 2019 in light of allegations made against the PIC board at the commission of inquiry into its activities (see Public Investment Corporation).

On the way up

Referenced in conversation whenever the fall of Jacob Zuma is discussed, Gungubele is a hero among ANC supporters who witnessed how he managed a motion of no confidence against the former president in 2017. One of the few ANC MPs brave enough to break ranks and publicly say how they would vote in a secret ballot, he admitted he had lost confidence in Zuma and would vote consistent with that attitude. And Zuma champions called for his head.

But Gungubele never shied from speaking his mind. He was one of Cyril Ramaphosa's ardent backers ahead of the ANC's Nasrec elective conference in December 2017, having known him since the founding of the National Union of Mineworkers (NUM) in the early 1980s. And his ability to ask the most pointed questions during Parliament's Public Enterprises Portfolio Committee probing state capture literally moved people onto their feet.

Ramaphosa showed full confidence in Gungubele by appointing him as the

Deputy Minister of Finance in 2017.

He first got involved in ANC politics as a nurse campaigning for workers' struggles. Elected chairperson of the Vosloorus ANC branch before he served as the party's regional chairperson in the Ekurhuleni area outside Johannesburg, Gungubele became a member of the ANC's NEC in 2012.

He previously served as mayor of the Ekurhuleni Metropolitan Municipality and holds a BComm (Law) degree and a national diploma in nursing.

The Guptas

Notorious 'family friends' of former president Jacob Zuma

Protagonists of state capture | Under investigation

Once holed up in a luxury pile in Saxonwold, one of Johannesburg's most expensive suburbs, the Guptas wrought a vile influence that will be felt for decades, if not generations, to come.

Atul Gupta was first to arrive in South Africa, in 1993. Joined not long afterwards by brothers Ajay and Rajesh, they started a computer company, Sahara, which had no relation to the IT giant of the same name, building their empire in South Africa through Department of Education tenders.

The family empire grew to include a media component, starting with a national daily newspaper, *The New Age*, set up in 2010 to push the government agenda, which rapidly segued into reflecting the agenda of the Jacob Zuma faction within the ANC.

By 2013, the family had also started a 24-hour TV news channel, notable both for its amateurish production and unabashed Zuma-centric agit-prop. But the Guptas began over-reaching themselves that year when a wedding party for a family member landed in a commercial jet at Waterkloof Air Force base, a privilege reserved for government business and visiting heads of state. The blue light escorts and the grotesque expense of the protracted Bollywood-styled wedding at Sun City brought the Gupta family four-square into the South African conversation – and finally turned them into a target for the Economic Freedom Fighters (EFF) and other opposition parties.

Undaunted, the brothers moved to get control of a coal mine which, it is alleged, they contrived to get Eskom to pay for, and it was contended that they extended their influence over Zuma to the extent that they were able to vet Cabinet appointments and offer ministries to capture politicians. They also employed Zuma's son, Duduzane, and other members of the president's extended family, appearing horribly impregnable at that point. But by 2016, shortly after Atul Gupta was named the seventh richest man in South Africa, the big four South African banks disowned the family.

The following year, the release of the so-called 'Gupta leaks', a trove of millions of incriminating emails, laid bare the extent of their devastation, embedding 'state capture' in the South African lexicon, and destroying reputations well beyond the Zuma family. One of the most high-profile looked to be Ace Magashule, the former Free State premier and secretary-general of the ANC; another, the former minister of

Mineral Resources, Mosebenzi Zwane, who was axed by President Cyril Ramaphosa in February 2018.

There was a blow to elite investigations unit, the Hawks, when the Asset Forfeiture Unit's attempts to place around R250 million of the Guptas' assets under curatorship in early 2018 were denied by the courts.

Equally disappointing was the state's inability to ready its case in time against the so-called 'Estina 8' who were linked to allegations against the Guptas regarding a failed dairy farm project in the Free State.

Meanwhile infamous individuals linked to the Guptas, including some members of that family, remained fugitives of justice, believed to have fled South Africa for Dubai.

'Gupta leaks'

Massive trove of emails recovered from spy cables

Led to recovery of information leading to State capture allegations

Sam Sole and Karabo Rajuili of the amaBhungane Centre for Investigative Journalism described the leak of South African Secret Service (SSA) papers as 'embarrassing' when this became public knowledge through the Al Jazeera international news service, in 2015.

At the beginning, Sole explained, the 'bulk of the leaked documentation (appeared) to come from the records of the foreign branch of the agency, whose targets – other states and their spies – (were) inherently less controversial than those whom the domestic branch chooses to watch'. But it wouldn't take long before the details of 'domestic scandals that had plagued the agency, scandals stemming largely from the politicisation and factionalisation of the services' started to filter into public view, too.

Al Jazeera's Investigative Unit's scoop revealed papers written by Israel's Mossad, Britain's MI6, Russia's Federal Security Service of the Russian Federation, Australia's Australian Security Intelligence Organisation and South Africa's SSA. Together with *The Guardian* in London, Al Jazeera published an array of analyses exploring the stories contained within the spy cables.

If it were not for the Gupta Leaks, it's unlikely much of the incalculably damaging corruption which has been revealed over the past two years in South Africa would have come to light, or been able to be remedied. In fact, Jacob Zuma may himself have sustained a seeming 'untouchability' which was the case during most of his time as president.

H

Hadebe, Phakamani

CEO of Eskom | Previously worked at the International Monetary Fund (IMF) | Previously worked at National Treasury | Previously CEO of the Land Bank

Power broker | Star

CONFIRMED TO HEAD THE TROUBLED, IF NOT BANKRUPT, electricity utility in May 2018 by the minister of public enterprises, Pravin Gordhan, Hadebe had shown his mettle, successfully acting in that position for four months.

Previously an asset to the International Monetary Fund, National Treasury and Absa, he had also reported a massive turnaround at the Land Bank just a year after he took over as CEO there in 2008. Unprecedented corruption at the Land Bank before his time would eventually lead to the conviction of its former CEO, Philemon Mohlahlane, as well as former Gauteng housing MEC Daniel Mofokeng, former ANC MP Reuben Mohlaloga, and lawyers Dinga Rammy Nkhwashu and Dingamanzi ka Dinga.

Hadebe's time at Absa was remarkable for the banking giant having overlooked him for a key position. Media attention was drawn to his departure in 2017, for 'personal reasons', when more than a dozen employees staged a walkout in protest at his resignation.

Hadebe was an economics lecturer at the University of KwaZulu-Natal when he was recruited by Treasury to steer government debt and sovereign risk management.

Hanekom, Derek

Minister of Tourism | Former minister of Science and Technology | Former minister of Agriculture and Land Affairs | Chairperson of the ANC's National Disciplinary Committee | Deputy chairperson of the Board of the Ahmed Kathrada Foundation | An original member of the Government of National Unity (GNU) | Former political prisoner | Member of the ANC's National Working Committee (NWC)

ONE OF THE FEW CURRENT ANC LEADERS to have served on the party's NEC since 1994, and a member of its NWC, Hanekom worked his way up the party ranks.

He spent years familiarising himself with the struggles of ordinary people, labouring on farms, in factories and on building sites, and becoming involved in the trade union movement before he was jailed and, upon release, went into exile with the ANC in Zimbabwe with his wife, Trish, in 1987. Hanekom returned in 1990 and first worked at the ANC's Johannesburg headquarters, where he was responsible for policy formulation on land and agricultural matters.

His insight into land saw Nelson Mandela appoint him minister of agriculture and land affairs from 1994 to 1999, allowing Hanekom to play a crucial role by driving reform bills through Parliament according to his preferred means of redistribution. Not many South Africans may know that the changes under way in this sector – however slow – were significantly the work of Hanekom, who was also the chairperson of the ANC's national disciplinary committee. He chaired the panel that suspended former ANC Youth League (ANCYL) president Julius Malema and other ANCYL leaders, including its deputy president Ronald Lamola, treasurer-general Pule Mabe and spokesperson Floyd Shivambu in 2011. They were accused of sowing division and bringing the party into disrepute. The national disciplinary committee of appeal, chaired by Cyril Ramaphosa, confirmed their suspension in 2012.

In 2018, he was serving as minister of tourism in his second stint in the post after he was booted out by former president Jacob Zuma in 2017 when he spoke out against Zuma's corrupt relationships, and the decline this had brought within the ANC and to the country's prospects.

Hanekom remained an ANC MP even after he had filed a motion of no confidence against Zuma.

The Hawks

The Directorate for Priority Crime Investigation (DPCI) | Government agency

THE HAWKS WAS ESTABLISHED AS AN INDEPENDENT unit within the South African Police Service (SAPS) in 2008 to replace the Scorpions by then president Jacob Zuma.

The Scorpions did not fall under the SAPS structures and the decision to replace it came out of a resolution taken by the ANC Polokwane elective conference in 2007, when Zuma was elected party president. Pro-Zuma delegates there argued that 'government oversight' was needed so that such an agency couldn't be used as a political tool, but at its core appeared to be Zuma's urgency to escape prosecution himself.

By keeping the Hawks under the control of the SAPS, the unit automatically fell under the control of the executive, which was, of course, led by the president.

The Scorpions had been investigating Zuma when it was disbanded, its probe into his activities around weapons procurement already having led to the successful prosecution of his 'financial adviser', Schabir Shaik. It wanted Zuma prosecuted on charges of fraud, but these were dropped by the National Prosecuting Authority (NPA) early in 2009, and, within weeks, Zuma was the state president.

By 2018, however, the chances of a successful prosecution of Zuma, at last, looked a little more promising for the Hawks, with a date set down for trial in May 2019. But many other high-level prosecutions, particularly those concerning the Gupta family, revealed the paucity of its investigations, and the serious negative impact that Zuma's interference in its work had had in stripping it of its forensic talent.

Health Ombudsman

Independent authority tasked with enforcing health and safety standards within the Department of Health

Change agent

THE OMBUDSMAN'S OFFICE ADDRESSES, among other issues, complaints of mis-communication against health practitioners as a mediator. Acting as a 'public protector' of health, it falls under the Health Professions Council of South Africa (HPCSA).

Former University of KwaZulu-Natal vice-chancellor, Professor (Dr) Malegapuru Makgoba was appointed as the country's first health ombudsman in 2016 by Minister Aaron Motsoaledi, at a time described as a 'crisis point' by him. With a massive burden of disease, a failing public healthcare system, fewer specialists and increasing costs, there was also an overwhelming number of medical negligence claims. MacRobert Attorneys in Pretoria estimated these claims to have seen a 537% increase in 13 years. The ombudsman reports directly to the Minister of Health.

One of Makgoba's most significant acts was to intervene after the Life Esidimeni tragedy in 2018 in which dozens of mental health patients died after government cancelled its contract with a private provider and sent them to often-unregistered NGOs. Makgoba participated in the subsequent inquiry chaired by Deputy Chief Justice Emeritus Dikgang Moseneke, and found that the Gauteng Health MEC Qedani Mahlangu, Head of Department Dr Tiego Ephraim Selebano and Director Dr Makgabo Manamela's 'fingerprints were peppered' throughout the project. He said their decision was 'unwise and flawed, with inadequate planning and a "chaotic" and "rushed or hurried" implementation process'.

The Heher Commission into the Feasibility of Fee-Free Higher Education and Training

State probe

JACOB ZUMA ESTABLISHED THE HEHER COMMISSION in January 2016, appointing Judge Jonathan Heher, assisted by advocate Gregory Ally and Leah Khumalo. The presidency – which had been under extreme pressure to resolve the crisis in higher education after significant protests by students – received its report in August 2017, in which it acknowledged that everyone had a right to further education and that the state had a duty to make this possible 'progressively ... in time'.

It found, however, that totally free education was 'not in the best interests of South Africa's higher education sector' and that those who could afford to pay 'must pay'.

Existing schemes for funding higher education were 'inequitable, inadequate and unsustainable', but praised the Technical Vocational Education and Training (TVET) colleges, which offered tuition for selected qualifications, primarily higher certificates. It recommended adding R50 billion into the TVET sector.

The commission said the additional funding from the state should come from the estimated R99-billion surplus from the Unemployed Insurance Fund (UIF).

An income contingent loan (ICL) could also be established through public–private partnerships with financial institutions. Government would underwrite these.

It was recommended that application and registration fees for higher education and training institutions should be scrapped.

The report was released after Zuma had been briefed and won over by a plan to introduce fee-free tertiary education, which researcher and former University of the Witwatersrand Student Representative Council leader Makovhe Masutha had presented. It required government to find R40 billion to fund a free-education policy for families who earn less than R350,000, and contradicted the Heher Commission's report, which said that students should be funded through a cost-sharing model of government guaranteed 'Income-Contingency Loans' sourced from commercial banks – but irrespective of their family background.

State entities specifically involved in examining the Heher Commission report were the Inter-Ministerial Committee on Higher Education Funding led by the then minister in the Presidency, Jeff Radebe, and the Presidential Fiscal Committee led by then finance minister Malusi Gigaba.

The Heher Commission recommended students pay when they graduate and are earning a specific income, and if they do not reach that level by an agreed time government would be liable for the fees.

The Helen Suzman Foundation

Independent advocacy organisation | Liberal

AVOWEDLY LIBERAL, THIS JOHANNESBURG-BASED think-tank has gradually involved itself in more relevant and critical battles to secure South African democracy against corruption. Many of these battles – including fights to keep the Hawks, the Judicial Services Commission (JSC) and other public institutions free of kleptocrats and cronies – have given the foundation an identity in society.

Political scientist, economist and former head of the School of Public Management and Development at the University of the Witwatersrand (Wits), Francis Antonie was the director of the foundation in 2019.

Helen Suzman was a beacon of hope internationally as the single voice of dissent in parliament during some of apartheid's darkest days. Among her acts of social justice were seeing conditions for prisoners alleviated on Robben Island

Among the cases in which the Helen Suzman Foundation has been involved are: a review application against the Judicial Service Commission in terms of deficiencies in the selection of judges; securing Independent Police Investigations Directorate from undue political interference, and a review of unlawful, improper and corrupt exercises of public power at Eskom.

Heywood, Mark

Former executive director of SECTION27 | Former deputy chairperson of the South African National AIDS Council (SANAC) | Former chairperson of the UNAIDS Reference Group on HIV and Human Rights | Linked to the SaveSouthAfrica and #UniteAgainstCorruption activist campaigns

Change agent | Star

One of the country's best-known protagonists of social justice and development, Heywood became the backbone of SECTION27, a public-interest law centre.

An Oxford graduate, he worked for the Marxist Workers Tendency of the ANC, first in London and then from 1989 to 1994 in South Africa. He engaged in tough local campaigns, joining the Leeukop Political Prisoners' Support Committee and the Johannesburg Inner City Community Forum. But it was when Heywood was elected deputy chairperson of the South African National AIDS Council (SANAC) that he began to gain a much more prominent place in political society.

Among his most important roles was chairing the UNAIDS Reference Group on HIV and Human Rights, which led to his becoming a member of the Ministerial Advisory Committee on the National Health Insurance (NHI). Heywood became an expert on HIV, human rights and the law, having been on the legal teams of the AIDS Law Project and the Treatment Action Campaign (TAC) which were involved in all the major litigation around those subjects in South Africa. Together with other activists, he helped secure anti-retrovirals (ARVs) for people living with HIV, textbooks for poor schools and a future democratic agenda through campaigns like SaveSouthAfrica and #UniteAgainstCorruption.

Heywood's 2017 memoir, *Get Up! Stand Up! Personal Journeys Towards Social Justice*, provided a guide to ongoing struggles for rights.

HIV/AIDS policy

William 'Willie' Madisha was disgraced when he was fired as Congress of South African Trade Unions (Cosatu) president and South African Democratic Teachers Union (Sadtu) president in 2008. But if there is one powerful act for which Madisha – now a Congress of the People (COPE) MP – ought to be remembered from when he was a trade unionist, it was his federation's support of people living with HIV.

Speaking at the lowest point in the battle against stigma and for the distribution of generic Anti-Retroviral Drugs (ARVs) after then president Thabo Mbeki had earned scorn for his denialism, Madisha said HIV would be the 'litmus test of our revolution'.

He said he had voted for an ANC government 'in the belief it would look after its most vulnerable citizens' – including at least 200,000 people who, at that time, needed access to ARVs. Madisha and Cosatu were indeed revolutionary then for having effectively broken ranks with Mbeki, leader of the federation's alliance partner, the ANC, over his government's destructive AIDS policy.

Yet the confusion around and downplaying of HIV didn't start with Mbeki.

Despite the publicity given to Nelson Mandela's 46664 campaign, Mandela's Health Minister Dr Nkosazana Dlamini-Zuma had emphasised prevention of HIV transmission, when it seemed clear treatment is important.

By the time Mbeki came into power, the government had already failed in its duty of care around the provision of drugs and support for the HIV+ community, and so Cosatu's demands were also political – and would help change history.

Nearly a decade after Mandela effectively failed to provide sustainable leadership on HIV/AIDS, 5 million South Africans had contracted the virus.

South Africa has not been able to turn this around and remains among the five countries with the highest HIV rate in the world. The others are Swaziland, Botswana, Lesotho and Namibia. Nonetheless, South Africa has the largest treatment programme in the world and the life expectancy of those living with HIV/Aids has increased dramatically over the last 15 years.

Mbeki's Health Minister, the late Manto Tshabalala-Msimang, was among the most disgraced public figures in the AIDS tragedy. Infamous for confusing the eventual ARV distribution with her backing of nutritional 'African treatments', Tshabalala-Msimang would be somewhat sidelined by Mbeki's deputy president Phumzile Mlambo-Ngcuka, now head of UN Women, when Mlambo-Ngcuka oversaw the introduction of a five-year National Strategic Plan.

It was, however, only during Jacob Zuma's administration that universal access to ARVs was widely rolled out, initially championed by Barbara Hogan, appointed health minister by Zuma's predecessor as president, Kgalema Motlanthe. (Motlanthe was in office for eight months before Zuma.)

Zuma's health minister Aaron Motsoaledi had the executive, legislative and judicial backing for universal access, and South Africa then had the world's largest ARV therapy programme in the world, but there were still problems around provision.

Meanwhile, the numbers of those contracting the virus were not significantly down, with concern about rates among young women.

Astonishingly, while HIV/AIDS remained South Africa's most serious health crisis, it was not much of a political issue. A marginal percentage of politicians campaigned around HIV, openly gave their support to those living with HIV or even mentioned it. And since the demise of Mandela 'magic' and his 46664 razzmatazz, neither did celebrities who were once among the loudest advocates of universal access and against stigma.

Millions of South Africans have HIV and AIDS, but they were largely forgotten, and were it not for civil rights organisation Treatment Action Campaign (TAC), which celebrated its 20th anniversary in December 2018, they might have been forgotten entirely.

Hlabisa, Velenkosini

A likely next leader of the Inkatha Freedom Party (IFP) | Former IFP Youth Brigade leader | Former mayor of Hlabisa in the uMkhanyakude District Municipality in KwaZulu-Natal

On the way up

A MEMBER OF THE IFP FOR NEARLY as long as the party's founder, Mangosuthu Buthelezi, Hlabisa led in all party structures. That was why it was no surprise when he was endorsed by Buthelezi as his successor – or so it seemed – in October 2017 after four decades at the helm. Buthelezi had described Hlabisa as a 'leader of integrity' who would assist the party to play a necessary role, but while he, Hlabisa, may have been a favourite, he had not yet been elected by the beginning of 2019.

At 52, Hlabisa was, however, a significantly younger choice than even the ANC had made in some of its structures. The IFP's Extended National Council agreed to nominate him, having seen him lead from the party's youth brigade to branch level, to becoming its secretary in KwaZulu-Natal in 2011.

Hlabisa was a teacher who became a ward councillor in 1995 and then the mayor of Hlabisa in the uMkhanyakude District Municipality in KwaZulu-Natal.

Hofmeyr, Steve

Rightwing celebrity | Singer, performer | Leader of the ToekomsVonk minority rights organisation

ONCE A LONG-HAIRED, GOOD-TIME GUY WHO SANG, wrote poetry and acted in popular Afrikaans TV dramas, Hofmeyr turned overtly political in 2010 when he suddenly began actively campaigning for the security of white farmers and railing against the ANC Youth League (ANCYL) president Julius Malema's singing of the pro-black apartheid-era chant, 'Shoot the Boer/ Kill the Farmer' (Dubul'ibhunu).

But it was when Hofmeyr showed up at the funeral of murdered Afrikanerweerstandsbeweging leader, Eugène Terre'blanche, and delivered a eulogy, that he began to segue into a full-blown racists' apologist, defending the old apartheid ('Vierkleur') flag and tweeting in 2014 that 'blacks were the architects of apartheid'.

The response was concomitant. His concerts were cancelled in New Zealand and in South Africa, with pressure brought to bear on corporate sponsors for Afrikaans cultural festivals. But Hofmeyr only grew his taste for white supremacists' approval and remains the rightwing's most visible celebrity.

He was, however, able to capture more mainstream headlines when Congress of the People (COPE) leader Mosiuoa Lekota teamed up with him to lay charges against Black First Land First leader Andile Mngxitama for threats Mngxitama made against white people in December 2018. Hofmeyr represented his organisation, ToekomsVonk, under which he has formally styled himself as an activist for Afrikaner/Boer re-actualisation. Its events for 2019 range from National Milk Tart Day to memorialising apartheid holidays Van Riebeeck Day, Republic Day and

Kruger Day. Lekota and Hofmeyr were believed to have partnered in a call to United States president Donald Trump to intervene to stop land expropriation.

Holomisa, Bantu

Leader of the United Democratic Movement (UDM) | Member of Parliament | Former deputy minister of Environment and Tourism | Former ANC leader, expelled | Former Transkei general

Power broker

MAVERICK BY INSTINCT, THE FORMER MILITARY STRONGMAN will be well remembered for standing up against corruption and greed in the early days of ANC rule.

The only homeland 'ruler' to defy the apartheid regime's tradition of Uncle Toms, Holomisa was a brigadier in the Transkei Defence Force when he drove former Transkei prime minister George Matanzima to resign and into exile in 1987. Holomisa then helmed the overthrow of Matanzima's successor, Stella Sigcau. He was appointed head of the Transkei Defence Force and major-general that year. Holomisa gave harbour to South African Communist Party (SACP) and ANC leader Chris Hani, among others, before Transkei was reintegrated into South Africa.

By 1994, Holomisa was elected onto the ANC's National Executive Committee (NEC) and Nelson Mandela made him Deputy Minister of Environment and Tourism. But Holomisa was never one to keep quiet, and spoke out against mistakes of the 'reconciliation' while he was testifying before the Truth and Reconciliation Commission (TRC) in 1996.

He alleged that senior ANC leaders, including then deputy president, Thabo Mbeki, and now late sports minister, Steve Tshwete, accepted favours from hotel magnate Sol Kerzner in return for protecting Kerzner from prosecution. He also alleged the ANC had accepted financial assistance from Kerzner for its 1994 general election campaign. Holomisa further implicated now late public enterprises minister Sigcau in corruption. He said she had accepted a R50,000 cut from a R2-million bribe paid by Kerzner to Matanzima for exclusive gambling rights, and that she was not alone in 'accepting certain favours'.

Holomisa said Kerzner had also funded social events of leading ANC members, including Mbeki's 50th birthday party, and that various ANC leaders, including Tshwete, had accepted free accommodation when they attended British boxer Chris Eubank's world title defence at Sun City in 1994.

The ANC and Kerzner denied everything and Holomisa was fired as a deputy minister for 'political indiscretions'. He faced an ANC disciplinary inquiry after complaints by Sigcau and Tshwete, to which Holomisa's response was addressed to then ANC secretary-general Cyril Ramaphosa, urging that the NEC should choose 'whether we'll be perpetually influenced by people like Kerzner'. Ultimately expelled from the ANC in 1996, Holomisa was undeterred, but the events around his expulsion marked the moment at which many people finally saw the revolutionary colours start to fade on the ANC, post-1994.

Holomisa formed the United Democratic Movement (UDM) in 1997 with former ANC NEC member John Taylor and former National Party minister and Convention for a Democratic South Africa (Codesa) negotiator, Roelf Meyer. Holomisa represented the UDM as an MP after 1999 and aligned it with other political parties in many battles, particularly the fight against former president Jacob Zuma. He was present at the Economic Freedom Fighters' launch in 2013.

Holomisa is likely to garner a small number of votes for the UDM in 2019, especially among those voters who feel they have nowhere else to put their cross. This could allow the UDF to continue to engage in co-governing agreements, such as in Nelson Mandela Bay in the Eastern Cape where it had an executive mayor in Mongameli Bobani, or at the very least, remain a fearless voice in the National Assembly.

101 Stalwarts

Group of ANC veterans acting against the party's decline

This collective comprised former Robben Island prisoners, former leaders of the United Democratic Front (UDF), former Umkhonto we Sizwe (MK) combatants and former exiled ANC structure leaders. They began to gather in 2016 as the ANC started to unravel under the corrupt administration of then president Jacob Zuma.

Their intervention officially began with the release of a document titled, 'For the sake of our future', which laid bare the ANC's problems of disintegration. The group proposed a national consultative conference, which was eventually held in November 2017, but without the support of the current ANC leadership. The ANC had opted to discuss 'organisational renewal' at its key July 2017 policy conference, but the Stalwarts believed a more profound approach was necessary, and so boycotted that event.

Among the 101 were: former Cabinet ministers Trevor Manuel, Essop Pahad, Aziz Pahad, Siphiwe Nyanda, Sydney Mufamadi, Alec Erwin and Barbara Hogan; the first speaker of Parliament, Frene Ginwala; former United Democratic Front (UDF) leader Cheryl Carolus; Struggle heroes Ahmed Kathrada, Denis Goldberg, Andrew Mlangeni and Gertrude Shope; former ambassadors Barbara Masekela and Dumi Matabane, and activist cleric and former Tshwane mayor Father Smangaliso Mkhatshwa.

Zuma was reluctant to give the 101 Stalwarts air, and dubbed them 'divisive', but when Cyril Ramaphosa was elected president, he and deputy David Mabuza met with the group. Ramaphosa said he was 'saddened by the manner in which (they) were treated' by Zuma, and invited them to be active in party campaigns ahead of the 2019 elections.

I

Independent Communications Authority of South Africa (ICASA)

Chapter 9 institution

THE OFFICIAL REGULATOR OF COMMUNICATIONS, broadcasting and postal services, it issues and monitors broadcasting licences, plans and manages the radio frequency spectrum, and is required to protect consumers on the price of and access to communications networks.

ICASA's most controversial task, however, is to receive and act on complaints, and it's made headlines for some of its more unpopular decisions. In 2016, for instance, it took significant flak for not acting decisively enough when Hlaudi Motsoeneng, then the COO of the SABC, issued a directive to stop the public broadcaster from covering violent service delivery and anti-government protests.

ICASA's biggest challenge of 2017 and 2018 was that of mobile phone network data packages. Twitter responded vociferously to the issue through the #DataMustFall campaign. Ultimately, the authority got applause for ruling that data could be rolled over or transferred, and that networks could not simply use a consumer's airtime when their data package had been depleted.

ICASA was established in July 2000 when the South African Telecommunications Regulatory Authority (SATRA) and the Independent Broadcasting Authority (IBA) merged, and is a de facto Chapter 9 institution and a portfolio organisation of the Department of Communications.

Independent Police Investigative Directorate (IPID) (see McBride, Robert)

Government agency

FORMERLY KNOWN AS THE INDEPENDENT Complaints Directorate (ICD), the police watchdog is an agency of government designed to play a central role in the continuing post-apartheid reform of the South African Police Service (SAPS). Established in 1997, it investigates deaths in custody, crimes allegedly committed by police officers, violations of SAPS policy, and dissatisfaction with the service provided by the police.

It also became more politicised in recent years. Especially under Robert McBride, IPID found itself playing more of a key role in how the SAPS controls its own, especially high-ranking, members.

It was reported in March 2018 that Parliament wanted to alter the IPID Act to curb the powers of the police minister to suspend or remove the head of the police watchdog. In 2016, the Constitutional Court (ConCourt) had ruled that the police minister had no authority to dismiss the IPID head without Parliament instituting the necessary processes.

The ConCourt said in its ruling that IPID was an independent body established in terms of the Constitution, which had to function independently of the SAPS. It confirmed that IPID's oversight role was 'of cardinal importance'.

Industrial Development Corporation (IDC)

Fully owned by the government

ESTABLISHED IN 1940 BY AN ACT OF PARLIAMENT, the IDC was mandated to develop domestic industrial capacity, specifically in manufactured goods, to mitigate the disruption of trade between Europe and South Africa during the Second World War.

It established, among others, the petro-chemicals and minerals beneficiation industries and influenced the establishment of industries in fabricated metals, agriculture and clothing and textiles. During the 1990s, its mandate was expanded to include investment in the rest of Africa. Its investments in Africa include mining, agriculture, manufacturing, tourism and telecommunications.

The IDC's funding is generated through income from loan and equity investments and exits from mature investments, as well as borrowing from commercial banks, development finance institutions (DFIs) and other lenders. It aligns its priorities with government's policy direction, which meant it was centred on the National Development Plan (NDP), the New Growth Path (NGP) and the Industrial Policy Action Plan (IPAP).

Its funding activities focused mainly on the private sector, but it also worked closely with government agencies and sector organisations. Creating black industrialists was a strategic imperative for the continent's largest development finance with assets of nearly R130 billion.

After the inception of its Black Industrialists Development Programme in 2014/15, it approved 203 deals worth R11.4 billion to 185 companies. According to the IDC, this created and saved nearly 12,000 jobs.

The IDC CEO in 2019 was Tshokolo Nchocho, a former CEO of the Land Bank, and a development financier and banker with experience at the Development Bank. His appointment was approved by Cabinet in December 2018.

A priority for the IDC was to enable the Fourth Industrial Revolution to replace sunset sectors. It would have to move away from the mining sector and services, and from a highly financialised economy driven by the Johannesburg Stock Exchange (JSE) towards new technologies, clean energy, life sciences and food security.

Industrial Policy Action Plan (IPAP)

Government policy

THIS 'ROLLING ANNUAL ACTION PLAN' WAS ALIGNED to successive three-year cycles of government planning to spur industrial growth and reduce unemployment. It was originally launched in 2007 to focus on labour-intensive economic activity in the production sectors, led by manufacturing, and aimed for a more competitive South African economy with a higher global share.

But the Department of Trade and Industry (dti), which drives it, was by 2018 concentrating also on politics, with an emphasis on its Black Industrialists Scheme.

It was meanwhile setting out ways to try and meet the challenges and opportunities of the digital industrial revolution.

IPAP unlocked billions in private investments through companies like Toyota SA and the Beijing Automobile International Corporation, which were expected to create thousands of direct jobs.

Ingonyama Trust

A corporate entity established to administer the land traditionally owned by the Zulu people, represented by their traditional monarch, for the benefit of their nation

SET UP IN THE LAST DAYS OF THE apartheid regime, the Ingonyama Trust transferred all the land that was owned by or belonged to the bantustan KwaZulu government to be held for the 'benefit, material welfare and social well-being' of those living on the land. This amounts to 2.8-million hectares, or 30%, of what is today the province of KwaZulu-Natal.

The sole trustee of the land is King Goodwill Zwelithini, who also establishes and appoints its board.

The trust came into sharp relief following the 2017 release of former president Kgalema Motlanthe's Independent High Level Panel report, which called for the Ingonyama Trust to be fundamentally changed or abolished as it did not guarantee security of tenure to the people on the land. The king immediately hit back, even threatening secession.

Motlanthe responded by calling the administrators of the Trust 'rent seekers', receiving up to R96 million a year from businesses, but not accounting for the money. The issue spiralled further in the wake of the ANC's decision to expropriate land without compensation (EWC) at its December 2018 elective conference.

The Council for the Advancement of the South African Constitution ratcheted up the pressure with a court bid in 2018 to stop Zwelithini from forcing occupiers of Ingonyama land to pay rents of between R1 500 and R7 000 a month as part of a so-called 'conversion project' in which the Trust tried to move occupiers from the traditional right to occupy to 40-year leases.

As the EWC debate ballooned, President Cyril Ramaphosa personally went to Ulundi to reassure the king that neither the government nor the ANC had any intention of taking Ingonyama land as part of the expropriation process.

The EFF weighed in with its support for the king, while Contralesa – representing traditional leaders – opined that since the land was held 'by Africans for Africans', the EFF should concentrate on the EWC of white-owned land only.

The Ingonyama Trust stands in sharp relief to the Royal Bafokeng Nation of more than 100,000 Setswana-speaking South Africans, which owns 1000 sq km in North West – all purchased in the 19th century by Kgosi August Mokgatle (1834–1891), using donations from the community to buy land stolen from them by Boer farmers. Held in trust for the Bafokeng people, this proved to be an absolute bonanza when the Merensky Reef, the world's largest deposit of platinum, was discovered in 1924, enabling the community to secure royalties from mining companies.

Inkatha Freedom Party (IFP)

Centrist, Nationalist | Focus on isiZulu-speaking South Africans | Number of seats in Parliament in 2018: 25

Captured by the apartheid regime

THE INKATHA ('COIL OF GRASS') NATIONAL CULTURAL Liberation Movement (INCLM), invigorated by Zulu royal family member Prince Mangosuthu Buthelezi, became a political party in 1975. The INCLM was rooted in a cultural organisation established by Zulu King Solomon kaDinuzulu in the 1920s, and was part of the cultural and political imagination in large parts of KwaZulu-Natal when the IFP was founded.

As Buthelezi had once been a member of the ANC and its Youth League, the IFP and the ANC were, briefly, politically close, but by the time the United Democratic Front (UDF) was formed in the early 1980s, those links were severed.

So estranged were the IFP and the ANC that their split led to significant bloodshed in the Transvaal and Natal during the 1980s and early 1990s, with Buthelezi increasingly regarded as a puppet of the apartheid regime. But it wasn't only political rivalry. Buthelezi decided to collaborate with the South African Defence Force (SADF) and Zulu militia were given military training as part of what was known as Operation Marion. Several massacres involving these militia shocked the country, and the world, in the decade before the 1994 elections. The Trust Feed massacre of 1988 saw 11 people killed and the Boipatong massacre of 1992 resulted in the deaths of at least 45 people.

The IFP was instrumental to tensions in the months, weeks and days before the 1994 elections, too. On 28 March that year, thousands of its supporters marched to the ANC's first Johannesburg headquarters, Shell House, in protest against the elections that it said it would boycott. The ANC's security opened fire and 19 people were killed in what was a bloody and tragic reminder of the power struggle between the two at the end of apartheid.

The IFP only agreed to participate eight days before the poll as it sought a federal system while the ANC preferred a centralised system of governance. To that effect, the IFP collaborated with the Afrikanervolksunie (a forerunner of the Freedom Front Plus), the Conservative Party (the Official Opposition during the last years of apartheid) and bantustan leaders Lucas Magope (Bophuthatswana) and Oupa Gqoza (Ciskei) in a cohort known as the Concerned South Africans Group (Cosag) and, later, the Freedom Alliance. All wanted to retain a homeland-type system.

Once the IFP agreed to be part of the 1994 elections, its logo had to be printed on stickers, which were glued onto the end of every ballot by hand. It won a million votes, with Buthelezi serving for a time as a co-leader in the Government of National Unity, but the IFP limped through the third and fourth elections.

Those were the years when South Africa saw coalition politics begin to take hold, with the IFP, the Democratic Alliance (DA), the United Democratic Movement (UDM) and the Congress of the People (COPE) ultimately working in different partnerships at local government level.

A schism came in 2011 when the IFP's then chairperson, Zanele Magwaza-Msibi, broke away to form the National Freedom Party (NFP) when Buthelezi refused to give up his leadership of the party. But in 2014, the IFP showed some resurgence, although it would never reach the heights of 1994, with only half its seats in the National Assembly.

Inspector-General of Intelligence (IGI)

Key state appointee

Appointed by the President after a process of nomination by Parliament's Joint Standing Committee on Intelligence (JSCI). The nominated IGI must be approved by at least two-thirds of the members of the National Assembly. The IGI in 2019 was Dr Setlhomamaru Dintwe.

The office of the IGI is ratified to conduct independent civilian monitoring of the intelligence services, which include the National Intelligence Agency (NIA), the South African Secret Service (SASS), the intelligence division of the South African Police Service (SAPS) and the intelligence division of the South African National Defence Force (SANDF). The IGI has great oversight power and only reports to the JSCI. No access to intelligence or information may be withheld from the IGI in terms of the Intelligence Services Oversight Act of 1994, and they can only be removed or suspended by the President.

The IGI was particularly challenged in early 2015 when international news service Al Jazeera started publishing extracts from a massive cache of leaked documents of the South African State Security Agency (SSA). This was not long before the previous IGI, Faith Radebe, left office at the end of March. It took two years to replace her.

Originally, the focus for the ANC was heavily on seeing its candidate, MP Cecil Burgess, given the job. But a central difficulty was that, while it ordinarily needed only its 249 seats in the National Assembly to push through what it wanted, the ANC had to respect the constitutional requirement that an IGI can only be appointed with an absolute two-thirds majority, at 267 votes, which was more than it could muster.

A major criticism of the IGI is that it is largely free of public oversight. The office of the IGI does not make its documents transparent. All it does is send these to the JSCI, whose meetings are closed.

The Institute for Security Studies (ISS)

Research and publication | Non-aligned

A pan-African non-profit with offices in South Africa, Kenya, Ethiopia and Senegal, its work covered transnational crimes, migration, maritime security and development, peace-keeping, peace-building, crime prevention and criminal justice, and the analysis of conflict and governance.

The ISS was founded in 1990 as the Institute for Defence Policy by its former executive director, Dr Jakkie Cilliers. It was renamed in 1996, its motivation lying in an historic meeting between the Institute for Democracy in Africa (IDASA) and members of Umkhonto we Sizwe (MK), the armed wing of the ANC, in Lusaka in May 1990. Primarily an opportunity for security specialists and analysts from both sides to exchange views, it idealistically sought to collectively envisage a future military spectrum. Leading the dialogue was Cilliers – a former lieutenant-colonel in the old South African Defence Force (SADF) – and MK commander Chris Hani, who was assassinated in 1993.

After 1996, the ISS took on a regional and then more continental dimension, which was the radius of its work going forward.

J

Jacobs, Faiez

ANC Western Cape Secretary

JACOBS HAD A PARTICULARLY IMPORTANT ROLE to play for his party in the 2019 elections in the Western Cape, as its influence had been declining in the province run by the Democratic Alliance (DA). He felt there were concerns around race which had helped to dog the party's progress, and those issues reflected one of the most difficult topics in South Africa: the position of coloured people, who are 'a national minority, but a provincial majority'.

Jacobs drew to national attention the seeming diminishing of the role of coloureds, Indians and whites elected to the ANC's National Executive Committee (NEC), calling this 'an unintentional negative consequence of the "winner takes all" slate politics' of the party. He wrote in the *Daily Maverick* in January 2018 after the ANC's elective conference in Nasrec, Johannesburg, that, 'of the 86 elected members, there are only four coloureds elected to the NEC'.

Although Jacobs subscribed to the constitutional position that South Africans were either black (African, coloured or Indian) or white, and that the party's politics did not specifically discriminate on this issue, he noted, among other things, the alleged failure to recognise the Khoisan as traditional leaders, their culture as well as their First Nation status.

He also called to book the Draft Employment Equity (EE) regulations of 2014, which called for national demographics to apply to the top three echelons of management in all provinces. Although these were scrapped after the intervention of the ANC because of the prejudicial effect on the coloured and Indian populations in the Western Cape, Northern Cape and KwaZulu-Natal, there had been a re-emergence of the debate.

But by late 2018, Jacobs was at the centre of serious clashes between the ANC and its alliance partner, the SACP, with the latter feeling that Jacobs was undermining its role and manipulating the process of nominations for the 2019 elections. But he gained national prominence on 23 December 2018 after a private security company claiming to be enforcing Cape Town city by-laws, enforced an illegal curfew on 4th Beach in Clifton. Jacobs was on the beach having a family picnic when the security guards arrived. Jacobs, among others, refused to leave and by the next day, the unlawful crackdown on the formerly whites-only beach was on international headlines. Jacobs asked the Public Protector to investigate.

Jafta, Justice Chris

Constitutional Court (ConCourt) Justice | Former Judge President of the Transkei division | Former Supreme Court of Appeal judge

Jafta began his career in law as a court interpreter. By 1985 he was a magistrate, completing his LLB degree the following year. He resigned in February 1988 to begin his articles as an attorney, resigning again later that year to become a law lecturer at the University of the Transkei, where he would become friends with John Hlophe who was, in 2018, regarded a controversial jurist although he occupied the position of Western Cape Judge President.

Jafta practiced as an advocate in Mthatha, Eastern Cape, before being appointed as a judge in the Transkei division of the High Court in 1999, then acting as judge president between 2001 and 2003 before becoming acting judge of appeal at the labour appeal court on the invitation of Raymond Zondo, who would become Deputy Chief Justice in 2017.

Jafta was appointed to the Supreme Court of Appeal (SCA) in 2004, being elevated to the ConCourt in 2008. But that was a tough year. He and fellow ConCourt Justice Bess Nkabinde faced a serious challenge when they reported having been approached by Hlophe to rule in favour of an upcoming matter regarding then presidential campaigner Jacob Zuma's ongoing arms deal charges.

Eleven ConCourt justices signed a complaint to the Judicial Services Commission (JSC).

Over the next eight years, Nkabinde and Jafta would try to rescind their complaint. They felt the matter had been dealt with by their reporting it. But in 2016, the SCA ruled that the two judges would have to testify.

They appealed the decision to their own court, which upheld the SCA ruling. They then launched a second appeal, leaving many observers pondering their motivation since the ConCourt was not able to hear matters concerning its own judges – and even if it could, it would lack quorum, given the number of judges who would have to recuse themselves.

The net result was to emasculate the JSC from probing any other judges for misconduct. (Nkabinde retired from the ConCourt at the end of 2017, following the completion of her 12-year term.)

Jafta, Loyiso

Acting Director-General (D-G) of the State Security Agency (SSA) | Former head of the National Communications Centre of the Secret Service

Jafta was moved into the acting D-G post at the SSA – with which he had been associated previously – after controversial former DG Arthur Fraser was sent to the Department of Correctional Services by President Cyril Ramaphosa.

Jafta had long been in government structures, among other roles as an aide to Nosiviwe Mapisa-Nqakula, previously the Minister of Correctional Services.

He had been embroiled in the scandal that surrounded the recall of Thabo Mbeki and the ascendance of Jacob Zuma from 2006 to 2009, and left the National Intelligence Agency (NIA) after the departure of the former NIA DG Manala Manzini. Jafta had played an important role there as head of the National Communications Centre, which intercepted calls from outside the country.

Jafta was of the generation of spooks who fell within former Intellligence Minister Ronnie Kasrils's remit when he instituted a Ministerial Review Commission, headed by ANC veteran Joe Matthews, to assess the state of the intelligence services. The Matthews Commission's report was given to President Mbeki in 2008, but has never been completely made public.

Jana, (Devikarani) Priscilla

Deputy Commissioner of the South African Human Rights Commission (SAHRC) | Former ambassador to the Netherlands | Former ambassador to Ireland | Black Consciousness (BC) in political origin

Star

AFTER STUDYING MEDICINE IN INDIA, and then law, Jana opened her own law practice in 1979 with a focus on civil liberties and human rights. That led her to play a significant role in protest politics with her background in the Black Consciousness (BC) South African Students' Organisation (SASO), the Black People's Convention (BPC) and the Anti-Constitutional Committee and Federation of Transvaal Women (FEDTRAW).

Appointed Deputy Commissioner of the SAHRC in early 2017, Jana was distinguished for representing the ANC's Umkhonto we Sizwe (MK) soldier, Solomon Mahlangu, in 1978, and playing a pivotal role in international awareness and protest against his death sentence and then his execution by the apartheid state.

Jana was also notable for taking the South African Medical and Dental Council (SAMDC) on review in 1984 for its treatment of BC leader Steve Biko, who died as a result of police torture in 1977. The council was ordered to hold an investigation into the conduct of the doctors who were eventually found guilty of disgraceful conduct.

Jana represented many prominent activists in court, including Nelson Mandela, Walter Sisulu, Govan Mbeki, Ahmed Kathrada, Winnie Madikizela-Mandela and Archbishop Emeritus Desmond Tutu. She was also a member of the South African Law Commission, and sat on the Advisory Committee to the President during Nelson Mandela's time in office.

Ambassador in the Netherlands from 2001 to 2005 and then Ambassador in Ireland from 2006 to 2011, Jana was an ANC MP from 1994 to 1999, serving on numerous portfolio committees.

Jiba, Nomgcobo

Former Deputy Director of Public Prosecutions in the National Prosecuting Authority (NPA) | Qualified as an advocate

Linked to corruption and capture

JIBA ONCE HAD THE POWER TO MANAGE the performance of directors of public prosecutions and the lower courts around the country, meaning she oversaw all prosecutorial decisions made by the state. But in 2016, Jiba and another deputy director of public prosecutions, Lawrence Mrwebi, were struck off the roll of the General Council of the Bar of South Africa by the North Gauteng High Court for their disputed involvement in a number of matters with a high political content.

Dominant among these was a decision to drop corruption charges against former head of the South African Police Service's (SAPS) Crime Intelligence Division, Richard Mdluli, and a failed attempt to convict former Hawks official Major General Johan Booysen, who claimed Jiba had attempted to 'set him up' so as to prevent him from investigating corruption cases linked to Jacob Zuma.

Jiba was granted leave to appeal the decision in January 2017, whereupon Zuma decided not to suspend her or to institute a commission of inquiry into her conduct. Later that year, AfriForum announced it would institute legal action to privately prosecute Jiba on charges of fraud and perjury.

Jiba was previously suspended from the NPA while facing charges of dishonesty and bringing the organisation into disrepute after it was alleged she had abused her powers when trying to undermine corruption investigations into disgraced former National Police Commissioner Jackie Selebi, who was later convicted and jailed, before being given medical parole.

Mdluli was a character witness for Jiba in her subsequent legal challenges which led to disciplinary charges against her being dropped before the then head of the NPA, Advocate Menzi Simelane, appointed her as Deputy National Director. Zuma then appointed her acting head of the NPA when the Supreme Court of Appeal (SCA) found Simelane was not a 'fit and proper' person to run the organisation.

The North Gauteng High Court's decision on Jiba as an advocate was overturned by the Supreme Court of Appeal (SCA) in 2018, with the Constitutional Court to rule upon whether she should be struck from the roll after the General Council of the Bar (GCB) took the SCA's ruling on appeal. The application was laid down to be heard in March 2019.

In January 2019, Jiba took pole position in the high stakes race as to who could be cited for corruption out of the state capture project, when the Mokgoro Commission started in Pretoria. The Commission, chaired by retired Constitutional Court (ConCourt) Justice Yvonne Mokgoro, was established to look into Jiba and Mrwebi's fitness to hold office. Senior prosecutor Jan Ferreira said Jiba had committed perjury when she stated under oath that she had considered all available evidence when agreeing to press charges against Booysen.

Jim, Irvin

National Union of Metalworkers of South Africa (Numsa) general-secretary | Leftwing, politically non-aligned

Power broker

JIM DREW A LINE IN THE SAND BETWEEN the workers he led and Cyril Ramaphosa in 2018 when he described Ramaphosa as the 'Donald Trump of South Africa'. *City Press* newspaper reported that Jim had accused Ramaphosa of 'selling out black people to white monopoly capital' at a Workers' Day rally in Bloemfontein where he was addressing a South African Federation of Trade Unions (Saftu) rally.

With Jim and other union leaders at the fore, Saftu had held a march the previous week, protesting government's endorsement of a minimum wage of R20 per hour. To many workers, it had failed the working class with this number, considering the rate of renumeration of CEOs, and harrowing increases in the price of fuel, food and VAT. But for Jim, acrimony with government and particularly the ruling ANC, was not a new position. He was one of the most vocal protagonists of an exit from the Congress of South African Trade Unions (Cosatu) during the corrupt administration of Jacob Zuma.

In December 2018, Jim brushed aside rumours that Numsa would rejoin Cosatu after such overtures had been made by the National Union of Mineworkers (NUM), with whom Numsa had gone on strike during the year. It was said in some reports that 'a principled unity' with Cosatu had been discussed at a Saftu national executive committee meeting. But Jim said this was not the case, and described such efforts as 'electioneering' ahead of the 2019 polls.

As the leader of the biggest single trade union in South Africa, he situated Numsa outside the neo-liberal economic goals of the ANC, and described it as 'Marxist-Leninist' with the intention to create a 'socialist republic' in which the Reserve Bank, mines, land and monopoly industries would be nationalised without compensation.

Jim grew up the son of a farm worker in the Eastern Cape and told of how witnessing his father's exploitation and the family's enforced and unhappy nomadic life politicised him. Jim became a trade unionist when he had to abandon higher education and take a job at a tyre company in Port Elizabeth.

In early 2019, it was believed he could face a difficult choice if the Socialist Workers Revolutionary Party, which was established as the political party of the National Union of Metalworkers of South Africa (Numsa) at the end of 2018, were to contest the national and provincial elections. Jim was expected to lead the party to the polls, which would potentially create a void of charismatic leadership at Numsa.

Joemat-Pettersson, Tina

Former minister of Energy | Former minister of Agriculture, Forestry and Fisheries | Member of the ANC's National Working Committee (NWC)

Linked to corruption

A STUDENT ACTIVIST-TURNED-POLITICIAN, Joemat-Pettersson is among only a few ANC cadres from the Northern Cape to be recognised for a post in national government. And she went further than that, being given two Cabinet positions until she was fired and then resigned in 2017. Although she has been returned to the fold, with a place on the party's prestigious National Working Committee (NWC), the cloud over her time in office remains.

A young Joemat-Pettersson campaigned for the ANC in what was then a 'new' province in 1994 and was appointed as MEC for Education, Arts and Culture, a job she held in its legislature for a decade before serving as the MEC for Agriculture. She was popular and, on the face if it, performed well enough in the provincial legislature to be selected by Zuma for a much more senior role in 2009: the Minister of Agriculture, Forestry and Fisheries. But her time in fisheries was tainted by allegations that there were spurious quota allocations from government's side, and questions were raised about her role in an illegal fisheries patrol contract being given to businessman Dr Iqbal Survé.

Yet those who have examined Zuma's plans for state capture suggest there was more than just reward for a job well done. It's believed that in 2007, when Zuma was actively campaigning to win the ANC presidency and needed all the branch support he could get, Joemat-Pettersson was influential in getting the Northern Cape to back him. That, too, could have come with a reward.

Joemat-Pettersson was elevated again in 2014 when made the Minister of Energy by Zuma. Among other disputable acts, she signed off on what EyeWitness News (EWN) called 'a dubious deal at bargain-basement prices': the sale of South Africa's strategic oil stocks.

Former Public Protector Thuli Madonsela meanwhile found in her report, 'Costly Moves', that Joemat-Pettersson's 'blank-cheque attitude towards public funds' was problematic. Madonsela also questioned Joemat-Pettersson for her involvement in a controversial R800 million marine resources tender.

Joemat-Pettersson was finally relieved of her post in April 2017, and then she resigned as an ANC MP, along with two other ANC veterans, Dipuo Peters – the second premier of the Northern Cape – and Mcebisi Jonas, who were fired by Zuma. Yet she received a 'once-off gratuity' of R2.1 million in November 2017.

Jonas, Mcebisi

Economic Envoy | Former deputy finance minister | Former chairperson and non-executive director of the Public Investment Corporation (PIC) | Former Member of the Executive Council (MEC) for Economic Development and Environmental Affairs in the Eastern Cape province

Star

JONAS WAS A TEENAGE LIBERATION ACTIVIST steeped in Black Consciousness (BC) that distinguished the Port Elizabeth area. Later, his public political persona was as an organiser for the restricted Azanian Students Organisation (Azaso), but he was also leading underground structures in the Eastern Cape. Jonas would, however, switch from BC politics to ANC politics when he became involved in founding United Democratic Front (UDF) structures in that province.

He received military training in Angola and Uganda with the ANC's Umkhonto we Sizwe (MK), but was also noticed as having broader organisational and educational skills, and was employed by the United Nations to run an education programme for MK cadres.

Jonas returned from exile in the early 1990s and continued to develop structures for the ANC, and also for the South African Communist Party (SACP), in the Eastern Cape, where the ANC then made him a provincial administrator before he was elected onto its provincial executive committee.

Although Jonas was performing well in his position as Deputy Finance Minister under Minister Pravin Gordhan in the Zuma administration, it was when he alleged in 2015 that the notorious Gupta family had offered him R600 million to replace Gordhan, and then follow their agenda, that Jonas really entered public view. He refused what he claimed were the Guptas' 'offers' and 'demands' and, in 2017, Zuma axed him and Gordhan in a middle-of-the-night reshuffle of his Cabinet.

A vocal and outspoken antagonist of state capture, Jonas would then resign from government. Although he joined MTN as an independent, non-executive director, and was appointed as an economic envoy by President Cyril Ramaphosa in early 2018, it was only when he made his appearance before the Zondo Commission of Inquiry into state capture in September 2018 that he was back in the spotlight. Jonas's testimony was explosive. He explained how Ajay Gupta – regarded as the kingpin of the disgraced family – tried to 'buy' him in order to also facilitate the axeing of National Treasury Director General Lungisa Fuzile, head of Tax and Financial Sector Policy Ismail Momoniat, Treasury expert Andrew Donaldson and then chief procurement officer Kenneth Brown.

Jonas had immediately reported the meeting at the Guptas' infamous Saxonwold home where Zuma's son Duduzane was also present, to the ANC. Jonas said Ajay Gupta had claimed 'Lynne Brown (then Minister of Public Enterprises) and Brian Molefe (then CEO of Eskom)' were already captured and that the Guptas were 'in control of everything ... the NPA, the NIA, the Hawks' and 'the old man', which is a common reference to Zuma.

Jonas alleged he was also later approached by Major General Zinhle Mnonopi, head of the anti-corruption unit of the Hawks, who, he said, produced a draft statement for him to sign that would essentially make his R600-million bribe case – which had by then been reported to the Hawks by the DA – disappear.

Ajay Gupta denied Jonas's testimony but refused to return to South Africa to testify himself or cross-examine Jonas at the inquiry in Johannesburg.

Judicial Service Commission (JSC)

Government body

ESTABLISHED IN TERMS OF THE CONSTITUTION, the Commission consists of 23 members who advise government on matters relating to the judiciary or the administration of justice.

The Commission also interviews candidates for judicial posts and makes recommendations for appointment to the bench, as well as dealing with complaints brought against judges. Only the president can make appointments to it and can withdraw members from its panel. Complaints against judges are first reported to the JSC Secretariat which, like the JSC itself, meets bi-annually. The JSC meets for a week in April and October, generally in Cape Town.

Its members include the Chief Justice, the President of the Supreme Court of Appeal and the Minister of Justice, and its work can also call upon a Judge President, provincial premiers and various academicians and representatives of the legal profession. There was a clear plan after apartheid to ensure a democratic JSC, which resulted in each commissioner holding voting power equal to the respective votes of members of the National Assembly, and the same representation of opposition parties.

Thus, six politicians are appointed to the JSC by the NA, four by the National Council of Provinces and four designated by the President as the executive head. All parties represented in the NA are consulted.

The JSC holds considerable power as it chooses High Court and Supreme Court of Appeals judges and the president has no veto on those. In the case of the Constitutional Court (ConCourt), however, the JSC presents the president with four candidates from whom he or she must choose one.

kaMagwaza-Msibi, Zanele

National Freedom Party (NFP) leader | Former leader within the Inkatha Freedom Party (IFP)

THE ONLY WOMAN TO HEAD A PARTY among the 13 parties represented in Parliament, kaMagwaza-Msibi battled long bouts of ill health. Nonetheless, her NFP was able to strike at the heart of her former political boss, Mangosuthu Buthelezi's Inkatha Freedom Party (IFP) heartland, KwaZulu-Natal's rural areas, in 2014.

It is uncertain as to how the NFP will perform in 2019, although the IFP had been working on a resurgence strategy in order to combat some attempts by the Economic Freedom Fighters (EFF) to make inroads in KwaZulu-Natal.

Kasrils, Ronnie

Former minister for Intelligence Services | Former minister of Water Affairs and Forestry | Former deputy minister of Defence | SaveSouthAfrica and #UniteBehind campaigner

Change agent

MANY ANC VETERANS STEPPED FORWARD to berate their party for failing them and the nation. But few made the decision to openly declare their antipathy towards former president Jacob Zuma – targeted as a protagonist of state capture – as early as Kasrils. His knowledge of Zuma went back enough decades, to when they worked together underground in intelligence and as Umkhonto we Sizwe commanders for the ANC during apartheid, for Kasrils to be able to offer significant insights into Zuma's possible roles at the genesis of corruption.

Kasrils was in both Nelson Mandela's and Thabo Mbeki's cabinets, most prominently during Mbeki's time as Minister for Intelligence from 2004 to 2008. Prior to that, he was the the Deputy Minister for Defence, and Water Affairs and Forestry. He was also a member of the ANC's National Executive Committee (NEC) from 1987 to 2007 as well as a member of the Central Committee of the SACP from 1986 to 2007.

A crisis in intelligence circles would lead Kasrils to establish the Matthews Commission of Inquiry – chaired by ANC veteran Joe Matthews – to look at why spies were leaving the service, and the source of destabilisation in it. The report was finally partially revealed, but Kasrils left government just days after that when he resigned upon Mbeki's recall in 2008. The report has never been made completely public.

In April 2014, as government was preparing for the national and provincial elections which would see Zuma enter a second term as president, Kasrils launched the 'Vote No' campaign with other ANC members who feared the onset of state capture under Zuma. The aim was to encourage voters to either protest or spoil their ballots. That December, Kasrils continued with his bid to represent the views of ANC leaders whose pleas against corruption had been ignored. He was elected to the national working committee of the newly created United Front, which was dominated by trade unionists who had left the Congress of Trade Unions (Cosatu), the ANC's partner in its tripartite alliance.

Kasrils became a renowned author, whose autobiography, *Armed and Dangerous*, was first published in 1993 and updated and re-published in 1998 and 2004. The *Unlikely Secret Agent*, his personal account of his late wife Eleanor's contribution to the struggle, won the 2011 Sunday Times Alan Paton Award. His 2017 book, *A Simple Man*, detailed his experience of working with Zuma and offered profound insights into the rape of Fezekile Ntsukela Kuzwayo, alias Khwezi, who charged Zuma.

Kasrils explained in the book how state capture could have happened, and how the signs had been there for it since the time the ANC's headquarters were in Lusaka, Zambia.

Kekana, Pinky

Deputy Minister of Communications

Linked to corruption

THE ANC MP JOINED THE DEPARTMENT of Communications as its new deputy minister in February 2018 when President Cyril Ramaphosa appointed her during his first Cabinet reshuffle, replacing Tandi Mahambehlala.

When Kekana was chosen, she was a member of the ad hoc committee on the filling of vacancies in the Commission for Gender Equality, a position she had held since November 2016. But if she was something of a stranger to the wider South Africa, she was not such to the people of Limpopo, or to Economic Freedom Fighters (EFF) leader Julius Malema, or to the former Public Protector, Thuli Madonsela. In fact, Kekana had quite a history stretching behind her by the time she stepped up to be sworn in at a special ceremony in Tuynhuys, next to Parliament in Cape Town in 2018.

Limpopo knew the passionate former teacher well in one of her previous capacities, as its roads and transport MEC. But more than that, the province knew her for allegations that she had milked that position for political gain – and this is where Malema, and Madonsela, come in.

Those allegations were contained in Madonsela's provisional 2012 report into abuse of state power in which she described how Kekana had ordered an off-duty traffic officer to arrest Malema's then-rival, former provincial ANC Youth League (ANCYL) deputy secretary Thandi Moraka, at the League's chaotic Limpopo elective conference in Makhado. Kekana's side claimed Moraka had stolen conference documents. Moraka, meanwhile, waited for criminal charges to be laid against her. But she later became so agitated that, after her 'case' was 'dismissed', following several court appearances, she decided to lodge a complaint with Madonsela.

Kganyago, Lesetja

Governor of the South African Reserve Bank (SARB)

AN ECONOMIST AND CENTRAL BANKER, Kganyago was appointed as governor of the SARB in 2014 when the mandated term of his predecessor, Gill Marcus, came to an end. Marcus, an ANC veteran, was appointed in 2009.

Kganyago, who started his professional working life as a bank clerk, earned a Master's degree in development economics from the University of London, and further qualifications from the Wits Business School and Harvard University.

He served as the director of the National Treasury from 1996 to 1998, and then until 2004 as Chief Director: Liability of the National Treasury. From 2005 to 2011, he was the director-general of Treasury, before becoming the deputy governor of the SARB. Kganyago was also the chair of the International Monetary and Financial Committee (IMFC), the policy advisory committee of the board of governors of the International Monetary Fund (IMF), until 2020.

Attempts to suggest Kganyago had a bloated share portfolio came to nought when it was revealed that it was small and managed by a third party in line with SARB policy.

Kganyago was declared the world's best central banker by the authoritative publication *Central Banking*, which awarded him the title of Central Banking Governor of the Year in 2018.

But back home, there was trouble brewing as the Jacob Zuma faction within the ANC demanded the SARB be made to follow a resolution to nationalise it, which came out of the party's 2017 elective conference at Nasrec. Such resolutions can win positions for candidates at those key conferences. A further resolution was that the structure of private shareholders at the bank should be dismantled. Kganyago explained that shareholders had no say over monetary police and that buying them out would cost the fiscus.

Kingon, Mark

Acting South African Revenue Service (SARS) Commissioner | Former SARS Group Executive for Relationship Management within Business and Individual Taxes

MORE THAN THREE DECADES OF WORKING at SARS might not have been long enough to prepare Kingon for the supreme task of sorting out the Service from its political mire. But he took it on when then finance minister Nhlanhla Nene re-appointed him as acting SARS commissioner in June 2018 when Tom Moyane was suspended, accused of egregious leadership errors and corruption.

Moyane was fired on 1 November 2018, having fought a disciplinary process and the Nugent Commission of Inquiry, which sought to understand how SARS had dug a R100-billion hole in revenue collection over four years – the time in which Moyane was at the helm.

Kingon was then requested to continue in the acting commissioner role until Ramaphosa made a permanent appointment.

King Goodwill Zwelithini (Zwelithini Goodwill ka Bhekuzulu)

Traditional leader

THE 71-YEAR-OLD MONARCH HAS RULED his estimated 10-million subjects since his coronation on 3 December 1971. He is the longest reigning of the eight Zulu kings since Shaka formed the nation in 1816.

He did not assume power immediately after the death of his father, King Cyprian Bhekuzulu kaSolomon, in 1968, but went into exile on St Helena Island to avoid assassination. He was crowned on his return three years later at an event attended by 20 000 of his subjects.

An often controversial figure, Zwelithini is as well-known for his pleas for more money as he has been for his chauvinistic defence of Zulu culture – often in the face of the values enshrined in the same Constitution that allows for his existence. Dominant among these have been homophobic and xenophobic comments he made in 2012 and 2015 respectively.

The cost of running his household of eight palaces, six wives and their children was R66 million in 2018, on top of his own R1-million personal salary.

More recently, the king attracted headlines for a row around the Ingonyama Trust which provides him a further income of more than R98 million as he is the sole trustee of what is effectively almost a third of KwaZulu-Natal's land.

Zwelithini has been assiduously wooed by politicians because of the influence he wields; from the president to populists in opposition, but he seemed to eschew all of that to enter into a partnership with lobby group AfriForum in October 2018 to fight expropriation of land without compensation. Zwelithini urged his subjects not to vote for parties who propagated it.

Kodwa, Zizi

Former ANC spokesperson | ANC's head of monitoring and evaluating in the office of the president at Luthuli House | Member of the ANC's National Working Committee (NWC)

On the way up

KODWA SPENT MUCH OF HIS ENERGY for eight years in defending the ANC under Jacob Zuma, but by late 2017, he was firmly behind incoming president Cyril Ramaphosa, saying the ANC needed 'a leadership that restores confidence, people must have hope'. This was a couple of months after he'd penned an 'open letter' to the late ANC president Oliver Tambo, on the anniversary of Tambo's birthday, to express his dismay at how the ANC had failed the 'once glorious movement'.

'I'm saddened to report to you,' Kodwa wrote, 'that your glorious movement is more divided than ever before with some among us elevating personality cults above unity and cohesion of the ANC.'

His view of the 'revolutionary alliance' was that it could effectively collapse.

If there was a strategy to ingratiate himself with the architects of the inevitable – the departure of Zuma – it worked. By February 2018, Kodwa was among

Ramaphosa's selections to move permanently into the ANC's Johannesburg headquarters, Luthuli House, where an intense shakeup was intended to try and save the party from its own demise.

Not only that. Ramaphosa placed Kodwa in his own office and put him in charge of monitoring and evaluating the implementation of the party's resolutions, the performance of its deployees and to assess progress in service delivery.

KPMG

Disgraced auditing firm

Investigated for corruption

IT WAS SEEMINGLY THE MONEY FROM AN ARRAY of state contracts that had helped pay for the infamous 'Gupta wedding' in 2013, which involved a flight landing at Waterkloof base and massive celebrations at Sun City. But it was the fawning email – later leaked – from Moses Kgosana, a top executive at KPMG, that began the decline of the South African chapter of the top auditing company. Kgosana described the wedding as 'an event of the millennium'.

Regulators pressed the South African Police Service (SAPS) to investigate the Netherlands-based KPMG for its work for the South African Revenue Service (SARS) in 2015. KPMG acknowledged that elements of its work there 'should no longer be relied upon' and offered to pay back its consulting fees.

The executive's email was among other thousands of exchanges which were leaked to South African news organisations and the amaBhungane Centre for Investigative Journalism in 2015. These brought about national outrage at the Gupta family and at then president Jacob Zuma.

KPMG's links to the Guptas were drawn around an apparent order to a junior employee from a senior manager to allow the immigrant family to 'write off' some of the expenses of that family wedding as 'business costs'. KPMG has since acknowledged that its actions 'fell well short of the quality expected'. Investigations into it continued in 2018, while it announced that it would be retrenching up to 400 employees.

But there was more. By October 2018, calls had grown overwhelmingly loud for South Africa to seek damages from KPMG for the role it played in 'the great bank heist' of Venda Building Society' (VBS), in which, reported the South African Reserve Bank (SARB), at least R1.9 billion was stolen.

Two partners at KPMG – which had audited the bank's financial results – failed to disclose financial interests in VBS. Sipho Malaba, who was found to have committed fraud, and Dumi Tshuma later resigned. The company had already lost more than a dozen clients by the time the SARB report was made public by Advocate Terry Motau, who led the probe. Motau recommended an auditor's liability claim be instituted by the Prudential Authority, the curator and National Treasury against KPMG for recovery of their respective damages.

In December 2018, KPMG confirmed it would distribute R47 million in fees it earned from auditing the Gupta companies' books to 52 non-profit education organisations. There was no guarantee, however, that KPMG's charitable efforts would regain it some of the top clients it lost. Among these were Nedbank, Absa bank and the office of the Auditor General of South Africa.

Kriel, Kallie

AfriForum CEO | Rightwing

Formerly a driving force within the mostly white trade union Solidarity, and a teacher by profession, the CEO of lobby group AfriForum was never believed to be much of a liberal, let alone a progressive force. But it was when he earned the disgust of Radio 702 and Cape Talk listeners, and thereafter thousands on social media, after he told radio host Eusebius McKaiser he didn't think apartheid was a crime against humanity, that Kriel revealed himself.

The AfriForum CEO, however, claimed the 'definition' of a crime against humanity 'is when there are mass murders like in the case of Nazi Germany'. He then used incorrect statistics from the apartheid years that 'only about 700 people' were murdered by the apartheid security forces. According to the submissions made by the SA Human Rights Commission at the Truth and Reconciliation Commission in 1996, at least 21,000 black people were killed. Kriel said the racial policy that saw the killing, torture and dispossession of black people 'was not as bad as some other systems in the world'.

Kriel, nonetheless, insists that white rightwing tendencies do not influence AfriForum, which, instead, represents a 'new Afrikaner' who is 'dynamic and forward-thinking'.

He was accused of playing race politics, though, when he and AfriForum pursued a charge against EFF leader Julius Malema, who had been accused of money laundering, racketeering and corruption in a public protector's report. AfriForum said the report had not had its remedies attended to by government, but it was notable that the intention to charge Malema came in the wake of government's announcement around land seizure without compensation – a goal towards which the EFF had been working in its original 2013/2014 campaigns for public office as well as in its 2019 elections campaigns.

Kubayi-Ngubane, Mmamoloko

Minister of Science and Technology | Former minister of Communications | Former minister of Energy | ANC-aligned

On the way up

The former minister of Communications had shadows to walk in after her predecessors, Dina Pule and Faith Muthambi, were portrayed as possibly corrupt via the #GuptaLeaks. This meant Kubayi-Ngubane had political obstacles to dodge from the moment she was appointed in April 2017.

With anyone linked to or associated with Zuma deemed likely corrupt, she had her work cut out to prove herself. And that was not only within her own party, but also from the Economic Freedom Fighters (EFF), where she had attracted a formidable 'enemy' in her former ANC Youth League comrade, EFF leader Julius

Malema. They were in conflict when they worked together in the ANCYL and it was against this backdrop that they had to again work together in Parliament, as Malema chaired the Telecommunications and Postal Services Portfolio Committee.

Kubayi-Ngubane entered Parliament as the youngest minister in the Cabinet, presiding over a department which had been affected by the ANC's resolution at its policy conference in July 2017 to re-merge communications, telecommunications and postal services. Kubayi-Ngubane was not destined to remain in the post, however, considered talented enough to gain wider experience.

President Cyril Ramaphosa appointed her Minister of Science and Technology in February 2018 when he reshuffled his Cabinet after Zuma resigned.

KwaZulu-Natal

Province | Led by the ANC

Deeply divided

FACTIONAL DIVISIONS WITHIN THE KWAZULU-NATAL ANC all but tore the party apart there, with much infighting as to the legality of its elective conference there in 2017 and 2018. Behind it all lay the complication of Jacob Zuma, who had once been all-powerful in KZN, but as he fell deeper into the mire of corruption, the KZN ANC also started to come undone, to the point where violence between its own supporters was a regular occurrence.

This placed the party's National Executive Committee (NEC) in the invidious position of having to intervene while Zuma was still in power and see through the suspension of the provincial leadership. But a 'Hands off Zuma' campaign in early 2018 did not assist the process of peacemaking, as supporters of President Cyril Ramaphosa, who included Police Minister Bheki Cele – a leader in the KZN ANC – were targeted for insults. Factions had been brewing since 2015.

The split had seen two leaders emerge: Senzo Mchunu, an SACP and former ANC provincial chairman, a former KZN premier, and a man described as Ramaphosa's 'proxy' in the province, and Sihle Zikalala, the provincial ANC leader before the NEC suspended the leadership. That was after the Pietermaritzburg High Court found that the November 2015 KZN elective conference, won by Zikalala against Mchunu, was null and void. Zikalala then found his way to Ramaphosa.

The Premier of KZN in 2018, Willies Mchunu, was regarded as a Zuma ally, to the extent that he even participated in activities of the Twelve Apostles Church in Christ, whose leader Bishop Caesar Nongqunga was a confidante of the former president. But Mchunu hasn't endeared himself to the broadest population of KZN, and was also castigated for making 'anti-Indian' comments.

Mchunu was, however, a long-time ANC member and former chairperson of the South African Communist Party (SACP) in KZN, which may account for his ability to accede to the premiership, but there was no guarantee that he would retain it after the 2019 elections.

L

Lamola, Ronald

ANC politician | Former deputy president of the ANC Youth League (ANCYL) | Former general-secretary of the Young Communist League (YCL) of the South African Communist Party (SACP) | Former Speaker in Mpumalanga | Member of the ANC's National Working Committee (NWC)

On the way up | Star

THE YOUNGEST ANC NATIONAL EXECUTIVE COMMITTEE (NEC) member in its history, and also a member of the party's National Working Committee (NWC), Lamola earned his second Master's degree in law in 2018, and said he hoped it would inspire the #FeesMustFall movement and 'all African children yearning for education by showing them that despite being poor, nothing is impossible'.

News24 reported that his older sister, Constance, used her salary to pay for his schooling, with Lamola explaining: 'I am a product of "black tax". My sister taking all her salary to pay for my fees motivated me to work hard during my undergraduate years.' His parents were farmworkers and could not afford to send him to school.

Lamola's second Master's, completed at the University of Pretoria, was in extractive law in Africa, finding that the Department of Minerals and Energy's enforcement unit is 'inadequately resourced to ensure compliance', affecting mining communities negatively. Lamola's first Master's was in corporate law.

The former deputy president of the ANCYL made substantial progress in leadership in the party, despite his conversion from being an acolyte of former president Jacob Zuma to campaigning for Zuma to be recalled within the space of five years. He took significant political blows from Economic Freedom Fighters (EFF)'s chief, Julius Malema, as a result, but there may be a deeper motive for that, as the two young political stars are perhaps likely to face off as presidential candidates in the years to come.

Lamola was deputy to Malema when he was ANCYL president before Malema was expelled by the party, and the EFF leader believed Lamola had not been as honest as he could have been about why he, Lamola, survived the party's chop while others did not.

Lamola was a reluctant acting ANCYL leader in 2012 after Malema was ousted, and his adverse comments about an ANCYL National Task Team (NTT) appointed to investigate the structure did him no favours. Mzwandile Masina – for some time a vocal supporter of Zuma, and in 2018 the mayor of Ekurhuleni – was appointed convenor of the NTT. Insisting he remained deputy president rather than acting president, Lamola said the NTT was 'distorting history and wishing away the ANCYL's leadership collective and programmes under … Malema'.

Lamola's achievements in higher education and internal support from other factions of the party afforded him intellectual leverage in the ANC, however, and by 2018 he was, for instance, its most public voice on the topic of land expropriation without compensation.

But this was a theme that the ANCYL under Malema had developed and presented years before it was trending as ANC policy in government. And so, when Lamola addressed a conference on land reform at the University of South Africa in early 2018, the resentment was quickly laid bare. He was heckled by EFF supporters until a brawl broke out, and the conference had to be cancelled.

The Land Claims Court

Government body

Established in 1996 to deal with disputes that arise out of land reform, this court has the same status as any High Court. Any appeal against a decision it makes lies with the Supreme Court of Appeal (SCA) and, finally, the Constitutional Court.

Its main seat is in Randburg, Johannesburg.

It was expected that the Land Claims Court would be increasingly in the spotlight with trade unions, formations on the Left and some political parties, predominantly the Economic Freedom Fighters, insisting on state ownership of all the land in the country.

Leader of the Opposition

As the leader of the largest minority party, the Leader of the Opposition enjoys a special status in Parliament. The post is specified in the Constitution and the Rules, and is accorded a specific salary, though no duties in terms of the Rules are specified.

The Leader of the Opposition in 2018 was Mmusi Maimane of the Democratic Alliance. He took over the role from Helen Zille.

Lebeya, Advocate Godfrey

Head of the Hawks (the directorate for priority crime investigation), Former deputy national commissioner of police in charge of crime intelligence and detective services

Star

Lebeya was widely praised when he was appointed in June 2018 in the wake of his tainted predecessor, Berning Ntlemeza, whose appointment was declared unlawful and invalid in 2017. Although Ntlemeza had a powerful support base which approved of his determination to bring down former South African Revenue Service (SARS) Commissioner Pravin Gordhan using fake news and other tactics to conjure up activities for a 'rogue unit' at SARS, he couldn't escape being exposed.

Lebeya's PhD in Criminal Law with a specific focus on organised crime was one of the reasons why he was identified as a talent by his peers. But he became a danger to the state capture project, and was dismissed in 2016.

It was the Jacob Zuma era and Lebeya was proving to be an obstacle when he stood against the 'protection' of Richard Mdluli, then head of crime intelligence in the South African Police Service. Lebeya – who had worked in the National Prosecuting Authority's Asset Forfeiture Unit and in the Special Investigating Unit of the Department of Justice – also clashed with National Police Commissioner Riah Phiyega, seemingly over murder suspect Mdluli.

Legoete, Dakota

Secretary of the North West ANC | Former ANC chief whip in Tlokwe municipality, North West Province | Former municipal manager, Tswaing municipality, North West province | Member of the ANC National Working Committee (NWC) | Acting ANC spokesperson

LEGOETE TOOK THE NATIONAL STAGE IN December 2018 when he was appointed ANC acting spokesperson after Pule Mabe took leave following a sexual harassment complaint by his PA. This gave Legoete – who accused Kgalema Motlanthe of 'playing to the gallery' when the former president appeared to endorse late ANC veteran Ahmed Kathrada's call for Jacob Zuma to step down in 2017 – a prime spotlight.

Previously, Legoete's name had made headlines only through factional politics in North West. A member of the ANC's National Executive Committee (NEC), Legoete was suspended by the Tswaing municipality in Sannieshof, in 2009 after allegations of fraud and corruption, but he challenged his suspension in court and was later appointed a municipal councillor in the divided Tlokwe municipality.

Mostly involved in the fraught politics of North West, Legoete defended former Eskom CEO Brian Molefe in a dispute over Molefe's ANC branch membership.

In October 2017, he led a political protest by the North West ANC's Provincial Executive Committee (PEC) in distancing it from ANC presidential hopeful Cyril Ramaphosa's visit. The PEC had previously said it would endorse the party's National Executive Committee (NEC) member Nkosazana Dlamini-Zuma as its preferred presidential candidate.

Lekganyane, Barnabas

Head of the Zion Christian Church (ZCC) | Courted by politicians

Potential power broker

AS LEADER OF THE BIGGEST CHRISTIAN DENOMINATION in South Africa, Lekganyane and his brethren have a following of at least 15 million worshippers. Established in 1910 by Lekganyane's grandfather, the ZCC's headquarters is in Zion City, Moria, Limpopo, and is the scene of an extraordinary annual pilgrimage every Easter when several million congregants commune with one another.

Access to the church grounds is limited to ZCC members, although leading politicians are often allowed to address the faithful. Apartheid supremo P.W. Botha did so in 1985 and received a 'freedom award' from Lekganyane. Nelson Mandela did so in 1992, along with apartheid president F.W. de Klerk, and Inkatha Freedom Party (IFP) leader Mangosuthu Buthelezi was also hosted at a prayer meeting. The ZCC has attracted the favour of every president, as well as former Democratic Alliance leader Helen Zille and Economic Freedom Fighters (EFF) Commander-in-Chief Julius Malema.

Lekganyane is, however, only the leader of one of two 'sects' of the ZCC after the church split in 1949 – a year after the death of his grandfather. His father retained the ZCC and his uncle formed the St Engena Zion Christian Church.

The ZCC of Lekganyane hit the headlines in 2017 when the church called for its members to boycott Tiso Blackstar, the media company which published *Sowetan*, *Sunday World* and the *Sunday Times*, among other titles, for its stories that the church was 'crisis-ridden, morally questionable and devoid of leadership'. The following week, *Sunday World* published a prominent apology.

Lesufi, Panyaza

Gauteng MEC for Education | Former special adviser to the Minister of Basic Education | Former head of communications for the Department of Basic Education | Former spokesperson of Scorpions | Former spokesperson for the South African Police Service (SAPS | ANC politician | Former political detainee

On the way up | Star

A YOUTH, STUDENT AND COMMUNITY LEADER from Tembisa outside Johannesburg, Lesufi was arrested during the 1988 State of Emergency regulations for belonging to the then banned Congress of South African Students (Cosas). He was also giving his tacit support to the ANC and Umkhonto we Sizwe underground.

Thirty years later, Lesufi is usually cited as one of the ANC's strongest assets in his position as Gauteng MEC for Education.

He is an experienced politician, having served as a special advisor to the Minister of Basic Education, and as head of communications for the Department of Education, the now defunct Scorpions and the SAPS.

He has had extensive experience at ANC branch level in Tembisa, Kyalami and Ekurhuleni, and has been a member of the Provincial Executive Committee (PEC) in Gauteng since 2007. But being the MEC of Education in Gauteng brought an extensive list of societal problems, as well as political questions, to his door, as Lesufi worked hard to be recognised at an even higher level of government.

A plus was his drive towards Information Technology Communication (ICT) curriculum delivery. A downside was the exposure of the deep race fault lines across Gauteng as parent took on parent in township battles, and others refused to allow teachers or head teachers to operate because of their race.

Children, too, revealed themselves in shocking acts of racism and even violence, while language and admission policies became conflated as a lever for race. Lesufi had to deal with all of these, in addition to aggression against teachers and an ever-growing youth population due to migration.

It is testament to his plan for his own political career that Lesufi turned down a position on the ANC's National Executive Committee (NEC) at Nasrec in December 2017 to concentrate on growing his profile in his province. But it was unlikely that a politician of Lesufi's calibre would remain in provincial government forever.

Limpopo

Province | Led by the ANC since 1994

History of massive corruption

ONCE KNOWN AS THE ANC's 'ELECTION BASKET' province because of the high number of votes it could 'harvest' for the ruling party, Limpopo has a deep connection with the ANC because of its distinguished resistance history. In particular, the University of Limpopo, popularly known as Turfloop (formally, the University of the North), was a place of extensive political education and mobilisation from the late 1960s. Among its alumni are: President Cyril Ramaphosa; Reverend Frank Chikane and Black Consciousness (BC) hero Onkgopotse Tiro.

Despite this, Limpopo has been mired in massive corruption scandals in the post-democratic years. In 2012, finance minister Pravin Gordhan placed it under government administration after it emerged that the Limpopo treasury was effectively bankrupt, needing a bailout of R2 billion.

The Hawks and its law enforcement partner, the Special Investigating Unit (SIU), probed tender rigging and kickbacks, and it was shown that a culture of impugnity which pervaded ANC politics was rife in Limpopo.

Primary figures in corruption there included: former premier Cassel Mathale; former ANC Youth League (ANCYL) president and now leader of the Economic Freedom Fighters (EFF), Julius Malema; Mathale's business partner Selby Manthata; Lesiba Gwangwa, the CEO of On-Point Engineering, which was co-owned by Malema's Ratanang Family Trust; and former Limpopo ANCYL secretary Jacob Lebogo.

In particular, On-Point was central to the tender rigging, having been 'awarded' a prize deal with the Limpopo Department of Roads and Transport. Jacob Zuma would later purge several MECs and mayors.

Corruption by politicians and businesspeople was also evident in the sale of residential plots in Bendor, a smart suburb of Limpopo's capital Polokwane. Fronting, 'double transfers' and payouts to middle men were evident in that matter. A 'double transfer' had also been alleged in Malema's purchase of a property in the affluent Polokwane suburb of Ster Park, nicknamed 'Tender Park' for the number of corrupt individuals it housed in luxury mansions.

Limpopo was under ANC rule after 1994, but after the 2016 local elections, the EFF held sway as the opposition, having toppled the Democratic Alliance. Limpopo remained a fairly open book in terms of the 2019 national and provincial elections, although the EFF was clambering for greater power.

Its premier in 2019 was Stan Mathabathe.

Local government

Prior to the Constitution being ratified in 1996, local municipalities existed only at the mercy of provincial governments. These were fragmented, racially segregated and provided massively unequal services to different communities. After 1996, the concept of proper 'local government' became entrenched as a vehicle for society's integration and the sharing of municipal services from the well-off to the poor.

It went through a few phases: the first, pre-interim phase, which came with the Local Government Transition Act of 1993 and the establishment of negotiating forums in local authorities pending the first local government election; the second phase, which saw the first local government elections held in 1995–96 simply to integrate the municipalities but not always through a democratic vote, and the third and final phase of local government elections in December 2000, establishing the current municipalities.

The Constitution elevated local government to a sphere of government, firmly establishing its autonomy. A municipality now had the right to govern, on its own initiative, the local affairs of its community. While national and provincial governments could supervise the functioning of local government, this had to be done without encroaching on the institutional integrity of local government.

The developmental mandate of local government was effected through metropolitan municipalities in the eight largest urbanised and industrialised centres in the country. These were charged with addressing the legacy of urban apartheid as the providers of primary services, making them central to transformation.

Losi, Zingiswa

Congress of Trade Unions (Cosatu) president | Political activist for the ANC

On the way up | Star

The top trade unionist joined the Congress of South African Students (Cosas) when she was at school, and then the ANC Youth League (ANCYL) structures in the Eastern Cape.

With two brothers in exile, training with the ANC's military wing, Umkhonto we Sizwe (MK), Losi was conscientised from childhood. Too young to be part of MK herself, Losi later joined the South African National Defence Force (SANDF) before she began work as an operator in the assembling division for car manufacturer Ford in Port Elizabeth. After she was promoted to quality inspector, she became a shop steward for the National Union of Metalworkers (Numsa), and was soon a senior leader of that organisation.

Losi rose within the ANC too, and was said to have lost the position of deputy secretary at the party's national elective conference at Nasrec, Johannesburg, in December 2017 to party veteran and deputy secretary-general Jessie Duarte for political reasons. Losi was, however, elected onto the ANC's National Executive Committee (NEC) at that conference and was expected to be an asset to the party going into the 2019 elections.

She was elected President of Cosatu – the first woman in that position – after she was nominated unopposed at its 13th national congress in Midrand, outside Johannesburg in September 2018.

Love, Janet

Electoral Commission Commissioner | South African Human Rights Commission Commissioner | National director of the Legal Resources Centre | Former member of the Constitutional Committee of the Constitutional Assembly which created the Constitution | Former political prisoner

Change agent

The activist was unanimously elected by all three major political parties in the National Assembly to fill the vacancy left by Democratic Alliance (DA) MP Reinette Taljaart's resignation as an Electoral Commission (IEC) Commissioner in 2015. That was the second time Love had been nominated for the position.

She became an activist as a student at the University of the Witwatersrand (Wits) in the early 1970s before going into exile for the ANC and joining Umkhonto we Sizwe (MK). Later, Love was a key member of Operation Vula, which was active from 1986 to 1990. Vula was MK's plan to maintain a structure inside South Africa prior to Nelson Mandela's release and then kept in place as a 'guarantee' in case the peace process collapsed.

Love was part of the ANC negotiating team at the Convention for a Democratic South Africa (Codesa) in the early 1990s and served as an ANC MP after 1994, notably as a member of the 22-person constitutional committee which helped create the Constitution.

She left Parliament for a stint at the South African Reserve Bank (SARB) as the head of strategic analysis, after which she became national director of the Legal Resources Centre, as well as serving a seven-year term on the South African Human Rights Commission (SAHRC).

Lucas, Sylvia

Northern Cape premier | ANC politician

Linked to corruption

Lucas was a typist for the National Party before she joined the ANC in 1992 as a branch member. Such was her personality and dedication to the party that, from 1995–2000, she was a councillor for the //Khara Hais Local Municipality in Upington while also working for the regional structures of the ANC in that remote area.

She became chairperson of the ANC in the Siyanda region, which falls within a predominantly Afrikaans-speaking area of the Northern Cape, and was there elected to serve on the Provincial Executive Committee (PEC) of the ANC while she moved up the ranks of the ANC Women's League (ANCWL).

In 2009, Lucas was appointed as MEC for Environment and Nature Conservation in the Northern Cape and then, upon Premier Hazel Jenkins's illness and subsequent resignation, as premier in 2013. Lucas was reappointed in 2014 after that year's general election.

Despite the ANC's decision to have a 50/50 gender representation, Lucas was the only woman appointed as a premier in the eight ANC-run provinces in 2009. But she earned a humiliating nickname, the 'Fast Food Premier', when she spent R53,000 on personal groceries with her government-issued credit card.

Lungisa, Andile

Former ANC Youth League (ANCYL) deputy chairperson | Eastern Cape ANC politician

Jailed for assault with the intent to cause grievous bodily harm

ANC Eastern Cape heavyweight Lungisa was sentenced to three years' imprisonment by the Port Elizabeth Magistrate's Court in May 2018 for assault with the intent to cause grievous bodily harm.

He had pleaded not guilty to smashing a glass jug over the head of former member of the mayoral committee Rano Kayser, during a Nelson Mandela Bay (NMB) council meeting in October 2016. Magistrate Morne Cannon said Lungisa had shown no remorse, but by June 2018, Lungisa was back in the NMB council.

Also in October 2016, as a member of the Eastern Cape Provincial Executive Committee (PEC), Lungisa was involved in a court action involving the Johannesburg Commercial Crimes Unit. He stepped back from participating in the PEC until the matter was resolved and charges were withdrawn, with the ANC saying at the time it 'welcomed back' Lungisa 'to help us in our process of self-introspection'.

In March 2017, Lungisa was elected to lead the NMB municipality. This meant he eventually – and reluctantly – resigned from the PEC, according to the party's constitution. But the backdrop was dramatic as the Eastern Cape had been without a regional body for two years after Jacob Zuma disbanded it due to factionalism. Lungisa defied an ANC Top 6 instruction to vacate the regional chairperson position as he had been irregularly elected, violating the party's constitution around occupying two seats simultaneously. Lungisa claimed his situation was 'special' because it was about having a 'revolutionary cause' to reclaim the metro (from the Democratic Alliance (DA)).

Lungisa and the ANC ultimately lost the election in the NMB metro to a governing agreement between the DA, the Economic Freedom Fighters (EFF) and other, smaller parties including the Patriotic Alliance (PA).

Luthuli House

The ANC headquarters

Based in Pixley Seme Street in the centre of Johannesburg, the building, which houses subsidiary organisations of the ruling party as well as its own administration and leadership, is named after Nobel laureate, Chief Albert Luthuli.

Luthuli was the first African and the first person outside the Americas and Europe to be awarded the Peace Prize in 1960. He was named for his role in the struggle against apartheid.

Luthuli House has become a metonym for the ANC's leadership, much like the Oval Office has become for the United States government.

M

Mabe, Pule

ANC spokesperson (took leave in 2018 pending the outcome of a complaint against him) | Former ANC MP

Linked to corruption

THE LONG-TIME ANC MEMBER might have thought the only flak he would take when he was named Zizi Kodwa's successor as ANC spokersperson in February 2018 was that he was not as fluent, glib and informed as Kodwa. It went much further than that.

Mabe was widely ridiculed for his tendency for foot-in-mouth statements, which included retracting press statements which had already gone out. He had left his job as an ANC backbencher in Parliament where he didn't particularly shine over the three years he was there. He was notable, however, for dissenting and supporting a parliamentary motion of no confidence against Jacob Zuma in September 2017, along with other ANC MPs.

But by May 2018, scandal surrounded Mabe with the *Mail & Guardia*n alleging he was implicated in a multimillion-rand tender, which had apparently been awarded to Mvest Trust, a business in which he was involved, by the North West government. It was claimed proper procurement processes were not followed for the tender to establish dry cleaning and laundry services in the province.

Mvest Trust held Mabe's patent rights for the development of an app.

Mabe was previously in a conduct crisis when Parliament's Ethics Committee fined him R40,000 for not declaring that KG Media, a company with which he was closely associated, had received benefits from a seemingly improper tender with the Passenger Rail Agency of South Africa (Prasa), to produce its magazine, Hambanathi.

Mabe was also linked to a R29-million deal allegedly involving Gauteng ANC MEC Lebogang Maile. The Democratic Alliance (DA) in the province revealed that the deal – for the delivery of three-wheeler vehicles to be given to waste pickers to collect recyclable goods – was unlawful in terms of provincial treasury rules.

In December 2018, Mabe asked the ANC for leave, pending the outcome of a sexual harassment complaint laid against him by his former personal assistant. ANC North West veteran Dakota Legoete was appointed in an acting position as party spokesperson.

Mabuyane, Oscar

ANC party chairperson in the Eastern Cape

On the way up | Power broker

A STALWART IN THE TROUBLED EASTERN CAPE ANC, Mabuyane was brought into the key position of party chairperson in a new Provincial Executive Committee (PEC) in 2017. The Eastern Cape ANC had grown ever more politically divided as its leadership had failed on many socio-economic fronts, and the election of the new PEC had been troubled.

Upon joining the leadership team of ANC secretary Lulama Ngcukaitobi and his deputy Mlungisi Mvoko, a former teacher and trade unionist, Mabuyane was identified as a future premier. But the backdrop was chaotic as Ngcukatoibi and a group of other Eastern Cape ANC leaders had to travel to the ANC's Johannesburg headquarters, Luthuli House, in 2017 to push for then premier Phumulo Masualle, and six of his MECs to be axed.

Masualle and the MECs had refused to recognise the PEC's election, including Mabuyane as party leader. Masualle survived, but the events surrounding him were symptomatic of the way the Eastern Cape ANC had degenerated along factional lines. The new PEC became the first formal ANC structure to publicly call for Jacob Zuma's removal.

Mabuyane was also made MEC for Economic Development in the Provincial Legislature in the reshuffle that followed in 2017.

The expectation was that the 2019 national and provincial elections would bring about the acceptance of that new PEC, and that this would be desirable for a turnaround in the Eastern Cape's fortunes.

Mabuza, David

Nickname: 'DD'; the Cat | Deputy President of South Africa | Leader of government business in Parliament | Former Mpumalanga premier

Linked to corruption and capture

THE FIRST PREMIER OF MPUMALANGA, Matthews Phosa, is credited with bringing 'DD' Mabuza into the ANC when he recruited Mabuza into the organisation when Mabuza was a student.

Phosa and Mabuza operated out of the same ANC underground cell and their association would continue when Phosa endorsed Mabuza in the post of Mpumalanga MEC for Education. But their relationship turned sour when a scandal over matric (final school year) results unravelled in 2008, showing the results had been inflated. Phosa axed Mabuza.

But 'DD' wasn't making light when he once dubbed himself 'the cat'. He indeed survived, even after his administration was implicated in the 2009 murder of stadium tender whistleblower Jimmy Mohlala, who was the Speaker of the Mbombela municipality. At least 16 more assassinations deemed political took place in Mpumalanga, with no conclusions in the investigations to date.

Mabuza vanished from public sight for months after he fell ill in late 2015, saying he had been poisoned. When he returned, he again took full flight. Mabuza was again said to be ill and seeking medical treatment, this time in Russia, in 2018 when he fell out of public view for a few weeks. But there was speculation that his trip may not have been about his health, and rather about government deals, perhaps even dating back to the Jacob Zuma era.

His ascendancy to the deputy presidency of the country was controversial, yet those who understand the workings of the ANC say it made sense in terms of how President Cyril Ramaphosa had to manage the party's factions until the 2019 elections. Mabuza had, in effect, been the kingmaker at the ANC's elective conference at Nasrec, Johannesburg, in 2017, with many believing Ramaphosa stood little chance of victory over his rival Nkosazana Dlamini-Zuma. Mabuza's 'betrayal' of the Zuma faction saw him throw his substantial weight behind Ramaphosa instead, and that swayed the vote.

As deputy president, Mabuza also became Leader of Government Business in Parliament. The Leader of Government Business is appointed from the Cabinet by the president to take care of the affairs of the executive in Parliament. That includes arranging the attendance of Cabinet ministers in Parliament. Cabinet ministers appear in the national legislature to account to the nation, and it was Mabuza's task to ensure they did so.

Mabuza, Jabu

Eskom chairperson | President of Business Unity South Africa (BUSA) | Chairperson of Business Leadership South Africa (BLSA) | Chairperson of the Regional Business Council for the World Economic Forum (WEF) | Chairperson of the Casino Association of South Africa (CASA) | Former chairperson of Telkom SA | Former Group Chief Executive of Tsogo Sun Holdings | Former deputy chairperson of Tsogo Sun Holdings | Former chairperson of South African Tourism | Former country advisor to the Union Bank of Switzerland (UBS)

Change agent

Mabuza was appointed chairperson of Eskom at the beginning of 2018, at the height of an appalling crisis involving state capture, mismanagement and financial doom at the energy utility. As it was lost of all its credibility, his task was to stabilise it through a proper system of governance and stem its growing debt burden on the state, with Phakamani Hadebe as the group's acting chief executive – later confirmed as CEO – and a new board of 13 members.

Mabuza started his working life as a clerk of the court at the then Department of Bantu Affairs. But it was when he decided to start driving taxis to raise his university tuition fees, and later became a taxi owner, that his life began to take its upward trajectory. Mabuza joined the South African Black Taxi Association (SABTA) and later became its commercial head.

In 1988, he was a founding member of the Foundation for African Business and Consumer Services, becoming its CEO in 1990, and that got him noticed by Meyer Kahn, CEO and later chair of SABMiller plc. Kahn asked Mabuza to join SAB as Group Advancement Manager in the Chairman's Office, exposing him to affiliates in the group. Mabuza then sat on the boards of, among others, OK Bazaars, ABI (Amalgamated Beverage Industries) and the Southern Sun (hotel group).

Others on the Eskom board under Mabuza included Sifiso Dabengwa, Sindi Mabaso-Koyana, Mark Lamberti, Professor Tshepo Mongalo, Professor Malegapuru Makgoba, Busisiwe Mavuso, Nelisiwe Magubane, Dr Rod Crompton, George Sebulela, Dr Pulane Molokwane, Dr Banothile Makhubela and Jacky Molisane.

But Mabuza was not in for a smooth ride.

At least two of the members – Dabengwa, previously the CEO at MTN, and Lamberti – faced serious challenges. Dabengwa was identified by Economic Freedom Fighters (EFF) leader Julius Malema as being 'too close' to President Cyril Ramaphosa in what the EFF steered into a jobs-for-pals scandal. Ramaphosa said he had recused himself from the selections. Lamberti, meanwhile, has resigned as a director of the Eskom Board and as CEO of Imperial Holdings after Adila Chowan, a former group financial manager at Associated Motor Holdings and Imperial, accused him of race and gender discrimination.

Madikizela, Bonginkosi

Democratic Alliance (DA) Western Cape leader | Former ANC and United Democratic Movement (UDM) politician

On the way up, or down, depending

THE LEADER OF THE DEMOCRATIC ALLIANCE (DA) in the Western Cape has had a chequered political history, having once been loyal to former ANC Western Cape premier, Ebrahim Rasool, who left his position under a cloud and became a diplomat before he made his return to provincial politics in 2018.

Madikizela, originally from the Eastern Cape, was in a group of disaffected ANC members who had been supportive of Rasool in his party leadership battle with Mcebisi Skwatsha. Skwatsha won the battle, but Madikizela and others felt they had been marginalised by their party for the local government elections in 2006. They opted to go independent for that poll, but the party expelled them instead.

Madikizela then joined the United Democratic Movement (UDM) in 2007, but the UDM believed him to be disreputable after Madikizela was discovered recruiting its members to join the DA.

He finally threw his lot in with the DA in 2008 when he became Mayor Helen Zille's spokesperson, and then Housing MEC. When he was the MEC for Human Settlements in the Western Cape, his role became somewhat uncertain as an internal political split threatened the DA in 2018. But there were those who believed Madikizela had his eye on, and could even become, the premier – possibly in 2019.

Madlanga, Justice Mbuyiseli

Constitutional Court justice | Chief evidence leader at the Farlam Commission | Chief evidence leader at the investigation into National Police Commissioner Bheki Cele's fitness to hold office | Represented South Africa at the International Court of Justice at The Hague | Former chair of the Exchange Control Amnesty Unit

MBUYISELI MADLANGA EARNED HIS LLB AT RHODES UNIVERSITY before he returned to the University of the Transkei, his first alma mater, to lecture. He then studied at the University of Notre Dame in Indiana, United States, where he graduated cum laude with an LLM before interning at Amnesty International.

Madlanga was the youngest judge in the country at 36 when he was appointed to the Transkei division of the High Court in 1996. Three years later he was appointed as an acting judge of appeal at the Supreme Court of Appeal (SCA) and a judge of appeal at the Competition Commission.

He had to give up his SCA appointment to return to Mthatha as acting judge president of the division. While there, Madlanga also acted as a justice in the Constitutional Court (ConCourt). He stepped down from the bench in 2001 citing financial reasons, as the father of a family of six, and began practising as a silk in Johannesburg and Mthatha.

His highlights as a judge included being the chief evidence leader in both the Farlam Commission into the Marikana massacre and the investigation into National Police Commissioner Bheki Cele's fitness to hold office. He also represented South Africa at the International Court of Justice at The Hague and chaired the Exchange Control Amnesty Unit.

Madlanga was permanently appointed to the Constitutional Court in August 2013, replacing Justice Zac Yakoob, who retired at the end of his 12-year tenure.

Madonsela, Professor (Advocate) Thuli

Former Public Protector | Helped draft the Constitution | Formerly a United Democratic Front activist | Now non-aligned | Launched her Thuma Foundation in 2018

Change agent | Star

THE FORMER PUBLIC PROTECTOR (PP) got positive reviews from the Twitterverse and analysts as a choice to run the National Prosecuting Authority (NPA) when Advocate Shaun Abrahams left the position in 2018.

But those who understand ANC politics were less excitable. After all, it was not only the former president, Jacob Zuma, who had found her confidence, not to say, independence, as PP either intimidating or going beyond her mandate. And, in fact, despite enormous support from the citizenry, Madonsela herself may not have been partial to the idea, having become a professor based at Stellenbosch University's law department as its Chair of Social Justice, and lecturing at other institutions around the world.

Madonsela was appointed PP by Zuma for a non-renewable seven-year term commencing in October 2009. He had the unanimous support of the National Assembly. Madonsela would, however, never be forgotten, particularly for her report, 'A State of Capture', which eventually led to the demise of Jacob Zuma – even if that demise took a while, and a fight, to reach fruition.

In the end, it was the Constitutional Court (ConCourt) and the High Court that had to pronounce to Parliament and the President on the requirement to adhere to the PP's recommendations. As a result, Zuma was compelled to institute an inquiry into state capture.

Madonsela was certainly unable to leave the office of the PP quietly. She was targeted by her successor, Advocate Busisiwe Mkhwebane, when Mkhwebane sought a police investigation into her, claiming Madonsela had acted illegally when she released a video of an interview she conducted with Zuma during the state capture investigation, in which Zuma clearly refused to answer questions. Madonsela did so as she wished to prove that Zuma was lying after he told the public and the ConCourt that he had 'never been given an opportunity' to answer allegations against him.

Mkhwebane's intentions against Madonsela came to nothing.

Madonsela – who helped draft the final Constitution of South Africa, which was ratified in 1996 – graduated with a BA degree in law from the University of Swaziland in 1987, and an LLB from the University of the Witwatersrand in 1990. She earned a Doctor of Laws from both the universities of Stellenbosch and Cape Town.

Madonsela was a long-time ANC supporter, and served the United Democratic Front (UDF) in the 1980s. She turned down the chance to become an MP in 1994 and invitations to again join government in a political capacity during the national elections in 2014.

Magashule, Ace (also see Premier League)

ANC secretary-general | Former Free State premier

Linked to capture

THE ANC'S LEADER IN THE FREE STATE after the first democratic elections in 1994, Magashule's history within the party is somewhat contested once he was linked to state capture.

For instance, when Winnie Madikizela-Mandela died in 2018, there were those who claimed Magashule had been close to her and that she had been a catalyst to his political career. Others scoffed, decoding his rise as more subversive. Nonetheless, Magashule's entry into formal provincial politics had nothing to do with a Mandela, but rather happened under the first Free State premier, Mosiuoa Lekota.

That relationship did not end well, with Lekota claiming Magashule had stolen government funds. Lekota's wish for Magashule to be disciplined was overruled by none other than Jacob Zuma, who was the ANC's chairperson at the time, in 1994. By coincidence or design, Magashule was appointed Free State premier in 2009 when Zuma became president.

Magashule was believed to be linked with corruption and was seen as a poor administrator who oversaw the demise of several Free State government departments, with the auditor-general bemoaning 'a lack of accountability and commitment towards clean administration'.

But it was when he was associated with the disreputable Gupta brothers through the 'Gupta leaks' emails, and his son, Tshepiso, employed by them, that his reputation came under more serious scrutiny.

Magashule, who became the ANC's secretary-general in December 2017, appeared central to the controversial Estina dairy project in Vrede, Free State, when he was the premier of the province.

According to court papers filed by Peter Thabethe, a former head of the provincial Department of Agriculture and one of the co-accused in the Estina 8 matter – which was withdrawn in the Bloemfontein magistrates court in November 2018 due to 'unreasonable delays' on the part of the state – Gupta 'lieutenant' Ashok Narayan served as an 'advisor' to Magashule when plans were put in place to establish the project. Thabethe claimed, for instance, that Magashule approved a trip to India for discussions about the project 'at the state's expense' in 2012. Later, it was alleged that a chain of companies may have been used to launder around R84 million of Estina's proceeds.

Since Magashule's rise to become ANC secretary-general, he has been accused of secretly plotting to unseat Ramaphosa and re-establish the Zuma faction's control of the ANC. In September 2018, he said he would be prepared to testify at the Zondo Commission of Inquiry into state capture.

Magashule was chosen as the ANC's secretary-general at the Nascrec elective conference in December 2017 through a compromise of factions.

Mahlobo, David

Former state security minister | ANC MP | Former director of transformation in the Department of Water Affairs and Forestry

Linked with corruption

Suspicion was cast on Mahlobo after revelations of his visit to a Mpumalanga massage spa owned by Guan Jiang Guang, a self-professed rhino horn trader who claimed to have grown 'close' to Mahlobo and his wife. The revelation was made by the Al Jazeera news network in 2016, leading Mahlobo to face questions from MPs.

That suspicion around possible corruption was, however, dismissed by Mahlobo and government, even as it became clear he was not suitable for a position at State Security.

Mahlobo would again be discredited when he was asked by former Inspector General of Intelligence Faith Radebe to conduct a forensic investigation around the Principal Agent Network, established by Arthur Fraser, the former Deputy Director-General of the National Intelligence Agency – and failed to do so.

Eventually axed from his ministerial job, the son of Chief Mandlenkosi Mahlobo of the KwaMahlobo Traditional Community in Mpumalanga still had credentials from his days with the ANC Youth League and the South African Students Congress.

A BSc Honours graduate, Mahlobo was appointed the director of transformation in the Department of Water Affairs and Forestry, before becoming head of the Department of Co-operative Governance and Traditional Affairs in Mpumalanga.

Appointed to the ANC's National Executive Committee (NEC) at Mangaung in 2012, off the back of an increasingly close relationship with Jacob Zuma and then Mpumalanga premier, David 'DD' Mabuza, Mahlobo was investigated by the Hawks on the allegations of the rhino horn trader.

Mahumapelo, Supra (also see Premier League)

Nickname: Black Jesus; 'the essence of the absence of presence' | Former North West Premier | Head of the ANC's cadreship programme

Linked to corruption

SEVERAL NICKNAMES WERE AFFORDED MAHUMAPELO, including the one he gave himself, 'Black Jesus'. But when he presented the budget address at the provincial legislature in May 2018 in Mahikeng, at the apex of the fight by his party to have him resign or be fired, his description of himself as 'the essence of the absence of presence' was an instant classic.

Yet there was no mirth around violent protests that erupted over Mahumapelo's premiership.

Mahumapelo had himself entered office after the 2014 national and provincial elections amid the kind of violence that characterised his exit from the premiership in 2018.

He was widely expected to resign at the beginning of May 2018 after holding firm for weeks against the mayhemic scenes. But he waited for the Provincial Executive Committee (PEC) to give his resignation the nod. Three weeks later, he left office.

Mahumapelo was a political 'strongman' who could exact patronage. It was irrefutable that an irregular R1.1 million bursary had been given to his son by State-owned arms enterprise, Denel. There were those who even believed his axing could affect the ANC's outcome in North West in the 2019 elections.

Mahumapelo was quiet for a short while after his left office, and then appeared on the podium behind former president Jacob Zuma when Zuma was addressing crowds gathered outside the Durban High Court for his second appearance ahead of his expected corruption trial.

There was scorn when it was announced in June 2018 that Mahumapelo would run the ANC's OR Tambo Political School, a party institution which has yet to properly get off the ground, which would be based in North West province.

Maile, Lebogang

Economic development member of the Executive Council in Gauteng | Former Gauteng MEC for Education, Finance and Scrutiny | Former president of the Congress of South African Students (Cosas)

On the way up | Power broker | Linked to corruption

MAILE WAS APPOINTED TO SENIOR LEADERSHIP in the Gauteng Provincial Executive Committee (PEC) after years of making his way through the party from its youth formations. He was made Gauteng MEC for Economic Development, Agriculture, Environment and Rural Development in 2018, having entered the race as the frontrunner against Gauteng MEC for Education Panyaza Lesufi and former City of Johannesburg mayor Parks Tau.

Maile – an ANC loyalist – displayed passion about uplifting marginalised communities and re-aligning the economy to be inclusive.

Tipped as a potential premier of Gauteng, the young politician was, however, drawn into allegations of 'handing' a R29-million deal to ANC spokesperson Pule Mabe in Mabe's personal capacity as a businessman in 2018. He denied it. The Democratic Alliance (DA) in the province claimed that the deal – for the delivery of three-wheeler vehicles to be given to waste pickers to collect recyclable goods – was unlawful in terms of provincial treasury rules.

Maile was also accused in the same year by the DA of 'interfering' in the disciplinary hearings of two Gauteng staff members at the departments of Agriculture and Rural Development, with allegations being that while this department consistently failed to meet its targets, it was a popular source of enrichment for Maile.

Maimane, Mmusi

Nicknames: Mini-Mandela; MyMoney | Democratic Alliance (DA) leader | Former DA federal leader | Former national DA spokesperson

ONE OF THE COUNTRY'S YOUNGEST POLITICAL PARTY LEADERS, Maimane headed the Official Opposition in Parliament. His rise began when he was named the party's electoral candidate for mayor of Johannesburg in 2011, having stood unopposed for the position of federal leader at the party's congress that year.

But after the highs in 2016 and 2017, when he delivered scathing attacks in Parliament against President Jacob Zuma and seemingly spearheaded the DA's many legal actions against Zuma and corruption, it was his ineffectual response to his party's handling of two crises that first threatened his public image. These were the water crisis in Cape Town, dubbed 'Day Zero'; the other, the political fallout over the attempted ousting of Cape Town mayor, Patricia de Lille, in 2018.

Maimane was castigated by political rivals for seemingly being 'controlled' by so-called DA neo-cons, led by white members of the party's caucus. Some analysts felt it was those individuals who had also tried to force out De Lille, 'a black woman leader', without proper explanation. It was claimed that Maimane's public urging for transformation in the party ranks had not gone down well with that lobby either.

Maimane himself conceded that lost opportunities to show leadership could negatively affect his election ambitions in 2019. But by June 2018, he was fighting back, telling the *Sunday Times* in a front-page story that former leader of the DA, Helen Zille, should have been removed from decision-making structures after she stepped down. During the rest of that year, Maimane's fortunes more waned than waxed as he ultimately failed to really take the reins of the party in an increasingly demanding political scene ahead of the 2019 elections. Maimane was starting to come under increasing pressure from within his own ranks in early 2019, when there were even rumours of an internal putsch.

He has drawn attention for his marriage to a white woman, Natalie Maimane, who became his girlfriend when they were at school together in Johannesburg.

Maimane has a degree in psychology from the University of South Africa, a Master's in public administration from the University of the Witwatersrand and a Master's in theology from Bangor University, Wales.

Maine, Collen

Nicknames: Oros, Comrade Oros | Incumbent ANC Youth League president | Former ANC MP

Linked to corruption

MAINE HAD AN EMOTIONAL MOMENT at a Potchefstroom memorial service for Winnie Madikizela-Mandela in March 2018 when he revealed that he had indeed been introduced to the disreputable Gupta brothers by North West premier, Supra Mahumapelo, in 2016. 'Mama Winnie refused to go to the Guptas when many of us were willing,' Maine said. 'We must be honest about this, comrades.'

This came after Maine had ardently denied the same on other occasions, and so the response to his confession was not kind. Many said he was, in fact, using the moment to 'blame' Mahumapelo for his own alleged involvement with the Guptas, even though it was previously revealed that the Guptas may have played a role in helping him and his wife Kelebogile to buy a large personal residence in Pretoria.

Mahumapelo was unimpressed by Maine's revelations, but while some of Maine's comrades in the ANCYL demanded his head, in the end the League stood by him. Not the ANC Women's League (ANCWL), which took aim. The ANCWL's deputy secretary-general, Thandi Moraka, went so far as to label Maine 'a sellout'. Maine would later say, in 2017, that he believed Jacob Zuma should resign for the good of the country.

Prior to becoming an MEC in the North West government, and then the ANCYL president, Maine was an ANC MP. A delegate at the National Council of Provinces (NCOP), he was also a member of the select committees on Economic Development, Trade and International Relations, and a member of the Defence joint committees.

Maine was then shoehorned as 'a pair of safe hands' to take over the ANCYL with about six months to spare in terms of his age. The upper end for membership of the League is 35.

Majola, Bongani

Chairperson of the South African Human Rights Commission (SAHRC) | Former assistant secretary-general of the United Nations, to Ban ki-Moon | Previously the deputy chief prosecutor for the United Nations International Criminal Tribunal for Rwanda | Former national director of the Legal Resources Centre

MAJOLA WAS AN ADVOCATE WITH AN LLM from Harvard when he realised notable achievements at the helm of the Legal Resources Centre, but it was when he became Deputy Chief Prosecutor of the United Nations International Criminal Tribunal for Rwanda (ICTR) – which prosecuted suspects indicted for international crimes against humanity and war crimes during the genocide of 1994 – that Majola gained international respect.

After a decade in that role, he was appointed Assistant Secretary-General of the UN to former secretary-general, Ban ki-Moon, and Registrar of the ICTR. As Registrar, he supported the organs of the ICTR, including the judges, the Chambers and the Office of the Prosecutor. The ICTR successfully concluded its mandate and closed in December 2015.

Former president Jacob Zuma then appointed Majola as the chairperson of the SAHRC in December 2016. His seven-year term commenced in January 2017.

Makhaya, Trudi

Economics advisor to President Cyril Ramaphosa | Former deputy commissioner at the Competition Commission

On the way up | Change agent

MAKHAYA, A RHODES SCHOLAR, earned postgraduate degrees in business and economics from Oxford University and the University of the Witwatersrand (Wits). She held management or consulting roles at Deloitte South Africa, Genesis Analytics and AngloGold Ashanti, served as an advisor and angel investor to a number of companies, and held non-executive directorships at Vumelana Advisory Fund and MTN South Africa.

But it was her appointment by President Cyril Ramaphosa as his economics advisor in April 2018, following a period at the Competition Commission, which properly drew attention to Makhaya.

Ramaphosa made the announcement at the same time as he said he had appointed former Minister of Finance Trevor Manuel, former deputy minister of Finance Mcebisi Jonas, executive chairperson of the Afropulse Group, Phumzile Langeni and chairperson of the Liberty Group and former Standard Bank head, Jacko Maree as economic envoys.

Makhura, David

Premier of Gauteng | Former ANC provincial secretary in Gauteng | Former secretary-general of the Congress of South African Students (Cosas)

INVOLVED IN POLITICS SINCE HE WAS A TEENAGER on the streets of Mara Buysdorp in the Soutspanberg area of Limpopo province, Makhura went on to hold various positions within student movements, the ANC and South African Communist Party (SACP) before he became the premier of South Africa's richest and most powerful province, Gauteng.

But as the 2019 national and provincial elections beckons, there is no certainty that the ANC – and, therefore, its political leaders like Makhura – will survive at the top into the next five years. He had led the province's charge against Jacob Zuma, and won that battle, but the polls will be another story.

Even his Master's in public policy and management from the University of London and studies towards a Master's in energy futures at Stellenbosch University couldn't prepare Makhura for the difficult years of 2017 and 2018, where a form of co-governance in Gauteng's two most important metros – Tshwane and Johannesburg – had removed power from the ANC.

The Democratic Alliance (DA) and the Economic Freedom Fighters (EFF) had embarked upon a confidence-and-supply agreement in the metros whereby the EFF would vote with the DA – if it agreed on a particular policy. This was by virtue of the DA having needed the EFF's support to govern the cities.

For Makhura, this could be a certain threat. That model of governing could work on a provincial level as well if the DA won the 2019 elections with the support of the EFF. A May 2018 vote of no confidence in Makhura – brought by the DA, with the EFF voting with it – would not have assisted his confidence. Although the motion failed, with 27 members voting for it, 38 against, six members absent and one abstaining, it was a low point after Makhura had failed to take full responsibility for the Life Esidimeni tragedy in his province, which saw at least 144 mental health patients die after the province cancelled an agreement with the private healthcare provider and moved them to often-unlicensed NGOs.

That was not the first no confidence motion brought against Makhura, as the EFF had previously attempted it, in 2016.

Makgoba, Thabo

Anglican Church leader | Chancellor of the University of the Western Cape (UWC)

Change agent

MAKGOBA MADE HISTORY AS THE YOUNGEST Anglican archbishop at only 48, when he was elected to replace the retiring Archbishop Njongonkulu Ndungane, in 2008.

Educated at Soweto's Orlando High, he studied at the University of the Witwatersrand (Wits), earning a Master's in educational psychology and later a PhD in workplace spirituality from the University of Cape Town.

He attended St Paul's in Grahamstown to study for the priesthood and, after ordination, returned to Johannesburg where he ministered to a number of parishes before being sent back to Grahamstown as suffragan bishop, then bishop and finally archbishop, which saw him move to Cape Town.

Makgoba taught MBA students on spirituality and ethics and has served as Chancellor of the University of the Western Cape (UWC).

Politically outspoken, Makgoba vocalised consistently against the excesses of the Jacob Zuma administration and state capture, as he championed the plight of the most vulnerable in the country and railed against cases of sexual abuse by priests in his own church.

Malema, Julius

Nickname: Juju | Commander-in-Chief (CIC) of the Economic Freedom Fighters (EFF) | Member of the EFF's Central Command Team (CCT) | Member of the Pan-African Parliament (PAP) | Former ANC Youth League (ANCYL) president

On the way up | Identified as corrupt by the former Public Protector Thuli Madonsela | Power broker

In 2002, Malema led a chaotic Congress of South African Students (Cosas) march through the Johannesburg CBD in protest against the Gauteng education department's directive that schools close their gates during learning hours. It was anarchic. Everything that could go wrong went wrong, and it left the 21-year-old from Limpopo who was at its lead with much to consider. In later years, Malema said he regretted it, and that there had been no proper political preparation for how to control a march of that size and that level of emotion.

But this did not hold Malema back from achieving in the party he had held dear since childhood, and soon the former Cosas leader was elected president of the ANC Youth League (ANCYL) in April 2008 at a riotous elective conference. He was re-elected unopposed in 2011 when contender Lebogang Maile, now a Gauteng MEC, decided to withdraw.

With his militant rhetoric and disposition as a champion of the working class, the poor and the youth, Malema amassed support from those constituencies, to the extent that he began to be able to challenge then ANC president, Jacob Zuma, and the old guard. From his open support for Zimbabwean president, Robert Mugabe, and calling for regime change in Botswana, to publicly criticising Zuma and his many run-ins with the law, Malema became the quintessential enfant terrible.

Where once Zuma had said Malema could be a future leader of the ANC and the country, the two men parted ways as Malema became a political threat. Then Malema gifted the ANC an opportunity to get rid of him as allegations of corruption in Limpopo started unravelling. Malema was charged with fraud, money-laundering and racketeering in 2012, and Malema and other leaders of the ANCYL were ultimately expelled by the ANC that year.

That was the second time Malema had faced his party's disciplinary committee, the first being in 2010 when he was believed to have entered into a plea bargain for taking a stand against Jacob Zuma as president of the ANC at an ANCYL conference, and given a 'suspended' sentence of two years.

His legal woes – exacerbated by a report in 2012 by Public Protector (PP) Thuli Madonsela which identified him as corrupt and sought redress, but was never resolved – were dismissed by the courts in 2015 due to excessive delays by the National Prosecuting Authority (NPA).

In 2018, Afrikaner minority rights group AfriForum said it planned to mount a private prosecution of Malema related to the PP's report.

The EFF was formed in 2013 and, against all odds, considering the short time it had in which to organise support on the ground, won 25 seats in the National Assembly in the 2014 general election. Malema was sworn in as an MP that year.

Two months later, he was dismissed from Parliament after refusing to withdraw a remark he made accusing the ANC government of murder in the Marikana miners' strike. That was only the beginning of rancour between the EFF and other parties in Parliament.

Although Malema and his party were regarded as disruptors in South Africa's political landscape and it was expected that the 2019 elections would allow them even greater leverage as the Democratic Alliance (DA) was threatened with infighting, and the ANC struggled to find unity, the latter part of 2018 proved challenging.

First, in October 2018, Malema had to field allegations that his deputy, Floyd Shivambu, may have been the recipient of money which appeared to have been unlawfully gained by Shivambu's brother, Brian, in the VBS Bank scandal. Then, in December 2018, Malema was himself a target of allegations that he was too close to EFF funder Adriano Mazzotti – a suspected cigarette smuggler and tax evader – when it was revealed that Malema's wife and children lived in a mansion owned by Mazzotti.

Malema denied all allegations of corruption.

Malunga, Advocate Kevin

Deputy public protector | State legal adviser and spokesperson during the Farlam Judicial Commission of Inquiry into the Marikana massacre

BORN IN BULAWAYO, ZIMBABWE, MALUNGA arrived in South Africa in 2005 and became a citizen by naturalisation in 2010, having renounced his Zimbabwean citizenship. He has an LLM from Georgetown University, United States.

Malunga worked as the state's legal adviser for the Farlam Judicial Commission of Inquiry into the Marikana massacre. He had previously acted as legal advisor dealing with policy co-ordination and monitoring at the Ministry of Justice, and as an aide and researcher to the Committee on Institutional Models in former Chief Justice Sandile Ngcobo's office at the Constitutional Court (ConCourt), where he was the chief-of-staff.

Malunga applied to be the Public Protector when Advocate Thuli Madonsela, for whom he was also deputy, ended her time in office. But there were issues which were believed to have held him back, including: being axed from the Wits Law School; problems related to his citizenship; and his negative comments about Jacob Zuma having appointed Ngcobo over Deputy Chief Justice Dikgang Moseneke as Chief Justice.

Manana, Mduduzi

Former ANC MP | Former deputy minister of Higher Education

Convicted woman-beater

MANANA HAD INSISTED HE WAS A CHANGED MAN after he was found guilty of assaulting three women at a Sandton nightclub in 2017. He escaped a jail sentence, opting to pay a R100,000 fine, do 500 hours of community service and attend an anger management programme.

But he faced fresh allegations of assault, crimen injuria and intimidation after allegedly trying to push his domestic worker down the stairs of his double-storey Fourways home in April 2018. Manana's former helper Christine Wiro laid the charges against the former deputy minister of higher education at the Douglasdale police station in northern Johannesburg. And although she would soon withdraw them, allegedly under pressure from Manana, the investigation would continue – both from the police and the ANC itself. The National Prosecuting Authority ultimately decided not to prosecute him.

Despite his conviction of assault for the earlier nightclub attack, Manana remained an ANC MP, although Parliament's Joint Ethics Committee announced in June 2018 that it would be investigating him after the incident involving his helper. This, after many weeks of outrage about its inaction on the matter. Manana resigned as an MP not long after that announcement, saying the charges were 'a politically motivated smear campaign against me'.

Mandela, Nkosi Zwelivelile Mandla

Chief of the Mvezo Traditional Council, Eastern Cape | ANC MP | Nelson Mandela's grandson

THERE HAD BEEN CONSIDERABLE CONTROVERSY around the heir to Nelson Mandela's traditional legacy within the AbaThembu nation by the time the former president died in December 2013. Some of it is related to the three different families that had come about through Nelson Mandela's three marriages to Evelyn Mase, Winnie Madikizela-Mandela and Graça Machel.

The most headline-grabbing was the controversy when the Mthatha High Court had to intervene in July 2013 to force Mandla Mandela to return the remains of three of his grandfather's children to Qunu, Nelson Mandela's home village. Mandla Mandela had moved these to his own home village of Mvezo, nearby, without consulting the Mandela family. Mandla Mandela – who is the chief of the traditional council in Mvezo – was instructed to exhume and rebury the bodies. He did so.

But there were other issues that drew scandal, rather than emotional, familial or political attention to the ANC MP. These were his own marriages to: Tando Mabunu (married by civil ceremony in 2004, divorced in 2017 after she accused him of bigamy); French citizen of Réunion, Anaïs Grimaud (known as Nkosikazi Nobubele after they married in a traditional ceremony in 2010); and Mbali Makhathini (known as Nodiyala Mandela after they married in a traditional ceremony in 2011). His marriages to Grimaud and Makhatini were annulled.

Mandela married Rabia Clarke by Muslim rites in Cape Town in 2016. She is now known as Nkosikasi Nosekeni Rabia Mandela. Mandla Mandela embraced Islam, his wife's faith, before their marriage. He has, since then more dominantly, shown public and vocal support for the Palestinian liberation struggle.

For instance, Mandela prevailed upon Minister of International Relations and Co-Operation Lindiwe Sisulu and government to support a United Nations General Assembly vote condemning Apartheid Israel in June 2018. He said the Royal Mandela House was against acts of 'aggression and brutality' such as those that Israel perpetrated against the Palestinian people. In this, Mandela sought to align South African with Turkey and Algeria, the countries that had called for the UN vote.

Mandela attended the prestigious Waterford Kamhlaba School in Swaziland and went on to attain a BA in politics from Rhodes University.

'mantash' (a verb)

ANC national chairperson Gwede Mantashe may not have thought he'd ever be responsible for the coining of a new South African word, but that was indeed the case in 2018 when he was ANC secretary-general.

After publicly stating his discomfort around President Jacob Zuma's controversial Cabinet reshuffle, Mantashe suddenly adopted the completely opposite position at an ANC National Working Committee (NWC) briefing.

Social media users quickly created the verb 'mantash', meaning 'to change your mind abruptly'. It quickly gained popular usage.

Mantashe, Gwede (also see Chamber of Mines)

Minister of Mineral Resources | ANC chairperson | Former ANC secretary-general | Former chairperson of the South African Communist Party (SACP) | Former trade unionist

President Cyril Ramaphosa's decision to appoint Mantashe to the National Assembly in his first Cabinet reshuffle after the departure of Jacob Zuma came as something of a surprise to some, and a shock to others. Although Mantashe had the ideological credentials and much political experience, his reputation for seeming arrogance, his outspokenness and his maverick disregard for protocol had not always gone down well with all constituencies.

This would now include big business, 'white monopoly capital' and others invested in maintaining the ANC and government's neo-liberal agenda. It may also have included young people, especially students who had held him verbal hostage outside the ANC's Johannesburg headquarters, Luthuli House, during a #FeesMustFall march in 2016.

It was also mining communities, particularly the increasingly vocal Mining Affected Communities United in Action (MACUA) network, which was immediately unhappy with Mantashe's apparently laissez-faire approach towards consultation upon him taking up his post. And in the case of MACUA, it was serious, because there was a court order to consult with their network before the Department of Mineral Resources could make any decision.

But in November 2018, Mantashe had to concede when the Gauteng High Court in Pretoria ruled that consent had to be given by communities living on ancestral land before government could give the go-ahead for mining rights. The case that brought the issue to a head was that of the Xolobeni community in the Eastern Cape, represented by the Amadiba Crisis Committee, which had approached the court to prevent the department from issuing a mining licence to Australian mining conglomerate Transworld Energy and Minerals.

Although Mantashe took to the ground running in his new government portfolio, despite wielding the blows from all sides, he was a focus of negative attention during the Zondo Commission of Inquiry into State Capture when it was revealed that he had been present at a meeting with Standard Bank officials to question them about the closure of Gupta-linked accounts in 2016. He was the secretary-general of the ANC at the time. Mantashe would testify at the commission himself in late November 2018, confirming that such a meeting happened and that the ANC's National Working Committee (NWC) had indeed summoned representatives of the four big banks to meetings at the ANC's headquarters, Luthuli House, to discuss why the banks would not accept the Guptas as clients. But Mantashe was criticised for failing to explain why the NWC would do such a thing when the banks had already clearly explained that they considered the Guptas to be a risk. The NWC's position was that the banks were stifling black business and abusing their power. Mantashe was also criticised for his testimony in failing to explain why the ANC's NWC and then its National Executive Committee (NEC) would intervene on behalf of private individuals – which is what the Guptas were – at all.

But there was a bigger issue to come during the Zondo Commission in January 2019 when Mantashe was named as having allegedly received security upgrades through a subsidiary of the controversial Bosasa group of companies.

Mantashe has a BComm degree from the University of South Africa and a Master's from the University of Witwatersrand.

Manuel, Trevor

Economic envoy | Former minister in the Presidency | Former minister of Finance | Former minister of Trade and Industry | Former head of the National Planning Commission (NPC) | Member of the ANC's 101 Stalwarts | Chancellor of the Cape Peninsula University of Technology | Professor Extraordinaire at the University of Johannesburg | Chairperson of the Board of Old Mutual plc; representative in various capacities at the United Nations Commission for Trade and Development, the International Monetary Fund, the G20, the African Development Bank, the Southern African Development Community (SADC) and the Global Commission on Growth and Development

MANUEL WAS PORTRAYED AS AN ACTIVIST'S ACTIVIST in romantic histories of his life before he joined government.

He had helped establish the Cape Areas Housing Action Committee (CAHAC) in the 1970s before he found a more prominent political home in the United Democratic Front (UDF) in 1983. Manuel became a national executive member of the UDF with a slew of comrades, including Cheryl Carolus, Valli Moosa, Murphy Morobe and Johnny Issel.

He was elected to the ANC's National Executive Committee (NEC) in 1991 and became the head of economic planning in 1992. Made an ANC MP in 1994, he was then appointed Minister of Trade and Industry by Nelson Mandela before being moved up to Finance in 1996 – a post in which he remained until 2009, when Jacob Zuma entered power. Zuma instead appointed him Minister in the Presidency for the National Planning Commission from 2009 to 2014. Although the Commission launched a National Development Plan (NDP) in 2012, by 2018, the head of the secretariat of the NPC, Tshediso Matona, was reported as saying it was 'far off target' and 'very ambitious, given the current context'.

Manuel's Struggle reputation was, however, not matched by his behaviour in government. He was criticised for fundamental decisions which, say his detractors, had he not made them, or allowed them, or put his signature to them, could have stemmed the corrupt course of South African politics.

A neoliberal, Manuel presided over at least six currency crashes between 1996 and 2009 as finance minister. But there were other issues that he either inherited, or was party to, which many – particularly on the Left, representing workers and the poor – find hard to understand. This included the repayment of the US$25-billion, apartheid-era foreign debt, which many believe Manuel (and others) should have ensured was scrapped.

Manuel's adoption of government's flawed macroeconomic policy, Gear (the Growth, Employment, and Redistribution programme), is regarded by many of his critics as a low point.

In 2017, Manuel – who had been out of government for three years by then

– would be drawn into Jacob Zuma's protracted efforts to undermine and nearly destroy the model for the South African Revenue Service (SARS). Manuel and Jabu Moleketi, Manuel's former deputy in the Finance Ministry, were targeted by the Hawks (the Directorate for Priority Crime Investigation) to provide information on SARS' 'High Risk Investigation Unit' which, among other functions, allegedly spied on politicians.

After Manuel left government – where he was Finance Minister under Nelson Mandela, Thabo Mbeki and Kgalema Motlanthe from 1996 to 2009, and then Minister in the Presidency for the National Planning Commission under Zuma until 2014 – he took a number of positions in the world of capital.

These included being deputy chair of the South African franchise of British multinational investment bankers Rothschild and chairperson of Old Mutual plc.

Manuel's qualifications included a National Diploma in Civil and Structural Engineering from the Peninsula Technikon in Cape Town and the completion of an Executive Management Programme at Stanford University in the United States.

Fast forward to 2018 and President Cyril Ramaphosa announced Manuel as a special envoy on investment, deployed to attract US$100 billion in new investment into the country's economy, in April 2018. The other envoys were former Deputy Minister of Finance Mcebisi Jonas, executive chairperson of Afropulse Group Phumzile Langeni and former CEO of Standard Bank, Jacko Maree.

Manuel is married to Maria Ramos, the CEO of Absa Group Limited.

Manyi, Mzwanele

Member of the African Transformation Movement (ATM) national executive committee | ATM policy and strategy head | Former media owner | Former chairperson of the Black Management Forum (BMF) | Former chairperson of the Commission for Employment Equality | Former director-general of the Department of Labour | Formerly ANC-aligned

Linked to capture

MANYI SHOWED NO EMOTION WHEN he confirmed in January 2019 that he had left the ANC, which had been his political home for more than 30 years. He taunted the Twitterverse for days before holding a press conference, leading to speculation that he was joining Black First Land First (BLF). But Manyi threw a curveball when he said he had joined the ATM, which registered as a political party in June 2018.

Within a few days, he was, however, involved in a fracas with the All African Decolonisation Congress (AADC), which he founded. It 'dismissed' Manyi with immediate effect, saying he had 'blindsided' it by joining the ATM, and accused Manyi of wanting to use money he had raised from the Guptas for AADC, to fund the ATM.

Manyi had experience in management and presenting high-level entities to the public when his company, Afrotone Media Holdings, bought the TV channel formerly known as ANN7 and the newspaper formerly known as *The New Age* in a vendor financing arrangement in 2017.

A government spokesperson, the chairperson of the Black Management Forum and the Commission for Employment Equality, he also held the post of director-general (DG) of the Department of Labour. He did, however, attract controversy and anger in his role as DG when labour quotas were discussed in 2011, saying that there was a 'surplus' of coloured people in the Western Cape, and they would need to find employment in other parts of the country.

On the subject of Afrotone, Manyi bought the entities from the disgraced Gupta family's Oakbay Investments, with the Guptas themselves having 'loaned' him the money, and the 'deal' – then involving Manyi's new company Lodidox – was not a politically uncomplicated exchange. Manyi claimed in May 2017 that he had repaid the 'loan' in full. ANN7 had cost R300 million and *The New Age* R150 million.

By the time he announced three new shareholders for his rebranded company – as TV station Afro WorldView and *Afro Voice* newspaper – he was battling credibility on a massive scale. In August 2018, pay TV company MultiChoice cancelled his TV station's contract. By the end of that month, Manyi's station was off air permanently, and *Afro Voice* had already closed.

Marikana Massacre

State-sanctioned murder of 34 striking mineworkers | The bloodiest post-apartheid security operation

THE MEDIA WAS DRAWN TO THE MARIKANA platinum mine – operated by Lonmin, a British producer of platinum group metals operating in South Africa – at Nkaneng outside Rustenburg in the North West province on 11 August 2012. Violence was brewing between workers and their employer. Some 3,000 rock drillers had initiated a wildcat strike the day before when management would not meet with them over a proposed pay raise to R12,500, but there was also anger and rivalry between the unions representing the workers there: the National Council of Trade Unions (Nactu) affiliate, the Association of Mineworkers and Construction Union (AMCU), and its rival, the National Union of Mineworkers (NUM), an affiliate of Nactu rival the Congress of South African Trade Unions (Cosatu). Although NUM, an ANC supporter through its Cosatu links, had once held sway in Marikana, this was no longer the case, with its representation there having dropped to just below 50%.

Meanwhile, a key former leader of its own – NUM co-founder Cyril Ramaphosa – was a non-executive director of Lonmin. Ramaphosa is now the president of South Africa, but at the time of the massacre, he was a billionaire businessman whose company, Shanduka, was a minority shareholder in Lonmin, and his exchange with its management on the day before the massacre has haunted him. He said he believed 'criminal acts' had taken place and emails show that he had urged action from the police to control the strikers.

Ramaphosa testified the same to the Farlam Commission of Inquiry which then president Jacob Zuma eventually set up in the wake of massive outrage over 34 mostly state-sanctioned murders on 16 August. At least 112 people were injured, with the shootings having taken place at two locations about 500 metres away from each other.

Most of the dead were killed in R5 assault rifle police gunfire. Their deaths and those injuries followed the deaths of 10 people on or around the mine, including six mineworkers, two security guards who worked for Lonmin and two South African Police Service (SAPS) members between 12 and 14 August. But the violence had been sparked on that 11 August day when shooters linked to NUM opened fire on their own members embarking on the strike, seriously wounding two.

Since his inauguration as president, Ramaphosa has made a plea for action, effectively acknowledging that he is himself still tainted by the deaths.

He was, however, cleared by the Farlam Commission, whose 2016 report was widely criticised for failing to identify responsibility at a senior level of government and business and, thereafter, failing at adequate reparation.

Mashaba, Herman

Mayor of Johannesburg | Billionaire entrepreneur

THE FOUNDER OF THE BLACK LIKE ME hair products empire and a liberal businessman, who had no overt political identity before the Democratic Alliance (DA) recruited him, Mashaba burst onto the political scene in late 2015.

The DA allocated him the Johannesburg campaign for the local elections in 2016, with Mashaba promising he would end cadre redeployment, reduce the size of the department allocated to billing, link small and big business together and audit buildings, among other plans.

He won his seat once the hung metro was resolved in August 2016. But by 2018 Mashaba's results were a mixed bag, with the city's infrastructure crumbling ever more rapidly, billing still in crisis, and especially foreigners under a more challenging housing crunch than ever.

Mashaba likely realised his job as mayor was going to be tougher than he thought already in 2016 when the DA's press conference with its coalition partners, the Congress of the People (COPE), the United Democratic Movement (UDM), the African Christian Democratic Party (ACDP) and the Freedom Front Plus (FFP), was marred by its most important coalition partner, the Economic Freedom Fighters (EFF) attaching a condition to its agreement that the DA could elect the mayor.

It said it would not approve Mashaba, leaving the DA's leader Mmusi Maimane in a difficult position, having to defend the party's candidate by saying the people of Johannesburg had been promised Mashaba. The EFF stated that Mashaba had 'backward views' on poor black people, while the EFF leader, Julius Malema, claimed that Mashaba 'wanted to be white'. Maimane was then drawn to say that, if the wrangle deepened and the EFF abstained from voting for council leaders, the DA may have to 'forfeit' the EFF's crucial 11.09% into the coalition, which would have allowed the ANC to keep Johannesburg as a minority government.

Mashaba in turn said he would step aside if requested by the DA, but the EFF's determination to keep the ANC out of governing won, and Malema then indicated it would be 'cowardly to abstain'.

Mashaba was dogged by accusations that he was anti-foreigners, as he tended to single out asylum-seekers and economic refugees when he referred to Johannesburg's social problems. In August 2018, the Socio-Economic Rights Institute (Seri) accused Mashaba and the city of acting in contravention of two court orders, which compelled it to provide temporary accommodation to evictees, but Mashaba said that under his leadership, the city would never build houses for foreign nationals.

In October 2017, Mashaba came under fire from social justice activists when illegal migrants were persistently cleared off the streets where they were hawking small goods, and evicted from hijacked buildings.

But by January 2019, the media had also been reporting on either a 'growing closeness' between the mayor and the EFF, or the mayor 'over-thinking' the EFF's role in city government.

Mashatile, Paul

ANC treasurer-general | Former minister of Arts and Culture | Former Gauteng premier | Former Gauteng ANC chairperson | Former United Democratic Front (UDF) general-secretary | Former political prisoner

On the way up | Linked to corruption

MASHATILE WAS A CRITIC OF JACOB ZUMA before it became politically fashionable and the former president saw enough of a threat in the long-time activist to fire him from his administration before Mashatile could put any more obstacles in the way of state capture.

It was more difficult for Zuma to control Mashatile as the Gauteng ANC chairperson, particularly as the Gauteng ANC itself was not a protagonist of his presidency of the party. It had felt aggrieved that its support had fallen by a dramatic 10% in the 2014 provincial (and national) elections, blaming a large proportion of this on Zuma's perceived corruption and mismanagement of the economy.

Zuma removed Mashatile as Gauteng premier, a position to which his party had appointed him, after only eight months in 2009, instead giving Mashatile what had become known as the 'charity' Cabinet post – Arts and Culture – in order to elevate an acolyte, Nomvula Mokonyane, to premier.

The Gauteng Provincial Executive Committee (PEC) was against Mokonyane becoming premier, but that is not the choice of the PEC, and rather the choice of the State President. It was Zuma's wish that Mokonyane become chairperson of the Gauteng ANC in 2012, but Mashatile won that vote.

When he left Cabinet, Mashatile returned to Gauteng as MEC for Human Settlements and Co-Operative Governance. He was elected ANC Treasurer and a member of its elite Top 6 at the party's elective conference at Nasrec, Johannesburg, in December 2017.

No matter his highs and lows on the premium political stage, it was likely

Mashatile would also be remembered for being the 'Don' of the so-called 'Alex mafia'. But that seemingly playful appellation came with dark undertones.

The other main 'members' of that clique – who mixed business and pleasure after they were liberation fighters in Alexandra township, Johannesburg during apartheid – were Mike Maile (brother of ANC politician Lebogang Maile), Nkenke Kekana – a former ANC MP who chaired the National Assembly's communications portfolio committee – and Bridgman Sithole.

Allegations of corruption entered their shared histories a decade after the first democratic elections when Maile was chief executive of the Gauteng Shared Service Centre (GSSC), which fell under Mashatile and which awarded tenders to a company called Business Connexion, of which Kekana and Sithole were shareholders and board members of its various firms. Mashatile both said he had shares, and then disowned them. Further, Mashatile's daughter, Palesa, was employed by Business Connexion, which won GSSC tenders.

There were allegations that a consultant known to Mashatile had paid the fees for his nephew's tertiary studies, while other business conflicts involving the 'Alex mafia' were also raised by the Mail & Guardian's investigations team in 2007.

Mashinini, Sam

Elected ANC Free State provincial chairperson in May 2018 | Former Free State leader of the National Union of Mineworkers (NUM)

On the way up | Power broker

A TRADE UNIONIST AND FORMER CONGRESS of South African Trade Unions (Cosatu) provincial secretary, Mashinini was elected unopposed in an election that was largely closed to the media. The election was expected to pave the way for Mashinini to take over as premier of the province after the 2019 national elections, taking over from Sisi Ntombela, who, in turn, assumed the position in April 2018 after former premier Ace Magashule was appointed as the secretary-general of the ANC in December 2017.

Mashinini – who served as Free State leader of the National Union of Mineworkers (NUM) when Cyril Ramaphosa was the NUM's general-secretary in the late 1980s – was adamant that the province should 'move forward' and support Ramaphosa. This was because the Free State had been cited as one of the 'Premier League' provinces which had supported former president Jacob Zuma and then ANC National Executive Committee (NEC) member Nkosazana Dlamini-Zuma as the preferred candidate to succeed Zuma as party president at the end of 2017.

Mashinini was not especially tainted by his association with Magashule in terms of corruption allegations, although he was accused of not acting against Sandile Msibi, a former department head, when he, Mashinini, was the MEC for Police in the Free State. Msibi, who died in 2017, was said to have illegally transferred money into friends' accounts.

Mashinini was previously an ANC MP.

Mashinini, Vuma Glen

Independent Electoral Commission (IEC) chairperson | Former deputy chairperson of the Presidential Review Committee on State-Owned Entities (SOEs)

MASHININI WAS INITIALLY SEEN AS A CONTROVERSIAL choice to head the IEC after Advocate Pansy Tlakula resigned following former Public Protector Thuli Madonsela's report that there had been a conflict of interest for her, Tlakula, in the R320-million lease of a new head office.

The reason for him being a 'controversial' choice was that Mashinini had been a special advisor to Jacob Zuma, after serving as the deputy chairperson of the Presidential Review Committee on State-Owned Entities (SOEs). But Mashinini was undoubtedly qualified for the role, having been part of the original team that established the IEC, laying the foundations for its ongoing success and going on to provide electoral advice to Nigeria, Mozambique and Angola.

He allayed his critics' concerns, and his greatest achievement by mid-2018 was to ensure that the IEC is mostly in place to meet the Constitutional Court's demand that the commission update the voter's roll with the addresses of individual voters within an allotted deadline.

Masina, Mzwandile

Ekurhuleni ANC chairperson | Mayor of Ekurhuleni | Former deputy minister of Trade and Industry | Former ANC Youth League national convener

On the way up | Power broker

AN ANC YOUTH LEAGUE (ANCYL) MEMBER when he was 14, Masina grew up in the self-defence units on the streets of Katlehong outside Johannesburg, where civil war threatened as the democratic age drew nearer. He steadied his political trajectory when he went to the University of the Witwatersrand (Wits) and the University of Pretoria, emerging with a Master's in entrepreneurship – and a number of youth leadership awards.

Masina was a programme manager, the chief operations officer at the Gauteng Department of Sport, Arts, Culture and Recreation and, in 2012, the CEO of the Gauteng Film Commission.

He was the Deputy Minister of Trade and Industry before he moved back into metropolitan politics, and is regarded as a frontrunner in the ANC's bid to open its top leadership to younger achievers.

This is despite his vocal antipathy towards Cyril Ramaphosa before Ramaphosa was elected president of the ANC. After Ramaphosa's election, Masina felt differently, saying he was 'very happy with the outcome'. He claimed that he had been 'quoted out of context' on his earlier remarks.

Masina had an unfortunate reputation for public insults and was summoned by the ANC's top leadership around his rants, in particular against then Public

Protector (PP) Thuli Madonsela, in 2014. At the time the ANCYL national convener, Masina insulted Madonsela after she released her report into the upgrades at Jacob Zuma's Nkandla homestead. He said the report had 'disgusted' the ANCYL and that Madonsela 'must go'. He accused the PP's office of acting like a 'kangaroo court'.

Among the ANC leaders who called Masina to account were Nosiviwe Mapisa-Nqakula, Gwede Mantashe and Jackson Mthembu.

Masondo, David

ANC MP | Former chief director for the Gauteng Department of Economic Development | Former chairperson of the Young Communist League (YCL)

On the way up | Star

Although South Africans may not have been familiar with Masondo before, by 2018 they may be, especially if he is selected to replace public services minister Pravin Gordhan as Gordhan is planning on leaving government by the 2019 elections. Gordhan had indicated it would be important to groom a younger politician to take up the post. Masondo fits the ANC's plans to bring in a younger generation of cadre who have the intellectual base and political credentials to take the ideological and class edge off a surging Economic Freedom Fighters (EFF) in the 2019 polls.

Masondo was elected into the ANC's National Executive Committee (NEC) at its elective conference at Nasrec, Johannesburg, in December 2017, after an intense period of campaigning against then president Jacob Zuma.

He had been the CEO of the Automotive Industry Development Centre, having been headhunted when he was a lecturer at the University of the Witwatersrand (Wits), where he had once been the Student Representative Council president.

Masondo went on to become MEC for Provincial Treasury in Limpopo, but his time in government was placed in limbo when, in December 2011, the national executive placed five of Limpopo's government departments under administration. The province appeared to have gone bankrupt, but Masondo alleged in *City Press* newspaper in February 2018 that there might have been more to this that met the eye. His suggestion was that Treasury could have created a situation where Limpopo needed to be 'saved', and was effectively withholding funds.

Masondo previously served as the chief director for the Department of Economic Development in Gauteng.

Born in Limpopo, he was a teacher when he joined the ANC's alliance partner, the South African Communist Party (SACP), and eventually served on its central committee before he completed his PhD.

He completed his doctoral studies at New York University, his thesis on the effects of the Motor Industry Development Programme on the South African automotive industry. Masondo was the recipient of the Ford Foundation International Fellowships PhD Program award and the MacCracken PhD scholarship – both regarded as among the highest PhD accolades in the world.

Masualle, Phumulo

ANC Eastern Cape premier

IT LOOKED LIKE TIME WAS ALMOST UP for Masualle as premier in May 2018 when the ANC said it had given him an instruction to either reshuffle his failing Cabinet or face the consequences. Summoned to the party's Johannesburg headquarters, Luthuli House, Masualle looked like he was on a road to nowhere, possibly having to fire some of his loyalists in the interests of the party's survival in the 2019 elections.

In the end, compromises were struck that would see him bringing in people outside his own faction, representing the faction of Eastern Cape ANC chairperson Oscar Mabuyane. But it was clear even from Masualle's own statements that he would not remain as premier after the 2019 elections.

The province performed very badly in terms of governance on Masualle's watch, and was identified by the auditor-general as the worst in the country, with R13.5 billion in irregular and wasteful expenditure.

Masutha, Advocate Michael

Minister of Justice and Correctional Services | Former director of the Disability Rights Unit at Lawyers for Human Rights | Former head of legal services in the Department of Social Development

Star

BORN IN LIMPOPO, MASUTHA WAS A human rights lawyer before he entered government as an ANC MP in 1999 under the Thabo Mbeki administration. He rose to become Deputy Minister of Science and Technology in 2013 and was then appointed Minister of Justice and Correctional Services in 2014.

Despite a visual disability, Masutha earned his BJuris degree from the University of Limpopo (then the University of the North) in 1988 and obtained an LLB from the University of the Witwatersrand in 1991.

Masutha founded and participated in movements for disabled students when he was a student himself, advocating for the provision of appropriate support, and challenging the apartheid regime's treatment of disabled people. In 1986, he was a founding member of the Northern Transvaal Association for the Blind and then served as a member of the National Council for the Blind's Executive Committee where he advocated for the removal of discriminatory laws against blind people, especially in protective employment.

In 1991, Masutha participated in a delegation of the Human Rights Committee of Disabled People to the United Nations and was a director of the Disability Rights Unit at Lawyers for Human Rights, which provided legal assistance to people who were unfairly discriminated against on the basis of their disability.

Four years later, in 1996, Masutha was admitted as an advocate of the High Court of South Africa. That year, he was also appointed as the head of legal services in the Department of Social Development, where he specialised in children's rights and social security law.

After he became an ANC MP, Masutha served on a number of committees, including the Justice and Constitutional Development Committee, the Rules Committee and the Constitutional Review Committee. He chaired the Social Development Committee, the Standing Committee on the Auditor-General, the Sub-Committee on Review of Rules, the Ad Hoc Committee on Delegated Legislation and the Ad Hoc Committee that nominated the Public Protector.

Among his more challenging decisions as Justice and Correctional Services Minister was denying parole to South African Communist Party (SACP) and ANC hero Chris Hani's killer, Janusz Walus. Walus's co-accused, convicted killer Clive Derby-Lewis, was granted medical parole in 2015 after being diagnosed with terminal lung cancer.

Masutha, Makovhe

Former #FeesMustFall activist | Businessman and academic | ANC-aligned

Suspected of being a State Security agent while a student leader

Masutha came to attention in 2017 when he was revealed as an 'advisor' to former president Jacob Zuma around the fight for free tertiary education.

The executive director and senior researcher at the Johannesburg-based Centre for Emerging Researchers (CER) – which listed among its projects the 'Higher Education Fees Commission' – Masutha was a pivot for the very expensive shifts that government suddenly had to make in that arena. Zuma cited Masutha's research as the motivation for a profound decision in government policy to immediately award greater numbers of students free tertiary education. This was irrespective of probes government had itself done that showed that while there was a willingness, there might not necessarily have been the resources to pay for everybody. The most important among these investigations was the Heher Commission, appointed in 2016, which delivered its report at the end of 2017.

Masutha, who has a Master's degree in local economic development, started his career as a policy and strategy analyst at the City of Tshwane's Division of Economic Intelligence, and then volunteered and helped build Thusanani Foundation, a non-profit organisation aimed at improving access to higher education.

The chairperson of the South African Students Congress (SASCO) and president of the Students Representative Council (SRC) at the University of the Witwatersrand (Wits), Masutha served on the University's Council for Readmissions Committee for seven years.

A prominent member of the #FeesMustFall movement, Masutha was later alleged to have worked undercover for the State Security Agency (SSA) and was reportedly listed as an employee of the SSA when he was a student activist at Wits. It was also alleged that, at the time he compiled his research on fee-free tertiary education, he was having a relationship with Zuma's daughter Thuthukile.

Mathabatha, Stanley

Limpopo premier | Former ambassador to Ukraine | ANC politician

A renowned Umkhonto we Sizwe (MK) cadre, Mathabatha was linked to the ANC from his childhood years. His closest friend at that time was Peter Mokaba, an ANC activist whose detention under the Terrorism Act during apartheid only heightened Mokaba's resolve as he went on to become one of the party's staunchest and fieriest advocates.

Mathabatha was prominent in the United Democratic Front (UDF) in the 1980s, and selected to rebuild the ANC internally as the treasurer of the Northern Transvaal region in 1992. He served the ANC in various capacities in Limpopo, where politicians had to transform the former bantustan administrations of Lebowa, Venda and Gazankulu and the Transvaal Provincial Administration into one, democratic provincial administration.

With a Master's in development from the University of Limpopo and a trip to Harvard University in 2003, Mathabatha distinguished himself as a future top leader within the ANC.

As the general manager of the SMME directorate in the provincial Department of Finance and Economic Development in Limpopo (Limdev), he became the managing director of LimDev in 2005.

In 2010, he was the ambassador of South Africa in Ukraine, but returned in 2014 to take the chair of the ANC's Provincial Executive Committee (PEC) in Limpopo.

A bitter power battle in the province was won in June 2018 when its conference was ratified and Mathabatha declared leader.

Mathale, Cassel

Deputy minister of Small Business Development | Former Limpopo premier | ANC MP

Linked to corruption

Public sector contracts seemed to have been a source of personal wealth for Mathale whose links to Manaka Property Investments, which rented buildings in Pretoria to government departments, with Thaba Mufamadi, then chairperson of Parliament's finance committee and former MEC for Economic Development in Limpopo, and with property billionaire Jannie Moolman, then chairperson of the Limpopo Tender Board who was appointed by Mufamadi, turned out to be highly lucrative.

Mathale – who was premier of Limpopo from 2009 to 2013 – also oversaw the placing of his province under administration when it was claimed its treasury was effectively bankrupt, and Limpopo needed R2 billion to keep afloat.

A former ANC Youth League (ANCYL) leader and once an important ally of former ANCYL president Julius Malema – now leader of the Economic Freedom Fighters (EFF) – Mathale was accused of defying Treasury's supply chain management regulations. Moolman apparently awarded a number of tenders to spurious companies.

Finance minister Pravin Gordhan said there had been 'sufficient evidence that there have been attempts at sabotaging service delivery (in Limpopo) to blame non-delivery on the national government'.

Mathale resigned as Limpopo premier in 2013, having dared Jacob Zuma to have him arrested. He was then redeployed by the party to be an ANC MP.

Mathys, Leigh-Ann

Economic Freedom Fighters (EFF) treasurer-general | EFF MP

On the way up | Star

Mathys was a social justice activist who, by her own admission, became 'an accidental politician' after she joined the fledgling party, the Economic Freedom Fighters (EFF), in 2013. With a commitment to the cause of the EFF and a history of fundraising for community-based organisations rather than a background in formal politics, she was placed in the interim leadership and tasked with managing finances and administration.

In September 2016, Mathys was elected to the position of treasurer-general vacated by former EFF Commissar Magdalene Moonsamy in September 2016. (Moonsamy, who had left the ANC together with EFF leader Julius Malema and others in 2012, resigned to concentrate on her legal practice.) This placed Mathys on the party's Central Command Team (CCT), the party's highest decision-making body between its National People's Assemblies.

She was deployed to the National Assembly as an MP in 2014, whereupon she was selected as the party's National Council of Provinces (NCOP) delegate until 2016.

Maynier, David

Shadow Minister of Finance | Democratic Alliance (DA) politician

On the way up | Star

Maynier returned from Harvard in 2008 with a Master's in public administration and was appointed DA campaign manager in the Western Cape, where the party won an outright majority in the 2009 elections.

He was elected as a DA MP that year.

Maynier's association with the DA went back to 1999, when he joined the party as a researcher, rising to being its director of research, and then chief of staff to former party leader Tony Leon. In 2004, Maynier was named assistant to the chairperson of the federal executive, later promoted to director of fundraising, and then to the DA's deputy CEO with special responsibility for the Western Cape.

The DA won 51.3% of the vote in that province in 2009, up remarkably from 27% in 2004. The DA then took control of the Western Cape provincial legislature in an alliance with politician Patricia de Lille's Independent Democrats (ID).

Before Maynier was Shadow Minister of Finance, he was Shadow Minister of Defence, which allowed him the platform to make a number of significant revelations. Among these was that South Africa's National Conventional Arms

Control Committee appeared not to have taken cognisance of weapons deals being conducted between South African companies and then rogue states North Korea, Iran and Libya. Maynier also pushed for a parliamentary inquiry into what the DA believed was the South African National Defence Force's intervention in the Central African Republic (CAR) coup.

Mazibuko, Lindiwe

Former federal leader of the Democratic Alliance (DA) | Harvard fellow

Change agent

THE FORMER LEADER OF THE OFFICIAL OPPOSITION in Parliament, Mazibuko resigned in 2015 to take up a fellowship at the Harvard Institute of Politics and, through that experience, was enjoined to the ranks of the World Economic Forum (WEF) as a Young Global Leader.

After completing her Master's in public administration at Harvard, Mazibuko joined the London- and Berlin-based company apolitical – a global network that seeks to help public servants around the world find partners to solve challenges. The apolitical Academy, which Mazibuko launched to a South African audience in May 2018 in the presence of President Cyril Ramaphosa, was designed to train young people in public service.

Although Mazibuko resigned from the leadership of the DA, she continued to support the party, and in mid-2018, attempts to lure her back into active politics went public, especially as nominations were being accepted for the premierships of KwaZulu-Natal and Gauteng in the event there was a liberal victory in 2019.

Mazzone, Natasha

Democratic Alliance (DA) second deputy Federal Council chairperson | DA MP

HER SEEMINGLY NO-NONSENSE APPROACH during the Eskom inquiry in Parliament in February and March 2018 put the DA MP in the national spotlight. Populist, using catch-phrases from TV shows like *Game of Thrones* when she has grilled politicians purported to be captured, she was also gaining political experience as a member of the Parliamentary Portfolio Committee on Public Enterprises.

Then, seemingly out of the blue, Mazzone was elected as the DA's second deputy Federal Council chairperson, a new position, at the party's congress in April 2018. But she did not receive unqualified support from within her own party, where there were even threats of court action from those who believed her election was procedurally flawed. In particular, Gauteng South DA chairperson Khume Ramulifho, who contested for the same position, said he had found errors in Mazzone's appointment.

Her election seemed to spur on a fundamental debate in the DA between its white members and those black members who supported quotas for its seats under the mentorship of DA leader Mmusi Maimane. Maimane ratified Mazzone's appointment.

Her sudden rise was accompanied by a further drop in her appeal when she sounded shrill and authoritarian when she was publicly unsupportive of Patricia de Lille at the time of De Lille's war with the DA over the mayorship of Cape Town.

Mbalula, Fikile

Nicknames: Mr Razzmatazz; Mbaweezy; Mbaks; Mr Fearfokkol | ANC Elections head | Former minister of Police | Former minister of Sports and Recreation | Former deputy minister of Police | Former ANC Youth League (ANCYL) leader

MBALULA WAS ONE OF THE ANC's assets going into the 2019 elections. He had the personality, chutzpah and the down-to-earth approach that the party had lacked as it fell into disrepute under state capture allegations.

The former Cabinet minister was already a long-time member of the ANC National Executive Committee (NEC) by that time, and appeared to have overcome the potential disadvantages of being favoured by former president Jacob Zuma, with Mbalula's loyalty to Zuma having earned him political rewards.

Mbalula had many years of political experience under his belt, having been an area manager for the United Democratic Front (UDP) in 1989.

The ANC awarded him the extraordinary task of winning back the people in their numbers to put their crosses in its boxes on the 2019 ballot sheet, but this was not the first time the man known as 'Mr Razzmatazz' had performed that task for the party.

A political bellwether, Mbalula managed the ANC's successful election campaign in 2009 when Zuma was elected as state president, having previously also been credited as paving the way for him to become ANC president at the highly contested Polokwane elective conference in 2007 over Thabo Mbeki. Mbalula had previously been credited with having smoothed the path for Mbeki to become ANC president in 1998.

Despite receiving mostly praise for insisting on quotas in sport when he was the minister responsible for that area, he did not impress as a credible politician.

Mbalula's tweets have become legendary, however – for their comedy, naivete and sometimes ignorance. But there was a backlash on Twitter in January 2019 when his former adviser, Bongani (Bo) Mbindwane, was implicated by the Independent Police Investigative Directorate (IPID) in a plot allegedly involving top South African Police Services and crime intelligence officers.

It was claimed Mbindwane had met with the officials in the week before the ANC's national conference at Nasrec in 2017 to discuss the unlawful procurement of a 'grabber' – at three times its commercial price – for spying purposes to support Nkosazana-Zuma's presidential bid.

Mbalula, who was police minister at the time of the alleged events, said he had no knowledge of the meeting. IPID's affidavit also cited video evidence purporting to show that national police commissioner Khehla Sitole was there.

It was unlikely to be forgotten that Mbalula was linked to one of South Africa's most notorious 'corruptors', mining magnate Brett Kebble, when Mbalula was in the ANC Youth League. Kebble – who orchestrated his own suicide in 2005 – was believed to have 'mentored' Mbalula and other ANCYL leaders, as well as funding their lifestyles.

And while 2019 looked to be a challenge, 2018 hadn't ended well for Mbalula. Public Protector Busisiwe Mkhwebane found he had violated the Constitution by asking South African Sports Confederation and Olympic Committee (SASCOC) supplier Sedgars to foot the bill for a family hoiliday in Dubai in 2016.

Mbalula called it a 'loan', but Mkhwebane said instead that it would have been 'inappropriate' for him to enter into a 'loan agreement' with a company supplying SASCOC. She ordered the National Prosecuting Authority to investigate 'possible money laundering'.

Mbete, Baleka

Speaker of the National Assembly | Former deputy president of South Africa (under Kgalema Motlanthe) | Former National Council of Provinces (NCOP) deputy chairperson | Representative to the Pan-African Parliament (PAP) | Former national chairperson of the ANC

Inappropriate use of her position | Possible links with corruption

MBETE WENT INTO EXILE IN 1976, first teaching in Mbabane, eSwatini, and then working for the ANC in Tanzania, Kenya, Botswana, Zimbabwe and Zambia, returning from exile in 1990.

Mbete was elected secretary-general of the ANC Women's League after her return, and then as an ANC MP, having been voted onto the party's National Executive Committee (NEC). She was appointed chairperson of the ANC parliamentary caucus in 1995 and was Deputy Speaker of the National Assembly (NA) from 1996 to 2004. During that time, she was a member of the Presidential Panel on the Truth and Reconciliation Commission, and was selected for the original group of five South African parliamentarians to serve on the Pan-African Parliament.

In 2004, Mbete became the Speaker of the National Assembly and, three years later, the ANC's national chairperson by vote at the party's explosive elective conference in Polokwane, Limpopo.

It's been speculated on more than one occasion that Mbete would become state president, markedly in 2008 when Thabo Mbeki was recalled by the ANC. Instead, she assumed the position of deputy president to caretaker president Kgalema Motlanthe. Even when Jacob Zuma was elected president in May 2009, he chose to appoint Motlanthe as his deputy, and not Mbete.

Although she was returned to the position of Speaker in 2014, Mbete would begin a more difficult period in that seat. Her first battle would be with five opposition parties – led by the Democratic Alliance (DA) and the Economic Freedom Fighters (EFF) – planning to take action against her for holding both the ANC chairperson position, and that of Speaker. The plan was to institute a motion of no confidence in her but, in the end, it was rejected because those five parties had walked out of Parliament after the ANC interfered with the process.

That would not the last time Mbete – believed to be the highest-paid official in Parliament – faced opposition. On other occasions, she was accused of favouring the ANC, particularly former president Jacob Zuma. In fact, she was regarded by some as wilfully merging party and state affairs because of her dual position of being both the ANC's chairperson and Speaker.

An improperly issued driver's licence, chartering a jet at massive tax-payers' expense, spurious links with corrupt members of the ANC and dubious, perhaps corrupt, private business interests did not assist Mbete's reputation. Neither did her unfortunate description of the EFF as 'cockroaches', which brought to mind the deadly use of the word just before the genocide in Rwanda in 1994.

Mbindwane, Bongane (Bo) (see Mbalula, Fikile)

Mboweni, Tito

Nickname: Sha sha | Minister of Finance | Former Reserve Bank governor | Former minister of Labour | Former ANC NEC member | Former ANC National Working Committee (NWC) member | Former chair of the ANC NEC's Economic Transformation Committee and of the ANC's Policy Department | Advisor to Goldman Sachs | Non-executive director at the New Development Bank | Former chancellor of the University of the North West | Former professor of economics, Stellenbosch Univerity | Member of the board of governors at the Asia School of Business | Honorary professor in the School of Economic and Business Sciences, University of the Witwatersrand

Power broker

MBOWENI APPEARED TO HAVE MADE HIMSELF quite a comfortable and independent life outside of government and the ANC's bureaucratic cut-and-thrust when he was suddenly thrown right back into it after finance minister Nhlanhla Nene resigned and President Cyril Ramaphosa appointed him, Mboweni, in Nene's stead in October 2018.

Mboweni had gained a fairly inclusive following. He had been a successful governor of the South African Reserve Bank (SARB) – the first black South African to hold the post – which allowed capital and especially white people to be drawn to him, while he had also shown some Leftist leanings on Twitter during his time outside government, which had pleased protagonists on that side of the fray.

A founder member of Mboweni Brothers Investment Holdings and international advisor of Goldman Sachs International, Mboweni was also a non-executive director for South Africa at the New Development Bank at the time of his appointment by Ramaphosa.

But he has deep ANC roots, having been an activist throughout his youth, even while he was studying towards his BA in economics and political science at the National University of Lesotho. By 1988, Mboweni had attained a Master's in development economics from the University of East Anglia in England.

He was the first post-apartheid Minister of Labour, regarded as an architect of South Africa's new labour legislation. His experience within the Department of Economic Policy in the ANC assisted greatly, and he had a significant enough portfolio to represent the liberation movement and then the party on local, African and international platforms.

Upon joining the SARB as advisor to then governor Dr Chris Stals in 1998, he resigned all of his elected and appointed positions in the ANC. He succeeded Stals in 1999. Mboweni was himself succeeded by ANC stalwart Gill Marcus in 2009.

McBride, Robert

Head of the Independent Police Investigative Directorate (IPID) | Former Chief of Police, Ekurhuleni municipality | Former death row inmate

THE POLICE OMBUDSMAN'S WORDS WERE CHILLING: 'We are turning into a mafia state.' That was September 2016 and McBride, the head of IPID, had just been reinstated in his job after the Constitutional Court ruled his suspension by then police minister, Nkosinathi Nhleko, unlawful.

McBride gave a little more detail: 'It's a power game to loot, rob and steal.' He might have been right.

It had previously been said McBride would be charged with alleged racketeering and he was rumoured to face imminent arrest but, customarily unemotional, he showed no fear. The background – involving former acting National Police Commissioner (NPC) Kgomotso Phahlane, who had been under scrutiny from IPID for his alleged corrupt activities – was, however, disturbing.

McBride would regain some stability in his key position after Police Minister Fikile Mbalula, South African Police Service (SAPS) National Commissioner General Khehla Sitole and former acting NPC Lesetja Mothiba, spoke out. It was suggested that Phahlane had a 'protection squad', which may have been seeking to 'undermine a legitimate investigation of massive corruption in the SAPS without anybody telling them to stop'.

Yet the drama continued, McBride summarising it in May 2018 by saying 'when there are investigations against officers, there will be some pushback'.

But that was not McBride's only drama. He had also been accused of violating the Children's Act after he allegedly physically attacked his 15-year-old daughter, but those charges were later dropped.

McBride led the Umkhonto we Sizwe (MK) cell that bombed the Why Not Restaurant and Magoo's Bar in Durban in June 1986 in which three were killed and 69 injured. He was convicted and sentenced to death, but the sentence was later commuted to life. He was released in 1992 after his actions were classified as politically motivated, and granted amnesty at the Truth and Reconciliation Commission (TRC).

McBride's first experience in the police force was when he was Chief of the Metropolitan Police of Ekurhuleni Municipality. He was sacked in 2008, two months before his contract expired, while he was still on trial for drunk driving after he crashed his state vehicle following a work party. McBride denied all the charges and was paid out for his full contract with his legal fees for existing cases also to be paid by the government.

He would experience more 'pushback' in January 2019 when Minister of Police Bheki Cele said he would not be renewing his (McBride's) five-year contract. McBride – who was at the time giving his support as executive director to a number of high-level probes involving key officials – claimed Cele was violating IPID's 'legislated independence'.

This reverts back to that Constitutional Court (ConCourt) ruling in his favour in 2016, which confirmed that the Minister of Police does not have the power to intervene in IPID matters. A decision not to renew the executive director's contract is vested in the National Assembly's Portfolio Committee on Police, which also makes appointments to the post.

The IPID head is not a public servant employed by the Minister of Police.

Cele had advised that McBride's last day would be 28 February 2019.

McCauley, Ray

Pastor | Head of the National Interfaith Leaders Council

LARGER THAN LIFE, RAY MCCAULEY, the bodybuilder and night club bouncer-turned-pastor to the stars and the elite, has worked hard to position himself as one of South Africa's religious leaders.

Born in Johannesburg in 1949, he dropped out of school in Grade 10 (then Standard 8) to train as a hairdresser, but left this to become a bodybuilder, ultimately coming third in the 1974 Mr Universe which Arnold Schwarzenegger won.

He and his first wife, Lindie, went to a Bible college in Tulsa, Oklahoma, in the United States, returning to his parents' home in Blairgowrie, Johannesburg to start their church, Rhema, in the lounge – with 13 congregants. Within a year this had grown to 1800.

Today the church has a sprawling Johannesburg campus, a TV channel and branches the length and breadth of the country spreading a revivalist prosperity gospel to an increasingly transformed upper-middle-class elite tithing in the millions of rand every month.

McCauley meanwhile managed to get himself elected as the head of the National Interfaith Leaders Council of South Africa by former president Jacob Zuma.

Never one to shy away from courting celebrities, he was the pastor to whom disgraced cricketer Hansie Cronje confessed about his match-fixing scandal, but McCauley has also wooed politicians, chief among them, Zuma. The church also provided a refuge for two disgraced high-fliers, former newspaper editor Vusi Mona and perpetual fraudster Carl Niehaus – both of whom act as Rhema spokespersons.

Mchunu, Senzo

Former premier of KwaZulu-Natal | Former provincial chairperson of KZN ANC | Redeployed to the ANC's headquarters, Luthuli House, to assist in organising the party ahead of the 2019 elections | Member of the ANC's National Working Committee (NWC)

A HIGH SCHOOL TEACHER WITH A BA in education and international relations, Mchunu's career took a different path after he married Thembeka Mchunu, who would become the uThungulu District Mayor. (uThungulu includes the town of Richards Bay and former president Jacob Zuma's hometown Nkandla.)

It's unlikely that, at the time he was appointed scribe and then first secretary of the party's regional interim committee in northern Natal in 1991, Mchunu would have envisioned the political drama that would explode around him and the ANC in KZN in 2016 and 2017.

By 1994, he was KZN provincial secretary and that afforded him the opportunity to become a Member of the Provincial Legislature (MPL) and, later, chairperson of the Agriculture Portfolio Committee.

Mchunu then did a Master's in political transformation at the University of the Free State, returning to KZN to become the chairperson of the Social Development Portfolio Committee and chair of the Education Portfolio Committee.

By 2009, he entered a more influential arena as Member of the Executive Committee (MEC) for Education in KZN. Then came the seat of provincial chair and, finally in 2013, the premiership.

During that time, the ANC's tectonic plates started shifting, and Mchunu was replaced as provincial chair in 2015 by rival Sihle Zikalala during a disputed provincial elective conference. A lengthy court battle followed, with complicated debates over the legality and meaning of the conference itself.

Although Mchunu would not return to his old position as he had joined the campaign to see Cyril Ramaphosa elected ANC president in 2017, there were reports that he was expecting to be named Minister of State Security in Ramaphosa's Cabinet. But he was instead given a full-time position at Luthuli House as head of the organising subcommittee for the governing party.

He was narrowly pipped by Ace Magashule to become ANC secretary-general at the party's elective conference at Nasrec in Johannesburg in December 2017.

McKinsey

Disgraced consulting firm

Investigated for corruption

A CRIMINAL INQUIRY WAS EXPECTED INTO MCKINSEY, the American consulting giant with offices in South Africa, over its relationship with Trillian Asset Managers, a front company linked to the controversial Gupta family, which had engineered a billion-rand contract involving Eskom, the state-owned utility.

The firm fell on its sword in 2017, saying there had indeed been 'multiple transgressions', including the fact that McKinsey had not provided Eskom with any service that could be invoiced for that amount, and that there had been no bidding process. McKinsey allowed South Africa senior partner Vikas Sagar to resign.

But its mea culpa would not necessarily be its saviour.

The R1 billion, which McKinsey was paid by Eskom for the illegal contract, was frozen, with McKinsey insisting it would pay it back. Eskom had taken legal action to recover the funds from McKinsey.

The National Prosecuting Authority (NPA) filed papers in the North Gauteng High Court in Pretoria in May 2018 in an application for a forfeiture order against McKinsey.

Mdluli, Richard

Former head of the Police Crime Intelligence Unit | Deputy head of the Gauteng police | Former member of the apartheid Security Police

Investigated for kidnapping, assault, murder, unlawful appointments and the misuse of public money | Relieved of his position in 2018

MDLULI'S CAREER AS A POLICEMAN LOOKED to finally be over in January 2018 when he was finally relieved of his duties by the Minister of Police. He had been under suspension for seven years, staying at home on a full salary with benefits.

Mdluli was arrested in 2011 on 18 charges relating to the murder of his ex-girlfriend's husband. These included intimidation, kidnapping, assault with the intent to do grievous bodily harm, and defeating the ends of justice. Thereafter, he was suspended by then National Police Commissioner (NPC) Bheki Cele, and charged also with unlawful appointments and the misuse of police money.

His suspension would be lifted, and then applied again, the charges thrown out and then effected or dropped again in an ongoing saga which cost taxpayers about R10 million.

His trajectory – joining the apartheid South African Police Force in 1979, to becoming part of its reviled Security Police, and then being integrated into a new, post-democracy SAPS – was not necessarily that different to other policemen of his era who achieved seniority.

But Mdluli – who became a station commander and the deputy head of the Gauteng police, before he was placed in charge of the key Crime Intelligence Unit in 2009, the year Jacob Zuma was elected president – seemed to be protected by Zuma. Crime Intelligence grew in influence under Mdluli's watch, including being given control over the VIP Protection Unit.

Mdluli left his job on a full pension with benefits.

Meshoe, Reverend Kenneth

Founder and president of the African Christian Democratic Party (ACDP) | ACDP MP

MESHOE WAS A MEMBER OF THE Parliamentary Portfolio Committee on Small Business Development, but failed to distinguish himself – except in one contrarian arena.

Consistent in his view that Israel is not an apartheid state, Meshoe made headlines for his strong stance against Palestinian rights and for Israeli settlement, and was the most outspoken member of the South African government in support of United States President Donald Trump's announcement that Jerusalem was Israel's capital.

Meshoe was a teacher before he became a pastor and then a political leader. He founded the ACDP in December 1993 and was a member of the National Assembly from 1994.

Awarded an honorary doctorate by Bethel Christian College of Riverside, California in 1994, Meshoe and his wife Lydia had more than 30 years of experience in Christian ministry work, having started their church, Hope of Glory Tabernacle, in the Vosloorus township outside Johannesburg, in 1988.

They had previously worked for the evangelical Christ of All Nations Church for more than 10 years.

Mfeketo, Nomaindia

Minister of Human Settlements | Former deputy minister of International Relations and Co-Operation | Former deputy speaker of the National Assembly | Former ANC mayor of Cape Town | Member of the ANC's National Working Committee (NWC)

MFEKETO DID NOT START HER POLITICAL career as an ANC cadre. Instead, she was an activist in NGOs during apartheid. These included the Zakhe Agricultural College and Training Institute, the Social Change Assistance Trust (SCAT) and the Development Action Group (DAG), all in Cape Town.

It was her work with DAG that introduced her to formal politics, when she was elected chairperson of the first democratically elected city council in Cape Town during the 'pre-interim phase' (see Local Government separate entry) in 1996–98. She then found herself in the mayor's seat by 2002, having ousted Gerald Morkel of the Democratic Alliance (DA). Mfeketo held the post until the DA regained control of the Cape Town city council in 2006, after which Helen Zille took office.

Elected to the ANC's National Executive Committee (NEC) in 2007, Mfeketo was accused by the DA in 2009 of having received a government-funded, custom-built mansion worth R8 million, allegedly in her capacity as Deputy Speaker of the National Assembly. This, despite Mfeketo owning her own private residence about 9 km away.

Mfeketo had also been accused of flouting the Constitution and the rules of the National Assembly in 2012, seemingly to protect then president Jacob Zuma from criticism by opposition party members. But in January 2019, it looked like the minister was taking particular strain. She had placed the Housing Development Agency (HAD) under administration after its chief executive officer Pascal Moloi and a number of executives and senior managers were suspended following allegations of 'financial irregularities' and 'sexual misconduct'.

Mhlantla, Justice Nonkosi

Constitutional Court (ConCourt) Justice

A B Proc graduate, Mhlantla had her own firm of attorneys for 10 years before being permanently appointed to the Eastern Cape High Court in 2002. She served there until 2009 when she was elevated to the Supreme Court of Appeal (SCA) in Bloemfontein. In 2012 she was asked to join the Constitutional Court (ConCourt) bench in Johannesburg. Mhlantla acted for a year before returning to the SCA. She was confirmed as a ConCourt justice in 2015.

Mhlantla's appointment, filling an 18-month-long vacancy brought about by the retirement of Justice Thembile Skweyia, was partly made to address the severe gender imbalance at the ConCourt of two female judges in an 11-member bench.

Mkhaliphi, Hlengiwe

Deputy secretary-general of the Economic Freedom Fighters (EFF) | Member of the EFF's Central Command Team (CCT) | EFF parliamentary whip | EFF MP

On the way up

Mkhaliphi (previously Hlophe-Maxon) had been an ANC supporter from the age of 14. Later, she also joined the Young Communist League (YCL), the youth wing of the South African Communist Party (SACP), rising to become its deputy national chairperson.

After working as an ANC councillor in the Durban area of the eThekwini municipality, Mkhaliphi became disillusioned with the party, and briefly joined the ANC breakaway, the Congress of the People (COPE), before the EFF was formed in 2013.

Mkhaliphi serves on Parliament's Home Affairs and International Affairs portfolio committees. She has been an MP since 2014.

In 2018, she raised the hackles of the home affairs minister, Hlengiwe Mkhize, when she questioned her about the notorious Gupta family's ability to get South African citizenship. Mkhaliphi's reasoning and approach on that occasion drew applause, as it revealed her to be a formidable parliamentary polemicist, if given the chance by her party.

Mkhize, Zweli

Minister of Co-Operative Governance and Traditional Affairs | Former premier of KwaZulu-Natal | Former chancellor of the University of KwaZulu-Natal | Former ANC treasurer-general

Moving from the Top 6 of the ANC into Cabinet seemed to have been a relatively quiet affair for Mkhize, a medical doctor, after the party's elective conference at Nasrec, Johannesburg, in December 2017. Then came the bombshell.

In June 2018, he was denying to the *Sunday Times* that he had ever facilitated a loan from the Public Investment Corporation (PIC), in his capacity as its treasurer-general, for a 'fund-raising' fee. This was as the newspaper exposed a letter of demand from a Johannesburg law firm which alleged there had been a R4.5-million kickback for Mkhize and other ANC supporters for helping oil company Afric Oil – which described itself as South Africa's 'first BEE (Black Economic Empowerment) fuel distribution company' – get a R210-million loan from the state's investment corporation.

The flurry was over almost as soon as it began, but it left Mkhize's reputation somewhat tainted at a time when he was trying to establish himself within President Cyril Ramaphosa's administration.

Having gone into exile with the ANC, he returned in 1991 and joined its national health secretariat to develop the country's democratic health policy. He was then appointed the KwaZulu-Natal MEC for Health in 1994, becoming the longest-serving provincial Health MEC by holding the position until 2004.

Mkhize then moved into the job of MEC for Finance and Economic Development, before he was elected KwaZulu-Natal premier. When he was selected as ANC treasurer-general at the party's elective conference in Mangaung, Free State, in 2012, he stepped down as premier, citing constitutional provisions. He did, however, maintain his position as ANC chairperson in the province.

Mkhize was long identified as a possible ANC president, and put himself up for nomination for the explosive context that would unfold at Nasrec, but when it became clear that it was a two-horse race – between Ramaphosa and Nkosazana Dlamini-Zuma – he saw his support dwindle.

Mkhwebane, Advocate Busisiwe

Public Protector (PP) | Former director for refugee affairs at the Department of Home Affairs | Former acting chief director in Asylum Seekers Management | Former counsillor for immigration and civic services in South Africa's embassy in Beijing, China | Former director on country information and co-operation management at the Department of Home Affairs | Former analyst for the State Security Agency (SSA) | Believed to be aligned to the ANC

Suspected of giving special treatment to certain corrupt individuals in the ANC

A CONTROVERSIAL PP FROM THE TIME SHE was nominated for the job, Mkhwebane experienced her toughest challenge in 2018 when it was revealed that she may have changed her report into the Vrede Dairy scandal in Free State to protect two senior ANC leaders – former Free State premier Ace Magashule and former Free State MEC for Agriculture and Cabinet minister Mosebenzi Zwane.

This was revealed in a court application brought by Lawson Naidoo of the Council for the Advancement of the South African Constitution (CASAC) in February 2018, the information linked to ever-more detailed revelations about possible corruption by the Gupta family.

Mkhwebane was accused not long before that of having hired state intelligence agents to work in the PP's office. She said they were on secondment due to her budget constraints.

Damaging, too, was Mkhwebane's early announcement that she was considering requesting a South African Police Services (SAPS) investigation into her predecessor. This was deemed an act of loyalty to Zuma on Mkhwebane's part, as the 'investigation' she wanted related to Madonsela's release of a state capture interview she conducted with Zuma in which he refused to answer questions. Madonsela released the video after Zuma claimed he had never been given such an opportunity.

Mkhwebane was later widely criticised for her report into the apartheid-era economic bail-out relating to Bankorp and other institutions. In the Bankorp-CIEX Report, she challenged the Constitution by recommending that the mandate of the South African Reserve Bank (SARB) be changed. The PP drew this conclusion from the finding that the SARB's R1.125-billion bail-out for Bankorp between 1985 and 1995 was unlawful. She also recommended that Absa bank, which bought Bankorp in 1992, be compelled to pay back more than a billion rand to the state. Both the SARB and Absa said the money had already been paid back and the North Gauteng High Court in Pretoria set aside her report.

Mkhwebane was appointed PP over another four candidates on the final shortlist: Judge Sharise Weiner, Judge Siraj Desai, Advocate Muvhango Lukhaimane and Advocate Bongani Majola.

Mkhwebane started her career at the Department of Justice as a public prosecutor, later a senior investigator, and also worked at the South African Human

Rights Commission (SAHRC) as a senior researcher before she moved properly into government, working at home affairs and at the State Security Agency.

In December 2018, Mkhwebane was more castigated than praised for issuing adverse findings in reports on Western Cape premier Helen Zille, ANC leader Fikile Mbalula and Treasury director-general Dondo Mogajane.

Modise, Thandi

Deputy speaker | Chairperson of the National Council of Provinces (NCOP) | Member of the Pan-African Parliament (PAP) | Former ANC North West premier | Member of the ANC's National Working Committee (NWC)

MODISE'S NAME IS ASSOCIATED WITH THE CRUELTY on her North West farm when dead and starving animals were discovered there in 2014.

Modise was also the subject of another controversy, relating to her official CV in which she claimed she was studying towards a Master's degree in economics at the 'University of Jordan' in the United States. The claims were later found to be inaccurate.

But there is more to the chairperson of the NCOP than controversies that have followed her political life. And although she had not served in the ANC National Executive Committee (NEC) since 2012, Modise's role in the NCOP saw her political influence rise sharply. The NCOP is one of the two houses of Parliament that ensures provincial interests are taken into account in government.

Modise was experienced in ANC politics, having served as deputy president of the ANC Women's League from 1994 to 2004, serving as its president in 2004. She was previously the Speaker of the North West legislature and its premier. In her capacity as deputy Speaker of the National Assembly, Modise presided over violent ejections of opposition party members from Parliament during former president Jacob Zuma's tenure.

She had particular political battles with Economic Freedom Fighters (EFF) leader Julius Malema, dating back to her days as deputy secretary-general of the ANC. Malema was eventually expelled from the party.

In 2016, Modise lost a case in the Supreme Court of Appeal (SCA) in Bloemfontein against him after she had ejected Malema from the National Assembly when he said the government had massacred Marikana mineworkers in 2012.

Moerane Commission

State-appointed inquiry

AN INQUIRY INTO FINDING ANSWERS TO THE VIOLENCE that has plagued particularly the ANC and its councillors in KwaZulu-Natal was set to be one of the most important events of the pre-election year of 2018.

The province had had only brief respites from bloodshed over these post apartheid 25 years, and was once known as 'the killing fields' when the ANC and the Inkatha Freedom Party (IFP) were at war for power, especially in its rural areas.

But by 2017 and 2018, the deadly conflict seemed centred largely within the ANC itself, as analysts and party members publicly concluded that the turf war was most likely about employment opportunities in a party that offered fewer places for those without an education and without experience at a higher level of politics.

There was shocking evidence from KwaZulu-Natal provincial electoral officer Mawethu Mosery in February 2018 when it was revealed that 'hundreds of thousands of rand were spent on convening unscheduled by-elections following the deaths of councillors by unnatural causes'. This tragedy has also been promoted by the breakaway of the National Freedom Party (NFP) from the IFP in 2011.

Mogajane, Dondo

Director-General (DG) of National Treasury | Director of New Development Bank

On the way up | Star

MOGAJANE JOINED TREASURY IN 1999 AS A DEPUTY DIRECTOR and served in various portfolios, including inter-governmental relations, provincial budget analysis and international economic relations. He represented the country as a senior adviser for Africa Group 1 countries on the World Bank Group's executive board from 2007 to 2010. (The World Bank Group, not to be confused with the World Bank, is a family of five international organisations that make leveraged loans to developing countries. It is the largest development bank in the world and is an observer at the United Nations.)

Between 2010 and 2014, Mogajane served as the chief of staff in the Ministry of Finance and, later, as the acting COO from May 2014 to May 2015.

He has two Honours degrees in public management, HR and industrial relations from the University of Durban-Westville (now the University of KwaZulu-Natal), as well as a Master's in public management from the University of Maryland, United States.

Mogajane's appointment in 2017 followed former Treasury Director-General (DG) Lungisa Fuzile's shock resignation that May.

The Democratic Alliance (DA) Shadow Minister of Finance David Maynier said upon Mogajane's appointment that the party 'wished him well, because he is going to have his hands full fighting off the fixers, rent-seekers and state-capturers who are desperate to get their hands on National Treasury'.

Respect for Mogajane seemed only to grow after Public Protector (PP) Busisiwe Mkhwebane ordered President Cyril Ramaphosa to take disciplinary action against him as he had not declared he was a 'criminal offender' for having had a speeding ticket. The PP's report on Mogajane drew howls of derision, even as she said his failure to declare his 'crime' reflected poorly on his honesty.

Mogoeng, Mogoeng

Chief justice | Former judge president of the North West High Court

Power broker | Change agent | Star

BORN IN A NORTH WEST VILLAGE IN 1961, Mogoeng Thomas Reetsang Mogoeng was a controversial nomination by former president Jacob Zuma. Derided as a 'bantustan prosecutor', Mogoeng came under immense criticism during his appearance before the Judicial Service Commission (JSC) for his fundamental Christian beliefs, alleged homophobia, alleged lack of legal intellect and apparent gender insensitivity, among other concerns.

Mogoeng quickly proved he was not the president's man, but a courageous jurist and keen defender of the independence of the judiciary.

Mogoeng obtained his B Juris from the University of Zululand and his LLB at the University of Natal. He worked as a prosecutor in the bantustan of Bophuthatswana until 1990 when he resigned to do his pupillage in Johannesburg.

Mogoeng returned to Mahikeng where he was an advocate until becoming a judge in the North West High Court in 1997. This was followed by his appointment to the Labour Appeal Court in 2000 and then as Judge President of the North West High Court in 2002.

He was elevated to the Constitutional Court (ConCourt) in 2009.

Five years after his appointment, Mogoeng shocked his detractors by writing and delivering the unanimous Constitutional Court judgment upholding former Public Protector Thuli Madonsela's State of Capture report, excoriating Zuma, and Parliament, in the process. This was followed by a number of ConCourt judgments which found against Zuma in his myriad legal battles, but strongly offset at the end of 2017 by Mogoeng's minority – and angry – judgment against his fellow judges for 'judicial overreach' in the so-called impeachment judgment.

Mokgoro Commission of Inquiry (see Jiba, Nomgcobo)

Mokgoro, Job

North West premier | Former director-general (DG) of the North West government

LEGENDARILY A GOVERNANCE EXPERT, Mokgoro took over from the disgraced Supra Mahumapelo as North West premier in the nick of time in June 2018. After a chaotic period in the province, where some parts of its government had had to be placed under administration during the divisive premiership of Mahumapelo, Mokgoro was announced days short of a what would have been a Constitutional requirement for an election.

Formerly with the University of the Witwatersrand's School of Governance, and with a Master's in public administration from the University of Toledo, United States, he came with a strong reputation as a disciplinarian and intellectual – but not necessarily as a politician.

Such was the adversarial nature of North West ANC politics that almost a month was spent after the eventual resignation of Mahumapelo deciding on who would be the best compromise candidate – and, at 70, Mokgoro was deemed that.

However, if his appointment somewhat assuaged problems for the party in the province, it did not please the opposition, especially the Economic Freedom Fighters (EFF), who were likely to be the ANC's biggest rivals there come the 2019 elections.

The EFF pointed out that it was during Mokgoro's tenure as acting DG in the office of the premier that *The New Age*, the national daily newspaper once owned by the notorious Gupta brothers, was 'illegally awarded a tender' to be distributed in North West. The party also alleged that Mokgoro was merely 'an extension of the corrupt cabal of the disgraced Supra Mahumapelo'. Its view was that Mokgoro had 'laid the foundation for the prevalence of corruption'.

Mokonyane, Nomvula

Minister of Environmental Affairs | Former minister of Communications | Former minister of Water and Sanitation | Former Gauteng premier | Honorary president of the South Africa-China People's Friendship Association | Former political detainee | Member of the ANC's National Working Committee (NWC) | Chair of the ANC's Disciplinary Appeals Committee

Linked to possible corruption

Mokonyane, who has called herself 'Mama Action', had strong credentials in the former liberation movement. Unlike many others, she was not an Umkhonto we Sizwe (MK) operative, but remained inside the country where she was a student activist, then joined the United Democratic Front (UDF) while organising for the Federation of Transvaal Women (Fedtraw), which supported the families of detainees.

Mokonyane was never free of harassment from the apartheid regime and spent time in detention before she was integrated into ANC and South African Communist Party structures after 1990. Thereafter, she served in the Gauteng Legislature from 1994.

She was elected to the ANC's National Executive Committee (NEC) at the 2007 conference in Polokwane, Limpopo, where Jacob Zuma was chosen as party president. A favourite of Zuma, Mokonyane was made premier of Gauteng by the national ANC despite not being placed first on its list for the provincial legislature. Paul Mashatile – who was, by 2018, one of the ANC's Top 6 – was widely expected to return as premier.

It was an event like that which did not add up for some ANC supporters. Another was her response to an anti-government demonstration in Bekkersdal, Johannesburg, in 2013 where she told protestors that the ANC did not want their 'dirty votes' in the 2014 elections. She had to be ferried out of the crowd by police, but while she apologised later for her remarks, the community said it would not forgive her.

Then there was concern about the lucrative Lesotho Highlands Water Project.

Mokonyane was the minister responsible for the development whose budget escalated as its deadline was extended. Mokonyane said this was in order to bring in more black-owned companies, but later there were reports that said only one company had been awarded the contracts.

Her decision to have Dudu Myeni – controversial chairperson of South African Airways (SAA) and founding chairperson of the Jacob Zuma Foundation – oversee a merger between the Umgeni and Mhlathuze Water boards in KwaZulu-Natal, also drew consternation.

The Department of Water and Sanitation ended up deep in debt, believed to have be mismanaged, and Mokonyane was redeployed to Communications by President Cyril Ramaphosa in February 2018, before he reshuffled her to Environmental Affairs in November 2018 amid calls for him to fire her.

Some of Mokonyane's dubious 'friendships' started to make sense in January 2019 when the untested and uncorroborated allegations of Angelo Agrizzi, a former CEO at the security and catering company Bosasa, threw a spotlight on her. Agrizzi claimed Bosasa had paid Mokonyane thousands upon thousands of rand, and 'sponsored' her extravagant lifestyle in order to secure her support in tender fraud. Mokonyane denied all allegations.

She couldn't, however, deny having left the Water and Sanitation ministry in some crisis when she was moved to the Communications Ministry and then to Environmental Affairs, both in 2018.

Mokonyane left Water and Sanitation virtually bankrupt, with the country in a worse-off position in terms of water provision. Irregular expenditure was at an all-time high on her watch, and it was only the arrival of new minister Gugile Nkwinti that saved the department from being taken under administration due to gross negligence and even corruption.

Molefe, Brian

Colonel in the South African National Defence Force (SANDF) | Former ANC MP | Former Eskom CEO | Former Transnet CEO | Former Public Investment Corporation (PIC) CEO

Alleged to be a chief enabler of state capture

ANTAGONISTS OF THE FORMER STATE-OWNED ENTITY (SOE) boss were invigorated to hear that Molefe could face criminal charges laid by the Democratic Alliance (DA) after he allegedly misled the Transnet board into approving inflated purchase prices for locomotives to benefit the notorious Gupta brothers.

A draft forensic report further accused Molefe of conducting financial transactions without board approval linked to Gupta associates Salim Essa, Iqbal Shara and Anoj Singh. Singh had been the chief financial officer at Eskom. The plan was to buy a thousand locomotives at nearly three times the regular cost price. Others who could have been implicated with Molefe in the presumed widescale looting included former public enterprises minister Malusi Gigaba and former Transnet CEO Siyabonga Gama and his executive.

It was claimed Molefe and others involved may have breached the Public Finance Management Act (PMFA).

All of this happened while Jacob Zuma was president and, had it not been for timely interventions, it even seemed possible for Zuma to have finance minister Nhanhla Nene replaced with Molefe. (As it turned out, Zuma replaced him with Gigaba.)

It is a pity Molefe was corrupt. He was an enviably talented civil servant in his earlier years, beginning as an institutional specialist at the Development Bank of South Africa (DBSA), moving on to be Chief Director of Strategic Planning in the Office of the Limpopo Premier, then on to National Treasury for nearly a decade, ending up a deputy director-general for asset liability management.

Then came Eskom and almost R1 billion for a dubious coal tender that probably bought Optimum Coal Mine from Glencore for the Guptas. Then came dozens of mobile calls between Molefe and Ajay Gupta and an extraordinary number of visits by Molefe to the Guptas' luxurious neighbourhood of Saxonwold, Johannesburg.

That Molefe ended up an honorary colonel in the South African Defence Force (SANDF) was a unique, final 'honorarium' from Zuma.

Yet it is unlikely that those who saw Molefe break down on TV in November 2016 at Eskom's results presentation have forgotten how it delivered a metonym for state capture. As Molefe tried to spin his way out of Public Protector Thuli Madonsela's damning State of Capture report, which linked him to alleged corruption in a multimillion-rand coal contract awarded to a Gupta-owned company, he had to find a reason for his ubiquitous presence in Saxonwold.

Thus, speaking about the luxurious suburban site of the Guptas' residence in Johannesburg, Molefe said there was 'a shebeen' there, but would not admit nor deny that he 'was going (there)' when he was frequently in the area. And so the expression 'Saxonwold shebeen' was born to describe a particular form of corruption associated with the Gupta brothers.

Molefe, Popo

Chancellor of North West University | Former premier of North West | Former chairperson of the Passenger Rail Agency of South Africa (Prasa) | Founding member of the United Democratic Front (UDF) | Former political prisoner | Member of the ANC's 101 Stalwarts

Change agent

PRESIDENT CYRIL RAMAPHOSA MADE IT CLEAR from his inauguration in February 2018 that stabilising the state-owned entities (SOEs) was a priority. Several had been severely affected by corruption during former president Jacob Zuma's time in office, and public enterprises minister Pravin Gordhan was under pressure to get these working again.

He needed an experienced troubleshooter and former UDF leader and Delmas treason trialist Popo Molefe had shown no fear or mercy when he was chairperson of Prasa in clearing it of its dirt. Thus, it made sense for Gordhan to place Molefe at the helm of one of the state's biggest problems: Transnet.

By mid-2018, Molefe was already having an impact as its interim chairperson, having overhauled a board riven with allegations of links to the notorious Gupta brothers who were, in turn, associated with Zuma and his son, Duduzane Zuma. Of special interest for Molefe at Transnet was a massive locomotives deal that had seen the SOE referred to the Special Investigating Unit (SIU).

Molefe had, meanwhile, refused to bow even to a state agency when it came to the work he was asked to do. In his previous capacity as Prasa chairperson, he launched a Pretoria High Court application against the Hawks, wanting it declared that the police super unit hadn't properly investigated alleged irregular tenders under former rail agency CEO Lucky Montana.

Molefe won that battle.

Montana, Lucky

Former CEO of Passenger Rail Agency of South Africa (Prasa)

Found responsible for maladministration and wasteful expenditure

MONTANA WAS REMOVED FROM PRASA IN 2015 after the country's biggest and most expensive tender scandal saw him oversee the purchase of Spanish locomotives that were too high for South African infrastructure.

It was a protracted removal, after which Montana seemed to disappear from public life until April 2018 when it was alleged that a R13.5-million Johannesburg property he owned had been partly funded through a beneficiary of shady contracts worth R4 billion from Prasa.

That beneficiary was identified as 'controversial Pretoria tender mogul Mario Ferreira', and Montana as his 'former business partner'. The property was 'registered to Montana's name, even though it was paid for by third parties linked to Ferreira'. It had been suspected that Montana had benefitted through substantial contracts awarded by Prasa to Siyangena Technologies, which was a subsidiary of Ferreira's TMM Holdings group.

Siyangena was to have installed security-related products at stations.

But the political consequences of Montana's appalling management paled in comparison to the human tragedy playing out on the railways in part due to the corruption which took place at Prasa. Public Protector Thuli Madonsela's Derailed report of 2015 showed how up to R3.9 billion was wasted on Montana's watch, this while thousands died and more than 15,000 were injured since 2010 – a great number of these people being commuters dramatically affected by derailments. Drivers and other Prasa staff have also been killed or injured.

Madonsela recommended criminal charges be laid against the Prasa board and a number of officials, including Sfiso Buthelezi, who was the chair at the time (he was Deputy Minister of Agriculture in 2019). By January 2019, no action had been taken.

Moseneke, Justice Dikgang

Deputy Chief Justice Emeritus | International Relations Special Envoy to South Sudan and Lesotho | Chairperson of the Life Esidimeni arbitration hearings | Former deputy chairperson of the Independent Electoral Commission (IEC) to oversee the 1994 elections | Helped draft the Interim Constitution

Power broker | Change agent | Star

MOSENEKE'S CAREER BEFORE THE BENCH and after has catapaulted him to a status far beyond the cloistered calm of Constitution Hill. Once famed as the youngest prisoner on Robben Island at the age of 15, he added an LLB to the matric, BA and B Juris he obtained on the island and began practice as an attorney, before switching to the Bar.

Moseneke helped draft the interim Constitution and served as deputy chair of the Independent Electoral Commission (IEC) which oversaw South Africa's watershed 1994 elections. He relinquished an acting judgeship to pursue a corporate career, including chairing Telkom, before returning to the bench in Pretoria in November 2001, moving to Johannesburg and the Constitutional Court (ConCourt) almost exactly a year later. In 2005, he was elevated to the ConCourt.

The first time Moseneke was overlooked to become chief justice rankled, but the second time, the promotion of, by his rank legal junior, Mogoeng Mogoeng, sparked outrage, reminding observers of the double snubbing of Deputy Chief Justice Oliver Schreiner in 1957 and 1959 in favour of chief justices more amenable to the apartheid regime.

Moseneke was as widely praised for his legal acumen as he was for his humanity. Never one to shy from speaking truth to power he, together with Advocate Sisi Khampepe, exposed the Zimbabwean 2002 general elections for the sham they were.

He interceded as Chancellor of the University of the Witwatersrand (Wits) in person during the #FeesMustFall movement of 2015 and 2016.

Moseneke cemented his place as the natural successor to Archbishop Emeritus Desmond Tutu as the conscience of the nation with his Solomonic handling, after his retirement from the bench, of the Life Esidimeni tragedy which claimed the lives of dozens of mental health patients in Gauteng.

Moseneke was appointed as special envoy to South Sudan and Lesotho by international relations minister Lindiwe Sisulu as part of her establishment of a review panel to steer a new direction for the country's foreign policy in May 2018.

Motion of No Confidence (Section 102)

IN A PARLIAMENTARY DEMOCRACY LIKE SOUTH AFRICA, MPs (or councillors, in the case of local government) can propose a motion of confidence or of no confidence in the government or executive, or in the leader of such. It is formally known as Section 102, which is different to Section 89, which is a vote of impeachment.

The results of such motions show how much support a government or a leader has, and if a motion of no confidence passes, a resignation would be expected to follow. A simple majority in the National Assembly is all that is needed to remove the head of state: in the case of South Africa, 200 members plus one.

As the ANC has 249 seats in the National Assembly, it shouldn't need the support of the opposition for such a motion, but there are always vacancies and it is difficult to ensure that all MPs are in the House when a vote is called.

If there are 201 'yeas', the government would be expected to resign as a whole, to allow the formation of a new government through an election.

It is, however, unusual for motions of no confidence to be passed even at local or provincial level in South Africa, never mind at national level, as was seen by the two attempts to have Jacob Zuma removed in this way by opposition parties in 2017. The last motion of no confidence was decided by secret ballot, after Speaker Baleka Mbete agreed this could be the case, but that does not mean that every motion of no confidence thereafter would be by secret ballot.

The most high-profile passing of a motion of no confidence was in April 2018 when the DA's caucus in the City of Cape Town won enough support to remove mayor Patricia de Lille. It took another four months for this to take effect due to a number of legal actions but, ultimately, De Lille did leave office.

Motlanthe, Kgalema

Known as: Mkhuluwa (the older one) | Former president of the Republic of South Africa | Former deputy president of the Republic of South Africa | Former deputy president of the ANC | Chairperson of the High-Level Panel on the Assessment of Key Legislation and the Acceleration of Fundamental Change (HLP) | Former ANC secretary-general | Former general-secretary of the National Union of Mineworkers (NUM) | Former political prisoner

When South Africa navigated its greatest crisis of the post-democratic period, it was Motlanthe who took the helm in the interregnum between the ousting of Thabo Mbeki in 2008 and the appointment of Jacob Zuma as state president. But it was as if Motlanthe – who grew up in Alexandra and almost went into the Anglican priesthood – had been born into negotiating conflict.

The apartheid regime denied him a passport to go to Swaziland to study, so, instead, he ended up in the ANC's military wing, Umkhonto we Sizwe (MK), first as a courier and then as a soldier, before being arrested, tortured and jailed on terrorism and sabotage charges.

A former Robben Islander, Motlanthe ascended through NUM, replacing Cyril Ramaphosa as general-secretary in 1992, before becoming secretary-general of the ANC in 1997 and then deputy president of the party to Zuma after the ANC's elective conference in Polokwane, Limpopo, in 2007. On that occasion, his support outweighed that for Nkosazana Dlamini-Zuma, who would lose another key election – for party president – in 2017.

Motlanthe's own challenge to be ANC president failed at its elective conference in Mangaung, Free State in 2012, and that spelt the end of Motlanthe's formal political career. He'd lost against Zuma in that election, and then decided he would not make himself available to be re-elected to the ANC's National Executive Committee. The plan was for Motlanthe to run the party's new political school.

Regarded as a principled man, he did not hesitate to sail against the wind of prevailing party opinion, whether the issue was moves to muzzle the media through state regulation or speaking out against the kleptocracy of state capture.

Motlanthe worked for many months, perhaps too quietly, on the High-Level Panel on the Assessment of Key Legislation and the Acceleration of Fundamental Change (HLP), which travelled the country assessing the impact new legislation had had on ordinary people. The panel submitted its final report to the Speaker's Forum in September 2017.

His political achievements notwithstanding, it was likely Motlanthe would also be remembered for headlines about his private life. In 2008, when he was 'interim' president, his affair with Luthuli House staffer Gugu Mtshali became public knowledge. It appeared she had left and then divorced her husband, who was identified as businessman Dumisani Mtshali, after several years of being in an extra-marital relationship with Motlanthe, while Motlanthe's wife Mapula and he were living apart. They eventually divorced, and Motlanthe and Mtshali got married in 2014.

But it wasn't only his affair with Mtshali that attracted sensational headlines to Motlanthe. There were also allegations that Mtshali – who was a personal assistant to the late former ANC treasurer Mendi Msimang and Cyril Ramaphosa when he was the ANC's secretary-general, and then to former Mpumalanga premier Mathews Phosa – had become a director of various companies while working at Luthuli House.

In 2010, while she was Motlanthe's official partner, she was linked in business terms to Zuma's son Duduzane, identified as a co-founder and shareholder of Imperial Crown Trading, in which the Guptas were also shareholders. The company won prospecting rights worth billions at the giant Sishen iron ore mine.

Mtshali was also linked to a R104-million bribe to obtain support from government agencies for 360 Aviation, a South African company, which was hoping to sell helicopters to the Islamic Republic of Iran – despite weapons sanctions against that country. Motlanthe asked Public Protector Thuli Madonsela to investigate and Madonsela cleared both Motlanthe and Mtshali.

It appeared the allegations may have had something to do with Motlanthe's intention to run for ANC president at the party's elective conference in Mangaung in December 2012. Zuma won the presidency.

Motshekga, Angie

Nickname: Minister of Broken Promises | Minister of Basic Education | Former ANC Women's League (ANCWL) president | Member of the ANC's National Working Committee (NWC)

A MEMBER OF THE ANC's NATIONAL Executive Committee (NEC), Motshekga has a Master's degree from the University of the Witwatersrand (Wits) and began her career as a teacher in Soweto in the early 1980s, before she lectured at Wits from 1985 to 1994.

Motshekga then served as the director in President Nelson Mandela's office from 1994 to 1997 and as MEC for Social Services and Education in Gauteng. President Jacob Zuma appointed her Minister of Basic Education in his first Cabinet in 2009 and she was reappointed in 2014.

Motshekga attracted controversy in her role as minister for seemingly undermining basic education. For example, in 2016, her department instructed public schools to condone children in Grades 7 to 9 who obtained a mere 20% in mathematics. Then, in 2017, it dropped mathematics as a compulsory subject to pass those grades. This came against the disturbing backdrop of South Africa having the reputation of one of the worst education systems in the world.

Motshekga and her department were also decried by the Supreme Court of Appeal (SCA) for their 'woeful' inability to deliver textbooks to schools in Limpopo three years after a new curriculum was introduced. The court said the department's failure to provide each pupil at public schools in Limpopo with a textbook for each subject, before the start of the 2014 school year, was an infringement of their rights.

But the most serious of all the allegations against Motshekga was what earned her the sobriquet, 'Minister of Broken Promises', from campaigners Equal Education. She failed to honour a law, that she had adopted, which detailed infrastructure standards for every public school. The law said that by the end of November 2016, schools had to have been provided with access to water, electricity and decent sanitation. It explicitly stated that plain pit latrines were not allowed at schools. However, by mid-2018, Motshekga and her department's provincial MECs had still failed to take action.

Two children – six-year-old Michael Komape in Limpopo and five-year-old Lumka Mketwa in the Eastern Cape – had drowned in pit latrines at their schools. Even those tragedies did not spur action. Instead, Motshekga was able to blame other government departments for downgrading the status of her department's infrastructure budgets to afford free higher education.

Yet, the Department of Basic Education had made little progress by its own deadline, some time before the fees-free tertiary environment had been accepted. Hundreds of schools remained in dire straits. It was only in November 2018 that the bell finally tolled when the Constitutional Court declared that government had no choice but to fix all infrastructure.

Motshekga, Dr Mathole

Former ANC chief whip | ANC MP | Founder of the Kara Heritage Institute

Motshekga served as a representative of the ANC in the Judicial Services Commission (JSC) and as chairperson of the Portfolio Committee on Justice and Correctional Services. He earned an LLM from Harvard Law School and a Doctor of Laws from Unisa, and taught Law at Albert-Ludwigs University in Germany and the University of South Africa (Unisa).

Motshekga came out publicly in mid-2017 to endorse Cyril Ramaphosa for president. He was castigated by opposition parties in June 2018 for seemingly supporting controversial Public Protector Busisiwe Mkhwebane when the issue of her removal from office was discussed.

One of his most critical tasks in 2018 was to chair the Justice Committee studying the Prevention and Combating of Hate Crimes and Hate Speech Bill. The committee had heard that, should a person be convicted of hate crimes, the Bill provided for the courts to impose sentencing, including imprisonment, a fine and correctional supervision depending on the base crime. But Motshekga said they should be careful that it did not have 'unintended consequences' like criminalising people over 'moral issues'. He called for a national dialogue on the issues so as 'to not create problems like sending people to prison because of intolerance'.

It was a pity, therefore, that Motshekga himself failed to extend that to then Public Protector Thuli Madonsela when, as chair of the portfolio committee, he said she had 'become a law unto herself' and that she had 'a lack of understanding of her mandate'. He would later be moved from that committee, when Mkhwebane was PP.

Motshekga is the founder of the Kara Heritage Institute in Pretoria, which educates communities in indigenous cultural heritage and African tradition, and trains them in skills development.

Motsoaledi, Dr Aaron

Minister of Health | Former head of the ANC Elections Commission | Former head of the ANC Economics and Infrastructure Desk

A MEDICAL DOCTOR, MOTSOALEDI WAS FIRST a member of the Black Consciousness (BC) movement as a leader in the Azanian Students' Organisation (Azaso). He later became involved with the United Democratic Front (UDF) and the ANC's armed wing, Umkhonto we Sizwe (MK).

A long-time health and political activist, Motsoaledi was the deputy chairperson of the ANC in the then Northern Transvaal and then the head of the ANC Elections Commission, the head of the ANC Economics and Infrastructure Desk and the head of the ANC Research and Briefing of the Election Task Team in Limpopo in 1994. He served as a member of the Limpopo Provincial Legislature from 1994–2009, as Education MEC from 1994–1997, MEC for Transport from 1998–1999 and MEC for Agriculture, Land and Environment from 1999.

Zuma made Motsoaledi his Minsiter of Health and a comprehensive HIV/AIDS treatment, policy and a dedicated follow-through regimen was quickly introduced. Two of Motsoaledi's predecessors in that post – Nkosazana Dlamini-Zuma (1994–1999) and Manto Tshabalala-Msimang (1999–2008) – had adopted erratic, denalist or insubstantial policies on HIV and AIDS which, especially under then president Thabo Mbeki (1999–2008), were believed to have contributed to the AIDS-related deaths of hundreds of thousands of South Africans. Motsoaledi took an HIV-focused approach and administered the first fixed dose combination (FDC) anti-retroviral tablet to a state patient in April 2013 in GaRankuwa outside Pretoria.

That said, Motsoaledi's popularity took a knock in 2017 and 2018. The ARVs distribution programme was not in perfect shape. Then, he was mocked for not being 'able' to take responsibility for the deaths of dozens of mental health patients in the Life Esidimeni tragedy after a contract with a private health provider was cancelled, allegedly to save costs, and the patients were moved to NGOs.

Motsoaledi repeatedly claimed the Constitution had made it legally impossible for him to intervene in provincial health affairs and that this had to be changed. Until then, his 'hands were tied'. This would also be his reason when oncology collapsed in KwaZulu-Natal and possibly even Tshwane, and when the North West public health system was placed under administration.

Politically, Motsoaledi is enigmatic, although he was among 32 ANC MPs who were absent during the motion of no confidence against Zuma in November 2016, despite having spoken out against Zuma previously.

But he was finding himself increasingly under pressure on the public stage in 2018 and 2019 as the demand for National Health Insurance (NHI) – a resolution out of the pivotal 2007 ANC elective conference at Polokwane – mounted. Zuma won the ANC presidency at that conference.

The projected costs of NHI were staggering, pilot projects around it had been hit-and-miss, private healthcare – which catered to a minority of the population – believed it had the moral high ground after a Competition Commission inquiry into its profits was soft on it, and many public health facilities were still under-resourced and even dangerous.

Motsoeneng, Hlaudi (also see South African Broadcasting Corporation)

Leader of the African Content Movement | Former acting Chief Operating Officer of the SABC | Former SABC group executive editor

Corrupt

When the Western Cape High Court ruled in 2016 that Motsoeneng's appointment as group executive editor at the SABC was unlawful, it was a vindication for thousands at the SABC or in other state institutions (including the National Assembly) who had had to tolerate his corruption and predilection for outrageous lies and bombast for years.

The court was clear: Motsoeneng – who infamously lied about having a Matric – was not entitled to occupy any position at the SABC. His ability to ingratiate himself with politicians for their and his nefarious purposes, and his tendency to steal and exaggerate, sounds almost comical, but it allowed state capture to bed down. Motsoeneng wouldn't allow objective coverage of the Zuma era.

Public Protector Thuli Madonsela's 2014 report When governance and ethics fail highlighted his dishonesty and abuse of power at the SABC, which included his own salary hike of R1 million. Before Motsoeneng was finally fired in June 2017, the SABC had fallen into a R600-million hole.

His 'comeback' as the leader of the African Content Movement, which was launched at the end of December 2018 and claimed to be contesting the 2019 elections, was identified by many analysts as just an aspect of the continuing factional plot of political interference and malfeasance.

Moyane, Tom

Former South African Revenue Service (SARS) commissioner | Former national commissioner of the Department of Correctional Services | Former chief executive of the Government Printing Works | Former advisor to the State Information Technology Agency

Alleged to be a chief enabler of State Capture | Suspected of assault

MOYANE WAS FIRED FROM HIS POSITION AS SARS commissioner by President Cyril Ramaphosa in November 2018 after four major charges were laid against him, including the violation of his duties and responsibilities in terms of the SARS Act, the Public Finance Management Act (PFMA), the SARS code of conduct as well as his fiduciary duties, and his duties prescribed by the Constitution.

The charges were: gross mishandling of a Financial Intelligence Centre (FIC) report of May 2016 looking into SARS official Jonas Makwakwa; unauthorised bonus payments of R3 million which Moyane had earmarked for his executive committee; misleading Parliament; and instructing SARS official Helgard Lombard not to co-operate in auditors KPMG's SARS investigation.

Lombard was a former State Security operative who had been tasked by then state prosecutor Gerrie Nel with installing surveillance equipment in some meeting rooms at SARS. This was apparently to flush out a 'spy' who was said to be giving information to politicians ahead of time about their impending prosecutions.

Daily Maverick investigations writer Pauli van Wyk wrote in May 2018 that it was the last charge against Moyane, of 'actively sabotaging' an investigation, which could 'prove cataclysmic not only for Moyane, but also for the National Prosecuting Authority (NPA)'.

That charge was detailed on Moyane's disciplinary charge sheet and alleged that, in May 2015, Moyane had 'instructed (Lombard) not to co-operate with the KPMG investigation into the SARS High Risk Investigative Unit by instructing ... Lombard to feign illness on the day that he was scheduled to be questioned by KPMG in relation to the investigation'. This action, it said, 'constituted an abuse of the Office of the Commissioner of SARS, a violation of the SARS Code of Conduct and egregious misconduct'.

These events happened against the backdrop of SARS Deputy and then Acting Commissioner Ivan Pillay, and SARS executives Andries Janse van Rensburg and Johann van Loggerenberg being charged for alleged fraud and intercepting the NPA's communication emanating from the offices and boardrooms of NPA officials, including those of Nel. It was nicknamed Project Sunday Evenings. Moyane was the NPA's complainant in their case against Pillay, Van Loggerenberg and Janse van Rensburg.

Moyane had a contract at SARS until September 2019. Ramaphosa instructed that he would have to fund his own defence.

Once so highly regarded that, while in exile with the ANC during apartheid, he had worked for the Mozambique and Guinea-Bissau governments, Moyane's reputation looked to be in tatters in 2018. His suspension at SARS had already dragged him into public view and then he was accused of 'ninja-kicking' the 17-year-old mother of his grandchild.

Moyane's conduct at SARS became part of the Nugent Commission of Inquiry into the country's tax administration, which started its work in June 2018.

Mpofu, Advocate Dali SC

Economic Freedom Fighters (EFF) national chairperson | Member of the EFF's Central Command Team (CCT) | Former South African Broadcasting Corporation (SABC) Chief Executive Officer

Power broker

THE LEGAL FIXTURE, WHO IS ALSO A BUSINESS EXECUTIVE, was the CEO of the SABC until he was dimissed in 2009 amid allegations of financial mismanagement, political interference and sidelining his critics.

Mpofu was a prominent member of the ANC until 2013, when he joined the Economic Freedom Fighters (EFF).

Among other major cases, Mpofu represented miners who were injured during the August 2012 Marikana Massacre at Lonmin mine in North West, and some others who were arrested at the subsequent Farlam Commission of Inquiry established to investigate the state-sanctioned killings.

Mpofu served as Winnie Madikizela-Mandela's deputy on the ANC's Department of Social Development, but was dismissed in 1992 when there were allegations that funds had been misappropriated. Madikizela-Mandela resigned. Rumours had meanwhile abounded that he and Madikizela-Mandela had been involved in a romantic relationship while she was still married to Nelson Mandela.

Mpofu was selected for the National Anti-Corruption Task Team in 1999 and as chairperson of the National Anti-Corruption Forum since 2001.

Among other positions, he was chairperson of Victim Support South Africa/ Business Against Crime until 2005, when he became a member of the International Marketing Council of South Africa.

In 2006, Mpofu was named as the chairperson of the board of Proudly South Africa and the president of the Southern African Broadcasters Association. He is also an acting judge for the Labour Court of South Africa and the chairman of the Information and Communication Technology (ICT) Black Economic Empowerment (BEE) Charter Working Group.

Mpofu's association with EFF leader Julius Malema goes back to 2011 and 2012 when Mpofu represented Malema at the ANC disciplinary hearing that resulted in Malema being expelled from the party.

There was a suggestion in 2018, however, that Mpofu's work as an advocate was starting to clash with his political work with the EFF. Among other matters, Mpofu represented former SARS commissioner Tom Moyane in his fightback, which failed, as well as former DA member Patricia de Lille, in her bid to retain the position of mayor in Cape Town, which succeeded.

Mpumalanga

Province | ANC-led since 1994

Significant corruption

The ANC had two decades of seemingly overwhelming support in the popular tourist province, but the 2010 World Cup laid bare a much darker truth shadowed by assassinations, tender fraud, poor governance and troubling political conflict.

If factionalism was always an issue in the modern ANC, it seemed nowhere more so than in Mpumalanga – notable from 2008 when Premier Mathews Phosa took action against an errant Education MEC by the name of David Mabuza.

These days, Mabuza – better known as 'DD' – is not only the former premier of the province himself, but also the deputy president of South Africa. And the story of how 'DD' reached that elevated level in the country is integral to the story of Mpumalanga over a decade of despair.

So too is the story of sometime presidential contender Phosa.

Phosa squared off with his successor, Ndaweni Mahlangu, over a R100-million investment, which the latter said had been misappropriated during his predecessor's tenure. And while Mahlangu, who caused a stir for his statement that it is 'common for politicians to lie', may have had a short-lived stint as premier, his presence in the mire only intensified concern from inside and outside about the party's morality.

Former ANC Umkhonto we Sizwe (MK) operative Thabang Makwetla followed as premier, and then came 'DD'. After Mabuza was elected as deputy president at the ANC at its elective conference at Nasrec, Johannesburg, in December 2017, Limpopo's MEC for Co-operative Governance and Traditional Affairs, Refilwe Mtsweni, became the Premier.

But hers was probably the most difficult of all those deployments as she took on a deeply divided province, riven with violent factions, showing no end to its corruption.

Msimang, Mavuso

Chairperson of Corruption Watch | CEO of South African National Parks (SanParks) | CEO of the Oliver and Adelaide Tambo Foundation | Chairperson of the iSimangaliso Wetland Park, a World Heritage site | Former director-general (DG) of Home Affairs | Former secretary to ANC President OR Tambo | Member of the 101 Stalwarts

Change agent | Star

Msimang gained positive public attention when he was DG at Home Affairs for putting systems in place that greatly improved turnaround times in the issuance of identity documents, birth certificates and passports.

Government corridors were far away from the life he had known when he served on the Umkhonto we Sizwe (MK) Military High Command from 1966 to 1969, before being appointed secretary to ANC President O.R. Tambo, a position that he held from 1969 to 1971.

Msimang would go on to be involved in the transformation and restructuring of a number of state-owned entities (SOEs). In 1994, he took on the country's unpopular tourism marketing organisation, then called Satour, and, together with his board, laid the foundation for the establishment of SA Tourism.

As CEO of South African National Parks (SanParks), Msimang oversaw the implementation of the organisation's financial, environmental and social responsibility programmes.

Before his return to South Africa in 1994, Msimang worked for a number of NGOs in international development, including the United Nations Children's Fund (Unicef), the World Food Programme and the UN Development Programme.

His non-executive board directorships included the African Parks Network and the Peace Parks Foundation. Msimang was also chairperson of the iSimangaliso Wetland Park, a World Heritage site.

Msimang was the chairperson of Corruption Watch in 2019. Exposing rot was his priority. He found himself on the receiving end of Human Settlements Minister Nomaindia Mfeketo in December 2018 when she fired him as chair of the Housing Development Agency after the board demanded the suspension of CEO Pascal Moloi and other managers after allegations of sex-for-jobs and financial irregularities.

Msimanga, Solly

Former mayor of the Tshwane Metropolitan Municipality | Democratic Alliance (DA) politician | DA Candidate for Gauteng premier in 2019

Made a seemingly nepotistic senior appointment | Linked to a suspicious tender for the Tshwane municipality

Msimanga joined the DA in 2006, rising through its ranks until he became the leader of the DA's Gauteng North region in 2011, the same year he was elected to the Tshwane City Council. In 2014, Msimanga was elected as a member of the Gauteng Provincial Legislature and succeeded Mike Moriarty as DA provincial chairperson in 2015.

He was then announced as the DA's mayoral candidate for the City of Tshwane for the 2016 elections in which the party emerged as the largest in the election, but without a majority in the hung metro. It then formed a coalition with several smaller parties, with the vital support of the Economic Freedom Fighters (EFF), whose leader, Julius Malema, described Msimanga as 'genuine'.

Msimanga was the first DA member to hold the post of mayor in the Tshwane metro. But his relationship with the EFF was not all plain-sailing. Msimanga faced two votes of no confidence, and by the later part of 2018 was believed to be an unstable force in the city's chambers.

Msimanga had faced his first major, personal controversy in the job in May 2018 when it was shown that he had allowed the appointment of an under-qualified, unsuitable candidate to be his chief of staff. It was alleged by rival political parties that Marietha Aucamp did not have a tertiary education and had lied about her qualifications. Msimanga, who was on the panel that interviewed Aucamp and gave her the top position which was renumerated at more than R1 million per year, asked her to resign.

Msimanga faced another, more serious challenge, in December 2018 when the ANC in Tshwane laid charges against him for contravening the Municipal Structures Act in relation to allegations of tender irregularity that led to engineering company GladAfrica securing a R12-billion contract with the City of Tshwane to provide project management support. And it was this which likely assisted in his decision to step down as mayor in January 2019, although the official reason given was that he needed to focus on his provincial campaign.

Despite the turbulent waters of Tshwane politics, Msimanga was named the DA's Gauteng premier candidate for 2019.

Mthembu, Jackson

ANC chief whip | ANC's former national spokesperson | Former political prisoner

A FORMER MEC FOR PUBLIC ROADS and Transport in Mpumalanga and the chair of the portfolio committees on Local Government, Education, Sport and Recreation, Arts and Culture and Environmental Affairs, Mthembu in 2017 defied then president Jacob Zuma and some members of the caucus he led, by supporting a comprehensive investigation into state capture.

He openly supported Cyril Ramaphosa for president during 2017 and at the ANC's Nasrec, Johannesburg elective conference at the end of that year.

A former student leader who was expelled for his political activity by the University of Fort Hare, Mthembu frequently saw the inside of apartheid's jails, ultimately being charged with treason. He led the South West African People's Organisation support group to Namibia's first democratic elections in 1988.

Mthembu managed to overcome a reputation he picked up for drinking when he was arrested for drunken driving in 2010 and pleaded guilty.

Mthethwa, Nathi

Minister of Arts and Culture | Former minister of Police | Former ANC chief whip | Member of the ANC's National Working Committee (NWC)

MTHETHWA BECAME KNOWN AS 'THE MINISTER OF TRIBUTES' in 2018 after it seemed that the only times he made speeches in public anymore was to pay the government's respects to an artist or a public figure prominent in South African culture who had died.

Indeed, Mthethwa seemed to have receded into the background as factionalism and blood-letting in his party happened around him. It seemed largely by default that South Africans had a sense of him as a civil servant, either – particularly in his designated field of culture and the arts.

It wasn't always like that. Mthethwa, who'd been an ANC MP since 2002, was the one to announce that President Thabo Mbeki had resigned in September 2008 in his role as ANC chief whip. That was a new job for Mthethwa at the time, but the pronouncement of a party hack propelled him into public view.

Mthethwa then continued to come out strongly in support of Zuma, even in mid-2017 as allegations of state capture involving Zuma associates, the Gupta brothers, gained momentum.

But he seemed to have vanished from the spotlight after the Marikana Massacre in 2012. The state-sanctioned murder of 34 striking workers on Lonmin mines' property in North West happened on Mthethwa's watch as he was Minister of Police at the time. The Farlam Commission of Inquiry, which was established by Zuma, cleared Mthethwa of wrongdoing.

Muthambi, Faith

ANC MP | Former minister of Public Service and Administration | Former minister of Communications

Linked to corruption and nepotism

Muthambi had wide political experience before Jacob Zuma introduced her to his second Cabinet in 2014. Among other roles, she was the provincial treasurer of the ANC Youth League (ANCYL) in Limpopo from 2005–08, a leading member of the ANC Women's League (ANCWL) in Limpopo, an ANC MP and a member of the Pan-African Parliament.

With a B Proc from the University of Venda and certifications from the Wits Business School, among other institutions, Muthambi ought to have been a valued member of government. Instead, she seemed to dig herself an ever-deeper hole.

In 2017, an ad hoc parliamentary committee found her 'incompetent' and guilty of misleading Parliament – potentially, a criminal offence. The Portfolio Committee on Communications had been given a legal report recommending that Muthambi be investigated for possibly lying to MPs during an inquiry into the South African Broadcasting Corporation (SABC) board in 2016. It was reported that she had said she 'did not pressurise the broadcaster's board to appoint (its disgraced former COO) Hlaudi Motsoeneng to his former position', but that 'minutes of board meetings showed she wasn't being truthful'.

Muthambi was also perverse about explaining an amount of R300,000 spent on transport for friends and family to watch her deliver a speech, and accounting for the bloating by 17 people of her personal staff, where there was also believed to have been nepotism on her part.

Muthambi was relieved of her post in February 2018 by President Cyril

Ramaphosa but remained an ANC MP and a member of the Portfolio Committee on Labour.

Government spokesperson Phumla Williams testified at the Zondo Commission of Inquiry into state capture that Muthambi had 'tortured' her to such an extent that she relived the torture she, Williams, had endured during apartheid. Williams was close to tears as she recounted her harrowing experience in which Muthambi, as communications minister, stripped her of her powers and neutralised the capacity of the Government Communication and Information System (GCIS), a key state institution.

Muthambi denied all allegations.

Myeni, Dudu

Businesswoman | Former chairperson of South African Airways SOC Limited | Chairperson of the Jacob G Zuma Foundation | Chairperson of the South African Association of Water Utilities | Director of Trade and Investment in KwaZulu-Natal

Linked to corruption

A former teacher who lied about her tertiary qualification (she told SAA she had a BA in Administration, but had not yet completed it), Myeni's friendship with Jacob Zuma was believed to be a key driver of the high office she reached at SAA.

Originally a social development consultant, Myeni worked with government and the private sector before she joined SAA's board of directors in 2009, the year Zuma was inaugurated as president. Three years later, she was appointed chair and successor to former United Democratic Front leader Cheryl Carolus, after the majority of board members resigned at the same time.

Her time at SAA was fraught from the beginning, and complaints were even directed to then public enterprises minister Malusi Gigaba in 2014, when the airline's chief executive Monwabisi Kalawe accused Myeni of corruption before she disciplined him.

Not long after Gigaba appeared to support Kalawe, he was moved by Zuma from public enterprises to home affairs. The disgraced Lynne Brown replaced Gigaba at public enterprises.

Brown was in charge when Myeni was suspected of corruption in an apparently maverick 'deal' she signed with Airbus, in which she failed to consult SAA executives, claiming a 'third party' would rather be involved in the purchase of a number of new planes.

This was seemingly the start of Myeni's undoing at the airline as its legal position stated that if normal procurement processes were not followed, an agreement would have to be signed off by the Minister of Finance.

At that time, 2015, the minister was Nhlanhla Nene, and he would not give his approval. Within days, Zuma replaced Nene with ANC backbencher David van Rooyen, resulting in massive losses on the Stock Exchange before Zuma replaced

Van Rooyen with Gordhan, who had been the Minister of Finance before Nene. Gordhan also threw out Myeni's request.

Finally removed as chair in October 2017, Myeni disappeared from view until allegations were made that she had given confidential National Prosecuting Authority documents to Angelo Agrizzi, former Chief Operations Officer at Bosasa – a private security and catering firm linked to corruption – and Bosasa's CEO Gavin Watson in 2015.

Agrizzi made the bombshell claim at the Zondo Commission.

Meanwhile, SAA – which received more than R5 billion in bailouts and had an outstanding debt of R5 billion, with accumulated losses of more than R15 billion when Myeni left in 2017 – was still on crutches when the Inquiry into State Capture heard Agrizzi's testimony. Government support for SAA was believed to be almost R25 billion in the decade when Myeni was at the airline.

N

Naidoo, Lawson

Executive secretary of the Council for the Advancement of the South African Constitution (CASAC) | Non-aligned

Change agent

LAWSON MADE NEWS IN 2018 when he filed an affidavit on behalf of CASAC at the North Gauteng High Court, charging that Public Protector (PP) Busisiwe Mkhwebane had made serious alterations to the provisional report of her predecessor, Thuli Madonsela.

This related to the Vrede Dairy scandal in which, it was claimed in the original report, former Free State premier Ace Magashule and former Free State MEC for Agriculture Mosebenzi Zwane had benefitted from the alleged laundering of state money for their own purposes. Mkhwebane was said to have removed their names from the final report.

CASAC said the case was destined to help decide the political direction of the PP's office into the 2019 election.

Naidoo was the special assistant to Frene Ginwala, the speaker of the National Assembly, from 1994 to 1999, and Deputy Secretary of the Ginwala Enquiry, which was established by former president Thabo Mbeki in 2007 to examine whether then National Director of Public Prosecutions (NDPP) Vusi Pikoli was fit to hold office.

Naidoo is a prominent legal and political commentator.

CASAC was described as 'a project of progressive people' who sought to advance the Constitution as a platform for democratic politics and the transformation of society. It entered into litigation and monitored political and legal developments in the country.

Nasrec

The ANC's 54th conference, 2017

THE ANC HAS TRADITIONALLY ADOPTED populist proposals and turned them into propaganda at its four-yearly elective conferences.

The Nasrec conference in Johannesburg in 2017 was no different, although it featured a mighty contest for leadership between billionaire businessman and party stalwart Cyril Ramaphosa and former Cabinet minister and former leader of the African Union (AU) Commission Nkosazana Dlamini-Zuma. Dlamini-Zuma, who was supported in her bid for party power by the soon-to-be former president, Jacob Zuma, lost – although by the most slender of margins.

The Nasrec conference also came at a time when the ANC was at its most challenged, mired in factionalism and corruption.

Ramaphosa did not escape the stain of Zuma's legacy, having to contend with at least three Zuma champions – former Free State premier Ace Magashule (as secretary-general), former Mpumalanga premier David 'DD' Mabuza (as ANC deputy president) and ANC veteran Jessie Duarte (as deputy secretary-general) – in his 'Top 6'. The other two members of the Top 6 were veterans Paul Mashatile (who had supported Ramaphosa, as treasurer-general) and Gwede Mantashe (as national chairperson).

Among the proposals adopted by the ANC at Nasrec were the nationalisation of the Reserve Bank and the expropriation of land without compensation.

National Assembly (NA)

SOUTH AFRICA HAS A BICAMERAL PARLIAMENT (two Houses) supported by a joint administration. The National Assembly is the house directly elected by the voters, while the National Council of Provinces (NCOP) is elected by the provinces to ensure their interests are taken into account in the national sphere.

The NA has 400 members. The number of seats that a party has is in proportion to the number of voters who voted for it in the elections. The Speaker is the presiding officer and is assisted by whips, who are party-political functionaries. The leader of the largest minority party (or largest party that is not in government) is the Leader of the Opposition and enjoys a special status in Parliament.

The leader of government business is appointed from the Cabinet by the president to take care of the affairs of the executive in Parliament. The Speaker may also select two members of the NA to act as parliamentary counsellors – one to the president and the other to the deputy president.

The final decisions on all matters are taken by the House, which is the final authority, but the NA also establishes a range of committees, which make recommendations for debate and decision. A large part of the NA's role in the law-making process happens in committees and much of its oversight over the executive is also done through committees, particularly the portfolio committees.

Individual MPs have several ways of bringing matters to the attention of the House. They may give notice that they intend moving a motion, which is a way of asking the House to take a decision on or to debate it.

The Rules also make provision for members' statements on certain days. During members' statements, 15 members get an opportunity to make a statement for a minute and a half on a topic of their choice. At least six ministers are then afforded two minutes each to respond to any of the statements.

A Cabinet member may ask the Speaker for an opportunity to make a statement. Each political party is allowed an opportunity to then respond to the statement. An important mechanism the NA has of holding the executive to account is questions by MPs to the president and Cabinet ministers. The answers are published in Hansard, the official record of the debates in Parliament.

The NA has many other tasks and roles, including the ratification of international agreements and the appointment of certain office bearers such as the Auditor-General and the Public Protector.

National Council of Provinces (NCOP)

THE UPPER HOUSE OF PARLIAMENT, the NCOP replaced the old Senate. It comprises 90 provincial delegates – 10 for each of the nine provinces, regardless of the population of the province.

Provincial delegations include six permanent delegates and four special delegates, while party representation in the delegation must proportionally reflect the party representation in the provincial legislature. The permanent delegates are selected by the nine provincial legislatures. The four special delegates include the premier of the province and three other special delegates allocated from members of the provincial legislature. They are nominated from Members of the Provincial Legislature (MPLs), contingent on the subject matter being considered by the NCOP.

Organised local government is also represented in the NCOP through the South African Local Government Association (SALGA), which is permitted 10 delegates who may participate, but have no voting rights.

The chairperson of the NCOP in 2019 was the ANC's Thandi Modise, who also occupied the seat of Deputy Speaker of the National Assembly. Her deputy was ANC MP Raseriti Tau, while the leader of the opposition in the Council was the Democratic Alliance's Cathlene Labuschagne.

National Development Plan (NDP)

Government policy

A LONG-TERM PLAN DEVELOPED BY the National Planning Commission (NPC) 'in collaboration and consultation with South Africans from all walks of life' was launched in 2012.

Former finance minister Trevor Manuel, who was national planning minister under President Jacob Zuma, stated in a speech at the launch: '(This) is a plan for a better future ... in which no person lives in poverty, where no one goes hungry, where there is work for all, a nation united in the vision of our Constitution.'

The NDP envisioned 'a transformation of the domestic economy and focused efforts to build the capabilities of both the country and the people'. It was 'founded on six pillars' that represented 'the broad objectives of the plan' which had to be realised by 2030. These were: 'uniting South Africans around a common programme to eliminate poverty and reduce inequality; encouraging citizens to be active in strengthening democracy and in holding their government accountable; raising economic growth, promoting exports and making the economy more labour-absorbing; focusing on key capabilities, including infrastructure, social security, strong institutions and partnerships; and building a capable and developmental state.'

According to the NDP, by 2030 there should be: 'a reduction in the number of people who live in households with a monthly income below R419 per person, from 39% to zero; a reduction in inequality as measured by the Gini coefficient, from 0.69 to 0.6, by redirecting the focus of policy making from short-term, symptom-based policies to longer-term policies based on evidence and reason, and a 'decent standard of living', which included housing, water, electricity, sanitation, safe and reliable public transport, quality education, skills development, safety, security, quality healthcare, social protection, employment, recreation, leisure, a clean environment and adequate nutrition.'

But if Manuel's speech received a rousing response at the launch of the NDP, that was somewhat short-lived. The Congress of South African Trade Unions' Strategies Co-Ordinator, Neil Coleman, wrote in the *Daily Maverick* in 2014 that the plan was 'a deeply problematic document', which failed to address 'the structural problems in our economy'.

Its detractors, like organised labour, said its proposals entrenched 'existing power relations' and that the NDP represented a 'fightback' by conservative economic forces, led by National Treasury and conservative business elites.

The NDP model of wage repression was also seen to contradict government's New Growth Path (NGP) of 2010.

Wage repression is the deliberate undermining of wages by particularly private sector employers to control their payroll, but the state – which is the largest employer in South Africa – also does this. It is a typical means of 'economic efficiency' in a neoliberal state such as South Africa and is based on examples of this same ideology. The Conservatives in Britain have used this method throughout their terms in power, dubbing it 'austerity'.

The NGP, on the other hand, proposed a cap on salaries at the top end, wage moderation in the middle of the wage structure, and more rapid wage growth at the bottom. Many analysts and economists believed this to be the better route, but the NDP has confused the way forward.

Cyril Ramaphosa occasionally referred to it in his many announcements around the economic or new structures related to building the economy after he became president in February 2018. In particular, he noted that total fixed investment in the South African economy stood at 24% of GDP in 2008 but had declined to around 19% by 2017. The NDP said this would need to increase to at least 30% of Gross Domestic Product (GDP) by 2030.

The National Council of Trade Unions (Nactu)

Influenced by Black Consciousness (BC)

One of South Africa's largest trade union federations, it represents more than 400,000 workers across the mining, chemical, food and transport industries. Its largest and most politically prominent affiliate is the Association of Mineworkers and Construction Union (AMCU), which came to wider public attention during the industrial action that preceded the Marikana Massacre. After AMCU, the three largest affiliates in Nactu are in the chemical, food and transport industries.

The federation was founded around the same time as Congress of South African Trade Unions (Cosatu), in 1986, and the current general-secretary is Cunningham Ngcukana. Joseph Maqhekeni was elected Nactu president in 2001 and is still in office.

Anti-privatisation campaigns united smaller trade union federations such as the Federation of Unions of South Africa (Fedusa), the Confederation of South African Workers' Unions (Consawu) and Nactu into considering operating as one federation called the South African Confederation of Trade Unions (Sacotu).

The Council of Unions of South Africa (Cusa) and the Azanian Confederation of Trade Unions (Azactu) had made the decision to merge and analysts believed it would make sense for the proposed new body, Sacotu, to form a new union federation with them, as all were to some degree influenced by the Black Consciousness Movement.

While agreeing on non-racialism, their leadership insisted that the leadership of such a united federation, too, must be black. (During Cosatu's formation, there were discussions surrounding the possibility of both Azactu and Cusa joining it, but these talks were halted over the issue of Cosatu allowing whites to take up positions of leadership.)

By 2014, while Sacotu was formally a trade union federation, an agreement had still not been reached over the merger of different formations with it. And so, the unions effectively still operated as distinct entities.

The National Economic Development and Labour Council (Nedlac)

Established through a 1994 Act of Parliament

Nedlac was launched in 1995 to bring government, organised labour, organised business and community-based organisations together to 'develop and strengthen co-operative mechanisms to address challenges facing South Africa's democracy'.

Its tasks were: sustainable economic growth; facilitating wealth creation; creating greater social equity in the workplace and in communities; increasing participation by all major stakeholders in economic decision-making; and ensuring the equitable distribution of wealth. Nedlac was conceptualised as crucial to the success of the Reconstruction and Development Programme (RDP). It was established through an Act of Parliament in 1994 and operates in terms of its own constitution.

Tito Mboweni, then the governor of the South African Reserve Bank (SARB), signed off on Nedlac in 1995 on behalf of government, John Gomomo on behalf of the Congress of South African Trade Unions (Cosatu), the National Congress of Trade Unions (Nactu) and the Federation of South African Labour (Fedsal), and David Brink, then chairperson of Murray & Roberts Holdings, on behalf of organised business.

Nedlac was expected to consider all proposed legislation relating to labour market policy before being introduced in Parliament. It was also expected to consider all 'significant changes' to social and economic policy before being implemented or introduced in Parliament. It was anticipated that government would be an 'active partner' in Nedlac's policy and legislative engagement processes, and that policy and legislation would, therefore, be revised by government on the basis of consensus reached at Nedlac, before this was submitted to Parliament.

Importantly, however, Parliament was given the sovereign right to determine on these issues whether or not there was agreement from all social partners.

National Energy Regulator of South Africa (Nersa)

State regulatory authority

NERSA IS THE REGULATORY ENERGY AUTHORITY whose mandate is to regulate the electricity, piped-gas and petroleum pipelines industries. Its structure consists of nine members, five of whom are part-time and four full-time, including the Chief Executive Officer. The Energy Regulator is supported by personnel under the direction of the CEO.

There is a view that Nersa and Eskom should be complementary, if not compatible, formations. While the one regulates electricity, the other produces it. Yet, at key junctures over the past few years, the two entities have been at loggerheads. It could be deduced that this was because Eskom's management was digging itself an ever-deeper hole of corruption, and, due to flailing finances and a lack of governance, the power utility needed more money, and that money had to come from consumers. And the only way a cost hike could happen was with Nersa's approval.

At times Nersa has agreed to this, but in 2018, as Eskom sought a staggering R44 billion to cover some of its losses over the 2014/15, 2015/16 and 2016/17 financial years under successive captured individuals, the regulator pushed back. (The R44 billion was 67% of the R66 billion Eskom needed to cover its entire debt portfolio.)

The utility's request to Nersa may have sounded reasonable on paper. It wanted a regulatory clearing account (RCA), which would reconcile a variance in revenue from what Nersa gave Eskom during those years based on Eskom's own projections, and what Eskom's true costs were in the end. An RCA could have eased its liquidity, with Eskom claiming coal contracts were partly to blame as more mines were fixing prices than ever before, and there had also been a lower demand for electricity due to the slump in the economy.

But any additional charges Nersa agreed to would have sent costs up for consumers already under pressure through fuel and VAT increases, leading to a spike in other fees. Nersa then decided to hold public hearings on Eskom's RCA request, which started in June 2018. The last day for consumers to have their say was on 29 November 2018.

Jacob Modise was the chair of Nersa and Maleho Nkomo the deputy chair in that year. Modise was previously the CEO of the Road Accident Fund, the CEO of Johnnic Holdings Limited (the company of which Cyril Ramaphosa was once chairperson), the head of the corporate finance division at Eskom and the financial planning manager at Johannesburg Consolidated Investment Limited (JCI). Nkomo was previously acting chairperson of the National Credit Regulator (NCR) and acting deputy commissioner at the Competition Commission.

(ANC) National Executive Committee (NEC)

Highest organ of the party between its national conferences

Power brokers | Corrupt and captured individuals in its ranks

The NEC has the authority to lead the ANC, subject to the provisions of its Constitution. It is obliged to carry out the decisions and instructions of the national conference and the National General Council (NGC) and supervise and direct the work of the ANC and all its organs, including national, provincial and local government caucuses.

It oversees the work of the ANC Veterans League, ANC Women's League (ANCWL) and the ANC Youth League (ANCYL), and manages and controls all the national and international property and assets of the ANC.

The NEC, importantly, annually appoints a national list committee of not fewer than five and not more than nine people for the selection and adoption of candidates for Parliament. It draws up regulations for the procedures to be followed in such a selection and must report to the NEC prior to the implementation of its recommendations.

The NEC may not consist of less than 50% women and must be elected by secret ballot by the national conference. It holds office for five years and is constituted of the president, deputy president, national chairperson, secretary-general, deputy secretary-general and treasurer-general who are elected separately by the national conference.

There are 80 additional members of the NEC.

The chairperson and the secretary of each elected ANC Provincial Executive Committee (PEC), as well as the presidents and secretary-generals of the ANCWL, the ANCYL and the ANC Veterans League are ex-officio members of the NEC.

The NEC may also co-opt not more than five additional members 'at any time' during its term of office 'in order to provide for a balanced representation that reflects the true character of the South African people'. It fills its own vacancies.

National Freedom Party (NFP)

Nationalist, centrist | Number of seats in Parliament in 2018: 6

Holding on

NEARLY A DECADE AGO, THE NFP EXPLODED into the political scene in KwaZulu-Natal by gaining enough votes during local government elections (LGE) to overtake the Inkatha Freedom Party (IFP) and the Democratic Alliance (DA) to become the biggest party in the province. Fast forward to 2016, the start-up party that secured six seats in Parliament after the 2014 national and provincial elections was on the brink of implosion, beset by infighting that saw it booted out of the LGE in 2016 for failing to pay a deposit to participate.

Its leader, Zanele KaMagwaza-Msibi, had become more of a ceremonial president due to ill health, leaving notable MP and NFP founding member Munzoor Shaik-Emam and his fellow MP Nhlanhlakayise Khubisa to keep the party's profile on the national agenda. But its outlook was not strong for the 2019 elections and its municipal representation had been reduced to one, countrywide.

National Planning Commission (NPC)

Government-funded body | Supports the National Development Plan (NDP)

THE COMMISSION WAS APPOINTED BY then president Jacob Zuma during his first administration in 2010 with the expectation that it would bring fresh ideas and insight to a National Development Plan (NDP), which would advance growth.

The Commissioners would, collectively, have expertise and practical experience in areas including finance, business, politics, labour, economics, sociology, technology, science, demographics and development.

They would be critical advisors to government and would be allocated to expert panels both inside and outside government. These panels would concentrate on issues such as water security, food security, economic development, social security, education, climate change, social cohesion, spatial issues, health and human resource development.

A secretariat would remain in place after the NDP's realisation, and an expert would be positioned in every government department identified in the Plan, whose job it would be to take forward the Commission's proposals.

The goal would be integrated policies and programmes aligned to the NDP.

It was decided the NCP should be chaired by then deputy president Cyril Ramaphosa. His task would be to feed the work of the Commission into Cabinet and government. Then minister in the Presidency for Planning, Monitoring and Evaluation, Jeff Radebe, was named deputy chairperson.

In 2015, Zuma announced new members of the NCP for a further period of five years, with Radebe named chairperson, and Professor Malegapuru William Makgoba deputy chairperson. But the NCP remained largely a background operation, with very little of its work filtering into public knowledge or discussion.

National Prosecuting Authority of South Africa (NPA)

Government body

Mired in corruption

THE CONSTITUTION AND THE BILL OF RIGHTS created this body in 1996, with the Office of the National Director of Public Prosecutions established in 1998, also in terms of the Constitution.

The NPA comprises a National Director, deputy national directors, directors of public prosecutions and special directors.

The Constitution provides the prosecuting authority with the power to institute criminal proceedings on behalf of the State.

The NPA is structured into the following Core Business Units: the National Prosecutions Service (NPS); the Asset Forfeiture Unit (AFU); Sexual Offences and Community Affairs (SOCA); the Specialised Commercial Crime Unit (SCCU); the Witness Protection Unit (WPU) and the Priority Crimes Litigation Unit (PCLU).

The National Union of Metalworkers of South Africa (Numsa)

Workerist union | Rejects allegiances to political parties | Falls within the South African Federation of Trade Unions (SAFTU) fold

Power brokers

NUMSA WAS A LONG-TIME AFFILIATE of the Congress of South African Trade Unions (Cosatu) before it grew ideologically restless, ever-more distanced from Cosatu's tripartite partner the ANC under Jacob Zuma's leadership, was expelled from the federation and eventually fell under another collective's umbrella.

Formed in 1987 as a merger of the Metal and Allied Workers Union (Mawu) and three others, it benefitted when the General and Allied Workers Union and the Transport and General Workers Union, which were Cosatu members, 'gave' Numsa their metal members. Its strongest influence was from Mawu, a conceit of intellectuals and workers whose legacy negated Cosatu's 'populists' and 'nationalists' who had 'allowed' the federation to be 'pacified' through its alliance with the ANC from 1992 onwards. This, despite it remaining on the Left.

Numsa's general secretary Moses Mayekiso originally agitated for a split with Cosatu to form a workers' party after the Constitution was ratified in 1996, but the National Union of Mineworkers (NUM) – then, as now, Cosatu's biggest affiliate – opposed it.

Increasingly distanced from the ANC and the SACP – which Numsa later regarded as having abandoned a socialist direction – Numsa's affiliation with SAFTU indicated its valiant hope for more revolutionary tactical opportunities, including the establishment of the Socialist Revolutionary Workers Party in November 2018. It was expected that Numsa general-secretary Irvin Jim would take up its leadership, although there were concerns this could negatively affect the union if the party contested the national and provincial elections in 2019. But Numsa's critics said it had concentrated too much on the intellectual aspect and neglected actual shop-floor issues, especially those affected by the rapid arrival of the Fourth Industrial Revolution.

Numsa was among those unions that seemed to be leaving its members largely unprepared in an economy mired in the Second Industrial Revolution where electricity and fossil fuels still steered production.

Meanwhile, international metal players took decisions in their parent countries or through global or regional trade deals unconcerned with the drawbacks for metalworkers trained only for South Africa's old world economic model.

The National Union of Mineworkers (NUM)

The largest affiliate of the Congress of South African Trade Unions (Cosatu)

Power brokers | Gupta links

THE UNION ONCE CREDITED WITH THE HIGHEST MEMBERSHIP in South Africa, the NUM has a close history with Cyril Ramaphosa, who became State President in 2018, as he founded it in 1982 for black mineworkers.

Many analysts put its bargaining recognition from the Chamber of Mines at that time down to Ramaphosa's skill and experience in traversing the worlds of business, labour and liberation politics.

Among NUM's achievements during the last years of apartheid was driving the end of job reservation for whites. Its fierce lobbying also brought about the Leon Commission of Inquiry into Safety and Health in the Mining Industry in 1995, which ultimately led to significant changes in underground safety and health conditions. But nearly 20 years of economic turmoil, political infighting and a failure to materially alter the prospects for workers within government's neoliberal model took their toll on NUM which was, by 2012, a union in serious trouble with itself.

Then came mid-year labour conflict on Lonmin's mines in Marikana, North West, which, by August 2012, had reached breaking point. NUM took a devastating blow when the state-sanctioned massacre unfolded in the middle of that month, deeply affecting many of its members.

Organised mine labour had been steadily dividing between NUM and the Association of Mineworkers and Construction Union (Amcu, known as 'the yellow union'), largely along political lines, but Marikana speeded that up while NUM was already seeing its membership gradually dropping in a crisis-hit sector. Some bargaining structures said it failed threshold requirements to be recognised.

NUM organised in the mining, construction and energy sectors, all of which were struggling due to a poor growth and investment outlook for the country. The mining sector was especially embattled as more retrenchments loomed in the years ahead. The union took further strain for its seeming closeness to employers and government as an affiliate of the ANC's partner, Cosatu.

Antipathy meanwhile grew towards NUM's general secretary Frans Baleni, who finally bowed out under pressure and amid controversy in 2015 after nearly 10 years in the post. Baleni had succeeded ANC heavyweights Gwede Mantashe and Kgalema Motlanthe who were also NUM general secretaries.

By 2016, the union's own action plan said it had failed to 'eradicate tribalism, factionalism, cliques, gossip and rumour-mongering'. Baleni's successor David Sipunzi had failed to unite NUM, and there were concerns that Sipunzi had been captured.

In 2017, Sipunzi admitted that his 2012 campaign for NUM office had been funded by the Shiva Uranium Mine, which was owned by the notorious Gupta family. But it wasn't only Sipunzi's faction that had links with the Guptas. NUM itself in 2017 confirmed it had received R1.5 million in donations from the family's Oakbay Resources.

The union's former deputy president Joseph Montisetsi was elected new president of the NUM at its national congress in June 2018. He defeated former president Piet Matosa for the position, while Sipunzi retained his position after defeating contender Mbuyiseni Hibana.

NUM resolved to put all of its muscle into ending mine fatalities, calling for an arbitration process similar to the Life Esidimeni hearings into the deaths of dozens of mental health patients in Gauteng, in order to fight for compensation for the families of mineworkers who died on the job.

(ANC) National Working Committee (NWC)

Pivotal body within the party's leadership

The constitution of a new NWC happens as soon as possible after the conclusion of the ANC's national conference held every five years. Thereafter, the National Executive Committee (NEC) meets and elects the NWC, which does not necessarily only include full-time functionaries of the ANC.

The ANC Veterans League, ANC Women's League and the ANC Youth League appoint one representative each to serve on the NWC. Not less than 50% of members must be women.

The NWC carries out decisions and instructions of the NEC, conducts the current work of the ANC and ensures that provinces, regions, branches and all other party structures, including parliamentary caucuses, also fulfil its decisions.

In 2018, the members of the NWC were: Nkosazana Dlamini-Zuma, Lindiwe Sisulu, Naledi Pandor, Jeff Radebe, Angie Motshekga, Derek Hanekom, Thoko Didiza, Nomvula Mokonyane, Nathi Mthethwa, Ronald Lamola, Tina Joemat-Pettersson, Dakota Legoete, Senzo Mchunu, Zizi Kodwa, Tony Yengeni, Bathabile Dlamini, Nomaindia Mfeketo, Barbara Creecy and Thandi Modise.

Ndabeni-Abrahams, Stella

Minister of Communications, Telecommunications and Postal Services | ANC-aligned

On the way up

When Ndabeni-Abrahams was appointed in a reshuffle by President Cyril Ramaphosa in November 2018, there was widespread support for the decision, and for her. Previously deputy minister of Communications, Ndabeni-Abrahams also had solid ANC credentials, as a member of the Eastern Cape Provincial Executive Committee (PEC), and of the Eastern Cape ANC Provincial Working Committee (PWC).

She had been a strong supporter of Ramaphosa's 2017 ANC presidential campaign, and had been in the movement since the ANC Youth League (ANCYL) days of its former presidents Julius Malema and Fikile Mbalula and deputy president Ronald Lamola, serving as a member of the ANCYL in East London from 1990 to 1994 before becoming a member of its National Executive Committee under Malema, from 2008 to 2010.

At only 40, Ndabeni-Abrahams is one of the youngest people in government. She was the youngest minister in Jacob Zuma's Cabinet at the age of 34, but that did not stop her from standing up to senior adversaries in the party. When she was appointed as Minister of Communications, the media recalled how she earned headlines back in 2016 when it was revealed that she had asked Zuma to intervene because then communications minister Faith Muthambi – who is suspected of state capture – was treating her like a 'PA'.

Ndabeni-Abrahams has an advanced certificate in project management from Rhodes University, a Commonwealth Telecommunications Organisation diploma in telecommunications and management systems, and a certificate in telecommunications, policy and regulation management from the University of the Witwatersrand. She had enrolled for a Master's in telecommunications, policy and regulation management at the University of the Witwatersrand.

Ndabeni-Abrahams was elected as an ANC MP in 2009 after being a project manager for the Eastern Cape Socio-Economic Consultative Council from 2003–09.

She faced many challenges in her new post. In terms of administration, she would effectively have to undo what Siyabonga Cwele, former minister of Telecommunications and Postal Services, did under Jacob Zuma by overseeing the unification of two ministries. Cwele had to split Communications and Telecommunications and Postal Services.

Ndabeni-Abrahams would also have to lead a way forward in ICT (information and communication technologies) with government placing emphasis on the fourth industrial revolution, but not coming to grips yet with how it would impact on the country in terms of education, and job opportunities and job losses. But this placed her firmly in the sights of the millennials, whose concerns about the high cost of data were raised immediately upon her appointment on Twitter.

Ndabeni-Abrahams herself has recognised that Artificial Intelligence, Big Data and Machine Learning are imperatives to reskill South Africa's young workforce in a digital knowledge-driven future. When she was Deputy Minister of Communications, Cabinet approved the Ikamva National e-Skills Institute (*iNeSI*) Bill which came before Parliament in May 2018, and also approved the ICT SMME strategy and an accompanying implementation plan, while the Digital Development Fund Bill was still to be approved as public consultations had to be had.

But Ndabeni-Abrahams's greatest political challenge looked to be dealing with the SABC, and within a fortnight of her appointment, she had already raised the ire of its board by visiting the public broadcaster and talking to staff and unions about proposed Section 189 retrenchments, which the board favoured. Ndabeni-Abrahams said she hoped to find an alternative to job losses, but the SABC was bleeding money, and looked to collapse within months if it did not cut up to 2000 jobs. But in January 2019, the SABC board announced it had suspended retrenchments and job cuts owing to 'pressure' from the government and unions.

Ndlozi, Mbuyiseni

Nickname: People's bae | Economic Freedom Fighters (EFF) MP | EFF national spokesperson

On the way up | Star

A MEMBER OF THE SOUTH AFRICAN STUDENTS CONGRESS (SASCO), the ANC Youth League (ANCYL) and the Young Communist League (YCL) when he was at school and a student, Ndlozi was also well known for his internationalism, serving in the Cuban solidarity movement and working for Boycott Divestment Sanctions (BDS) which supports Palestinian liberation by way of isolating Israel.

He completed his doctorate at the University of the Witwatersrand (Wits) in 2017.

Ndlozi was among the EFF MPs who were forcibly and violently removed from Parliament during former president Jacob Zuma's State of the Nation Address in 2015. They had disrupted his speech, and repeatedly heckled him with the words 'pay back the money', which related to the upgrade costs on Zuma's private homestead in Nkandla, KwaZulu-Natal. They had been members of the National Assembly for less than a year at that point, but the impact of their heavy-handed removal was wide-ranging, and drew criticism even from their ideological opposites, the Democratic Alliance (DA).

Using a combination of revolutionary intellect and charm, Ndlozi quickly got the South African spotlight, grabbing the attention irrespective of party political affiliations. This allowed the EFF a unique reach, which the ANC and the DA simply did not have.

Nel, Advocate Gerrie

Nickname: The Bulldog | Former state prosecutor | Head of private prosecutions at AfriForum | Non-aligned

AFRIFORUM STARTLED THE COUNTRY WHEN NEL announced his resignation after many high-profile cases for the state and joined its ranks in 2017. He had worked for the justice system for 34 years, during which time he had successfully prosecuted former national police commissioner Jackie Selebi for corruption and former paralympian Oscar Pistorius for murder.

Nel was to become head of AfriForum's new private prosecuting unit, with South African legislation making private prosecution possible in cases where the National Prosecuting Authority (NPA) had decided not to prosecute someone suspected of an offence. Nel said he had decided to not accept the position at AfriForum because he was concerned about the NPA's 'tendency to selective prosecutions', and that not everyone was necessarily equal before the law.

Nel and AfriForum earned the spotlight in 2018 when they announced they were considering a private prosecution against Economic Freedom Fighters (EFF) leader Julius Malema for fraud. But there wasn't much uptake from analysts who believed the bid would fail.

Nel earned more public support for his attempts to see former Zimbabwean first lady Grace Mugabe prosecuted for her alleged assault on South African Gabriella Engels, who she was said to have attacked with an extension cord in a Sandton hotel room in 2017. The South African government's awarding of diplomatic immunity to Mugabe was overturned by the High Court and AfriForum sought to proceed with a criminal case against her.

Nene, Nhlanhla

Former finance minister | Former deputy minister of Finance | Former trade unionist | ANC politician

NENE WAS NO STRANGER TO THE JOB of Minister of Finance when President Cyril Ramaphosa appointed him in February 2018. He'd previously held the post in 2014 and 2015 when former president Jacob Zuma both appointed and axed him. The axeing was to 'promote' ANC backbencher David 'Des' van Rooyen who, it was believed, may have been more amenable to signing off on projects Zuma needed approved, whereas Nene was less pliable.

But it came as a shock to the nation when Nene resigned from his post in October 2018, after he testified at the Zondo Commission of Inquiry into state capture that he had met the notorious Guptas, at their Saxonwold compound, several times. He had earlier denied this in a TV interview after his firing, in 2016.

Nene was also linked to a spurious Public Investment Corporation (PIC) loan awarded to his son, Siyabonga Nene, and Siyabonga's Mozambican business associate, while he, Nhlanhla Nene, was the chairperson of the PIC. The EFF had been calling for an investigation into Nene's Gupta links as well as possible incursions relating to his son and the PIC.

Nene was nonetheless praised for having withstood pressure from Zuma to sign off on the disputed nuclear deal with Russia, which was given as a primary reason for his having been axed from his post in 2015. He also received some praise for having fallen on his sword when his Gupta visits were revealed.

Zuma's reason for Nene's departure in 2015 was that he, Nene, was moving to the New Development Bank (NDB) of BRICS (an association of five major emerging national economies, including Brazil, Russia, India, China and South Africa).

Two years later, Nene was still not with the NDB and, by that time, Van Rooyen had spent a mere weekend in the job while the market capitalisation of the Johannesburg Stock Exchange (JSE) went down by 1.49% to R11.18 trillion, a loss of R169.6 billion. Nene was finally named chairperson of the NDP in April 2018 when he was already back in his old job.

Zuma was compelled to bring back Nene's predecessor Pravin Gordhan to get the ship back in the water, but he would later reshuffle his Cabinet and turn Malusi Gigaba, an acolyte linked to state capture, into finance minister.

Ramaphosa quickly shifted Gigaba back to his old ministry of Home Affairs after he became president and restored Nene to Finance. Nene was then also finally elected to chair the NDB at a meeting in Shanghai, China.

Nene would meanwhile have to consider the implications of a R20.3-billion loan made available to South Africa (and the other members of the association) by the bank.

He would also have to consider the consequences of a decade of legislation, passed in 2008, which allowed Parliament more control over the budget, Nene being a stickler for macroeconomic stability.

Nene organised the first-ever strike in the financial sector, in 1990. He was a regional administrative manager at Metropolitan Life insurance company at the time, but also a shop steward of the South African Commercial, Catering and Allied Workers Union (SACCAWU).

New Development Bank (NDB)

Multilateral development bank | Financing arm of the BRICS (Brazil, Russia, India, China and South Africa) development bloc

Change agent

THE NDB, ESTABLISHED IN 2014, WAS REPORTED as 'ready to provide' US$8 billion for infrastructure in South Africa by mid-2018, yet there were serious concerns that it was neither 'ready', nor could meet expectations of due diligence and transparency. One of its main obstacles was that it was still denominated by the dollar, which opened borrowers up to currency risk and inevitably created high pressure around the cost of repayment.

NDB president, K.V. Kamath, said the bank would begin to issue loans in local currencies during the second half of 2018 'to reduce the effects of exchange rate volatility and the borrowing costs of member countries'.

The NDP was designed as an alternative to the International Monetary Fund (IMF) and the World Bank, but its funding model seemed to replicate that of those.

The bank's blueprint was to back infrastructure and 'sustainable development projects' in developing countries and emerging economies, particularly those in its bloc. It was to work alongside other multilateral banks and financial institutions, especially in the BRICS countries. In the case of South Africa, it wanted partnerships to co-finance projects with the Development Bank of South Africa (DBSA), the Industrial Development Corporation (IDC) and the African Development Bank (AfDB) or Banque Africaine de Développement – based in Abidjan, Côte d'Ivoire – as well as commercial banks. (South Africa is a beneficiary of the AfDB, a financial provider to African governments and private companies investing in the regional member countries.)

The NDB approved projects from all five BRICS members by 2018. Those loans indeed dominated its portfolio, aggregating $1.6 billion of its total amount of approvals of US$1.7 billion. Ultimately, it would be looking at 55% to remain owned by the five founding members and 45% to be split among other countries, according to Leslie Maasdorp, the NDP's vice president and chief financial officer.

Among its high-level commitments was $200 million (R2.5 billion) to South Africa's state-owned transportation company Transnet, specifically the Durban Container Terminal Berth Reconstruction Project. The aim was to bring Durban's port-petrochemical complex capacity up to world standard, but it was expected this may result in protests from environmental activists and communities which could be adversely affected by the build.

The remainder of the bank's $8-billion allocation to South Africa was also set to fund infrastructure. Power utility Eskom originally received a R2.4-billion loan but corruption investigations into the state-owned entity placed that in jeopardy, and it was held over.

Maasdorp, named vice president and CFO of the bank, was previously a president of Bank of America-Merrill Lynch for southern Africa for four years, a vice-chairperson of Barclays Capital and Absa Capital and the first African appointed as international advisor to Goldman Sachs International.

Before he became a global investment banker, Maasdorp served in government, first as special advisor to the Minister of Labour and then as deputy director-general of the Department of Public Enterprises. He also led the restructuring and privatisation of state-owned entities (SOEs). Maasdorp earned a Master's in economics from the School of Oriental and African Studies (SPAS) at the University of London.

South African Monale Ratsoma was confirmed as the head of the NDB's African Regional Centre in Sandton in 2017. The regional centre aimed to particularly develop the transport and energy sector. Ratsoma – who has a Master's in economics from the University of Johannesburg – was at Treasury for six years and previously headed its asset and liability management division. Before that, he was the chief economist for the Thebe Investment Corporation.

South African Dondo Mogajane, the director-general of Treasury, was named as Director for South Africa in 2017. Former Reserve Bank governor and struggle stalwart Tito Mboweni was the first director for South Africa. His term ran from 2015 to 2017.

New Growth Path (NGP)

Government economic plan

FORMER ECONOMIC DEVELOPMENT MINISTER Ebrahim Patel laid out the NGP in December 2010 with job creation as a priority, the goal being to reduce unemployment by 10 percentage points by 2020. As an emerging economy striving for development, South Africa seemed to offer the perfect framework for such a plan. The NGP fixed six priority areas to job creation: infrastructure development, agriculture, mining, manufacturing, the 'green' economy and tourism.

There was opposition to it from the start from both capital and labour, as they felt the programme lacked concrete measures to fight unemployment. It also appeared to contradict the National Development Plan (NDP), which sought to advance a neoliberal ideology, which essentially keeps wages at the bottom low.

Ngwenya, Gwen

Democratic Alliance (DA) MP | Former DA policy chief | Former University of Cape Town (UCT) Student Representative Council (SRC) leader

Not even 30 years old, Ngwenya – who was schooled in activism through the DA Student Organisation at university – quickly became a force in liberal politics.

With a degree in law from UCT, a Master's in international economics from the University of Paris and working towards her second Master's, in finance, at the University of London in 2018, she had gained experience in economics research in India and had been the chief operating officer for the Johannesburg-based liberal think tank, the Institute of Race Relations (IRR).

She described herself upon entering her top job at the DA as 'a gutsy liberal' who did not regard her party as 'anti-black'.

Ngwenya resigned as DA policy chief a month before the party's elections manifesto launch, apparently due to clashes with some leaders over the DA's disputed position on Black Economic Empowerment (BEE). After the party's federal council decided BEE was 'not working' in mid-2018, its internecine struggles over this issue went public on social media.

Nhlapo Commission of Inquiry

Government probe

The Department of Traditional Affairs during the Thabo Mbeki administration assigned Professor Thandabantu Nhlapo – a legal expert, former deputy ambassador to Washington D.C. and advisor to the Constitutional Assembly after 1994 – to head a commission to decide which of South Africa's royal family's kings would receive recognition certificates.

In 2006, it was announced that King Mpendulo Calvin Sigcau of the amaXhosa, King Ndamase KaNdamase of the amaMpondo of Nyandeni, King Makoke Enoch Mabhena of the amaNdebele, King Mbusi Mahlangu of amaNdebele of Ndzundza, King Lekunutu Cavandish Mota of Batlokwa and King Mopeli Thokoana Mopeli of the Bakwena would be the only kings allowed to name themselves as such. This caused significant conflict, especially when the inquiry's investigations revealed that the amahlubi, amaShangane, amaKwayi, amaKhonjwayo, amaSwati akaMlambo and amaMpondomise did not have kingships at all.

It also took longer than expected for recognition certificates to be awarded to King Goodwill Zwelithini of the amaZulu, King Zwelibanzi Dalindyebo of the abaThembu, King Thulare Victor Thulare of the Bapeli and King Toni Peter Mphephu Ramabulana of the VhaVenda.

Ramabulana became highly controversial in 2018 when he was identified as having been the recipient of disputed luxury goods purchased through the disgraced VBA Mutual Bank in Limpopo.

Cases that remained in ligitation were the kingship of the VhaVenda, the Bapedi Ba Marota and the amaShangane in Limpopo, the amaPondo of Nyandeni, amaMpondomise and amaRharabe in the Eastern Cape and the amaNdunza in Mpumalanga.

The most prominent objection lingered into 2018 when the royal family representing Wezizwe Feziwe Sigcau was told by the Minister of Co-operative Governance and Traditional Affairs that it should have instituted a legal challenge to review the Nhlapo Commission's decision and former president Jacob Zuma, who opposed her bid to become queen of the amaMpondo aseQaukeni. Instead, the commission had stated that Zanozuko Tyelovuyo Sigcau was the king of the amaMpondo nation.

Wezizwe was the daughter of the late amaMpondo aseQaukeni paramount chief, Mpondombini Justice Sigcau, who was removed as king by the decision of the commission in 2010. It replaced him with King Zanozuko. Wezizwe believed she should be queen to take over from her father, following a later setting-aside of Zuma's submission to the high court in 2014 for an order declaring she had no right to claim the position of queen.

But Norman Arendse SC for the president and the department said the approach favoured by Wezizwe would result in the duplication of the task the commission undertook when it investigated the claims for kingship. Judgment was reserved.

Niehaus, Carl

Former ANC MP | Former ambassador to the Netherlands | Former CEO of the Gauteng Economic Development Agency | Former political prisoner

Pathological liar | Perennial fraudster

UMKHONTO WE SIZWE VETERANS ASSOCIATION (MKMVA) leader and self-appointed campaign manager for Nkosazana Damini-Zuma's abortive bid to become president of the ANC December 2017, Niehaus packed many dubious achievements into his life.

He was studying theology at the old Rand-Afrikaanse Universiteit (RAU, now the University of Johannesburg) when he was expelled for putting up ANC posters. He later studied at the University of the Witwatersrand (Wits) but was arrested and jailed for 15 years for high treason. During that time, he completed two degrees through Unisa and married his co-accused, Jansie Lourens, while they were both in jail.

On his release in 1991, Niehaus became part of the ANC's negotiating team, a member of its Provincial Executive Committee in what would become Gauteng, and one of Nelson Mandela's spokespersons. He became an MP after 1994 and was then made the ambassador to the Netherlands.

Niehaus then held a series of short-lived corporate and government appointments, including as the Chief Executive Officer of the evangelical Rhema church and the Gauteng Economic Development Agency. It was when he was working for the Gauteng government that he admitted forgery.

Married multiple times, Neihaus made headlines for the debts he had run up, landlords trying to evict him and the many schemes he came up with to get funds from friends and family, including paying for the fictitious funerals of his parents – both of whom were still alive at the time.

Despite all this ignominy, Neihaus was elected to the leadership of the splinter Umkhonto we Sizwe Military Veterans Association (MKMVA) led by former deputy minister of Defence, Kebby Maphatsoe, himself a controversial figure.

Northern Cape

Province

SOUTH AFRICA'S LARGEST, THOUGH MOST SPARSELY POPULATED, province was established in 1994 as one of three to emerge out of the Cape province. With its capital in the historic diamond city of Kimberley, the Northern Cape has traditionally been ANC-ruled, but its dominance is not guaranteed. Infighting within the party, most notably in the success of the wake of the breakaway Congress of the People (COPE), coupled to the steady growth in popularity of the Democratic Alliance (DA), make this one of the key provinces to be contested in 2019.

The DA has made no secret of its desire to wrest control of the province, along with Gauteng, while the ruling ANC has mirrored the factional splits in the parent organisation – and its own high-profile corruption case culminating in the conviction of former provincial leader John Block.

The figures back this up: ANC support at a hairline 49.8% in 1994, grew as high as 68% in 2004, before subsiding to between 60% and 64%, while the 2016 local government elections took it below the 60% threshold to 58.3%. The DA on the other hand has grown from just over 1% in 1994 to 24% by 2014. COPE polled a highly credible 16.7% on debut in 2009, but all but disappeared five years later. The EFF entered provincial politics in 2014 at just under 5%, receiving 8.6% support two years later during the local government elections.

Control of the province will be more than just bragging rights, beset by welfare problems from foetal alcohol syndrome to unemployment, it also sits atop a treasure trove of minerals – from diamonds to iron ore, bauxite, zinc, lead and manganese.

North West

Province | Led by the ANC since 1994

Mired in corruption

THE PEOPLE OF THIS POOR-PERFORMING REGION where poverty and unemployment were high witnessed corruption on a grand scale.

National Treasury Director-General (DG) Dondo Mogajane told the Public Financial Management (PFM) conference in May 2018 that 'fruitless and wasteful expenditure' had risen in North West from R2 billion to R14 billion in the 2016 to 2017 period. That was around the time people were not being cared for, and even dying, in its non-performing health facilities.

Small wonder North West's health department was placed under administration by President Cyril Ramaphosa in 2018, at around the same time as he appointed an inter-ministerial committee to assess the state of the province.

At the centre of all of this was former premier Supra Mahumapelo. Believed by some to be so dubious and dangerous an individual within its own ranks, the ANC sought his voluntary resignation. He refused at first, adding fuel to a divisive political environment, which was further challenged by threats from party supporters in the province to boycott the ANC in the 2019 elections if Mahumapelo was pushed out.

Mahumapelo faced off against the Provincial Executive Committee (PEC) in May 2018, saying he was under pressure from Luthuli House to resign. The ANC was certainly facing its own worst scenario in North West at the time, having seemingly taken the province's support for granted for far too long.

Political commentator and author Ralph Mathekga, a fellow at the University of Johannesburg, described North West as having been a 'home run' for the ANC. In the 2004 elections, it secured a resounding 80.71% electoral support. That was followed by another convincing victory in the 2009 elections, with the party securing 72.89% support. Its winning streak carried into the 2014 elections where it secured 67.39% electoral support. But that support was shown to be waning by 2018, and it was predicted that it could even reach 'a severe decline' in 2019.

After political wrangling that went on for months inside the ANC, former North West DG of administration Job Mokgoro was appointed premier.

Ntombela, Sisi

Free State premier | ANC politician

NTOMBELA HAD A MAJOR TASK TAKING OVER from her controversial predecessor, Ace Magashule, and this was not only because the province itself had been run by a Provincial Task Team (PTT) for months by the time she entered office. It was also because she was identified as having been close to Magashule and her name had been supported for his old job by the ANC Women's League, in particular its controversial president, Bathabile Dlamini.

Magashule and Dlamini were in the camp that surrounded ANC presidential hopeful Nkosazana Dlamini-Zuma in the battle to be the party's leader in December 2017. Dlamini-Zuma lost to Cyril Ramaphosa, but there were many senior comrades sowing disunity or not actively practising unity.

Nonetheless, Ntombela quickly declared her support for Ramaphosa. But not only did she have to face issues of factionalism within the ANC in the province as well as massive allegations of nepotism and corruption from within Magashule's old administration, she also had to unravel serious financial trouble in municipalities.

Interventions had already happened in three – Maluti-A-Phofung, Mafube and Masilonyana – during which their executive powers were removed by constitutional means.

Upon her inauguration in early 2018, Ntombela recognised many of the socio-economic problems that had led to circumstances where homeowners were simply not paying for services, leaving some municipalities stricken. This pointed to far-wider issues within the country. Ntombela noted, for instance, that in Mafube 'about 90% of the people are unemployed and dependent on social grants'. But she also set a deadline of six months to her new executive to account for how money allocated to their departments was spent.

Free State politics was expected to shift and even fundamentally change in 2019 through possible national coalitions struck by opposition parties with ANC divisions high in the province. Despite his notoriety, Magashule had got the results the ANC wanted in elections, and his detractors were concerned that he might 'rule' Free State 'from Luthuli House'.

Equally, once trade unionist Sam Mashinini was named Magashule's successor as Free State chairperson at the party's provincial elective conference in May 2018, Ntombela was believed to be on her way out as premier by mid-2019. She was elected ANC treasurer in those elections, which had been stalled for months after a first round was declared null and void by the courts.

Ntsebeza, Advocate Dumisa SC

Chancellor of the University of Fort Hare | Visiting professor of political science and law at the University of Connecticut Storrs and Hartford campuses | Chairperson of the Desmond Tutu Peace Trust | Trustee of the Nelson Mandela Foundation | Founder and former president of the National Association of Democratic Lawyers (Nadel) | Former president of the Black Lawyers Association | Former commissioner of the Truth and Reconciliation Commission (TRC) | Politically non-aligned | Former political prisoner

Change agent | Star

A long prison sentence for his anti-apartheid political activities did not stop Ntsebeza either from completing his law studies or, later, from representing some of South Africa's most high-profile political prisoners.

His was a defiant political trajectory, neither Black Consciousness (BC) nor ANC, but an activist and leftwing to the extent that he was expelled from Fort Hare, and his association with struggle heroes like Matthew Goniwe (one of The Cradock Four who were assassinated by the apartheid regime in 1985) led to his torture and imprisonment.

Ntsebeza was the first black African South African to be conferred silk status in the history of the Cape bar, in 2005. He was a member of and spokesperson for the Judicial Service Commission (JSC) until then president Zuma replaced him in 2017.

Known for his independence and his refusal to remain quiet in the face of injustice of any kind, Ntsebeza was a thorn in the side of the Farlam Commission, established by Zuma to investigate the Marikana Massacre in 2012. When its report was released in 2015, he called it 'a disgrace'. Representing 36 families of Lonmin employees who were killed at the mine by the police, Ntsebeza earned the respect of the nation for his powerful, unyielding approach towards government and big business. He noted at the start that post-mortem reports, introduced by the evidence leaders, showed that no less than 14 of the striking miners were shot from behind, many in the back or in the back of the head.

That would have assisted the positive response to him heading up a South

African Institute of Chartered Accountants inquiry in 2018 into the conduct of former KPMG employees who were alleged to have contravened the code of their profession in their work on the notorious Gupta family's accounts and with the South African Revenue Service.

Nugent Commission of Inquiry into Tax Administration and Governance by SARS

State probe (also see Moyane, Tom)

President Cyril Ramaphosa set up the commission under retired Judge Robert Nugent to investigate the near-destruction of the tax collection agency under Commissioner Tom Moyane, who was appointed by Jacob Zuma. Its final report, which it submitted in December 2018, recommended the setting aside of a number of illegal contracts and the recovery of expenditure at an imploding revenue service.

Chief among its findings was that the disgraced Moyane should pay his own legal bills, and that the National Director for Public Prosecutions should consider criminal prosecution for Moyane having awarded a spurious contract to global management consultancy Bain & Co for the 'restructuring' of SARS.

Nugent said Bain had collaborated with Moyane in a 'premeditated offensive' to allow Moyane to effectively 'seize' SARS for his own purposes.

Bain, which has its headquarters in Boston, Massachusetts, admitted to 'serious lapses of judgement'. Moyane was fired by Ramaphosa in November 2018.

Nxasana, Mxolisi

Former national director of Public Prosecutions (NDPP)

Believed to have corruptly accepted a golden handshake

Nxasana was the focus of a corruption case when the North Gauteng High Court in Pretoria referred to him as being party to a bribe by accepting a R17-million settlement offer from then president Jacob Zuma. Advocacy groups Corruption Watch and Freedom Under Law challenged his 2015 golden handshake, with Advocate Jeff Budlender asking the court to declare the deal between Zuma and Nxasana unlawful, and set it aside.

Judge Willem van der Linde questioned Nxasana's suitability to be the NDPP, saying the facts revealed he was on the one end of a bribe, and questioned whether it was desirable to have a prosecutor who was willing to take a bribe lead the NPA.

Behind the scenes, it was believed Nxasana had fallen out with Zuma after he sent Zuma a memorandum recommending the suspensions of former acting NDPP Nomgcobo Jiba and NPA commercial crimes head Lawrence Mgwebi.

Nxasana later took court action in an attempt to have the president institute an inquiry into their conduct.

The Pretoria High Court had found that Jiba, deputy NDPP, and Mrwebi, a special director of public prosecutions, had brought the NPA and the legal profession into disrepute by failing to prosecute former police crime intelligence head Richard Mdluli. The duo was stripped of their right to practise as advocates.

Nzimande, Blade (see South African Communist Party)

Orania

Proto-white homeland | Rightwing

Its protagonists hoped Orania would form part of a balkanised South Africa of ethnic states founded on the principles of self-determination and created it as a prototype in what was an apartheid government town created in 1965 to house workers building the Orange River Scheme.

Professor Carel Boshoff, the son-in-law of apartheid supremo Hendrik Verwoerd, bought the town on 8 000ha of arid Karoo land for R1.3 million and it was opened in 1991 as an 'Afrikaner town' and a 'national state growth point'.

It continues to this day, and has never grown beyond much of a curiosity – a uniquely South African combination of a kibbutz and an Amish settlement that is determined to govern itself on cultural and religious lines, but has never achieved the momentum that Boshoff and his band of hardcore followers believed it could before the watershed 1994 elections.

The population grew to 1400 people led by Boshoff's son Carel Boshoff Jr. In 2017, it announced plans to take its currency, the ora – which is pegged to the rand – into the world of virtual currency.

It remains very much part of the Northern Cape, subject to the same laws and norms as the rest of South Africa.

O'Sullivan, Paul

Private forensic investigator | Loss control consultant | Self-styled corruption-buster

It was a rare private eye who would have the chutzpah to sue the state for R193.2 millon. But O'Sullivan – who seemed to be involved in every kind of high-profile legal matter, from that of jailed underworld boss Radovan Krejcir to Dudu Myeni, the former chairperson of SAA and the Jacob Zuma Foundation – was an embedded thorn in the ruling party's side.

The suit against the state came in 2018 after O'Sullivan's arrest off a Heathrow-bound flight at O.R. Tambo International in Johannesburg was dismissed by a court. He had been held on an alleged passport violation, but claimed the reason behind it was political as he had been probing cases against corrupt police officers, prosecutors, state-owned entity board members and top politicians. O'Sullivan wanted R22.6 million for loss of income and R164.8 million for estimated future loss of income, as well as R5 million for pain and suffering, and R700,000 in legal fees.

But his cases were seldom about himself. Also in 2018, for example, O'Sullivan and his associates teamed up with the non-profit, Forensics for Justice, to open criminal dockets against the food company, Tiger Brands, following the deaths of at least 180 people and the illnesses of nearly 500 from eating the company's products. O'Sullivan dubbed the affects of the listeriosis crisis 'mass deaths' and planned to work with the National Institute for Communicable Diseases to file charges of attempted murder and culpable homicide.

Politicians and state deployees in his crosshairs have included Deputy President David 'DD' Mabuza (over 'fake land claims'), former acting national police commissioner (NPC) Khomtso Phahlane, former Passenger Rail Association of South Africa CEO Lucky Montana and the late former NPC, Jackie Selebi.

OUTA (Organisation Undoing Tax Abuse)

Originally known as The Opposition to Urban Tolling Alliance | Non-profit | Linked with SaveSouthAfrica

Change agents

OUTA was originally established as a citizens' initiative to challenge Gauteng's contested e-tolls in 2012, but when it achieved a landmark judgment – with a court interdict against the multi-billion-rand project – OUTA's organiser, Avis chief executive Wayne Duvenage, saw an opportunity to develop it as a civic movement.

After all, if an ad hoc people's protest could realise a credit downgrade for the mighty South African National Roads Agency (SANRAL), which was behind the e-tolls, and the resignation of SANRAL's CEO, Nazir Alli (although he later returned), there had to be more to it than just one purpose. Indeed, OUTA's actions even saw government set up an inter-ministerial committee into the matter, as well as launch an appeal at the Constitutional Court. Duvenage, who later resigned from Avis, soon found himself in behind-closed-doors meetings with the president.

The organisation then grew into a body that could conduct litigation and research into other areas of inefficiency, maladministration and corruption in the state. It aimed to hold those responsible for poor governance and corruption to account, especially when it came to wasteful expenditure and 'irrational decisions'. This was to hold officials to account in terms of taxpayers' money.

Duvenage was the chief executive officer and Ferrial Adam the chairperson and non-executive director. Adam was previously well-known as an activist with Greenpeace Africa. Former ANC MP Makhosi Khosa, who stood up to her party around Zuma's alleged corruption, was also a non-executive director assigned with local government affairs.

Among OUTA's prominent campaigns were: against electricity tariff hikes for consumers which have to be applied for by Eskom and then agreed to by the National Electricity Regulator of South Africa; for the unbundling of Eskom into two divisions – electricity generation and transmission, and the 'nuclear deal', which it was feared would tie South Africa into a long-term relationship with Russia and see the country having to borrow between R600 billion and R1.2 trillion to finance it.

OUTA uses crowd-funding for its endeavours.

P

The Pan-Africanist Congress of Azania (PAC)

Black Consciousness (BC) in origin | Number of seats in Parliament in 2018: 1

On the way out

Depending on who you believed, there were two, parallel leadership groupings of the PAC, which both claimed to be legitimate, by the 2000s. Such was the sorry state of the once-mighty PAC – the first party in South Africa to advocate for the return of the land to Africans, and the driving force behind the powerful boycott campaigns that led to the Sharpeville Massacre in 1959 – that its voice was drowned out in the National Assembly before the 2019 elections.

At that time, it was thought the party was already at its end, despite it having earned five seats in the first democratic elections after initially refusing to participate when it felt the ANC had given up too much ground to the former oppressors. Yet the PAC wished to differ on predictions of its doom.

At its national policy conference in December 2017, its secretary-general Narius Moloto told about 3000 delegates that the PAC leadership had 'cleaned' the party and rid it of 'dirty things'. It intended to actively campaign for the next general elections.

The PAC's only seat by 2018 was occupied by Moloto after he was appointed its president, also in December 2017, following the expulsion of former president Luthando Mbinda. It took court action for the party to be able to remove Mbinda from his position in the National Assembly when he initially refused to go.

Torn apart by internecine strife and lacking a clear ideological direction, the PAC of 2019 was far removed from the ANC breakaway party of Robert Sobukwe, a great African hero.

Pandor, Naledi

Minister of Higher Education (in her second stint in the position, having previously held the post from 2009–12) | Former acting president of South Africa | Former minister of Home Affairs | Former minister of Science and Technology | Former minister of Education (different to Higher Education, as this department was reorganised under Jacob Zuma) | Former ANC deputy chief whip | Former chairperson of the National Council of Provinces (NCOP) | Member of the ANC's National Working Committee (NWC)

Of all the Cabinet ministers in Cyril Ramaphosa's administration, Pandor is one of only two who can claim an heroic struggle family history. The other was Lindiwe Sisulu. Pandor's grandfather was respected ANC stalwart and intellectual Professor Z.K. Matthews and her father was activist and lawyer Joe Matthews. Among her relatives was Sol Plaatje, the revered first general-secretary of the South African Native National Congress which developed into the ANC.

Pandor had a difficult path under Zuma, criticised by the anti-Zuma faction for not rising up against him, despite her power within the ANC. This was particularly the case in 2013, as the scandal around the notorious Gupta family and their influence on the ruling party began to come to light. Pandor was the Minister of Home Affairs when the family was allowed to use the government's Waterkloof Air Force Base, a national key point, to land a private plane carrying a wedding party.

Yet Pandor was still considered executive material, and Ramaphosa saw fit to make her his running mate in his 2017 campaign to be elected president of the party. Although he was indeed elected president, he had to select David Maduza as his deputy.

Pandor studied at the University of Botswana, earning a BA in history and English and later an MA at the University of London. She also earned an MA in linguistics at Stellenbosch University in 1997. She had been an English lecturer in Botswana, the UK and South Africa, and assisted in the reform of South Africa's education system.

Pandor was pivotal to South Africa being granted the rights to host the Square Kilometre Array (SKA), the large multi-radio telescope project in the Karoo, when she was the Minister of Science and Technology. She was a driving force in its implementation.

Passenger Rail Agency of South Africa (Prasa)

State-owned enterprise (SOE)

Riddled with corruption

Responsible for most passenger rail services in the country, Prasa consists of Metrorail (urban commuters), Shosholoza Meyl (regional and inter-city rail), Autopax (regional and inter-city coach services) and Intersite (which manages Prasa properties).

The former South African Rail Commuter Corporation (SARCC) was renamed the Passenger Rail Agency of South Africa in 2008. But seven years later, the ambitious SOE was mired in scandals, including one of shocking, and ludicrous, proportions when 'mismanagement' led to the loss of R2.65 billion through the acquisition of Spanish trains that were too high for South Africa's rail infrastructure. This led to the removal of the chief executive officer, Lucky Montana, and chief engineer Daniel Mtimkulu who had falsified his qualifications, in 2016. Former public protector Thuli Madonsela called out Montana in an official report in 2015.

In the wake of Montana came acting CEO Collins Letsoalo but he was also dismissed in early 2017 after allegations that he had irregularly increased his own salary from R1.7 million to R5.9 million a year. Montana was meanwhile linked to further corruption in 2018 when it appeared he might have benefitted R4 billion in Prasa contracts awarded to Siyangena Technologies, a company linked to TMM Holdings Group, owned by Montana's former 'business partner', Pretoria-based businessman Marco Ferreira.

Prasa's passenger rail services had also been adversely affected by breakdowns, derailments, which at times had led to injuries and death, violent crime, supply-chain management problems and industrial action, while its management remained in office for years, despite ongoing complaints of corruption.

In 2018, Transport Minister Blade Nzimande – who said the agency had 'been treated like an ATM' – appointed a new board chaired by Khanyisile Kweyama. She was previously Chief Executive of Business Unity South Africa (BUSA), served on the executive committee of the National Economic Development and Labour Council (Nedlac), was an executive director at Anglo American's South Africa division, and a board member at BMW SA, Barloworld Logistics Africa, Sovereign Foods, Kumba Iron Ore, Telkom and the SABC. She also served as the chairperson of Brand South Africa's board of trustees. This Prasa board appointed by Nzimande would serve a 12-month term.

But if Kweyama's appointment was applauded, not so widely Prasa's new interim group CEO Sibusiso Sithole, who was approved by Nzimande also in 2018. The former city manager of eThekwini municipality in Durban, Sithole's contract with that entity was to have ended on 31 December 2016, but he was asked to vacate his position immediately, two weeks early. The Democratic Alliance (DA) alleged at the time this was because Sithole would not accede to 'ANC demands' that he employ party loyalists at the municipality. The ANC denied the claims.

Patriotic Alliance (PA)

Political party | Describes itself as 'economically centrist' | Number of seats in Parliament in 2018: 0

Ex-convict, bank robber-turned-motivational speaker, author-cum-businessman Gayton McKenzie joined forces with ex-convict and fraudster-turned-businessman-cum-socialite Kenny Kunene to start a political party that would contest the national and provincial elections of 2014, with a special focus on the Western Cape.

It said it especially hoped to play peacemaker among the notorious gangs on the Cape Flats in Cape Town, and, while commendable to some, that added to an image problem for the PA in that it was dubbed 'the gangster party' – also for the fact that former inmates McKenzie and Kunene were its founding partners.

Kunene would, however, not last much beyond the ballot before he quit, with the PA earning a minuscule 0.07% of the national vote. But the party fared better than expected in the 2016 local government elections. It was able to gain seats in the metropolitan municipalities of Cape Town, Johannesburg, Ekurhuleni and Nelson Mandela Bay in Port Elizabeth, Eastern Cape, with a tiny, but evident support base in some coloured communities.

Former Democratic Alliance (DA) councillor Freddie Kearns later joined, as did another ex-convict, the infamous leader of the Hard Livings gang, Rashied Staggie, whose twin brother Rashaad was shot and then burned alive in 1996 by Cape Flats vigilantes known as People Against Gangsterism and Drugs (Pagad).

The PA attracted attention in April 2018 when, as an effective kingmaker, it put its co-governing coalition with the ANC in Ekurhuleni outside Johannesburg on notice by telling the ruling party it would leave that coalition – which would result in collapse for the ANC – if the ANC did not support Marlon Daniels, the PA's candidate for Nelson Mandela Bay deputy mayor. The position had been vacant for some time, and there was a concern that if that continued, the post would ultimately be dissolved.

Phahlane, Khomotso

Former acting National Police Commissioner (NPC) | Former general in the South African Police Service (SAPS)

Linked to corruption

PREVIOUSLY HEAD OF THE SAPS forensic service from 2012 to 2015, Phahlane was appointed as acting NPC in 2015 after the suspension of former NPC Riah Phiyega.

Phahlane was relieved of his duties in July 2017.

The head of the Independent Police Investigative Directorate (IPID), Robert McBride, then found himself in Phahlane's sights when the directorate began investigating suspicious activities linked to Phahlane's multi-million-rand house and the boot of his car, among others. Although Phahlane then actively sought McBride's arrest, IPID continued to investigate a relationship Phahlane had developed with companies Crimetech and Kriminalistik involving R96 million and linked to improvements to Phahlane's home and cash payments made to construction company employees directly from his vehicle.

There was no record of monies withdrawn from Phahlane or his wife, Beauty Phahlane's account to fund the construction-related improvements, but there were relatable withdrawals made from the companies' accounts. The two companies denied they had ever paid any private expenses of members of the SAPS or any SAPS personnel, including Phahlane.

The Police and Prisons Civil Rights Union (Popcru) also made allegations against Crimetech, while Phahlane may have gone into a spurious car deal with salesman Durand Snyman. The two men and Beauty Phahlane would find themselves in the Specialised Commercial Crimes Court in Pretoria to find out why Snyman had given the Phahlanes vehicles paid for by a police contractor who received billions in forensic contracts.

Snyman claimed he had 'sponsored' the cars, but IPID said it could prove this was not the case. Magistrate Nicola Setshoege, however, withdrew the case.

The police contractor was apartheid-era police officer Keith Keating, whose company Forensic Data Analysts (FDA) provided the police and the State Information Technology Agency (Sita) with infrastructure that allowed the police to track firearms and obtain access to clues needed for investigations.

Parliament's Standing Committee on Public Accounts (Scopa) agreed with IPID that something was not right in the relationship between Keating's company and the senior policeman.

Phiyega, Riah

Former National Police Commissioner (NPC) | Former chairperson of the Presidential State-Owned Enterprise (SOE) Review Committee | Former group executive at Transnet

PHIYEGA WAS THE ONLY NPC TO finish their term while on suspension. Former president Jacob Zuma had placed Phiyega on suspension in late 2015, pending the decision of a board of inquiry established to probe allegations of misconduct, her fitness to hold office and capacity to execute official duties efficiently.

The inquiry into her fitness to hold office, compiled by Judge Neels Claassen, stated that Phiyega was not fit and recommended she be dismissed. But Phiyega challenged the findings. She was suspended after the release of the Farlam Commission of Inquiry established by Zuma to investigate the massacre of mineworkers during the strike at Lonmin properties in Marikana, North West, in August 2012.

Phiyega had been appointed as NPC just two months before the massacre.

Prior to her appointment, Phiyega – who holds a Master's in social sciences from the University of Johannesburg – was a group executive at Absa Bank, a board member of Absa Actuaries and a trustee of the Absa Foundation.

She was also a group executive at Transnet and served on numerous Transnet subsidiaries. Phiyega was part of a team of senior executives there responsible for the restructuring of the old Portnet into separate entities, and then became part of the executive of the National Ports Authority of South Africa.

Among other roles, she served as director for development at the National Council for Child Welfare, the Road Traffic Management Corporation Investigation Task Team, the 2010 Bid Committee and as a commissioner for the Road Accident Fund Commission led by Judge Kathy Satchwell.

Immediately prior to joining the SAPS, Phiyega was appointed chairperson of the Presidential State-Owned Enterprise (SOE) Review Committee.

Plato, Dan

Mayor of Cape Town (a position he formerly held from 2009 to 2011) | Democratic Alliance (DA) politician | Former MEC for Community Safety in the Western Cape | Former DA ward councillor

PLATO WAS A STUDENT AND COMMUNITY activist in mass organisation against apartheid before he joined formal politics in 1996 when he was elected a ward councillor for the Cape Flats communities of Belhar, Uitsig and Ravensmead. A decade later, he had gained a substantial portfolio of political achievements, including serving two terms as the chair of the City of Cape Town's Economic Development, Tourism and Property Management Portfolio Committee, and becoming deputy chair of the DA Metro Region and the DA Caucus in the City of Cape Town before his first appointment as mayor in 2009 after Helen Zille resigned the position to become Premier of the Western Cape.

But it wasn't smooth-sailing for Plato as massive social issues landed on his desk, including that of open-air toilets in the township of Makhaza, Khayelitsha, which amounted to a human rights violation. The Western Cape High Court would later rule against these.

Plato left office in 2011 when the DA announced that former Independent Democrats leader Patricia de Lille would be its mayoral candidate in the local government elections. He was then appointed MEC for community safety, with the complex and violent issues of gang warfare on the Cape Flats becoming a primary concern.

Plato secured a peace treaty between notorious gangs the Americans and the Mongrels in 2012 in the working-class community of Hanover Park, but it failed to succeed. In 2013, the ANC claimed Plato had been working behind the scenes with gang leaders. The National Prosecuting Authority decided not to investigate.

Portfolio Committees

Bodies established by the National Assembly

MUCH OF THE NATIONAL ASSEMBLY (NA)'s law-making processes happen within the portfolio committees, which also assist Parliament greatly in oversight over the executive. Each portfolio committee corresponds to a government department and the composition of the committees reflects, as far as is practicable, the numerical strengths of the parties represented in the Assembly.

Committees deliberate on bills covering each department's areas of jurisdiction, and scrutinise and report on annual budgets and strategic plans.

As the people's representatives, members of the committees determine whether government departments are delivering on what was promised and whether public money is being spent in a responsible manner.

As part of oversight work, committees may also do site visits where people at ground level can comment on whether the government is delivering on its promises.

If a committee reports on a matter and makes certain recommendations, that report will be debated in a full sitting or plenary to give other members of the NA an opportunity to engage with the content of the report. Once the report has been debated, the house decides whether to adopt the committee's recommendations. The house may also decide only to note a report, or it may refer a report back to the committee with an instruction to do further work.

'Premier League'

Occasionally nicknamed the 'Maize Meal Cup' (after the South African football spectacular, sponsored by pap manufacturers Iwisa)

Regarded as a cabal of the corrupt

THIS WAS AN INFORMAL ALLIANCE OF PROVINCIAL premiers identified during President Jacob Zuma's time, and who supported him. It comprised former Free State premier Ace Magashule (later the secretary-general of the ANC), former Mpumalanga premier David Mabuza (later the deputy president of the country and the party) and former North West premier Supra Mahumapelo (later resigned, also as chairperson of the party in the province).

The 'Premier League' worked hard at elevating former Cabinet minister – and Zuma's first choice – Nkosazana Dlamini-Zuma to be president of the ANC, but when a mere 179 votes separated her from the victor, Cyril Ramaphosa, the three men would have to see the silver lining.

Two of them got into the ANC's prestigious Top 6, and one became Ramaphosa's second-in-command out of what could only be construed as serious political horse-trading. For Magashule and Mabuza, to have power out of the ANC's headquarters, Luthuli House, might have been a more significant – and potentially profitable – event even than being in the provincial heirarchies.

An important point, however, was that all three stumped up in the end for the Zuma faction, with their provinces delivering high numbers of ANC branch votes for Dlamini-Zuma, and it was unlikely that this would be quickly forgotten. It was, however, believed that, in throwing his province behind Ramaphosa, Mabuza had thrown his comrades under the bus.

Principal Agent Network (PAN) Project

Government-sponsored

Suspected of having links to corruption

The PAN Project was a campaign which Arthur Fraser, the former State Security Agency director-general and former deputy director-general of what was the National Intelligence Agency (NIA), set up in 2007.

Best-selling author and investigative journalist Jacques Pauw claimed in his book, *The President's Keepers*, that PAN was 'an orgy of wasteful expenditure, fraud and corruption ... (in which) Fraser and his cronies appointed 72 agents (never vetted ... some with criminal records ... others family members) ... for whom (Fraser) purchased 293 cars, including BMWs, Audis and Golf GTIs'. Pauw said these were 'stored in warehouses across the country that had been leased for R24 million'.

Further, it was claimed that PAN leased and purchased properties totalling R48 million and imported three 'technical surveillance vehicles' from the UK for more than R40 million.

Pauw alleged this was 'just the tip of the iceberg'.

Public Investment Corporation (PIC)

Government investment company | The focus of a Commission of Inquiry chaired by retired Supreme Court judge Lex Mpati

Suspected of corruption in its ranks

Established in 1911, the PIC is one of the largest investment managers in Africa, managing assets of over R1.928 trillion. The Minister of Finance is the shareholder representative.

The corporation invests funds on behalf of public sector entities, based on investment mandates set by each of those 'clients' and approved by the Financial Services Board (FSB). But the PIC has seen its reputation flounder in recent years amid allegations that it is too politically connected and that it has become something of a 'bank' for those who give the ANC support.

This was the case even when the PIC was chaired by the well-liked former deputy finance minister Mcebisi Jonas, who resigned as an ANC MP in 2017 after he was axed from his position by Jacob Zuma. (Jonas was appointed an economic envoy by President Cyril Ramaphosa in 2018.)

The chairperson must be a member of government as the PIC is owned by the state mainly through the Government Employees Pension Fund, which owns 88.2% of it. PIC strategies must be aligned with government finance and economic policy. The minister of Finance also appoints the directors.

Allegations of corruption reached a peak in 2018 under Dan Matjila, who was appointed PIC Chief Executive in 2014. Although National Treasury gave him its support in May 2018, the United Democratic Movement (UDM) especially was opposed to him remaining in charge.

It demanded Finance Minister Nhlanhla Nene suspend Matjila – who had joined the corporation in 2003 and was regarded as a highly experienced asset manager – over allegations that he had misappropriated PIC funds and, among other acts, steered these towards a woman with whom he was allegedly romantically involved.

The UDM wanted an independent inquiry into the claims and would not cease and desist. It even suggested that Nene, who was the PIC's chair during his time as deputy finance minister between 2009 and 2014, may have been party to spurious appointments at the corporation. In October 2018, it was reported by the *Mail & Guardian* newspaper and amaBhungane that Nene's son Siyabonga Nene had asked the PIC to fund part of a deal between a company he ran with business partner Muhammad Amir Mirza – Indiafrec Trade and Invest – to acquire 50% of the S&S Refinery LDA in Mozambique in 2014. The UDM got its wish in October 2018 when Ramaphosa announced the establishment of a Commission of Inquiry into governance issues and allegations of mismanagement and corruption at the PIC in October 2018. Retired Judge Lex Mpati was appointed chair of the commission, which started its work in Pretoria in January 2019.

Later in 2014 a new company owned by Mirza, called Zaid International, was mentioned in the deal, while Siyabonga Nene's name and Indiafrec fell away. A referral fee of $1.7 million (R18.5 million at the time) from the PIC was later paid to Mirza's company, Zaid International, which is registered as a United Arab Emirates free-zone company.

In his capacity as deputy finance minister at the time, Nhlanhla Nene was the chair of the PIC when the corporation paid the monies related to Siyabonga Nene. Nhlanhla Nene told the Zondo Commission of Inquiry into State Capture that he 'never acted inappropriately with any PIC investments', and his spokesperson later said Nene had only become aware of the deal in a 'casual father-son discussion'.

A senior ANC leader reportedly told the *Mail & Guardian* and amaBhungane that Nhlanhla Nene had asked his son to pull out of the deal after he had become aware of it.

The PIC board had cleared Matjila of contravening its rules in late 2017. He was also cleared by internal auditors. But other claims against the PIC came to light in June 2018 when Minister of Traditional Governance and Co-Operation Zweli Mkhize – who was previously ANC Treasurer – was identified in a *Sunday Times* report as having 'demanded a R4.5-million kickback for allegedly facilitating a loan to an oil company from the PIC'. Mkhize furiously denied the report.

At the same time, the PIC had given its chief IT executive, Vuyokazi Menye, a hefty golden handshake, although the corporation had signed an acknowledgment that Menye was not under suspicion. The head of IT security, Simphiwe Mayisela, had, however, been dismissed in the days before Menye's departure.

It was said that Matjila and the PIC board may have targeted the IT executives while searching for the identity of the whistleblower in the matter of the supposed misappropriation of funds. The South African Police Service (SAPS) was investigating the whistleblower's claims at the time, and it was believed that Menye and Mayisela had been suspended for not informing Matjila about the SAPS probe.

In October 2018, it was rumoured Matjila was 'ready to step down' and that he had told senior ANC and government leaders he was intending to ask his board to consider a golden handshake.

A forensic investigation into the PIC was already underway, as was a pending commission of inquiry announced by Ramaphosa.

Shortly after that, however, the Prudential Authority of the South African Reserve Bank (SARB) released its investigation into Venda Building Society (VBS Bank), and its main author, Advocate Terry Motau, revealed that Matjila might have received a R5-million bribe from the bank. Motau recommended this should be further investigated by the authorities.

Among the PIC's other much-debated investments was the acquisition of 55% in Sekunjalo Independent Media – a consortium led by Dr Iqbal Survé's Sekunjalo Investment Holdings – in 2013. The PIC would have to see a 50% repayment on that loan by August 2018.

It refused to invest in Survé's tech start-up Sagarmatha Technologies in April 2018 due to its technical non-compliance with the Johannesburg Stock Exchange's listing requirements. The PIC had, however, funded Survé's Ayo Technology Solutions in a deal that predated Sagamartha. There was a concern that the monies allotted to Ayo could be used to offset the original loan given to Survé to buy Sekunjalo Independent.

Ayo rebutted and said it would not hesitate to institute claims for reputational damage and loss of earnings arising out of what it termed 'malicious and illicit' allegations by some PIC representatives about the company during the Commission of Inquiry into the PIC.

Regarding the PIC itself, there was a fear that if there was not proper governance, it could be involved in bailing out embattled state-owned entities and ultimately collapse.

Matjila finally resigned in late November 2018, and in February 2019, the PIC chair (deputy finance minister Mondli Gungubele) and the board resigned as a result of allegations made at the commission of inquiry under Judge Mpati. In a letter addressed to Finance Minister Tito Mboweni, the directors said there was a 'concerted effort to discredit the board'.

The Public Protector (PP)

Chapter 9 institution

SOUTH AFRICA CAME TO PROPERLY UNDERSTAND the mandate of this office when former PP, Advocate Thuli Madonsela, held the position. A relatively unknown Chapter 9 institution before she popularised it through powerful reports and even more distinctive recommendations, the PP and its work was known to most citizens by the time of Madonsela's mandated departure in 2016.

Thanks to supportive court action by especially the Economic Freedom Fighters (EFF) and the Democratic Alliance (DA), the power of the PP was demonstrably upheld in the Constitutional Court (ConCourt). This was after the two political parties, and others, asked the Court to find that the then president, Jacob Zuma, had 'failed to assist and protect the Public Protector so as to ensure her independence, impartiality, dignity and effectiveness by failing to comply with her remedial action (as he was constitutionally required to do in terms of Section 181(3) of the Constitution)'.

This was in regard to Madonsela's 'Secure in Comfort' report into non-security upgrades at Zuma's private home in Nkandla, KwaZulu-Natal. His residence was at the heart of *Economic Freedom Fighters v Speaker of the National Assembly and Others*, and *Democratic Alliance v Speaker of the National Assembly and Others*, which – said constitutional law expert Pierre de Vos – 'affirmed several well-entrenched constitutional principles relating to the duties of the President and Parliament'.

De Vos explained that the Constitutional Court 'found that it was imperative for the proper functioning of the office of the Public Protector that she be empowered to provide' effective remedies'. 'It is for this reason that the Constitution imposed an obligation on organs of state to assist and protect the Public Protector so as to ensure her dignity.'

The PP is an independent institution established in terms of Section 181 of the Constitution, with a mandate to support and strengthen constitutional democracy. A supreme administrative oversight body, the PP has the power to investigate, report and remedy improper conduct in state affairs. It must be accessible to all people and all communities.

R

Radebe, Jeff

Minister of Energy | Chairperson of the National Planning Commission (NPC) | Former minister in the Presidency | Former minister of Justice and Constitutional Development | Former minister of Public Enterprises | Former minister of Transport | South Africa's longest continuously serving Cabinet member | Former political prisoner | Member of the ANC's National Working Committee (NWC)

RADEBE FOUND HIMSELF AT THE CENTRE of controversy the moment he took up the post of Minister of Energy in February 2018 under President Cyril Ramaphosa. If he had been serving rather quietly as Minister in the Presidency under former president Jacob Zuma, those days were over when he was appointed to head one of the most important sectors in South Africa.

Energy had become a highly contested field, following allegations of corruption against previous minister, Tina Joemat-Pettersson, who seemed unable to come to grips with policy.

It was inevitable that Radebe would face criticism when he announced in June 2018 that two new coal-fired power stations would be built at a cost of R400 billion, and these would be maintained by Independent Power Producers (IPP). Critics claimed this was 'privatisation via the back door' as the IPP were private-sector companies. Government's agreements with the IPP were, however, long-won, said Radebe, and part of government's commitment to renewables.

In the background still lay theories about a possible nuclear deal with Russia, the sale of South Africa's fuel reserves and battles between Eskom and the National Energy Regulator of South Africa (Nersa) over price hikes to consumers.

Radebe earned a B Juris from the University of Zululand and an LLM from Leipzig University. He was a long-serving ANC Policy Unit head, a member of the party's National Executive Committee (NEC) and National Working Committee (NWC), a member of the South African Communist Party (SACP) Central Committee and head of the ANC Policy Unit. Radebe also sat on the board of directors for the 2010 FIFA World Cup.

Radebe joined the ANC while he was still a student in 1976 and was first trained at the Lenin International School in Moscow.

Radebe's personal life has been of interest as he is a brother-in-law to billionaire Patrice Motsepe and to Ramaphosa, as he is married to Motsepe's sister Bridgette, whose sister, Dr Tshepo Motsepe, is married to Ramaphosa. But Radebe's private world took on a whole new public dimension in 2017 when he was still Minister in the Presidency.

Following a sensational report in a Sunday newspaper, he didn't deny his role in a 'sexting' scandal, which included him asking for nude pictures of a 29-year-old woman who worked at the Union Buildings in Pretoria.

Radical Economic Transformation (RET)

Economic Freedom Fighters (EFF) policy | ANC policy

IN 2017, FORMER PRESIDENT JACOB ZUMA claimed RET had always been ANC policy. To the EFF, whose leader Julius Malema was credited with having originally proposed it as a prevailing ideology for his former party when he was the ANC Youth League president, this was a bolt from the blue.

It was styled as a call to political arms.

But the contest over which party – the ANC or the EFF – could righteously claim RET as its concept to uplift poor communities, provide employment and alter the country's socio-economic model turned out not to matter as much as which could get the job done first.

Many South Africans were sceptical about either party ever being able to do it, considering the weight of government's international debt and its onerous requirements to fulfil near-impossible conditions of the World Bank and the International Monetary Fund (IMF).

Had the ANC not so quickly adopted a neoliberal economic framework, and rather pushed for South Africa's international debt to be scrapped in the early 1990s when those funding institutions may have been less inclined to milk the rainbow nation, the country might today have been in a rather different position.

Nonetheless, by 2018, the numbers of poor households were growing while the top 10% of individuals and companies were seeing their wealth increase. When Trevor Manuel was finance minister under Thabo Mbeki, he had endorsed policies that allowed significant offshore investment, sometimes amounting to divestment, and that had only deepened the divide.

RET was, thus, the gospel of the ANC and EFF in trying to lure workers, students, the unemployed, the rural poor and increasing numbers of protesters on the Left to support them in the 2019 elections.

The promise was black ownership of the economy, land expropriation without compensation, and – contradictions aside – a comprehensive social compact involving existing government economic policies the New Growth Path, the National Development Plan and the Industrial Policy Action Plan.

Ramaphosa, Cyril

Nickname: McBuffalo; His Excellency | State President | Former deputy president | Former chairperson of the National Planning Commission (NPC) | Former ANC secretary-general | Former ANC chief negotiator at Codesa | Former trade union leader

Power broker

RAMAPHOSA HAD BEEN LONG OUT OF OFFICIAL ANC politics when he appeared at the party's elective conference in Mangaung, Free State, in 2012. He had once been a favoured and popular leader – with credentials in establishing and then leading the National Union of Mineworkers (NUM) and being a co-founder of the Congress of

South African Trade Unions (Cosatu) – before he left and went into business in 1996, not long after the first democratic vote.

On reflection, considering the essential roles Ramaphosa played as the ANC's chief negotiator at Codesa and in drafting the interim Constitution which led to the final Constitution of 1996, it seems unlikely that the party would have been able to move as swiftly as it did to get beyond the Government of National Unity, had it not been for Ramaphosa.

One of the main reasons for this was that he was neither an exile – like Mbeki – or a member of the United Democratic Front (UDF), like so many others who were embraced by the ANC although he had a substantial presence in the Mass Democratic Movement. To a large extent, Ramaphosa was a bit of a lone political wolf, loyal to the ANC, but to no particular cause within it.

Yet speculation remains as to why Ramaphosa made the decision to leave in 1996, with the strongest suggestion being that he felt side-lined by Nelson Mandela who had selected Thabo Mbeki to be his deputy. This, despite Ramaphosa having garnered more party votes than Mbeki in 1991 – when Ramaphosa was elected ANC secretary-general – and again in 1996.

He developed his skills into becoming a successful businessman from 1996. Among his interests was Shanduka Group, a company he founded with investments in the resources sector, energy sector, real estate, banking, insurance and telecoms.

He was also chairman of The Bidvest Group Limited and MTN. His other non-executive directorships included Macsteel Holdings, Alexander Forbes and Standard Bank. In March 2007 he was appointed as the non-executive joint chairman of Mondi, a leading international paper and packaging group, when the company demerged from Anglo American plc. In July 2013 he retired from the board of SABMiller plc.

Ramaphosa's estimated wealth is R6.4 billion, with the Register of Members' interests, tabled at Parliament, revealing its extent in 2014. He had accumulated more than R76 million in company shares, and owned 30 properties in Johannesburg and two apartments in Cape Town.

During a visit to Uganda in 2004, Ramaphosa also became interested in investing in the Ankole cattle breed and bought 43 cows from Ugandan President Yoweri Museveni to be shipped to Kenya. By 2017, he had 100 Ankole breeding cows at his Ntaba Nyoni farm in Mpumalanga.

He returned with substantial flourish in 2012, and was elected deputy president of the ANC at Mangaung, having earlier handed down the ruling that dismissed former ANC Youth League (ANCYL) leader Julius Malema's appeal for his suspension from the party to be lifted. Malema was later expelled, with Ramaphosa seen as having presided over his demise.

Yet, there were significant political, and personal, setbacks for Ramaphosa in 2012. That was the year of the Marikana Massacre and he would forever be associated with Lonmin, the employer of the 34 slain mineworkers, in his position as executive chair of his company, Shanduka, which was a Lonmin shareholder.

Even after he was inaugurated as State President on 15 February 2018, after the eventual resignation of Jacob Zuma and a vote in the National Assembly, questions arose around Ramaphosa's position on capital's role in the massacre. He had been cleared by the Farlam Commission to probe events around the massacre, but the commission was regarded by many as a whitewash.

Nonetheless, the rand rose to a two-and-a-half-year high in 2018 after Ramaphosa was announced as ANC president at the party's elective conference at Nasrec, Johannesburg, in December 2017.

But the 'Ramaphoria' which followed – mostly at the expense of Nkosazana Dlamini-Zuma, his rival whom he beat by a slender margin due to lobbying of which the factional dimensions were never declared – was relatively short-lived, although it returned in fits and starts.

For instance, he was heartily praised when he publicly declared in 2018 that he would be donating half of his salary (R3.6 million annually) to charity in honour of late former president Nelson Mandela. Ramaphosa said the gesture was aimed at encouraging the wealthy to dedicate some of their pay to help build the nation.

Among Ramaphosa's achievements before he returned to active politics in 2012 was being appointed an inspector of the Irish Republican Army (IRA) weapon dumps in Northern Ireland.

He is the honorary consul-general for Iceland in Johannesburg.

Ramokgopa, Dr Gwendoline (Gwen)

Gauteng MEC for Health | ANC politician

Ramokgopa made her second appearance as Health MEC in 2017 after the resignation of disgraced Qedani Mahlangu, who had effectively presided over the deaths of more than 150 mental patients in the Life Esidimeni tragedy.

Ramokgopa returned to the post after four years as the mayor of Tshwane.

A former doctor and hospital manager at the state institution the George Mukhari Hospital she was the first black woman to chair the executive committee of the City Council of Pretoria.

Once labelled 'the worst mayor in the country' by the Empowerdex Service Delivery Index, Ramakgopa was identified as having failed even in adequate service delivery to the city's people. But there was believed to be worse to come for her if her implementation of health ombudsman Professor Malegapuru Makgoba's recommendations following Esidimeni, one of the country's biggest health disasters, was not successful.

Those outcomes would be closely monitored ahead of the 2019 elections.

Ramulifho, Khume

Democratic Alliance (DA) Shadow MEC of Education in Gauteng | DA Gauteng caucus whip | DA Johannesburg regional chairperson | Former member of the Gender, Youth and People with Disabilities Committee and Finance Portfolio Committee in the Gauteng Provincial Legislature | Former DA Youth provincial leader (Gauteng) | Former federal DA Youth leader

On the way up | Power broker

RAMULIFHO WAS DRAWN INTO POLITICS while he was a student and co-founded the Democratic Students Congress (now known as DA Student Organisation).

He earned an HR qualification with certificates in municipal governance from the University of Johannesburg, qualifications in governance and leadership from the University of South Africa (Unisa) and additional certifications from the University of the Witwatersrand (Wits), and attended the Leadership Development Program in France in 2011 and Germany in 2014.

Former ANC Youth League (ANCYL) leader Julius Malema once called Ramulifho a 'garden boy' in reference to his apparent submission to the white leadership of the DA, and upon an invitation to a public debate between them, Malema refused the opportunity.

Ramulifho meanwhile rose through his party's ranks to become the leader of the DA's biggest region, Gauteng South, which included Soweto.

He was among senior black party leaders who objected to the DA's federal legal commission decision to 'instal' MP Natasha Mazzone as its second deputy chairperson. Ramulifho wrote to federal executive council chair James Selfe to demand the party go to the High Court to have the controversial decision reviewed.

Rasool, Ebrahim

ANC Western Cape politician | Former Western Cape premier | Former ambassador to Washington D.C. | Former scholar-in-residence at the Al Waleed bin Talal Center for Muslim-Christian Understanding (CMCU), housed at Georgetown University's School of Foreign Service

Linked to corruption

THE PREMIER OF THE WESTERN CAPE during President Mbeki's administration, Rasool was unceremoniously booted from the post after the divisive ANC elective conference at Polokwane, Limpopo, in 2007, where Rasool was not a fan of Mbeki's rival for the ANC presidency, Jacob Zuma.

Yet much of the attention at the time of Rasool's recall was on a 'brown envelope' scandal which involved two Independent Newspapers journalists who, it was then alleged, were recipients of public funds channelled by Rasool to see stories favourable to him published. At the same time, his ANC opponents were to receive unfavourable coverage.

The ANC did its own investigation into the scandal with its report compiled by ANC member and deputy justice minister Andries Nel. Rasool found himself and his position threatened by others within the ANC Provincial Executive Committee (PEC) in the Western Cape at the time, predominantly senior members Mcebisi Skwatsha and James Ngculu.

Former *Cape Argus* journalist Ashley Smith revealed how a media company, Inkwenkwezi Communications, was set up with the assistance of Zain Orrie, a businessman close to Rasool and *Argus* political editor Joe Aranes. In a 2010 affidavit, Smith said it became clear that the main purpose of the enterprise was to use working journalists to support Rasool, then engaged in a battle for political survival against the Democratic Alliance (DA), but more acutely against a rival ANC faction under Skwatsha.

Just ahead of the DA's ascendance over the ANC in the Western Cape in 2009, Rasool was appointed special advisor to Kgalema Motlanthe, the caretaker president in 2008 and 2009, thereafter deployed to the National Assembly, where he served until 2010.

Zuma then appointed Rasool as South Africa's ambassador to Washington for the next five years.

After a period as scholar-in-residence at the the Al Waleed bin Talal Center for Muslim-Christian Understanding (CMCU) at Georgetown University's School of Foreign Service in Washington D.C., Rasool returned to boost ANC structures in the Western Cape ahead of the 2019 elections.

Right2Know

Non-profit advocacy organisation

Change agents | Stars

Established in 2010 to reduce state secrecy in the drafting of laws, Right2Know became expert in issues around access to information and freedom of expression – essentially transparency in government and the advancement of personal liberties. This would come to centre also on protection of whistleblowers.

This also meant that Right2Know became a target of corrupt officials, some of whom would later dub it an 'agent for foreign governments' or a CIA front.

It was, as it had been since the beginning, run by a leadership collective. Its national working group comprised Cleo Shezi, Dale McKinley, Ghalib Galant, Jacob Dube, Karabo Rajuli, Mhlobo Gunguluzi, Nomfundo Sibiya, Peter Zulu, Sinenhlanhla Manqele, Siviwe Mdoda, Sthembiso Khuluse and Thabo Maile.

Roets, Ernst

Deputy CEO of AFriForum | Rightwing

Roets studied for an LLB at the University of Pretoria and then did two years of articles at Hurter Spies, a Pretoria law firm specialising in civil rights issues involving Afrikaners. Trade union Solidarity and civil rights organisation AfriForum were its main clients.

Roets then joined AfriForum, where he was responsible for communications and youth affairs, having previously been the chairperson of AfriForum Youth. Today, he is the lobby group's deputy CEO, whose public profile vies for dominance in his sector with AfriForum founder and CEO Kallie Kriel.

Roets has been one of the central voices arguing that there is greater government involvement in the murders of mostly white farmers in South Africa than the public may realise. He wrote a book, *Kill the Boer: Government Complicity in South Africa's Brutal Farm Murders*, in pursuit of this argument, and produced a documentary, *Tainted Heroes*, in 2015, claiming the ANC was more intent on destroying rival majority black political parties and movements than it had been on overthrowing apartheid.

An indefatigable advocate for white rights, Roets also has an LLM focusing on constitutional law.

Rural development and land reform

Government policy

THE ANC DECIDED AT ITS ELECTIVE CONFERENCE in Polokwane, Limpopo, in December 2007 that the country would have a ministry dedicated to the social and economic development of rural South Africa. The Department of Rural Development and Land Reform was created when Jacob Zuma came into power in 2009, in line with the Polokwane resolutions.

The idea was that South Africans living in the rural areas would enjoy the same benefits as those in urban areas, by virtue of the Constitution. Government's plan for developing rural areas, the Comprehensive Rural Development Programme (CRDP) was aimed at 'curing the blight of poverty by the creation of vibrant, equitable and sustainable rural communities'. But agrarian transformation – its primary purpose – has been slow, and against the 2018 backdrop of significant agitation, not to say demands, for land expropriation without compensation, government is trying to steer it back onto the front page.

Agrarian transformation is also not a simple process. The state says this must translate into 'social mobilisation to enable rural communities to take initiatives', and it must provide access to basic services, economic opportunity and infrastructure development. Government also wants to see a growth in 'non-farm activities for strengthening of rural livelihoods'.

Local municipalities, traditional councils, provincial government and rural communities, as well as NGOs, faith-based organisations, community-based organisations and 'other organs of civil society' are supposed to work together to achieve these goals.

The ministry also touts what it calls 'a three-legged strategy': increasing agricultural production using natural resources and appropriate technologies; building of roads, community gardens, fencing and communal sanitation; and restitution, redistribution and land tenure reform.

The minister in the Department of Land Reform in 2019 was Maite Nkoana-Mashabane.

S

SAP (Systems, Applications and Products in Data Processing)

German-based European multinational software corporation

Investigated for corruption

THE CORPORATION WAS INVESTIGATED IN 2018 by the United States Department of Justice and the Securities and Exchange Commission after it voluntarily reported itself for possible violations of American law. Payments to intermediaries on state contracts in South Africa that may have contravened the US Foreign Corrupt Practices Act were disclosed. (In 2015, SAP agreed to pay US$3.9 million to settle civil charges in the US over a former executive's scheme to bribe Panama government officials in order to win lucrative technology contracts.)

International banks were ensnared in the Gupta-linked scandals. A British lawmaker accused both HSBC and Standard Chartered of laundering the family's ill-gotten gains, and HSBC said it had closed some accounts that belonged to front companies operated by the Guptas.

SAP was alleged to have paid CAD House, a Gupta-controlled company, R100 million to secure a deal with the state-owned entity, Transnet. This was revealed in the so-called 'Gupta leaks' trove of secret service emails made public by Al Jazeera.

SECTION27

Public interest law centre | Non-aligned

Power brokers | Change agents | Stars

SEEKING SUBSTANTIVE EQUALITY AND social justice in South Africa, and guided by the Constitution, SECTION27 used the law, advocacy, legal literacy, research and community mobilisation to achieve access to healthcare services and basic education.

Its board included broadcaster and writer Redi Tlhabi, Justice Johann Kriegler (formerly of the Supreme Court of Appeal), former Constitutional Court Justice Zac Yacoob and other eminent South African justice seekers.

With many women attorneys working for SECTION27, its work concentrated on access to healthcare, basic education, sufficient food, good governance and tracking the National Strategic Plan around TB and HIV/AIDS.

SECTION27 was a regular and vital contributor to national debates and campaigns that supported social justice and participated in some essential court actions on a pro bono basis. A good example was the key contribution it made to the inquiry into the Life Esidimeni tragedy in which dozens of mental health patients died due to a mismanagement and a lack of care on the part of the Gauteng Health Department.

SECTION27 also drove a court case on behalf of the family of six-year-old Michael Komape, who drowned in a delapidated pit latrine at his village school outside Polokwane, Limpopo, in 2014. Despite SECTION27's outstanding work, together with campaigners Equal Education, to compel the Department of Basic Education to take responsibility for failing to deliver vital infrastructure to all schools, government refused to submit.

Selfe, James

Chairperson of the Democratic Alliance (DA) Federal Council | Shadow Minister of Correctional Services

SELFE STARTED HIS CAREER IN LIBERAL POLITICS as a researcher for the Progressive Federal Party (PFP), the forerunner to the DA, in 1979, becoming the PFP's communications director in 1988, and a member of the president's council in 1989, before he was appointed an executive director of the party in 1992.

His first experience of post-democratic politics was being elected to what was then called the Senate in 1994. It was later called the National Council of Provinces (NCOP).

By 1999, Selfe was a DA MP and by 2018, the party's correctional services spokesperson and the long-serving chair of its powerful federal executive – since 2000. Selfe was described in the *Daily Maverick* in 2018 as 'being to the DA what Gwede Mantashe was to the ANC during his decade as secretary-general – an administrator, an implementer, an enforcer, and a bearer of vast institutional knowledge'.

Among areas covered by the chairperson were the federal legal commission and its many legal matters, and running the DA's candidate nomination and selection. Selfe also attended Parliament and the Portfolio Committee on Correctional Services.

Despite him apparently being the 'brains' behind his party's anti-Zuma campaigns, it appeared to be wanting to move Selfe in 2018, who had become unpopular, and replace him with DA chief whip John Steenhuisen. An idea was that Selfe could become the DA's CEO, but Steenhuisen decided against contesting Selfe at the federal council, and Selfe remained chair of the Federal Council ahead of the 2019 elections.

A significant shift, however, was that the chairperson received a second deputy in 2018. This was a new position, and, in Selfe's case, he got DA MP Natasha Mazzone, although her election was contested within the party.

Seoka, Jo

Former Anglican bishop of Pretoria | Dubbed the 'Bishop of Marikana' | Chairperson of the Bench Marks Foundation

Change agent

DR JOHANNES THOMAS SEOKA, THE FORMER Anglican bishop of Pretoria, will be most remembered for the work he did to try to avert the tragedy on the two koppies in Marikana in August 2012. Later at the Farlam Commission, he was outspoken blaming both police and mine management for the loss of life.

Seoka was also visible during the bitter #FeesMustFall movement on campuses and was a key voice in the Save SA campaign to oust Jacob Zuma. The chair of the Bench Marks Foundation, an ecumenical watchdog of corporate social investment programmes, he was also very outspoken on Zimbabwe.

Seoka was a student at the Eshowe College of Education before studying for the priesthood at St Bede's College in Mthatha, becoming ordained in 1975. He ministered in Umlazi, Greytown and Soweto, and Chicago in the United States, studying there and in Germany.

A contemporary of the late Black Consciousness (BC) leader Steve Biko and his fellow BC leader Barney Pityana, Seoka was appointed the dean of Pretoria in 1996 and the bishop two years later – a post he held until his retirement in 2015. He was shortlisted with Pityana to replace Archbishop Njongongkulu Ndungane in 2007, but the position was given instead to Thabo Makgoba.

In 2012, Seoka was in the headlines, identified as the church leader who 'closed down' the Cathedral of Pretoria parish after 'firing' the priest in charge. This was an unpopular decision with many members of the congregation who counter-claimed that Seoka had misappropriated R500 million in funds. He was also charged with assaulting a verger. A church committee exonerated Seoka, who then launched a lawsuit for defamation. This was, however, later resolved through Makgoba's intervention.

Ses'khona People's Rights Movement

Community activists | Previously linked to the ANC, later to the Democratic Alliance (DA)

Influential Cape Town community leader Andile Lili invoked the anger of the ANC in 2016 when he said the party had failed to fulfil its promises of improved service delivery to the poor. To that end, he and another 500 or so other members of Ses'khona left the ANC to join the DA ahead of the local elections that year.

DA mayor Patricia de Lille endorsed their membership at an official ceremony in Khayelitsha, an impoverished township on the outskirts of Cape Town. Ses'khona co-founder Loyiso Nkohla claimed at the time that he had been offered – and rejected – positions within the ANC. He had been an ANC councillor.

2016 was a fraught year politically, but it did bring to the country's attention the power of yet another community protest movement, which was struggling to find a home within the ruling party. Ses'khona had, however, taken protest to a whole new level when its members dumped buckets of human faeces at Cape Town International Airport in August 2013. Nine involved in the so-called 'poo protest' were later sentenced to three years in jail, suspended for five years, and community service in the Bellville Regional Court after being found guilty of contravening the Civil Aviation Act. They would later dump faeces on the steps of the Western Cape provincial government.

De Lille did not increase her popularity within the DA when she promoted Nkohla to be head of community liaison for various mayoral committee members.

She had originally employed him as an executive support officer to a mayoral committee member. Even DA leader Mmusi Maimane was against Nkohla's appointment, and other senior members of the party were incensed that his salary was allegedly pitched at more than R750,000 which was more than they earned after years of service.

The impasse – which included DA MP John Steenhuisen compiling a party report – resulted in Nkohla's 'preliminary suspension' in 2018 when he had a clash with Anda Ntsodo, the mayoral committee member for community services, over a housing development in Khayelitsha. Nkohla had wanted to 'fast-track' the development due to demonstrations by residents who were not receiving basic services like water and electricity.

Shaik, Schabir

Former 'financial adviser' to former president Jacob Zuma | Convicted of corruption and fraud in 2005 | Given medical parole in 2009

An early proponent of capture

SHAIK WAS A FIXTURE OF SOUTH AFRICAN LIFE since the early 2000s when he was identified as former president Jacob Zuma's benefactor and a go-between in a corrupt relationship to secure arms purchases for the multi-billion-rand strategic defence package.

Shaik's 'friendship' with Zuma dated back to 1990 when Zuma, intelligence master for the ANC in exile, returned to the country from Mozambique where he had been based. Essentially requiring financial support, Zuma – the chairperson of the ANC – accepted such from Shaik in the form of interest-free 'loans'.

Five years later, Shaik had established Nkobi Holdings against the backdrop of the ANC's unmanageable R40-million overdraft, apparently hoping to be able to see that cleared through international 'partnerships'. That did not happen and, instead, Shaik's brother Chippy – who worked for the Department of Defence and had access to its arms acquisition plans – was aware of Schabir's bid on a massive deal for patrol corvettes to the South African Navy. Schabir Shaik's company then went into a joint deal with a French defence contractor Thomson-CSF, establishing Thomson Holdings as a South African company to tender for contracts, including the upgrading of Durban International Airport, a national identity card, highway projects and mobile phone interests.

When Shaik went on trial before Judge Hillary Squires in the Durban High Court in 2005, he was Accused No 1 with 10 companies, which formed part of his private group.

Another corporate accused had been Thint, originally Thomson-CSF, the subsidiary of the company Shaik established with the French defence company and Nkobi Holdings. Charges were, however, withdrawn against Thint, although Thint would be an accused in Zuma's trial.

The main charge was that Shaik, or one or other of his accused companies, gratuitously made some 238 separate payments of money to Zuma, who was the

Minister for Economic Affairs and Tourism in KwaZulu-Natal before he became the deputy president and leader of government business in Parliament. Over the years 1994–99, a total sum of R1,340,078 was paid to Zuma, corruptly, to influence Zuma to use his name and political influence for the benefit of Shaik's business enterprises or as an ongoing reward for having done so from time to time.

Shaik – who admitted during his trial that he had also falsified his qualifications and business achievements – was found guilty on two counts of corruption and one count of fraud, with Squires stating in his 165-page verdict that there was 'overwhelming' evidence of a corrupt relationship between Shaik and Zuma. Shaik was given 15 years' imprisonment and Zuma was dismissed from his post as deputy president by President Thabo Mbeki in June 2005.

In March 2009, Shaik was released on medical parole, after serving two years and four months of his prison term. There have been several accusations of Shaik violating the terms of his parole since then.

After Zuma resigned as president in early 2018, it appeared Shaik may be willing to testify should Zuma be tried on fraud charges.

The Shembe

The Nazareth Baptist Church

THIS IS ONE OF THE LARGEST SOUTH AFRICAN indigenous Christian churches, second only to the Zion Christian Church. Established in 1910 as iBandla lamaNazaretha by Isaiah Indlimawafa Shembe as a healing ministry, the church's holy city is Ekuphakameni in KwaZulu-Natal.

Early in January every year, up to three million faithful walk for three days up to the holy mountain, Nhlangakazi, and two days back, barefoot for almost 60 kilometres. This is in fulfilment of the third book of Moses dating back to the divine revelation in 1916 to iNkosi Shembe that God would only speak to him on the mountain as He had done millennia before with Moses on Mount Sinai.

On the mountain, Shembe was struck by lightning, carried down and left for dead, but he came to – and thus was born the annual pilgrimage.

The sect is regarded by some as a personality cult, by others as a legitimate and important Africanised form of Christianity. But since 2011, the amaNazarethe have been riven by succession battles, first after the death of Vimbeni Shembe in 2010 and then after a court ruling declaring Vela Shembe the new leader.

By 2017, the church had split into two sects, one following Vela and the other his nephew Mduduzi Shembe. The courts then ordered that the faithful must elect a new leader.

Shivambu, Floyd

Economic Freedom Fighters (EFF) deputy commander-in-chief (CIC) | Member of the EFF's Central Command Team (CCT) | EFF MP | EFF chief whip | Former member of the Pan-African Parliament (PAP) | Former president of the University of the Witwatersrand (Wits) Student Representative Body (SRC) | Former ANC Youth League (ANCYL) spokesperson

Charged with an assault on a journalist | Linked to possible corruption (VBS Bank) | Power broker

SHIVAMBU IS MOST LIKELY TO BE THE NEXT MEMBER of the EFF to gain a PhD after his fellow fighter, Dr Mbuyiseni Ndlozi, having graduated with a Master's in political studies with distinction in 2014.

That he was the EFF's deputy CIC throughout, sat on parliamentary committees and maintained a high-level presence for his party in the National Assembly even when other leaders were unable to attend, gave Shivambu a consistent political presence.

Unlike EFF leader Julius Malema, or Ndlozi, however, Shivambu was not a charmer or an orator, but an ideologue who was seen to be developing the party's revolutionary position while other leaders gave it its more familiar, friendlier, public character. Shivambu did not seem to be troubled by conflict, some of which was engendered by himself, such as an unprovoked attack on a photojournalist on the Parliamentary precinct in 2018.

More debate followed reports about his alleged racism against National Treasury tax expert Ismail Momoniat. Shivambu's detractors said he had bemoaned Momoniat's constant appearances for the fact that he was 'Indian' and not black African. This was deemed to be racist. Shavambu's supporters said instead that his statements around Momoniat were not racist but reflected on a history that had effectively denied black representation. The EFF quickly dispatched the original video of Shivambu's words in Parliament onto social media and, in the end, the racism charge could not be adequately defended. However, Shivambu found himself at the centre of a critique of the EFF as being fascist and unable to tolerate dissension it its own ranks.

Then, in October 2018, it seemed there may have been an alternate reason for Shivambu to have agitated against Momoniat. This related to revelations by Advocate Terry Motau, who was the main author of a report commissioned by the South African Reserve Bank (SARB) into the Venda Building Society (VBS Bank). Among those stated to have received monies through a R1.9-billion routing of the bank, was Shivambu's younger brother Brian, who received R16 million.

There were allegations, which played out mostly on social media at first, that Floyd Shivambu, or a company associated with him or even the EFF itself, could have benefitted from Brian's money. Brian Shivambu had received the R16 million as a 'consultant' to Vele Investments, the company identified by Motau has being the driver of significant corruption at and through VBS.

Floyd Shivambu hit back, denying any payments were made over to him or any companies associated with him, or indeed to the EFF. However, his detractors cast their eye back on that Momoniat incident, and queried whether Shivambu had not perhaps been threatened by Momoniat's doggedness into governance. It was speculated that Shivambu might have known that SARS would be able to link Brian Shivambu to the VBS scandal, which was then unfolding behind the scenes.

A polemicist of note, Shivambu was the political editor of the Wits student newspaper, a researcher for the South African Communist Party (SACP) and a policy co-ordinator for the Chris Hani Institute, a joint venture of the SACP and the Congress of South African Trade Unions (Cosatu). The EFF put him in charge of its Policy, Research and Political Education Unit.

Shivambu was the editor and co-author of *The Coming Revolution: Julius Malema and the Fight for Economic Freedom* (Jacana, 2014) with Janet Smith and Dali Mpofu.

Sisulu, Lindiwe

Minister of International Relations and Co-Operation | Former minister of Housing (now Human Settlements) | Former minister of Public Works and Administration | Former minister of Defence and Military Veterans | Former political detainee | Member of the ANC's National Working Committee (NWC)

On the way up | Star

NOT LONG AFTER SISULU TOOK UP HER NEW Cabinet posting as Minister of International Relations in 2018, South Africa was elected as a non-permanent member of the United Nations Security Council. Sisulu said it would dedicate its tenure to Nelson Mandela.

It was an early triumph for Sisulu, but she had already made her mark on the international stage in May 2018 by withdrawing South Africa's ambassador to Israel from Tel Aviv and condemning the Israeli Defence Force's violence against Palestinians on the Gaza Strip. By the middle of June, the attacks had resulted in the murders of dozens of Palestinians and thousands of injuries.

Almost immediately after she moved into office, Sisulu had also issued a diplomatic démarche to the Australian High Commissioner over comments by the Australian Home Affairs Minister Peter Dutton that suggested white South African farmers were being persecuted and deserved protection with special visas from a 'civilised country'.

Sisulu intended to make a dramatic shift from the way her predecessor, Maite Nkoana-Mashabane, had operated. In her foray into overhauling South Africa's foreign policy, Sisulu indicated she would be concentrating on pan-African politics to reclaim South Africa's position as a major influence on the continent, and announced a review panel that would decide the direction it would take. It was believed the concentration would be on economic diplomacy, likely to match President Cyril Ramaphosa's appointment of economic envoys and an economic adviser to help bring in deals that could alleviate the country's financial burdens.

Sisulu's panel members included ANC head of economic transformation Enoch Godongwana, former deputy foreign affairs minister Aziz Pahad, former South African ambassador to Germany Lindiwe Mabuza, former international relations director-general Ayanda Ntsaluba and economist Xhanti Payi.

Deputy chief justice Emeritus Dikgang Moseneke was appointed as special envoy to South Sudan and Lesotho.

International relations seemed like a strong advancement for Sisulu, who was once believed to be a possible ANC presidential candidate, but who was not able to gain ground against Cyril Ramaphosa and his rival Nkosazana Dlamini-Zuma during that race in 2017.

The daughter of Albertina and Walter Sisulu, who are seen as ANC 'royalty', Sisulu has an MPhil from the Centre for Southern African Studies at the University of York.

A former assistant to Jacob Zuma when he was head of ANC intelligence in exile during apartheid, Sisulu has covered an immense amount of ground in government. But it is possible that her most stressful period was when she was housing minister. Her reputation was affected by her seeming lack of care towards communities in the Joe Slovo Informal Settlement outside Cape Town who rejected being relocated. Sisulu had hoped to use the ground on which they had settled to create the N2 Gateway, a development of bonded and free housing. Thousands were displaced into temporary relocation areas and onto the streets.

Sitole, General Khehla

National Police Commissioner (NPC)

From the time of his appointment in November 2017, Sitole's posting was highlighted for its lack of political interference. He had been in the service from his days as a police constable during apartheid, for 31 years.

Nelson Mandela started the trend of making political appointments as NPC, practising his tendency towards 'reconciliation' by naming George Fivaz – who was previously in the apartheid security forces – in 1995. Thabo Mbeki then appointed Jackie Selebi, who would be convicted of corruption and later die on medical parole, while Jacob Zuma appointed Bheki Cele and Riah Phiyega, both of whom would lose their jobs. Cele would be fired for corruption, while Phiyega was found unfit for office after the Marikana Massacre.

Sitole was, thus, given the opportunity to restore the role, but it would not be easy as the public no longer trust a police force that had not turned the tide on crime, and is seen as brutal and corrupt. It also did not assist his own image that he was alleged to have been at a meeting where, it is claimed, the illegal procurement of a 'grabber' eavesdropping device before the ANC's elective conference at Nasrec, Johannesburg, in December 2017, was discussed. The Independent Police Investigations Directorate took on the matter.

Sitole said he would concentrate on meeting the objectives around combating crime in the National Development Plan (NDP), as well as the National Crime

Prevention Strategy, which was approved by Cabinet in 1996. At that time, it intended to 're-engineer the criminal justice system' and improve 'inter-departmental co-operation'. The NDP said much the same thing in 2012, adding that the force needed to be professionalised and demilitarised.

Sitole was previously a divisional commissioner for protection and security services and an assistant commissioner in his home province, Mpumalanga.

Smith, Vincent

ANC MP | Key player in Parliament

Suspected of corruption

A 2018 PARLIAMENTARY AD HOC COMMITTEE TESTING land expropriation without compensation proposal placed Vincent Smith in a difficult place, but one where he appeared to be quite comfortable.

The ANC MP has served on a number of standing committees in the National Assembly after being elected in 1999. With long experience in the party – elected deputy chair of the ANC's Johannesburg region upon its unbanning and serving on the regional executive of the party until 2008 – he projected an unbiased leadership on those committees. Smith chaired the standing committee on the Auditor-General, the Ad Hoc Committee on the Auditor-General and the Ad Hoc Committee on African Peer Review in Parliament, as well as the Association of Public Accounts and the SADC Association of Public Accounts.

He gained national prominence in 2017 when he fearlessly faced down the South African Broadcasting Corporation (SABC) chief, Hlaudi Motsoeneng. Smith was also on the committees that called Eskom and Transnet to account.

One of his most challenging tasks would be to chair the ad hoc committee investigating party funding, which was to make recommendations on the regulation of private funding, as well as the model of public and private funding for political parties. But then came the revelation in September 2018 that Smith had 'assisted' former Bosasa chief operations officer Angelo Agrizzi's son to get a job at the ANC in Gauteng in 2015. In return, Agrizzi apparently facilitated a personal loan to Smith to cover his daughter's tertiary education fees. Agrizzi denied any loan agreement, and said Bosasa CEO Gavin Watson had instructed him to make the payments. Watson and Bosasa denied this.

Upon these revelations, Smith asked the ANC in Parliament to allow him to step aside from the various committees he serves on while an investigation by the ethics committee was in process. Despite public support from the ANC, Smith was also to face a probe by the ANC's integrity committee.

Socialist Revolutionary Workers Party (see The National Union of Metalworkers of South Africa and Irvin, Jim)

Solidarity

Afrikaans name: Solidariteit | Trade union for minority workers | Non-aligned, although closely linked with the mainly white Afrikaner community

SOLIDARITY'S ORIGINS DATE BACK MORE THAN 110 YEARS to a time when life in Johannesburg, a brand-new city and its fledgling satellite, was centred only on the Witwatersrand gold mines. Known as the Mine Workers' Union – a supremacist organisation – for 100 years before it changed its name to Solidarity in 2002, by that time, it had begun a significant recovery after near-financial collapse in 1997.

The credit for the recovery was given to Flip Buys, who, in 2019, was still Solidarity's general-secretary. Buys not only got it back on the ground financially but also shifted what was becoming an extreme rightwing organisation with increasingly low membership to one that represented minorities but did not speak for the fascists any longer. By 2018, it had 17 offices around the country and an estimated 2000 shop stewards affiliated with the Confederation of South African Workers' Unions and the International Trade Union Confederation.

Importantly for the trade union, it was also behind an independent initiative, AfriForum, the non-profit that sought to serve the interests of the Afrikaner minority community through legal and other means.

Solidarity ran a Growthfund which aimed to raise R500 million to empower the Afrikaans community. Its trade union members made a small monthly contribution to the fund as part of their membership dues. The Growthfund project was based on the concept of the Reddingsdaadbond (savings deed bond) of the early 20th century which, in turn, inspired successful Afrikaner companies like insurance firms Santam and Sanlam and the commercial Volkskas bank, which flourished under apartheid.

South African Airways (SAA)

State airline

Mired in mismanagement

SAA WAS IN A MAJOR FINANCIAL CRISIS and a political mire for years under Jacob Zuma associate Dudu Myeni, who was the national airline's acting chairperson and then chairperson from 2012 to 2017. The airline had made no profit since 2011, but matters were to get progressively worse. SAA's government guarantees had climbed to nearly R20 billion by the middle of 2018 – not only to pay some of its huge debt but also to allow it some 'working capital'.

Myeni – a teacher who lied about her qualifications, saying she had a degree in public administration from the University of Zululand when, in fact, she had two majors outstanding – was appointed to SAA's board in 2009, the same year Zuma became president. Three years later, she was appointed chairperson at a time when eight of 14 board members – including chairperson Cheryl Carolus – resigned.

Myeni's first casualty was acting chief executive Vuyisile Kona. By March 2014, the new chief executive, Monwabisi Kalawe, had accused her of corruption. When

Myeni hit back with counter-accusations of corruption, and then public enterprises minister Malusi Gigaba expressed his confidence in Kalawe, Gigaba was suddenly moved to the Department of Home Affairs in a Zuma reshuffle. But it wasn't as if he had been a success at SAA.

Carolus testified to the Zondo Commission in November 2018 that Gigaba had left the airline in a disastrous state.

It was on Gigaba's successor Lynne Brown's watch that SAA signed an agreement with Airbus in March 2015 to lease five of its aircraft. Then, without involving her executives, Myeni told Airbus in October that a 'third party' would instead be purchasing the aircraft on SAA's behalf, instead of leasing from them. As this by-passed procurement processes, a clause in the original agreement that any renegotiation of the agreement would need the finance minister's approval was invoked. Nhlanhla Nene, the minister at the time, refused, and was replaced by Des van Rooyen within days. A massive outcry and a bloodbath in the markets saw Van Rooyen in the job for only four days before Zuma replaced him with Pravin Gordhan, who also rejected Myeni's 'new deal'. It was clear at that point that SAA was in dangerous hands. There was a backlog of criminal and civil claims against the airline for price fixing and anti-competitive behaviour, and its balance sheet was in crisis.

Government then began to bail out SAA and continued to do so until as recently as June 2018. But a culture of impugnity seemed to have become embedded at the national flag carrier, as SAA was still wasting money on its executives, plus 13 new appointees in jobs created by new chairperson Vuyani Jarana. There was also a slew of 'consultants'.

SAA was meanwhile trying to pay R25 million to Deutsche Bank in a debt restructuring deal, while having lost nearly R4 billion in cuts to domestic and international routes.

South African Broadcasting Corporation (SABC)

State broadcaster

Functionally bankrupt

WHEN THE SABC BOARD ANNOUNCED the appointment of Madoda Mxakwe as CEO in June 2018, there was a collective sigh of relief. The destructive, litigious Hlaudi Motsoeneng, who had managed to become COO of the SABC through ingratiating himself with politicians and using lies and aggressive tactics to gain unwarranted promotions, had attempted widescale plunder.

The new board and management intended to save the public broadcaster from collapse, less than two years after the Western Cape High Court ruled that Motsoeneng was 'not entitled to occupy any position at the SABC'. Two years before that, public protector Thuli Madonsela's report, 'When governance and ethics fail', had called for the SABC board to take disciplinary action against Motsoeneng.

His world finally came crashing down in February 2018, when the Special Investigating Unit (SIU) issued him with summonses amounting to R21 million.

This was, in part, to recover an R11 million bonus Motsoeneng 'received' in 2016 for 'successfully negotiating' a controversial R533-million deal with pay-TV conglomerate, MultiChoice.

That deal gave MultiChoice access to the SABC's entire archive. Key to this sham was also that the SABC would support MultiChoice's proposal for encryption-free set-top boxes to be introduced as part of government's digital migration programme. (Most protagonists for competition were against the boxes being unencoded, in order to challenge MultiChoice's monopoly.)

Other compromised individuals in the SABC's meltdown included former acting CEO and CFO James Aguma and Communications Minister Faith Muthambi. In June 2018, the High Court in Pretoria ruled that ministers of communications could no longer influence appointments to the SABC board, which allowed it to fill the Corporation's vacant CFO and GCEO positions. Muthambi interfered constantly.

Mxakwe earned a Master's in global political economy from Sussex University and had qualifications in executive leadership and business administration from the London Business School and the Gordon Institute of Business School. He was previously Nestlé's country head for Mozambique, Namibia, Botswana, Swaziland and Lesotho. Motsoeneng did not pass matric.

The SABC board chairperson in 2018, Bongumusa Makhathini, a Harvard Business School graduate, was previously the chairperson of former first lady Bongi Ngema's foundation, although he resigned to prevent a conflict of interest. Makhathini had previously been a director for legal and external affairs at British American Tobacco.

Then came December 2018, and a number of board members had resigned after new communications minister, Stella Ndabeni-Abrahams, visited the SABC and spoke to staff and unions, bypassing the board. The conflict between the board and the minister related to Section 189 retrenchments which the board believed could save the public broadcaster from financial ruin within months. Ndabeni wished to discuss options other than retrenchment, including a bailout application. But in January 2019, the broadcaster said it would not renew a notice to invoke Section 189 but would instead conduct a comprehensive skills audit.

The resignation rumours reflected on the still-perilous state of morale at the broadcaster in the wake of Motsoeneng, who left the SABC needing a cash injection of at least R3 billion. An astonishing loss of R622 milllion had been recorded for the financial year ended March 2018, although Treasury granted the SABC a borrowing limit of up to R1.2 billion.

The South African Communist Party (SACP)

Partner of the ANC and the Congress of South African Trade Unions (Cosatu) in the Tripartite Alliance | Socialist

Some members of its leadership suspected of corruption

Its mantra – Defend. Advance. Deepen the National Democratic Revolution –

was designed for the vanguard. And while some SACP leaders – Ruth First, Bram Fischer, Joe Slovo, Chris Hani and Ronnie Kasrils – were lauded in revolutionary history, there were tricky moments for the SACP, ideologically speaking, in the Jacob Zuma era.

Critics asked how the 'voice of the proletariat' could allow its leaders to accept free luxury sedans when deployed into government. But materialism seemed to be a minor distraction for the senior deployees whose party was suddenly back in the frame again when Zuma took power. His predecessor, Thabo Mbeki, had not generally integrated the SACP into the work of the ruling party, but Zuma resuscitated the idea of the Tripartite Alliance, which included the ANC, the SACP and Cosatu.

But all was not well in that alliance, with the SACP complaining that even though some of its members were Cabinet ministers and MPs, the ANC still did not include the party in its major decisions. This irked the Communists who indicated they could contest elections independently of the alliance, following a party resolution in 2017.

The SACP's first attempt, a by-election in Metsimaholo, Free State, in December 2017, won it three seats. This was at the height of its antipathy towards Zuma, who, it rallied, had presided over the rot that led to state capture. (Zuma had also relieved SACP leader Blade Nzimande of his Cabinet position in October 2017 as divides widened again within the alliance.)

Under President Cyril Ramaphosa, such contestations seemed less likely as the SACP accommodated him politically, even as both it and the ANC struggled to define their dogma. Ramaphosa brought Nzimande back into his Cabinet in the position of Minister of Transport.

A challenge remained that, with around 250,000 members, the SACP's campaigning power outside the alliance was growing but limited, but if used as a lever within a revitalised alliance, it could help the ANC in key coalition negotiations. Cosatu also did not support the SACP contesting elections separately.

But Nzimande also said the SACP needed to stop being a doormat for the ANC. For instance, not a single member of the party was deployed to the ANC's National Executive Committee (NEC) at its elective conference in Nasrec, Johannesburg, in December 2017.

The South African Federation of Trade Unions (Saftu)

Leftist, Socialist in orientation

Power brokers | Change agents

UNDER THE SLOGAN 'ORGANISE OR STARVE', the country's second largest trade union federation was mandated at a workers' summit on May Day 2016, two years after its biggest affiliate, the National Union of Metalworkers (Numsa), was expelled from Cosatu, and another nine unions followed it into independence from the ANC-led Tripartite Alliance.

Representing 30 unions, or between 700,000 and 800,000 workers, across the sectors of municipal services, transport, the public sector, manufacturing, mining, construction, and commercial, cleaning and security services, Saftu's biggest partners were Numsa and the Food and Allied Workers Union (Fawu).

Saftu's members were required to be independent of employers and political parties, but not necessarily apolitical, socialist in orientation, and to place a high emphasis on anti-imperialism and internationalism.

It made its first significant display of political muscle in April 2018 when it organised a massive strike in the country's biggest cities. Thousands of workers took part in the mass action against government's announcement of a national minimum wage rate of R20 an hour. Other issues it was pushing at that time, such as its opposition to a strike-balloting provision in the Labour Relations Act, it said was highly detrimental to workers.

Gaining a more vocal presence through a revitalised former Cosatu general secretary Zwelinzima Vavi, Saftu's effective split from the ANC when its affiliates left Cosatu looked to be an important advantage as the working class has become increasingly distanced from the former liberation party.

South African Human Rights Commission (SAHRC)

Chapter 9 institution

After Lawrence Mushwana received a nearly R7-million golden handshake at the end of his tenure as Public Protector, he went on to head another Chapter 9 institution, the SAHRC – and ended up reducing it from a vibrant organisation growing in influence and stature under the previous commissioner, Judge Jody Kollapen, to one that people barely knew.

It was no surprise that Mushwana was criticised by some MPs at Justice portfolio committee hearings in 2016 when he sought reappointment to his position at the SAHRC. Among the reasons for their reticence was their confusion at the commission's parallel process in examining the August 2012 Marikana Massacre, its poor handling of complaints about inciting violence which were levelled against Zulu King Goodwill Zwelithini, and its apparent lack of concern when fears were raised about the plight of patients in the Life Esidimeni scandal.

But it was also a lack of faith in Mushwana's ability to revive an institution that should have been playing as vital a role in society as the Public Protector had under previous incumbent Advocate Thuli Madonsela.

Fortunately, the distinguished former United Nations deputy secretary-general, Professor Bongani Majola, also a previous director of the Legal Resources Centre, succeeded Mushwana in 2016.

An important first test for Majola would be to exercise the power of the SAHRC in compelling government to deal with the oncology crisis in KwaZulu-Natal (KZN).

South African Local Government Association (SALGA)

Constitutionally mandated organisation responsible for local government oversight

SALGA describes itself as having two strategic roles within government: that of 'protector' – enforcing the rights of the local government sector – and that of 'disruptor' – constructively reshaping existing systems that made it impossible for local government to deliver on its mandate. It supports efforts at sustainable, inclusive economic growth and spatial transformation, as well as the financial sustainability of local government and its greater fiscal equity.

Recognised as the government body representing local government, it is involved in training officials via its Centre for Leadership and Governance. It also serves as the facilitator between workers and employers in municipal wage and salary negotiations.

But SALGA – which was chaired by former mayor of Johannesburg, Parks Tau, in 2018 – had its own governance problems. (Tau was also the chair of the ANC in Johannesburg.)

Also in 2018, the Department of Labour confirmed that the Labour Registrar could act against SALGA for breaching sections of the Labour Relations Act. It had not submitted audited financial statements from 2012 to 2017, nor had it submitted minutes of meetings that elected office bearers.

Established in 1996 and gazetted in January 1998, it was created to represent most provincial organisations, which in turn were believed to represent most municipalities. It could designate 10 people to participate in the proceedings of the National Council of Provinces (NCOP), which it fell under in government.

Municipalities pay a membership fee to be part of SALGA.

South African National Civic Organisation (Sanco)

Broad-based community movement | Linked with the ANC

Change agents

THE HISTORY OF SANCO IS A FAIR REFLECTION of the history of liberation politics in South Africa in general. Launched in 1992, and building upon the widespread grassroots support for the United Democratic Front (UDF), it was designed to bring together as many as 4,000 disparate organisations that had operated from within civil society during apartheid.

But that was even more complicated than it looked by virtue of those numbers. There were profound divisions and ambitions even within each individual organisation, and that Sanco could be launched at all was an historic event. Even in 2018, it most certainly did not represent all civic movements.

Yet, it was believed to righteously represent millions of people, mostly in townships and informal settlements, operating under the slogan, 'People-Centred and People-Driven'. Sanco ran many powerful political campaigns and, by the 2019 elections, had been concentrating on the occupation of vacant land in the absence of reform.

Sanco had a unique political dynamic for a body, or a movement, of its size in that, at a national level, it did not always exercise its leverage as it had a number of leaders who represented both it and the ANC, hampering its independence. But at a branch level, it had a greater influence on black civil society.

It was drawn into law-making early on in the democratic process, working on local government and housing policy and being given representation at the National Economic Development and Labour Council (Nedlac).

South African Police Service (SAPS)

THE SAPS IS A PRODUCT OF THE AMALGAMATION of the 11 policing agencies that existed during apartheid. These were the 10 of the so-called 'homelands' – the TBVC states and the 'self-governing and development' territories – which had 'independent' status but were not widely recognised by the international community. In black communities in South Africa, these were known as 'bantustans' because the TBVC states – Transkei, Bophuthatswana, Venda and Ciskei – and 'self-governing territories' of Gazankulu, Kangwane, kwaNdebele, kwaZulu, Lebowa and Qwaqwa, were, in fact, only a 'legal' way of removing black people from gaining any meaningful political power.

There was no correlation between the policing agencies as each had its own heirarchy, uniform and structure, but the 1994 Interim Constitution provided for one service when the bantustans were abolished and nine provinces of a united South Africa established.

The first four National Police Commisioners – George Fivaz, Jackie Selebi, Bheki Cele and Riah Phiyega – were political appointees. General Khehla Sitole, who was appointed in November 2017, was the first career policeman to be given the job. Although Fivaz too had been in the police, he had a specific task as an apartheid-era official to ensure the loyalty of thousands of white police officers who had no knowledge of working in a democratic atmosphere.

South African Revenue Service (SARS)

Government's tax-collecting agency

ESTABLISHED BY LEGISLATION TO COLLECT revenue and ensure compliance with tax law, SARS was intended to support South Africa's integration into the global economy in a way that would benefit all citizens.

Administratively autonomous of the state, it does not fall within the public service, but within the public administration. So although South Africa's tax regime is set by the National Treasury, that regime is managed by SARS itself.

Its main functions are to: collect and administer all national taxes, duties and levies; provide protection against the illegal importation and exportation of goods; facilitate trade; and advise the Minister of Finance.

Structural reform at SARS under president Jacob Zuma appeared to have been to the benefit of some of his associates who were linked with corruption, fraud and money laundering. This was believed to have happened under the leadership of Tom Moyane, who was suspended as SARS Commissioner by President Cyril Ramaphosa in 2018, and later fired.

Ramaphosa set up the the Nugent Commission into tax governance and administration, but Moyane claimed when it started that it was nothing more than a 'witch hunt' against him. Retired Supreme Court of Appeal Judge Robert Nugent headed the inquiry which delivered explosive testimony.

It soon became clear that, as writer Jacques Pauw had showed in his best-selling book *The President's Keepers*, SARS was a key instrument in state capture.

Before Moyane was appointed by Zuma as the tax commissioner in October 2014, SARS was regarded as an exemplary organisation, contributing markedly to fiscal competence. Not long after Moyane took over, he disbanded a hard-working and efficient executive committee and soon, up to 55 senior managers left. Around that time, stories started emerging about a 'rogue unit' within SARS which was acting against the best principles of the organisation, and doing so illegally.

This 'rogue unit' was shown to be spurious and was, by late 2018, the reason why the *Sunday Times* parted ways with journalists Mzilikazi wa Afrika and Stephan Hofstatter. They had been part of the newspaper's team that had seemingly delivered fake news on the pre-Moyane era at SARS, inadvertently or deliberately assisting the destructive and costly power grab that then took place at the tax authority.

Among those who gave testimony at the Nugent Commission of Inquiry were former government spokesperson Themba Maseko, government spokesperson Phumla Williams, and Treasury officials Willie Mathebula, Dondo Mogajane and Ismail Momoniat. Among others, they showed how Moyane's new 'business model' profoundly undermined SARS.

It was known as the Receiver of Revenue during apartheid. The first Income Tax Act in South Africa was introduced in 1914.

South African Social Security Agency (SASSA)

Department of Government within the Department of Social Development

Mired in mismanagement and allegations of corruption

THE MANDATE OF THE AGENCY WAS TO ENSURE the provision of comprehensive social security services against vulnerability and poverty within the constitutional and legislative framework.

The grants allocated were: the Care Dependency Grant, the Child Support Grant and the Foster Child Grant, which are for South African citizens, permanent residents or refugees, designed to support the care of children under 18; the Disability Grant, for South African citizens, permanent residents or refugees aged 18 to 59 who are not in receipt of another social grant in respect of themselves; Grants-in-Aid, under which an applicant must be in receipt of a grant for Older Persons, a Disability Grant or a War Veteran's grant, and must require full-time attendance by another person owing to their physical or mental disabilities; Grants for Older Persons who are South African citizens, permanent residents or refugees, are 60 years or older and are not in receipt of another social grant for themselves; the Social Relief of Distress Grant, which is generally a three-month provision of assistance for South African citizens or permanent residents not receiving any other social grant who are in such dire material need that they are unable to meet basic needs because they are awaiting payment of a grant, are medically unfit, are not receiving maintenance, no longer have a bread winner in the house due to death or institutionalisation, or have been affected by a disaster, and the War Veterans' Grant, which is for South African citizens and permanent residents who are 60 or older, disabled, fought in World War 2 or the Korean War and are not in receipt of another social grant for themselves.

On paper, this was impressive, but SASSA was increasingly embattled during former social development minister Bathabile Dlamini's time, when her department failed to properly govern its relationship with Cashmaster Pay Services, a private company contracted to manage the payment of grants.

Speaker

Principal office bearer of the National Assembly

THE POSITION HAS MANY RESPONSIBILITIES, which include constitutional, statutory and procedural and administrative powers and functions.

The duties of the Speaker fall broadly into three categories: presiding over sittings of the house, maintaining order and applying its rules; acting as representative and spokesperson for the National Assembly and (with the chairperson of the Council) for Parliament; and acting as chief executive officer for Parliament, in conjunction with the chairperson of the Council.

The Speaker is equivalent in rank to a Cabinet minister. Although the Speaker is a member of a political party, they are required to act impartially and protect the rights of all parties.

In performing their functions, the Speaker is assisted by the deputy Speaker and three house chairpersons, each with specific areas of responsibility determined by the Speaker.

The Speaker in 2019 was ANC veteran Baleka Mbete.

Special Investigating Unit (SIU)

Independent statutory authority

Corruption-busters

ACCOUNTABLE TO PARLIAMENT AND THE PRESIDENT, the SIU's mandate is to recover and prevent financial losses to the state through corruption, fraud and maladministration.

The unit was established in 1996 and is funded by the Department of Justice. Its powers include subpoena, search, seize and interrogate under oath, and although all criminal matters it uncovers must be referred to the Hawks and the National Prosecuting Authority (NPA), it is permitted to take civil action. The South African Police Service and the NPA's Asset Forfeiture Unit are its closest partners in recovering the proceeds of crime.

Among the anti-corruption laws that the SIU utilises are the Constitution, the Public Finance Management Act, the Prevention of Organised Crime Act, the Municipal Financial Management Act, the Financial Intelligence Centre Act, the Prevention and Combating of Corrupt Activities Act and the Prevention of Corruption Act.

Its duties should fall within the scope of the government's Anti-Corruption Task

Team, established as an inter-governmental body in 2010 when Jacob Zuma was president. But it appears the task team all but ceased to function over a number of years. This, despite government insisting it had been 'strengthened' by another body – the Anti-Corruption Inter-Ministerial Committee – which was to be led by the Minister in the Presidency for Planning Monitoring and Evaluation.

When the task team head Zinhle Mnonopi was suspended in late 2018 after she was implicated in state capture by former deputy minister of Finance Mcebisi Jonas at the Zondo Commission, it looked to be in terminal decline. But the SIU was holding its ground.

Its head in 2019 was Advocate Andy Mothibi and the chief governance officer was Advocate Mahlodi Muofhe.

The Standing Committee on Public Accounts (Scopa)
Parliamentary body

Parliament has a number of standing or permanent committees, broadly representing the political make-up of the National Assembly (NA). Perhaps the most important is the National Assembly Standing Committee on Public Accounts, better known by its acronym Scopa.

Scopa is the parliamentary watchdog that checks how government (the executive) and state-owned enterprises (SOEs) spend budgets and scrutinises procedures and practices to ensure transparency and accountability.

Ministers and directors-general are regularly called to account before the committee, especially after the auditor-general tables the respective department's annual financial report. Scopa can recommend that the NA takes corrective actions if necessary.

The committee became ever-more important as state capture allegations grew and devastating mismanagement and corruption was revealed at SOEs like Eskom, Denel and the South African Broadcasting Corporation (SABC).

It had improved its independence under the chairpersonship of African People's Convention (APC) leader Themba Godi, formerly of the Pan-Africanist Congress (PAC). Where Scopa had lost almost all its credibility in the early years of democracy around the 'arms deal' scandal – which saw the resignation of both its then chairperson Dr Gavin Woods of the Democratic Alliance (DA) and deputy chair Andrew Feinstein of the ANC – over political interference from government, it is today a valued institution.

State banks

These include the Industrial Development Corporation (IDC), the Development Bank of Southern Africa (DBSA), the Land Bank and provincial development agencies.

Following years of mismanagement and corruption across a number of sectors which would have affected all of these, it was believed by 2018 that they needed to be recapitalised and properly capacitated.

Former Treasury official Andrew Donaldson said in 2017 that the DBSA, for example, had total assets of R83.7 billion, compared with the R1.95 trillion and R1.3 trillion balance sheets of Standard Bank and FirstRand – two of the 'big four' commercial banks - respectively.

The intention from the state, and ruling party the ANC, also came against the backdrop of pressure from the Economic Freedom Fighters (EFF) for a state-owned black-orientated bank. The EFF had become a protagonist of, for example, the beleaguered VBS Mutual Bank in Limpopo, which was tainted through its alleged associations with corruption and a bond out of the blue for former president Jacob Zuma to finance his private homestead, Nkandla, in KwaZulu-Natal.

The reason for the EFF's support was that it was black-owned, and had been seen to be increasing access to finance for black people. The state needed to be able to counter that with better marketing around its existing state banks, and opening those up for even deeper penetration into the black entrepreneurial market inside the country.

To that end, it would be important also to capacitate the National Empowerment Fund (NEF), established through an Act of Parliament in 1998 to promote black economic participation, and the Small Enterprise Development Agency (seda), established in December 2004 under the Department of Trade and Industry (dti).

Meanwhile, it was expected that the state-owned Postbank (a division of the Post Office) would be able to offer banking services to people living in poorer and more remote areas when it earned its banking licence in 2018. Postbank had a nationwide footprint, and was well supported with R7 billion in deposits and about 7 million depositors. A banking licence would mean it could offer unsecured loans, meaning borrowers would not have to have assets to apply, nor would they be subject to exorbitant interest rates such as those of the commercial banks.

This would be good news especially for informal traders, and people who, up until that point, might have been living in a backyard room saving up to buy a small property, but had been unable to do so because of prohibitive banking rules.

State-owned entities (SOEs)

Government enterprises

Many mired in corruption and mismanagement

A Presidential Council was established under President Cyril Ramaphosa to look at the balance sheet of every SOE when he assumed office in February 2018. This was because the situation within most SOEs was precarious and threatened both the economy and national security due to corruption, mismanagement and a lack of governance, which had allowed fraud and bankruptcy to thrive. An important reason for this was that the Department of Public Enterprises (DPE) – the shareholder representative of government with oversight responsibility for SOEs – was itself alleged to have been captured.

There is a long and corrupt history to these, as they were primarily established during the apartheid regime to counteract the effects of international sanctions against the country.

When the ANC took power in 1994, it unpopularly sold stakes in some of the SOEs. It also lowered import tariffs and so local producers were adversely affected. The ANC's partners in the Tripartite Alliance, the South African Communist Party (SACP) and the Congress of South African Trade Unions (Cosatu) were against its actions.

Although there are about 700 SOEs around the country, the DPE has oversight responsibility in full or in part for: Alexkor (diamonds), Denel (military equipment), Eskom (power generation), South African Express Airways; the South African Forestry Company (SAFCOL) and Transnet (transportation).

A number of former ministers and former CEOs and board members of SOEs were expected to be implicated or to give evidence in the Commission of Inquiry into State Capture which started its work under Deputy Chief Justice Raymond Zondo in March 2018.

State Security Agency (SSA)

Government body

Long beset by rumours of corruption

The SSA rarely features in the news, despite it playing a significant role in much of the work of government. But in 2018, the spotlight fell on its activities when Arthur Fraser, who was then its all-powerful director-general, was moved to the Department of Correctional Services in April 2018.

This move was welcomed by many, but it didn't come quietly.

Fraser was appointed as the spy boss in 2016 by President Jacob Zuma in a move which celebrated journalist Jacques Pauw called 'illogical, irrational and outright idiotic' in the *Sunday Times*. With Fraser's high-level permission quota extending to phone-tapping, wide surveillance and what Pauw called 'bags of dirt', Fraser had been accused of setting up a parallel intelligence network and possible treason. Pauw estimated the cost of Fraser's activities to have been around R1 billion.

It was Pauw, in his best-selling 2017 book, *The President's Keepers*, who had claimed Fraser was running such a 'parallel intelligence network', although this was during Fraser's time at the National Intelligence Agency (NIA, one of the organisations that preceded the creation of the SSA), before 2010.

Against the advice of his own intelligence sector's White Paper, Zuma decided to review the structures of the civilian intelligence community when he came into power in 2009. The SSA merged all, its mandate to advise government on domestic and foreign threats or potential threats to national stability, the Constitutional order, and 'the safety and wellbeing of our people'.

The final organisational structure would see the South African Secret Service (SASS), the South African National Academy of Intelligence (SANAI), the National Communications Centre (NCC), the Office for Interception Centres (OIC) and Electronic Communications Security (Pty) Ltd (COMSEC) collapsed into the SSA as branches, with each branch lead by a head accountable to the DG.

Oversight and legislation pertaining to the SSA include various Acts of Parliament such as the Regulation of Interception of Communications and Provision of Communication-Related Information Act (RICA), the Constitution and the IGI.

Among the missteps taken by the SSA in recent times included the bogus report that Zuma used to fire former finance minister Pravin Gordhan and deputy finance minister Mcebisi Jonas in 2017. Pauw alleges that the notorious 'spy tapes' which Zuma's attorney used to undermine former president Thabo Mbeki in 2007 and have him recalled in 2008 could have been supplied by Fraser through the then NIA, where Fraser was deputy DG at the time.

Statistics South Africa (StatsSA)

National statistical service of South Africa

The service has the goal of producing timely, accurate and official statistics to advance economic growth, development and democracy. It produces official demographic, economic and social censuses and surveys.

By the 2019 elections, StatsSA would have produced three censuses – in 1996, 2001 and 2011.

The statistician-general in 2019 was Risenga Maluleke who took office in November 2017 when the popular Dr Pali Lehohla's tenure expired. Maluleke had worked for StatsSA for 20 years, having joined as a manager at its Limpopo provincial office in 1997.

Steenhuisen, John

Democratic Alliance (DA) chief whip | DA MP | Member of the Joint Standing Committee on the Financial Management of Parliament

In 2010, Steenhuisen resigned as the DA's KwaZulu-Natal leader when news broke of his affair with the party's provincial spokesperson Terry Kass-Beaumont. He stayed on as an MPL and Caucus leader until his move to Parliament in 2011. But by the time Parliament had irrevocably altered to include the revolutionary spirit of the Economic Freedom Fighters (EFF), which was introduced from 2014, Steenhuisen's personal scandals had been brushed away.

To many South Africans who started taking a serious interest in Parliament when Speaker Baleka Mbete expelled the EFF leaders from the National Assembly not long after they had first entered it in 2011, Steenhuisen was either a brash liberal prat or a defender of democracy.

Nonetheless, he became the best known of the DA MPs, especially after President Cyril Ramaphosa instructed him to 'shut up' when Steenhuisen repeatedly heckled him during his question session in Parliament in May 2018. That interaction went viral.

Steenhuisen, a previous shadow minister of Co-operative Governance and Traditional Affairs, was considered a first option to succeeding long-serving chairperson of the DA's powerful federal executive in 2018, James Selfe, but then declined to stand against him and remain in Parliament.

By November 2018, however, Steenhuisen found himself at the centre of an alternately entertaining and angry storm when it was revealed that he only had matric, while having criticised his peers in other parties for their lack of education. Twitter had a field day, and the topics of whether MPs had to have a tertiary qualification, and whether whites could rise to the top without them, simply because they were white, were on every platform.

T

Tlhagale, Buti

Catholic archbishop

Change agent

TLHAGALE BECAME A CATHOLIC when he went to St Patrick's Primary School in Randfontein, Johannesburg. He entered priesthood shortly after high school, obtaining his BA from the University of Botswana, Lesotho and Swaziland (known as Roma, for the town in which it is situated near Maseru, Lesotho). Tlhagale then studied theology at Rome's Gregorian University.

He was ordained in 1976 and served as a parish priest across Soweto until 1999, when he became the archbishop of Bloemfontein. During that time, he played a key role in the establishment of the Azanian People's Organisation (Azapo) and worked in the justice and peace department of the South African Council of Churches (SACC). He later served for four years as secretary-general of the Southern African Catholic Bishops Conference.

Tlhagale was appointed bishop of Johannesburg in 2003 and, when the Pope elevated the diocese's status in 2007, Tlhagale became its first metropolitan archbishop – the post he holds to date.

He had written and published widely on black theology, labour and culture.

After becoming archbishop of Johannesburg, Tlhagale was especially outspoken on the Christian need to give succour to refugees in a country that often did the opposite with little effective condemnation by the state. He was also vocal about the scourge of state capture and corruption.

Trade Unions

ORGANISED LABOUR PLAYS A MIGHTY ROLE IN South African life, with at least 3 million people, or some 25% of the formal work force, represented by one of more than 20 federations or unions registered at the Office of the Registrar of Labour Relations.

The four biggest in 2019 were the Congress of South African Trade Unions (Cosatu), the South African Federation of Trade Unions (Saftu), the Federation of Unions of South Africa (Fedusa) and the National Council of Trade Unions (Nactu).

The others registered were the Confederation of Metal and Building Unions, the Federation of Trade Unions of Transnet, the SA Confederation of Labour, the Federasie van Mynproduksiewerkers, the Federation for Municipal Trade Unions, the Federation of Mining Unions, the Federation of Independent Trade Unions, the Federation of the Armaments and Allied Industries of South Africa, the United

Independent Trade Unions of South Africa, the United Independent Economic Trade Unions of South Africa, the South African Independent Trade Unions Confederation, the Movement for Social Justice, the Independent Trade Unions Alliance of South Africa, the Confederation of South African Workers Unions, the (South African chapter of the) International Federation of Building and Wood Workers, the (South African chapter of the) International Union of Food, Agricultural, Hotel, Restaurant, Catering, Tobacco and Allied Workers' Association, the (South African chapter of the) International Textile, Garment and Leather Workers' Federation, the (South African chapter of the) UNI (Union Network International) Global Union Federation and the Federation of Southern African Public Sector Trade Unions.

Traditional Courts Bill

Government legislation

THIS DIVISIVE BILL, FIRST BROUGHT BEFORE Parliament in 2008, exposed many of the conflicts surrounding customary entitlement. It took nearly another decade to somewhat unravel those difficulties and for Parliament to have more time to examine both unilateral chiefly power, tribal boundaries, the abiding problems of the bantustans and, seguing into all of these, land rights.

One of the country's most important researchers, Sindiso Mnisi Weeks of the University of Cape Town, laid much of this down in an analysis for *The Conversation* in 2017. She began by confirming that the Constitution recognises the institution of traditional leadership, in accordance with customary law and 'subject to the Constitution. But, government had 'erroneously interpreted' these provisions to mean that it should 'elevate the powers of traditional leaders in all customary law legislation'.

Instead, the Traditional Leadership and Governance Framework Act of 2003 allowed national or provincial government to, 'through legislative or other measures, provide a role for traditional councils or traditional leaders in respect of (among other things) administration of justice'.

In other words, through this Act, traditional courts were afforded the power to resolve civil and criminal disputes between observers of customary law. But many people objected, saying this was unconstitutional and that no ordinary people living in the rural areas were consulted; only traditional leaders and members of local government.

Things fell quiet until the Bill was reintroduced in 2012, but again, as Mnisi Weeks said in her analysis, it was 'profoundly flawed', so much so that government 'couldn't secure sufficient support to pass the Bill into law'. So it lapsed again in early 2014.

One of its biggest problems, as was the case in 2008, was that customary law is designed around 'distributed power and strives for participation and consensus among the members of a community'. Originally, there were disputes around who had the authority, with the Bill's detractors correctly questioning the emphasis being put on a 'senior traditional leader'. This created accountability questions and 'exacerbated the gender inequalities that exist under the patriarchal arrangements that prevail in many customary communities'.

The new Bill of 2016 no longer described the traditional leader as 'the presiding officer' in traditional courts. Instead, it recognised a central role for people from the community who were not traditional leaders. It wanted discrimination eliminated and traditional leaders to be prohibited from using these courts for personal benefit.

Transnet

South African rail, port and pipeline company | Chaired by Popo Molefe

Corrupt managers have been linked to state capture

WITH HEADQUARTERS IN THE CARLTON CENTRE in Johannesburg, Transnet was formed as a limited company on 1 April 1990. A majority of its stock is owned by the Department of Public Enterprises and it is categorised as a state-owned enterprise (SOE).

But its fate, which was to be a profitable enterprise assisting in the development of the country's infrastructure, changed from 2014 when CEO Brian Molefe was first exposed as a likely candidate for state capture. By 2018, court papers filed by Transnet showed that it needed to recover R189 million in inflated payments from the Gupta-linked Regiments Capital – that business 'partnership' revealing the level of collusion with the notorious family that had unfolded under Molefe and through senior executives at the SOE.

Former Transnet CEO Siyabonga Gama, former chief financial officers Anoj Singh and Garry Pita, and former group treasurer Robert Ramosebudi were said to have 'fraudulently colluded to cause Transnet to transfer to Regiments an overpayment of R151 million'.

The court papers showed that Singh, Gama, Pita and Ramosebudi had recommended that the board acquisitions and disposal committee approve the appointment of Regiments on a risk-sharing agreement, despite the company not being on risk, to provide 'transaction advisory services' related to a locomotives tender. And while Singh and Pita recommended in 2015 that Gama approve a payment of R166 million to Regiments, it was believed all should have known that Regiments was owed far less, which was R15 million.

This court action which was instigated by the board under Popo Molefe was set to begin a lengthy process to finally act against corruption at the SOE. Jacob Zuma was president during the time of the fraudulent transactions.

Treatment Action Campaign (TAC)

Activist organisation | Politically non-aligned

Change agents | Stars

CO-FOUNDED BY HIV-POSITIVE ACTIVIST Zachie Achmat and 10 others in 1998, the TAC originally aimed only to protest the government's refusal to distribute antiretrovirals (ARVs). The group's members became well known for wearing trademark T-shirts with 'HIV-POSITIVE' printed on them in large letters, and Achmat made a famous pledge to not use ARVs until they became available to all South Africans.

But it was soon clear that the TAC's battles would not begin and end with the provision of ARVs, even if they drew international attention to the debates unfolding in South African society under former president Thabo Mbeki, who was portrayed as an AIDS denialist for his recalcitrant and highly controversial views on HIV/AIDS.

The TAC's original campaign of the late 1990s saw AIDS activists and researchers call upon government to distribute an ARV drug called Zidovudine (AZT) to pregnant women. But all the provinces – all governed by the ANC at that time – rejected the use of AZT, based primarily on claims that it was 'too expensive to distribute'. Moreover, Health Minister Nkosazana Dlamini-Zuma openly opposed the drug and asserted that government's policy was to 'focus on prevention rather than treatment'. This argument seemed illogical to her critics, as the drug had been shown to dramatically reduce HIV transmission from pregnant women to their unborn children.

The Congress of South African Trade Unions (Cosatu), the ANC's partner in the Tripartite Alliance with the South African Communist Party (SACP), supported the TAC in its bid to provide ARVs to nearly five million South Africans living with HIV/AIDS.

Trillian Asset Management

Former financial advisory firm

Corrupt

In January 2018, the National Prosecuting Authority (NPA) lodged an affidavit at the North Gauteng High Court in Pretoria against international consulting firm McKinsey, 'boutique' financial advisory firm Trillian and state utility firm Eskom.

It said payments made by Eskom to McKinsey and Trillian were 'criminal, consisting of crimes including fraud, theft, corruption and money laundering', and requested a curator to preserve property worth R1.59 billion. That was allegedly how much McKinsey and Trillian received from Eskom, with the affidavit stating that R1 billion was paid to McKinsey and R595 million to Trillian.

The NPA claimed: there was no valid contract between the parties for the services it was alleged had been provided and therefore no legal obligation on Eskom to pay; there had been no competitive bidding in the appointment of either McKinsey or Trillian, and payments were made out of fake invoices or no invoices.

McKinsey's senior partner David Fine acknowledged that the purported contract was invalid and undertook to repay the money to South Africa. The NPA sought to show this as further proof that the entire R1.59-billion payment constituted the proceeds of unlawful activities.

The NPA's affidavit featured the names of some of the individuals who had appeared before Parliament during its inquiry into corruption at SOEs, including Trillian Asset Management's CEO and executive director Mosilo Mothepu. He said he had raised the alarm with Eric Woods, CEO of Trillian's parent company, Trillian Capital Partners, about it not having signed a contract with SOEs, including Eskom.

Another important figure was former Trillian CEO Bianca Goodson, whose signature was used without her permission on its invoices. She noted that Trillian did not even have the staff to do the work for which it billed Eskom in 2016.

Trillian was a modest financial advisory firm when it was sold to Gupta family associate Salim Essa.

Trollip, Athol

Federal chairperson of the Democratic Alliance (DA) | Former DA mayor of the Nelson Mandela Bay municipality | Former parliamentary leader of the Official Opposition | Former DA MP

TROLLIP WAS TESTED AS A POLITICIAN in 2018 when three motions of no confidence in him as executive mayor of the Nelson Mandela Bay metro in Port Elizabeth, came to nought. This was after the Economic Freedom Fighters (EFF), which had brought the motions, withdrew the final one. This was after several councillors in the contested metro were unable to attend a special council meeting to hear the motion.

Trollip was indeed ousted, however, when the ANC, the EFF and the United Democratic Movement collaborated. But those parties couldn't have brought an end to his power in Nelson Mandela Bay without the unexpected assistance of DA councillor Mbulelo Manyati's abstention in acknowledging the Speaker of the council, which led to the DA caucus leaving the chamber, allowing the opposition coalition to vote in the UDM's candidate Mogameli Bobani as executive mayor.

Shouting matches, arguments over the order of events and general unpleasantness had characterised the council's meetings under Trollip since the DA, the EFF and the ANC battled over who held control in the Eastern Cape metro after the 2016 Local Government Elections (LEC).

The subtext was ideological differences between the DA and the EFF, believed to be largely over the DA's refusal, through Trollip, to countenance the EFF's motion on land expropriation without compensation at a national level.

But Trollip – who had many years of political experience behind him, serving as a member of the Eastern Cape provincial legislature, as Parliamentary leader of the Official Opposition between 2009 and 2011 and as a DA MP – was not out of the national game. He remained DA Federal chairperson, which gave him an internal power-base to help determine the direction of the party towards the 2019 elections.

Tsenoli, Lechesa

Deputy Speaker of the National Assembly | Former minister of Co-operative Governance and Traditional Affairs | Former deputy minister of Rural Development and Land Affairs | ANC and South African Communist Party (SACP) politician | Former political prisoner

TSENOLI EARNED HIS GOVERNING STRIPES as a member of the Free State Provincial Legislature, but he had a long history of political activism in community, youth and civic organisations, including the United Democratic Front (UDF) and the South African National Civics Organisation (Sanco). He also operated underground for the ANC during apartheid.

Although he had been a member of Cabinet, by the time he was named Deputy Speaker, Tsenoli might not have been that familiar to all South Africans until he showed his mettle in Parliament.

Speaker Baleka Mbete has not always reacted well to vociferous debate in the National Assembly since the Economic Freedom Fighters (EFF) entered its space in 2014. This was to the extent that she allowed Parliament's security to forcibly and violently removed EFF members after they objected to former president Jacob Zuma's presence.

Tsenoli, on the other hand, became known for generally keeping his patience, although he was also criticised for seemingly not always understanding the processes underway, and for suppressing debate among opposition parties.

U

United Democratic Movement (UDM)

Political party | Centrist | Number of seats in Parliament in 2018: 4

Power brokers

SINCE ITS FOUNDING IN 1997, THE UDM of General Bantu Holomisa, with a mere four seats in Parliament, is a vocal lever of power. This was especially true of the one and a half terms of Jacob Zuma. From the scandal around payments for additional upgrades to Zuma's private homestead, Nkandla, to the massacre of mineworkers in Marikana in 2012, to insisting on a secret ballot for a motion of no confidence against Zuma, the UDM would not relent. And when it succeeded, as it did in the secret ballot issue, the UDM would lead the national discourse on accountability.

Perhaps there was no better place that summed up the UDM's political influence story than the Nelson Mandela Bay (NMB) municipality in Port Elizabeth, Eastern Cape. Once an ANC stronghold with a rich heritage, an area where foremost leaders like Govan Mbeki were buried, it would become a support-base for the UDM. Voters there gave it an unqualified thumbs up.

By extension, the NMB was also the story of the ANC's decline. It lost the municipality in the 2016 local government elections to a Democratic Alliance (DA)-led co-governing structure, which initially included the UDM. But then, after a DA councillor unexpectedly did not support his own party during a key vote, the UDM gained its first executive mayor, in Mongameli Bobani.

In Parliament, the UDM also found its voice, and its vibrancy. One of its youngest MPs, Nqabayomzi Kwankwa, became a leading figure after his arrival in the National Assembly in 2013. Kwankwa was a former ANC member who joined the UDM in 2007.

Yet the party's most influential figure would remain Holomisa, whose persuasive power would extend beyond the Eastern Cape, where he had once served as a military strongman as apartheid crumbled.

#UniteBehind

Civil society coalition | Politically non-aligned

Change agents

THIS CAMPAIGN INVOLVED MORE THAN 20 ORGANISATIONS that mobilised together around common struggles for a just and equal South Africa.

Activists from various peoples' movements, inspired to collective action after the Cape Town memorial for ANC veteran Ahmed Kathrada, formed the coalition. It included young people, struggle veterans, queer people, women, workers and unemployed people in the fight for women's equality, land justice, informal settlement upgrading, equal education, open, participatory and accountable governance, racial and economic justice and Constitutional rights. It also mobilised against State capture.

Its affiliates were: the Alternative Information and Development Centre (AIDC); the Centre for Environmental Rights; the District 6 Working Committee; Equal Education; the Financial Sector Campaign Coalition; Ndifuna Ukwazi; Parliament Watch; the People's Health Movement (PHM); the Philippi Horticultural Area (PHA) Food and Farming Campaign; Right 2 Know (Western Cape); the Southern African Faith Communities Environment Institute (SAFCEI); the South Africa First Forum; SaveSouthAfrica; SECTION27; Sonke Gender Justice; the Social Justice Coalition (SJC); the Treatment Action Campaign (TAC); the Women and Democracy Initiative; the Women's Legal Centre; the Trust for Community Outreach and Education; the United Democratic Front (UDF) Veterans; the Western Cape Religious Leaders Forum; and the Wellington Association Against the Incinerator.

Van Damme, Phumzile

Democratic Alliance (DA) National Spokesperson | DA MP | DA Shadow Minister of Communications | Former Head of Parliamentary Research and Communications for the DA

On the way up | Star

A GRADUATE OF RHODES UNIVERSITY, Van Damme majored in political science and law before joining the DA as a political staffer a few months after the 2009 election.

Her first five years with the party were spent largely in research and media, her election as an MP in 2014 making her one of the youngest Parliamentarians. Van Damme's political rise elevated her to the position of DA Shadow Minister of Communications by 2019.

Among her political campaigns was bringing a legal case against Bell Pottinger, the disgraced British public relations firm. Van Damme was one of the most vocal young politicians against its plot to provoke racial hate as a means of distracting South Africans from the state capture project of the Gupta brothers.

Van Damme was also unafraid of controversy within her own party, openly opposing Western Cape premier Helen Zille for her tweets about a tax revolt, and directly confronting the DA's former policy chief Gwen Ngwenya on ideological grounds, in 2019.

Vavi, Zwelinzima

Former general-secretary of the Congress of South African Trade Unions (Cosatu) | Organiser with the South African Federation of Trade Unions (Saftu) | Politically Left, but non-aligned

Power broker

Born on a farm in Hanover in the Northern Cape in 1962, two years after the National Party government banned anti-apartheid movements in the wake of the Sharpeville massacre, Vavi had memories of being an unpaid child labourer from an early age. Later a mining plant clerk and then an organiser for the National Union of Mineworkers (NUM), the victorious, seven-day 1987 mineworkers' strike – which routed mining capital and is still the biggest in South African labour history – was a turning point for him.

He then volunteered for Cosatu and was soon elected Western Transvaal regional secretary before becoming the federation's national organising secretary in 1992 and then its deputy general-secretary until 1999 when he succeeded Mbhazima Shilowa as general-secretary. This meant Vavi became the face of Cosatu in the Tripartite Alliance with the ANC and the South African Communist Party (SACP).

Among Vavi's other roles at Cosatu was serving as its proxy on the International Labour Organisation's commission of globalisation. But his relationship with the federation turned sour not long after Jacob Zuma became president when Vavi identified corruption among ANC leadership within the Public Investment Corporation (PIC) and parastatals.

He was widely quoted for calling South Africa under Zuma a 'predator state' led by 'a demagogic elite of political hyenas'.

A pro-Zuma faction within Cosatu agitated to have him expelled amid a sex scandal by 2015 after he sided with the National Union of Metalworkers (Numsa) in its battle to unseat the president and fight corruption in government and the ANC.

Vavi then championed and became a convenor of the steering committee of the rival South African Federation of Trade Unions (Saftu), whose launching congress was in April 2017.

Vavi has had allegations of sexual impropriety made against him twice. On both occasions, he indicated these were the result of campaigns to smear his name, although he did take responsibility for events that could have led to the collapse of his marriage in 2013.

VBS Mutual Bank

Formerly one of the few black-owned banks in the country | Formerly the Venda Building Society

Believed to be corrupt to the core

OFF THE BACK OF MIXED ANALYSIS as to its purpose and weight in a stable but predominantly white-run South African banking sector, the black-owned VBS was regarded by some as light at the end of the tunnel and by others as a front. It was established in 1982 as the Venda Building Society and became a mutual bank in the early 1990s with most of its customers living in Limpopo

In a market dominated by the big four – Standard Bank, First National Bank, Absa bank and Nedbank – its seeming attempts to direct business, especially state business, into its accounts was at first regarded as progressive. But by March 2018, it had been placed under curatorship for what South African Reserve Bank (SARB) Governor Lesetja Kganyago called its 'severe liquidity crisis'.

It had seemingly relied on 'large, illegal and short-term municipal deposits to fund long-term loans', according to *City Press* newspaper. And then, when VBS had what was first euphemistically described as a 'cash crunch', a number of municipalities were faced with disaster as hundreds of millions of rand could not be accessed. At least R1.1 billion of the deposits were believed to be related to eight Limpopo municipalities.

But the 'cash crunch' was later revealed to be much more than that. Vele Investments, VBS's controlling shareholder, was raided in May 2018 after the South African Reserve Bank (SARB) obtained a warrant under the new Financial Sector Regulation Act. By October 2018, a forensic investigator who looked into the bank on behalf of the SARB concluded that the rot ran too deep to salvage it.

Among those who benefitted from the looting was the lead auditor of the bank, Sipho Malaba who was linked to an amount of R34 million. Others linked to the corruption included ANC Limpopo treasurer Daniel Msiza, deputy director-general (DG) of Home Affairs Thulani Mavuso, two municipal officials from Gauteng, Vhavenda King Toni Mphephu Ramabulana, Brian Shivambu (brother of Floyd, the deputy commander-in-chief of the Economic Freedom Fighters) and KPMG auditors checking its books. A beleaguered KPMG later saw the aforementioned Malaba and another of its partners, Dumi Tshuma, resign before they could be disciplined as they had not disclosed the full extent of their financial interests in VBS.

It was claimed that VBS had given mortgage loans among others to its own directors, municipal officials and trade unionists linked to the South African Municipal Workers Union (SAMWU). SAMWU and VBS had conceptualised and launched a line of low-cost financial products for SAMWU members.

With only a R450-million mortgage book, VBS first drew attention when it gave Jacob Zuma a R7.5-million loan in 2017 to repay the state for his portion of the R246 million upgrades to his private home in Nkandla.

Meanwhile, as government and the SARB tried to come to grips with how to deal with the mess that was VBS, hundreds of ordinary people huddled outside the bank's branches in Limpopo waiting fearfully to withdraw their money as the collapse gained momentum.

Vrede dairy scandal

At the centre of state capture allegations | Linked to former Free State premier Ace Magashule and former Free State MEC for Agriculture Mosebenzi Zwane

Allegedly involved with the notorious Gupta family | Allegations of massive corruption

THE COUNCIL FOR THE ADVANCEMENT of the South African Constitution (CASAC) filed an affidavit in the Pretoria High Court in April 2018 which claimed that Public Protector Advocate Busisiwe Mkhwebane had altered a provisional report into the scandal compiled by her predecessor, Advocate Thuli Madonsela.

These 'alterations', CASAC said, were to 'protect' former Free State premier Ace Magashule and former Free State MEC for Agriculture Mosebenzi Zwane, as well as other politicians and managers.

CASAC's affidavit said that Mkhwebane had removed remedial action prescribed in Madonsela's provisional report, which apparently said the matter should be referred to the Special Investigating Unit (SIU) and the auditor-general. CASAC claimed Mkhwebane had instead deferred 'disciplinary' action to Zwane and removed Free State agriculture department head Peter Thabethe's name, recommending he move positions.

Thabethe was alleged to have effectively 'brokered' a deal seemingly to benefit the Guptas' Estina company by signing a contract, overseeing a 99-year leasehold and failing to use any oversight measures in a plan to develop a dairy farm to benefit poor farmers in the town of Vrede. That plan appeared to be marked by inflated pricing and exhibited a 'likelihood' of maladministration and fruitless expenditure.

But attempts by the Hawks to prove corruption amid claims that state money was 'engineered' out of the plan for a dairy to pay for a lavish Gupta family wedding stuttered, and a case against eight individuals allegedly linked to such was provisionally withdrawn in late November 2018.

Court documents showed the Free State province under Magashule paid Estina – a Gupta-linked company – US$11 million after officially terminating the dairy farm contract.

There were discomfiting events that took place that may or may not have been related to the scandal. For instance, Moses Tshake, a provincial government auditor. who inquired about projects in the agriculture department, was killed in a car-jacking in 2013. In Warden, a town near to Vrede where former minister Zwane had a large home, Vusi Mlaba, a politician who had campaigned against corruption in public housing, was fatally shot a dozen times just outside his home in 2016. Police investigations resulted in no arrests in either case.

The Vrede dairy scandal was not going to be an easy matter to resolve. Although the Asset Forfeiture Unit of the National Prosecuting Authority (NPA) seized about R250 million's worth of Gupta assets during its investigation in April 2018, by May, the High Court in Bloemfontein had freed those assets, which included luxury cars, aircraft and properties, as it found there were 'no reasonable grounds' to believe that those implicated in the Vrede case would be convicted. Thus, it appeared there were 'no grounds' to freeze the assets.

Western Cape

Province | Run by the Democratic Alliance (DA) since 2009

Among the most contested ahead of the 2019 elections

THE ANC WAS EXPECTED TO REINVEST with vigour politically, at a senior level, in 2018 and early 2019 in the only province it had not held since 2009. The DA saw its majority increase there in 2014, but in 2018, there was something of an implosion in the party's reputation with two major crises affecting the Western Cape and, in particular, the city of Cape Town.

These were its reponses to 'Day Zero', an impending drought in the capital, and attempts to axe Cape Town's mayor Patricia de Lille. Analysts and DA critics alike noted a chaotic response by the party to both issues, both having racial undertones that forced the party to come to terms with what the ANC described as 'racist, elitist ... (and reflective of) white privilege'.

As the Western Cape's leadership started to feel the rip at its political seams, the ANC there said the official opposition was in a 'perpetual state of crisis'. Meanwhile, Cape Town retained its notoriety as one of the most violent cities in the world, seemingly unable to contain the high levels of rape, assault and murder in its ghetto areas which the city's liberal government had failed to prioritise after nearly a decade.

In 2019, former DA leader Helen Zille was Premier of the Western Cape.

'White Monopoly Capital' (WMC)

South African phrase usually referring to the wealthy white elite that dominates large sectors of the economy

AS ALLEGATIONS OF STATE CAPTURE GREW from 2016 onwards, and as it became clear that Jacob Zuma might not have always had the country's best interests at heart, the term 'white monopoly capital' started to filter into the public realm. It had, however, been around for more than 50 years – during the struggle and after it.

The reason for its resuscitation turned out to have more to do with Zuma's benefactors and their desperate attempts to stave off allegations of state capture, than the real meaning of the words.

This was because top British public relations firm Bell Pottinger had been employed at great cost by the notorious Gupta family and their company, Oakbay, to divert attention from their allegedly corrupt relationship with Zuma, members of his family and members of his faction in the ANC itself. Bell Pottinger would use social media through fake bloggers and bots to sow racial division in South Africa and deliver fake news to support Zuma.

The Democratic Alliance (DA) complained about the firm to two British regulatory bodies, the Public Relations and Communications Association and the Chartered Institute of Public Relations, and by July 2017, Bell Pottinger CEO James Henderson had issued an apology and announced it had dismissed the lead partner involved and suspended another partner and two employees.

Ultimately, Bell Pottinger was forced to close its doors in disgrace, but WMC remained in the country's parlance.

Wierzycka, Magda

Richest woman in South Africa | Political commentator

WIERZYCKA ARRIVED IN SOUTH AFRICA IN 1983 a refugee from Poland, unable to speak English or any African languages. She graduated from Pretoria High School for Girls nonetheless, read for an actuarial science degree at the University of Cape Town and was by 2018 a self-made billionaire and the richest woman in South Africa. That was according to the annual *Sunday Times* Rich List.

Wierzycka took Sygnia, her fin-tech asset management company from R2 billion to R162 billion in 10 years – and learnt volumes from her friendship with controversial entrepreneur Mzi Khumalo. But she became better known to ordinary South Africans when she matched private forensic investigator Paul O'Sullivan's R500,000 bounty on the head of Atul Gupta, one of the notorious Gupta brothers, who had seemingly vanished as state capture allegations proliferated around his family and their government cronies in early 2018.

Outspoken to the point of being brash, Wierzycka broke the mould of corporate leaders not speaking truth to power and cultivated a considerable Twitter following – until she started to get it wrong. In March 2018, she made a highly unpopular call by asking middle-class South Africans to 'kick-start' employment by employing more domestic workers. And then, having raised the ire of Black Twitter, she quickly recanted by offering to seed a special job creation fund with R200,000 of her own money – from the R500,000 she'd originally pledged for Gupta's arrest.

Shortly afterwards came a Human Rights Day picture error on Twitter when she posted the iconic Soweto 1976 photo of a dying Hector Pietersen to commemorate the Sharpeville Massacre.

Wierzycka announced her intention to leave Twitter indefinitely, but was back within a few months, as incendiary and hard-hitting as ever.

Yengeni, Tony

Former ANC secretary general in the Western Cape | Former ANC chief whip in Parliament | Former ANC MP | Convicted of fraud and sentenced to four years in jail; served four months | Member of the ANC's National Working Committee (NWC) | Former political prisoner

YENGENI GAINED HIS STATUS WITHIN THE ANC for a number of reasons. He had survived obscene torture at the hands of the apartheid security police and bravely testified his experience at the Truth and Reconciliation Commission (TRC). He'd been a committed member of Umkhonto we Sizwe (MK), before which he did military training in Botswana, Zambia and Angola, and studied social science in Moscow.

Yengeni became a trade unionist, working as the regional secretary for the South African Council of Trade Unions (Sactu) in Lesotho during apartheid. But it was his militarism that helped drive him upwards in the liberation movement, becoming an MK leader in the Western Cape in the late 1980s before he was arrested and then spent four years awaiting trial for terrorism.

Upon his release, when he became the ANC general-secretary of the Western Cape, Yengeni was always a populist, but it was when he began to work in Parliament as chair of the Joint Standing Committee on Defence – which helped government make key decisions on arms purchases – that another side to him evolved.

Patricia de Lille and other MPs queried kick-backs and corruption linked to what then became a R43-billion 'arms deal' in 1999, and questions began to be asked about Yengeni's dark green Mercedes-Benz ML320 4x4 with its tinted windows and luxury upholstery. It would turn out that he indeed received a 'discount' on the car, courtesy of a company that benefitted from the arms procurement.

Although, at first, Yengeni would not declare his assets as required of all MPs to Parliament's Ethics Committee, he famously took out full-page advertisements in most Sunday newspapers to decry the 'witchhunt' against him. That didn't help as Yengeni still had to face charges of corruption, fraud, statutory perjury and forgery.

He spent a brief period of his four-year sentence behind bars and was later held for drunken driving in Cape Town, but after rumours of high-level interference in his case, it went nowhere.

Yengeni, who had, by 2018, been a member of the party's National Executive Committee (NEC) for nearly 20 years, remained active in the ANC even after his conviction, which prevented him from holding that office again. He was elected onto the ANC's National Working Committee (NWC) after Cyril Ramaphosa became president in 2018. And, with its liking for dark humour, Twitter found it alternately amusing and ironic that Yengeni was then put in charge of the party's crime and corruption committee.

Young Communist League

Nickname: uFasimba | Youth wing of the South African Communist Party (SACP)

UNDER THE SLOGAN, 'SOCIALISM IN OUR LIFETIME', the Young Communist League (YCL) was relaunched in December 2003 after 53 years in dormancy. The league – long part of a global chain of of YCLs – had been banned with the South African Communist Party (SACP) in 1950, but while the SACP was reconstituted underground, the YCL was not. Still, it had a strong history dating back to the 1920s when trade unionism was a vibrant and defiant aspect of early city life in Johannesburg.

While it was not ideologically ambivalent nor did it misunderstand the need for a class analysis, it was not an Africanist organisation. And even today, it lacks a South African identity, and is all but invisible on the national stage.

It did, however, support Julius Malema when he was the ANC Youth League president facing disciplinary proceedings, which ultimately led to his expulsion. But otherwise, it has not campaigned publicly on many issues.

Z

Zille, Helen

Former Democratic Alliance (DA) leader | Former DA mayor of Cape Town | Former MEC for Education in the Western Cape

Beset by criticism for her views on Twitter

ONCE A POLITICAL JOURNALIST AT THE *Rand Daily Mail*, Zille played a role in uncovering the story behind Black Consciousness (BC) leader Steve Biko's death after state-sanctioned torture in 1977.

A supporter of the courageous Black Sash social justice organisation in the 1980s, she and her husband John Maree opened their home as a safe house for political activists.

Zille joined what was then called the Democratic Party (DP), which merged with the New National Party (NNP) in 2000 to become the Democratic Alliance (DA), and was elevated to party leader seven years later.

It was when Zille became the premier of the Western Cape that her powerful rise – which accompanied her having taken the DA into the national realm – took a mighty dip. Mistakes were undoubtedly made, chief among them the wooing of Mamphela Ramphele of AgangSA, and it seemed that Zille tried to dominate younger politicians. But it was when she went on Twitter rampages and, in particular, seemed to approve of aspects of colonialism, blame poor people for their perilous state, or advocate a tax revolt, that the positive sides of her were irrevocably marred.

Yet there were those who believed the divisions she had created in the party through these public pronouncements had been a catalyst for the DA to finally confront its internal demographics and how to resolve these.

The Zondo Commission (the Judicial Commission of Inquiry into Allegations of State Capture)

State-appointed probe | Headed by Deputy Chief Justice Raymond Zondo

Change agent

Jacob Zuma was compelled by the High Court to institute this commission of inquiry in early 2018 after he failed to act upon the remedial recommendations of then-public protector (PP) Thuli Madonsela in her 2016 report, 'A state of capture', which detailed how he and others misused government resources.

Zuma appointed Deputy Chief Justice Raymond Zondo to head the commission.

Among former ministers alleged to have been involved in state capture were: Des van Rooyen (Co-operative Governance and, infamously briefly, Finance); Mosebenzi Zwane (Mining); Lynne Brown (Public Enterprises); Faith Muthambi (Public Service and Administration, and Communications) and David Mahlobo (Energy).

Former chief operating officer in the Department of Justice and Constitutional Development and former acting secretary-general of the Office of the Chief Justice, Dr Khotso Dewee, was named secretary of the commission in March 2018. But one of the major bombshells at the inquiry exploded when Angelo Agrizzi, the former chief operating officer of security and catering company Bosasa, testified in January 2019 that De Wee was one of the officials Bosasa bribed. De Wee was put on leave while an investigation started into Agrizzi's claims against him. Agrizzi said the bribe was linked to a 2013 tender for courts' security systems.

Zondo appointed Peter Pedlar, a former chief risk officer and head of strategy for the Gautrain Management Agency, and the former chief financial officer of Artscape, the main performing arts centre in Cape Town, in an acting position as secretary.

Former auditor-general, Terrence Nombembe, was named Head of Investigations, while Advocate Paul Pretorius, an acting judge in the High Court and the Labour Court, was named Head of Lawyers. Other members of the legal team included advocates Vincent Moleka, Leah Gcabashe and Nothandi Norman.

According to the regulations of the commission, if a person gave evidence before it, the evidence they gave could not be used against them in subsequent criminal proceedings. But if police had evidence from other witnesses or sources against those persons, that evidence could possibly be used against them. In other words, if an individual gave evidence to the commission, that would not mean they could not be prosecuted in the future.

Public hearings began in August 2018, with the inquiry said to have received 'extensive support' from the PP's office and the National Assembly Speaker's office in providing records relating to its investigation. It operated from Parktown, Johannesburg, and from the moment it began its hearings, it attracted massive attention.

Many of those who testified delivered significant and intricate detail into how the state was undone by corrupt individuals and cabals, with much focus on the notorious Gupta family and its grip on the ANC – and government – under Zuma.

Among the biggest news stories emanating out of the commission was the exposing of Finance Minister Nhlanhla Nene who admitted, almost out of the blue, on the stand, that he had had private meetings with the Guptas, and lied about it. This led to him resigning and being replaced in October 2018 by Tito Mboweni.

Other remarkable testimony came from government spokesperson Phumla Williams, who said former communications minister Faith Muthambi, believed to be a tool of the Guptas, had 'tortured' her to the point where it was reminiscent of the torture she, Williams, had endured during apartheid.

Former deputy finance minister Mcebisi Jonas revealed the extent to which he was threatened by Ajay Gupta who pursued him with an intended bribe of R600 million.

Capital was represented there, too, as the four major banks – Absa, FNB, Standard Bank and Nedbank – all said the ANC had wanted to question them at its headquarters, Luthuli House, when they closed the Guptas' bank accounts in 2017. And there was also much politicking, with a prime example being the Economic Freedom Fighters (EFF) attack on Minister of Public Enterprises Pravin Gordhan during his testimony. The EFF called him 'a dog of white monopoly capital'.

But it was Agrizzi's testimony in January 2019 that gained the most attention, as he recalibrated the inquiry which, up until then, had focused rather narrowly on the Guptas. Agrizzi described another world of corruption entirely, in which a 'Struggle hero', Gavin Watson, allegedly embarked on a looting spree that went on for more than a decade. Watson's connections within the ANC stretched back far enough for him to have the credibility in government to become part of the state capture project.

The best description of the state capture era came from former minister Ngoako Ramatlhodi who said the NEC had been riven by factionalism during a 'season of madness'.

Zondo, Raymond

Deputy Chief Justice | Chairperson of the Judicial Commission of Inquiry into Allegations of State Capture | Former judge-president for the Labour Appeal Court and Labour Court | Former chair of the governing body of the Commission for Conciliation, Mediation and Arbitration (CCMA)

Change agent

Born in rural Ixopo, KwaZulu-Natal, into poverty in 1960, Zondo gained the affection of the nation in 2017 when he told the story of how he had gathered support to study law at the University of Zululand, at his Judicial Service Commission (JSE) interview for Deputy Chief Justice.

A kindly shopkeeper, who he barely knew, had aided Zondo's mother through grocery donations while Zondo immersed himself in his books, upon the understanding that Zondo should graduate. Zondo's emotional retelling of that event offered South Africans a sense of the man when he was confirmed to the position.

By coincidence, current Chief Justice Mogoeng Mogoeng was a fellow first-year student and they developed a friendship.

Zondo graduated with a B Luris and an LLB from the University of Natal and went on to complete three separate LLM degrees. He helped draft the Labour Relations Bill and was the first chair of the governing body of the CCMA. Zondo then became a Labour Court judge in 1997 and a judge of the Pretoria High Court two years later.

In 2000 he was made Judge-President for the Labour Appeal Court and Labour Court. On completion of his 10-year term, Zondo returned to the Pretoria High Court before being elevated to the Constitutional Court in 2012. He was appointed Deputy Chief Justice in 2017 and was regarded as part of the Constitutional Court's more conservative 'wing'.

Zuma then gave Zondo a most challenging task: chairing the Judicial Commission of Inquiry into Allegations of State Capture, which started its work in March 2018.

Zokwana, Senzeni

Minister of Agriculture, Forestry and Fisheries | Chairperson of the South African Communist Party (SACP) | Former president of the National Union of Mineworkers (NUM) | Former president of the International Federation of Chemical, Energy, Mine and General Workers' Union | Former vice president of the Industrial Global Union

Linked to corruption

WITH A POWERFUL HISTORY OF TRADE UNIONIST leadership behind him, Zokwana became an ANC MP and was appointed as a Cabinet minister in the second Jacob Zuma administration in 2014.

It was especially disappointing that, with his struggle history, he was to become a target in an investigation by the Hawks in early 2018 as they probed Zuma for allegedly accepting a R1-million cash bribe from a Western Cape abalone dealer, Deon Larry, in exchange for keeping Zokwana in his Cabinet. It was further alleged that Zokwana, together with Congress of South African Trade Unions (Cosatu) president S'dumo Dlamini and Department of Agriculture deputy director-general Siphokazi Ndudane, had each taken a R30,000 bribe from Larry.

In 2018, Zokwana was asked to motivate why he should not be held personally liable for legal costs arising from the unlawful suspension of his director-general, Michael Mlengana. Zokwana had placed Mlengana on precautionary suspension in July 2017, pending an investigation into allegations of gross misconduct against him. But as rumours of his investigations into corruption in the department deepened,

Mlengana challenged this, and the high court ruled that Zokwana lacked the authority to suspend him. Mlengana was allowed to return to work.

Zuma, Jacob

Nicknames: uBaba kaDuduzane (the father of Duduzane); Msholozi | Former president of the Republic of South Africa | Former deputy president | Former political prisoner |

Faced 16 charges relating to 783 payments which he allegedly received in connection with the controversial multibillion-rand arms deal | Investigated on other allegations of corruption | Linked to state capture | Acquitted of rape in 2006

ZUMA'S LEGACY WILL BE INEXTRICABLY LINKED to his virility and his venality, the one complementing the other in a vicious circle until he was finally forced out of office in February 2018.

Zuma, who grew up extremely poor in KwaZulu-Natal (KZN), left school effectively uneducated to take up menial jobs in Durban. A master tactician and exceptionally wily politician, he forged alliances that would eventually see him unseating his one-time nemesis Thabo Mbeki at the ANC's elective conference in Polokwane in 2007. His was a coalition of the walking wounded.

By then, Zuma had escaped being convicted on charges of raping HIV-positive activist Fezekile Kuzwayo, who came to be known as 'Khwezi', in his own Johannesburg home, and narrowly sidestepping corruption charges.

With the exception of the recalibration of South Africa's policy on HIV/AIDS and making anti-retrovirals freely available, his time in office would be a bleak period of patronage, entrenched cronyism, emasculating law enforcement and intelligence agencies and introducing state capture.

The cost to the nation had been staggering.

'State capture' became a euphemism for a kleptocracy that preyed especially upon state-owned enterprises (SOEs) seemingly to benefit Zuma's extended family, some Struggle activists, many civil servants and the notorious Gupta family who would, it was claimed, even have sign-off on some of the former president's Cabinet appointments.

Enmired in controversy while ensconsed in his palatial rural KZN homestead, Nkandla, which was 'upgraded' at an eye-watering cost to taxpayers, Zuma saw the ANC narrowly vote in his deputy, Cyril Ramaphosa, at its elective conference in December 2017, rather than his preferred candidate – and former wife – Nkosazana Dlamini-Zuma.

From then, the writing looked to be on the wall.

Zuma eventually resigned in February 2018 in very bad grace, facing an unprecedented ninth motion of no-confidence in Parliament, allowing Ramaphosa to take over. Zuma returned to KZN to lick his wounds, mobilise support and prepare for the charges he had spent more than 10 years trying to have quashed – legally and extra-judicially – using millions of rands in taxpayers' money.

Yet Zuma would not give up his reputation as the strongman. In April 2018, virginity testing lobbyist Nonkanyiso Conco, aged 24, announced she'd given birth to his child on his 76th birthday and was about to marry him. This would be Zuma's 23rd child and Conco his fifth concurrent wife. He had two others: Dlamini-Zuma (mentioned above), who divorced him in 1998, while Kate Mantsho-Zuma committed suicide at the age of 44 in 2000. Mantsho-Zuma described her life with Zuma as '24 years of hell'.

By May 2018, Zuma's legal campaign to fight his corruption prosecution appeared to be in disarray – mainly, it would appear, because there would not be enough money to fund every aspect of it.

But there was life in him yet, as ad hoc groupings of potential funders and supporters started to rise up on the sidelines of the national story, chief among them the African Transformation Congress (ATC). This amalgam of taxi fleet owners, traditional and religious leaders, former members of the Economic Freedom Fighters (EFF) and other political parties, and long-time supporters were seen to be canvassing to bring the ANC to the brink in KZN, and then hope to replicate that in other areas.

Select bibliography

101 Stalwarts

https://www.scribd.com/document/329211634/ANC-stalwarts-backing-Gordhan

https://www.dailymaverick.co.za/article/2017-03-10-the-anc-vs-the-stalwarts-the-great-betrayal-the-fight-back/#.WzJSkaczbIV

http://www.702.co.za/articles/262573/zuma-lashes-out-at-101-anc-stalwarts-in-policy-conference-opening-salvo

Abrahams, Shaun

https://www.news24.com/SouthAfrica/News/criminal-charges-filed-against-npa-boss-shaun-abrahams-20180223

https://www.huffingtonpost.co.za/2017/10/13/huffpost-weekly-review-shaun-the-sheep-must-step-up-timol-verdict-opens-pandoras-box-and-fikile-crushes-the-wrong-balls_a_23242408/

Africa Check

https://africacheck.org/about-us/

African National Council (ANC) Youth League

https://www.sahistory.org.za/topic/african-national-congress-youth-league-ancyl

ANC Veterans League

https://www.iol.co.za/news/politics/stalwarts-veterans-agree-to-work-with-anc-leadership-13731222

African Transformation Congress

https://www.iol.co.za/capetimes/news/church-call-to-deposit-money-with-zuma-lender-2095519

AfriForum

Barron, C (2018), 'Q & A with Kallie Kriel', *Sunday Times*, Johannesburg, https://constitutionallyspeaking.co.za/afriforum-cannot-prosecute-julius-malema-but-a-public-protector-report-does-raise-questions-about-his-honesty/

https://www.afriforum.co.za/tuis/

https://citizen.co.za/news/news-cns/1926171/apartheid-was-not-a-crime-afriforum/

http://capetalk.co.za/articles/303586/watch-it-s-not-surprising-what-kallie-kriel-said-about-apartheid

Armscor

https://www.dailymaverick.co.za/article/2019-01-18-auditor-general-drawn-into-armscors-r8bn-covert-deal-battle/

Arms Deal

http://www.corruptionwatch.org.za/whos-who-in-the-arms-deal/

Azanian Peoples Organisation (Azapo)

http://azapo.org.za/about-azapo/this-is-azapo/

Bapela, Obed

http://www.justice.gov.za/trc/hrvtrans%5Calex/bapela.htm
https://www.pa.org.za/person/kopeng-obed-bapela/

Black First Land First (BLF)

https://citizen.co.za/news/south-africa/2049399/iec-warns-blf-to-refrain-from-further-hate-speech/

Black Twitter

http://www.bizcommunity.com/Article/196/669/127133.html
https://www.superlinear.co.za/the-evolution-of-south-african-politics-as-seen-through-twitter/

Bongo, Advocate Bongani

https://www.news24.com/SouthAfrica/News/da-lays-corruption-charges-against-state-security-minister-bongani-bongo-20171122

Bosasa (African Global Operations)

https://www.news24.com/SouthAfrica/News/exclusive-how-bosasa-bragged-about-zuma-npa-influence-20180926
https://www.news24.com/SouthAfrica/News/fact-checked-da-claims-over-bosasaramaphosa-contract-denial-misleading-20181210

Breytenbach, Glynnis

https://www.iol.co.za/news/breytenbach-suspended-to-silence-her-1483326
https://www.news24.com/SouthAfrica/News/breaking-glynnis-breytenbach-acquitted-of-all-charges-in-npa-case-20180228
https://www.iol.co.za/news/south-africa/gauteng/i-deleted-files-to-protect-my-privacy-glynnis-breytenbach-tells-court-11529765l
https://www.timeslive.co.za/news/south-africa/2012-12-05-simelane-out-of-the-npa/
https://www.biznews.com/interviews/2013/12/12/huge-relief-as-constitutional-court-rules-for-kumba-sends-gupta-owned-ict-packing/
https://mg.co.za/article/2013-12-12-concourt-puts-sishen-mining-right-dispute-to-bed
https://www.news24.com/SouthAfrica/News/Breytenbach-seeks-reasons-suspension-20120503

BRICS

https://mg.co.za/article/2018-01-29-there-is-more-for-south-africa-in-brics

The Brown Umbrella

http://www.sabcnews.com/sabcnews/five-small-parties-merge-to-contest-2019-elections/

Bulwane, William

http://www.sabcnews.com/sabcnews/william-bulwane-resigns-mpl/

Buthelezi, Sfiso

http://ewn.co.za/2017/12/07/da-opens-criminal-case-against-sfiso-buthelezi-and-lucky-montana

https://www.iol.co.za/news/politics/sfiso-buthelezi-im-not-guilty-of-any-corrupt-dealings-9804500
https://www.huffingtonpost.co.za/2017/06/11/charge-deputy-finance-minister-sfiso-buthelezi-treasury-investi_a_22136587/

Cardo, Michael

Haffajee, F (2018), 'What Mmusi Maimane should do to fix the DA', *Huffington Post*, https://www.huffingtonpost.co.za/ferial-haffajee/what-mmusi-maimane-should-do-to-take-the-da-forward_a_23429667/
https://www.iol.co.za/news/politics/da-mps-stand-their-ground-in-policy-row-on-race-14095801

Cele, Bheki

https://www.pa.org.za/person/bhekokwakhe-hamilton-cele/
https://www.iol.co.za/news/south-africa/police-must-shoot-to-kill-worry-later-cele-453587
https://www.news24.com/Archives/City-Press/Bheki-Cele-Back-I-was-never-gone-20150430
http://www.sabcnews.com/sabcnews/bheki-cele-snubs-ace-magashule/
https://www.iol.co.za/news/south-africa/kwazulu-natal/pro-zuma-anc-kzn-members-lambast-nec-bheki-cele-14563733
https://city-press.news24.com/News/there-can-only-be-one-general-20180310
http://amabhungane.co.za/article/2011-06-24-cele-fingerprints-all-over-kzn-lease

Chamber of Mines

https://www.iol.co.za/business-report/companies/change-of-heart-on-mine-principle-14611072

Chester Missing

http://www.702.co.za/articles/1231/the-life-and-times-of-political-puppet-chester-missing-and-ventriloquist-conrad-koch

Coalitions

https://mg.co.za/article/2018-04-20-00-coalitions-will-become-the-new-normal

Confidence-and-Supply model

https://www.businesslive.co.za/rdm/politics/2016-08-18-anc-squeezed-out-in-hung-councils-as-eff-chooses-better-devil-da/

Commission for Gender Equality

http://www.cge.org.za/
http://www.cge.org.za/commissioners/
https://city-press.news24.com/News/rapping-gender-boss-is-a-human-wrecking-ball-20181211

Commissions of Inquiry

http://sacsis.org.za/site/article/2347

Congress of the People (COPE)

https://www.enca.com/news/afriforum-cope-team-fight-land-expropriation-without-compensation

https://www.news24.com/SouthAfrica/News/copes-lekota-steve-hofmeyr-unite-against-fascist-formation-blf-20181212

Congress of South African Trade Unions (Cosatu)

https://www.news24.com/SouthAfrica/News/we-wont-appeal-cosatu-expulsion-alliance-is-dead-numsa-20151109
https://mg.co.za/article/2014-11-08-numsa-expelled-from-cosatu
http://www.cosatu.org.za/show.php?ID=13466
http://www.politicsweb.co.za/opinion/the-end-of-cosatus-hegemony

The Commission for the Promotion and Protection of the Rights of Cultural, Religious and Linguistic Communities (CRL Rights Commission)

https://www.news24.com/SouthAfrica/News/crl-rights-commission-to-go-to-concourt-after-ngcobo-massacre-20180226

Cwele, Siyabonga

http://www.brainstormmag.co.za/cover-story/36-cover-story/9332-martin-czernowalow

Denel

https://www.fin24.com/Companies/Industrial/denels-new-board-places-cfo-on-special-leave-20180618
https://www.news24.com/SouthAfrica/News/supra-must-pay-back-denel-money-for-sons-bursary-da-20180617

Development Bank of Southern Africa

https://businesstech.co.za/news/banking/238301/development-bank-of-southern-africa-appoints-new-cfo/
https://citizen.co.za/news/south-africa/1939725/brics-bank-signs-mou-with-development-bank-of-sa/
https://www.businesslive.co.za/bd/opinion/2018-06-12-how-eff-and-state-bank-proponents-ignore-perils-and-limitations/

Didiza, Thoko

https://www.timeslive.co.za/sunday-times/news/2016-06-26-how-thoko-didiza-went-from-minister-to-vendor/
https://mg.co.za/article/2016-06-20-who-is-thoko-didiza-3
https://www.pa.org.za/person/angela-thokozile-didiza/

Diko, Khusela

https://www.thesouthafrican.com/khusela-diko-cyril-ramaphosas-spokesperson/

Dintwe, Inspector General Setlhomamaru

https://www.news24.com/SouthAfrica/News/state-security-dept-seeks-greater-independence-for-igis-office-20180518
http://amabhungane.co.za/article/2015-04-14-new-call-to-lift-veil-on-igi-appointment
http://ewn.co.za/2018/04/19/security-minister-restores-full-security-clearance-to-igi
http://politicsweb.co.za/politics/finally-a-new-inspectorgeneral-of-intelligence-is-

Dlakude, Doris

https://www.pa.org.za/person/dorries-eunice-dlakude/
https://city-press.news24.com/News/sas-descent-into-amoral-society-20160703

Dlamini, Bathabile

https://www.pa.org.za/person/bathabile-olive-dlamini/
http://ewn.co.za/2016/04/15/Bathabile-Dlamini-cries-after-being-insulted-by-angry-residents-in-PE
https://www.timeslive.co.za/politics/2018-05-14-government-not-the-constitution-should-hold-me-accountable-says-bathabile-dlamini/
https://www.businesslive.co.za/bd/national/2018-05-07-judge-slams-bathabile-dlamini-for-her-testimony-in-sassa-probe/

Dlamini, Cathy

Yende, S (2018), 'I will do anything the ANC wants', City Press, https://mg.co.za/article/2011-09-16-nelspruit-mayor-cathy-dlamini-splurges-on-us-trip

Dlamini, Sdumo

https://m.news24.com/SouthAfrica/News/hawks-probe-zuma-for-r1m-bribe-20180325-3
https://www.news24.com/SouthAfrica/News/r1m-bribe-for-zuma-exposes-crisis-levels-of-abalone-poaching-da-20180325

Dlamini-Zuma, Nkosazana

https://www.pa.org.za/person/nkosazana-dlamini-zuma/
https://www.sahistory.org.za/people/nkosazana-clarice-dlamini-zuma
Jika, T & Skiti, S (2017), 'Dlamini-Zuma's R250,000 Gupta award prize was from laundered money, affidavit alleges', *Sunday Times*, Johannesburg, https://www.timeslive.co.za/politics/2017-06-09-dlamini-zumas-r250000-gupta-award-prize-was-from-laundered-money-affidavit-alleges/
https://www.iol.co.za/news/politics/cabinetreshuffle-meet-your-new-cabinet-ministers-8447591

Dlodlo, Ayanda

https://mg.co.za/article/2017-03-31-fierce-loyalty-reaps-big-rewards

Dodovu, China

https://www.sowetanlive.co.za/news/south-africa/2018-05-25-black-jesus-saw-himself-as-a-saint-dodovu-says-power-corrupted-supra-mahumapelo/

Dramat, Anwa

https://mg.co.za/article/2015-04-22-hawks-boss-dramat-quits-after-reaching-settlement

Electoral Commission of South Africa

http://www.elections.org.za/content/about-us/FAQ--About Us/
http://www.capetalk.co.za/articles/301476/judge-kriegler-recounts-how-the-iec-helped-pull-off-the-miracle-94-elections, https://www.news24.com/SouthAfrica/News/newsmaker-2019-elections-results-will-be-credible-20171015-2
https://www.news24.com/SouthAfrica/News/75-of-voters-roll-updated-to-comply-with-concourt-ruling-20180207

https://www.businesslive.co.za/bd/national/2018-03-13-three-iec-commissioners-may-not-be-able-to-work-on-2019-election/, https://www.dailymaverick.co.za/article/2017-10-29-analysis-elections-2019-time-to-be-alert-as-iec-seeks-to-fill-key-vacancies/#.Wuqh6qSFMdU, https://www.iol.co.za/pretoria-news/iec-marks-20-years-since-its-inception-10176197

Dudley, Cherilynn

https://www.timeslive.co.za/news/south-africa/2017-11-30-parental-leave-breakthrough-national-assembly-passes-bill/

Eskom

https://www.moneyweb.co.za/news/companies-and-deals/sa-faces-lights-out-unless-ramaphosa-can-fix-eskom/

Estina 8

https://www.iol.co.za/news/south-africa/free-state/vrededairy-case-these-are-the-accused-and-the-charges-they-face-13298962

Equal Education

https://www.businesslive.co.za/bd/national/2018-05-10-angie-motshekga-reveals-plunge-in-education-spending-per-pupil/

Expropriation of land without compensation

https://www.news24.com/SouthAfrica/News/no-willing-buyer-willing-seller-in-the-constitution-albie-sachs-20170530

#FeesMustFall

http://www.thepresidency.gov.za/press-statements/release-report-commission-inquiry-feasibility-making-high-education-and-training

https://www.news24.com/SouthAfrica/News/zuma-announces-free-higher-education-for-poor-and-working-class-students-20171216

Fraser, Arthur

Pauw, J (2018), 'Now is the time to clean the spy agency rot', *Sunday Times*, Johannesburg

https://www.news24.com/SouthAfrica/News/state-security-agency-dg-arthur-fraser-moved-to-correctional-services-20180417

Freedom Front Plus

http://www.anc.org.za/content/ifp-alliance-freedom-front-plus-senzo-mchunu

Free State

https://www.iol.co.za/news/politics/move-to-block-magashules-replacement-13799941

https://www.news24.com/SouthAfrica/News/free-state-mecs-off-the-hook-after-npa-withdraws-corruption-charges-over-a-technicality-20180731

Frolick, Cedric

https://www.news24.com/SouthAfrica/News/Firepool-also-a-recreational-facility-Frolick-20150722 https://www.pa.org.za/person/cedric-thomas-frolick/

Froneman, Justice Johan

https://www.news24.com/SouthAfrica/News/concourt-orders-investigation-into-bathabiles-liability-for-social-grants-case-20170615

Gana, Makashule

https://www.news24.com/SouthAfrica/News/das-makashule-gana-aims-to-become-gautengs-next-premier-20180411

Gardee, Godrich

https://www.sowetanlive.co.za/news/2015-05-09-former-anc-exile-ups-political-stakes/

Gigaba, Malusi

https://www.gov.za/about-government/contact-directory/malusi-knowledge-nkanyezi-gigaba-mr
https://www.businessinsider.co.za/finance-minister-malusi-gigaba-is-the-biggest-enabler-of-state-capture-business-leadership-south-africa-ceo-says-2018-2
https://www.news24.com/SouthAfrica/News/gigaba-survives-while-other-gupta-ministers-get-the-chop-20180227
https://www.news24.com/SouthAfrica/News/gigaba-fights-for-his-political-life-20180414
https://www.dailymaverick.co.za/opinionista/2017-04-11-malusi-gigaba-zumas-pawn-or-future-king/#.WwbC_EiFPIU

Godongwana, Enoch

https://www.timeslive.co.za/politics/2012-01-16-enoch-godongwanas-shock-resignation/

Gordhan, Pravin

https://www.pa.org.za/person/pravin-gordhan/
https://www.news24.com/SouthAfrica/News/decision-to-recall-gordhan-from-roadshow-an-embarrassment-for-sa-cosatu-20170328
https://www.sahistory.org.za/archive/pravin-gordhan-hawks

Gungubele, Mondli

https://www.pa.org.za/person/m-gungubele/
http://www.tambofoundation.org.za/trustees/mondli-gungubele/
https://www.news24.com/SouthAfrica/News/i-will-still-vote-for-zuma-to-go-anc-mp-gungubele-20170728

Guptas

https://www.businesslive.co.za/bd/national/2018-05-28-victory-for-guptas-as-court-releases-assets-related-to-estina-matter/

Gupta leaks

https://www.aljazeera.com/investigations/spycables.html

Hadebe, Phakamani

https://www.businessinsider.co.za/five-things-we-didnt-know-about-phakamani-hadebe-eskoms-new-ceo-2018-5

Hanekom, Derek

https://www.timeslive.co.za/sunday-times/news/2018-03-17-after-the-fire-derek-hanekom-ready-for-his-second-act/
https://www.pa.org.za/person/derek-andre-hanekom/

Heher Commission

https://www.news24.com/SouthAfrica/News/sa-doesnt-have-money-for-free-higher-education-heher-commission-20171113

Helen Suzman Foundation

https://hsf.org.za/litigation
https://mg.co.za/article/2013-04-26-00-suzman-was-against-apartheid-but-she-was-not-for-liberation

Hlabisa, Velenkosini

https://www.iol.co.za/dailynews/buthelezis-successor-believes-he-can-take-the-ifp-forward-11773488l

Holomisa, Bantu

http://www.justice.gov.za/trc/media%5C1996%5C9608/s960801d.htm

Independent Police Investigations Directorate (IPID)

https://www.timeslive.co.za/news/south-africa/2017-11-29-ipid-police-agree-on--who-investigates-whom/

Independent Communications Authority of South Africa (ICASA)

https://www.huffingtonpost.co.za/2018/04/26/5-big-wins-for-cellphone-users-from-the-icasa-ruling_a_23420851/

Industrial Development Corporation (IDC)

https://www.businesslive.co.za/fm/features/2017-08-03-how-idc-is-trying-to-create-black-industrialists/

Inkatha Freedom Party (IFP)

https://mg.co.za/article/2014-04-24-buthelezi-ifp-fought-for-good-citizenship
https://www.iol.co.za/dailynews/opinion/uncovering-the-truth-behind-the-trust-feed-massacre-1283657

Institute for Security Studies (ISS)

https://issafrica.org/about-us/how-we-work#history

Industrial Policy Action Plan (IPAP)

http://www.bizcommunity.com/Article/196/516/177007.html

Jacobs, Faiez

https://www.dailymaverick.co.za/opinionista/2018-01-29-western-cape-dynamics-the-anc-remains-committed-to-affirming-all-communities/#.Wwfa8kiFPIU
https://city-press.news24.com/News/sacp-fights-purge-from-anc-lists-20181122

Jiba, Nomgcobo

https://www.news24.com/Archives/City-Press/Husband-of-NPA-boss-

pardoned-20150430
http://ewn.co.za/2015/05/05/NPAs-Lawrence-Mgwebi-denies-being-unfit-to-be-advocate
http://www.702.co.za/articles/308604/what-business-is-nomgcobo-jiba-doing-npa-offices
https://www.businesslive.co.za/bd/national/2016-09-27-npa-boss-abrahamss-predecessor-claims-he-is-under-his-deputys-spell/

Jim, Irvin
https://www.huffingtonpost.co.za/2018/05/02/ramaphosa-is-the-trump-of-sa-irvin-jim_a_23424983/
https://www.dailymaverick.co.za/article/2012-06-15-profile-of-a-hawk-numsas-irvin-jim/#.WwgObUiFPIU

Joemat-Pettersson, Tina
http://ewn.co.za/2017/11/30/tina-joemat-pettersson-to-get-over-r2-million-bonus

kaMagwaza-Msibi, Zanele
https://www.timeslive.co.za/politics/2017-10-04-infirm-kamagwaza-msibi-says-the-embattled-nfp-is-not-dead-yet/
https://www.pa.org.za/person/veronica-zanele-msibi/

Kekana, Pinky
https://www.iol.co.za/news/politics/ex-mec-abused-position-to-benefit-malema-1364643

Kodwa, Zizi
https://www.news24.com/SouthAfrica/News/at-48-zizi-is-back-on-the-market-20180120
http://www.702.co.za/articles/278103/zizi-kodwa-s-feelings-on-zuma-apparent-in-his-open-letter-stephen-grootes
https://www.businesslive.co.za/bd/politics/2018-02-25-ramaphosas-new-cabinet-is-likely-very-soon/

KPMG
https://www.iol.co.za/business-report/companies/kpmg-must-pay-sa-back-over-vbs-scandal-sarb-17435294

Kriel, Kallie
http://legal.un.org/avl/ha/cspca/cspca.html

Kubayi-Ngubane, Mmamoloko
https://www.news24.com/SouthAfrica/News/from-pregnant-teen-to-powerhouse-20171216
https://citizen.co.za/news/news-eish/1606932/you-must-pay-for-your-nkandla-sins-we-wont-praise-you/

Lamola, Ronald
https://www.news24.com/SouthAfrica/News/i-am-a-product-of-black-tax-says-ronald-lamola-as-he-graduates-again-20180417
https://citizen.co.za/news/south-africa/1911226/malema-implies-ronald-lamola-did-deal-with-zuma-after-his-expulsion/

Land Restitution

http://www.sahistory.org.za/dated-event/native-land-act-passed
http://www.ruraldevelopment.gov.za/about-us/the-department#.WwKLfEiFPIU
http://www.plaas.org.za/news/land-recap-pmg
https://pmg.org.za/committee-meeting/20002/
https://www.huffingtonpost.co.za/2018/03/26/how-the-anc-plans-to-roll-out-land-expropriation_a_23395490/
https://theconversation.com/south-africas-traditional-courts-bill-2-0-improved-but-still-flawed-74997

Limpopo

https://mg.co.za/article/2011-08-19-polokwanes-landed-gentry
https://www.iol.co.za/news/south-africa/limpopo/limpopo-premiers-road-to-wealth-uncovered-1222475

Local government

https://www.salga.org.za/Municipalities%20AM.html

Lungisa, Andile

https://www.news24.com/SouthAfrica/News/lungisas-marching-orders-20170319-2
http://www.destinyconnect.com/2017/03/12/andile-lungisa-gets-not-lead-anc-nelson-mandela-bay/

McBride, Robert

http://ewn.co.za/2018/05/25/mcbride-not-surprised-by-cedrick-nkabinde-s-allegations-against-him
https://www.dailymaverick.co.za/article/2018-03-20-newsflash-ipid-head-robert-mcbride-off-the-hook-for-child-abuse/#.Wwuk9UiFPIU
https://www.dailymaverick.co.za/article/2018-03-20-newsflash-ipid-head-robert-mcbride-off-the-hook-for-child-abuse/#.Wwuk9UiFPIU
https://www.news24.com/SouthAfrica/News/breaking-ipid-head-robert-mcbride-faces-imminent-arrest-20180210

McKinsey

https://www.huffingtonpost.co.za/2018/05/02/mckinsey-execs-will-personally-pay-back-eskoms-money_a_23425865/
https://www.news24.com/SouthAfrica/News/npa-applies-for-forfeiture-order-in-mckinsey-eskom-matter-20180524

Mabe, Pule

https://www.dailymaverick.co.za/article/2017-09-01-anc-pule-mabe-leaves-parliament-to-seek-other-pastures/#.Wwu1KEiFPIU
http://www.702.co.za/articles/303159/anc-s-pule-mabe-tied-to-r49-million-north-west-tender
https://www.sowetanlive.co.za/sundayworld/news/2018-12-16-ancs-mabe-denies--harassment-allegations/

Mabuyane, Oscar

http://www.dispatchlive.co.za/news/politics/2017/10/07/lowdown-ancs-new-ec-pec/
https://www.news24.com/SouthAfrica/News/eastern-cape-pec-court-hearing-postponed-20171121

https://citizen.co.za/news/south-africa/1799963/eastern-cape-anc-wants-zumas-exit-to-be-fast-tracked/
https://www.news24.com/SouthAfrica/News/eastern-cape-premier-appoints-new-pec-20180510

Mabuza, David "DD"

https://www.thedailyvox.co.za/why-is-everybody-so-afraid-of-dd-mabuza-fatima-moosa/
https://citizen.co.za/news/south-africa/1849331/da-takes-dd-mabuza-to-task-over-cabinet-ministers-bunking-parliament/

Mabuza, Jabu

http://ewn.co.za/2018/01/21/new-eskom-board-chair-jabu-mabuza-ready-for-the-task-ahead
https://www.iol.co.za/capetimes/news/ramaphosa-recused-himself-from-process-to-appoint-eskom-director-13816358

Madonsela, Advocate Thuli

https://citizen.co.za/news/south-africa/1755780/calls-mount-for-thuli-madonsela-to-take-charge-and-head-npa/

Magashule, Ace

https://mg.co.za/article/2018-01-05-00-aces-future-in-free-state-and-top-six-in-the-balance

Mahumapelo, Supra

'Hogarth' (2018), 'Not losing a moment's sleep', *Sunday Times*, Johannesburg
https://www.news24.com/Columnists/Ralph_Mathekga/ancs-problem-with-replacing-mahumapelo-20180430

Maile, Lebogang

https://citizen.co.za/news/south-africa/1938625/investigate-lebogang-maile-for-r29m-favour-to-pule-mabes-company-da/

Maimane, Mmusi

'Mampara of the Week' (2018), 'Mmusi Maimane: Not even a mini-Mandela', *Sunday Times*, Johannesburg, https://www.timeslive.co.za/politics/2018-06-02-maimanes-big-zille-regret-it-was-a-mistake-to-keep-her/

Maine, Collen

http://www.thenewage.co.za/collen-maine-i-was-taken-to-the-guptas-by-supra-mahumapelo/
https://citizen.co.za/news/south-africa/1892251/2ancwl-slams-collen-maine-for-selling-out-to-ramaphosa-after-nasrec/

Makhaya, Trudi

https://www.fin24.com/Economy/meet-trudi-makhaya-ramaphosas-new-economic-adviser-20180417

Makhura, David

https://www.news24.com/SouthAfrica/News/gauteng-premier-david-makhura-survives-no-confidence-vote-20180515

Malunga, Kevin

https://citizen.co.za/news/south-africa/1249418/five-things-standing-between-deputy-public-protector-and-top-job/

https://www.theindependent.co.zw/2016/08/19/malungas-son-misses-big-sa-post-dark-cloud/

Manana, Mduduzi

https://www.sowetanlive.co.za/sundayworld/news/2018-05-02-mduduzi-manana-tries-to-stop-club-brawl/

Manuel, Trevor

https://www.iol.co.za/news/politics/a-life-in-the-service-of-others-1661929

https://mg.co.za/article/2016-01-12-why-south-africa-should-undo-mandelas-economic-deals

Manyi, Mzwanele

https://mg.co.za/article/2018-04-22-manyi-settles-gupta-loan-after-amount-due-lowered

https://www.fin24.com/Companies/ICT/mzwanele-manyi-reveals-afro-worldview-shareholders-declares-business-unusual-20180605

Marikana massacre

https://www.washingtonpost.com/business/south-african-police-open-fire-on-striking-mine-workers-several-injured/2012/08/16/c9c99e3c-e7ad-11e1-9739-eef99c5fb285_story.html "South African police open fire as striking miners charge, killing and wounding workers", Archived from the original on August 17 2012, *The Washington Post*, Washington

Mashaba, Herman

https://www.dailymaverick.co.za/opinionista/2018-05-14-mashaba-attacks-the-poor-so-long-as-julius-malema-lets-him/#.Wv2bCIiFPIV

Mashatile, Paul

https://www.iol.co.za/news/politics/anc54-meet-paul-mashatile-the-man-who-will-control-the-anc-purse-12468701

https://mg.co.za/article/2007-08-31-mashatile-and-the-alex-mafia

Mashinini, Sam

https://mg.co.za/article/2018-05-25-00-mashinini-steers-away-from-zuma

Masina, Mzwandile

https://www.news24.com/SouthAfrica/News/im-very-happy-with-the-outcome-i-will-work-with-ramaphosa-masina-20171220

Masondo, David

https://city-press.news24.com/News/changing-the-anc-the-new-young-blood-20180213

Masualle, Phumulo

http://ewn.co.za/2018/05/08/ec-anc-gives-premier-masualle-deadline-to-reshuffle-his-cabinet

Masutha, Mazuvho

https://emergingresearchers.org/research-projects/
https://www.fin24.com/Economy/zumas-alleged-fee-free-education-advisor-morris-masutha-joins-pff-20180107
https://www.news24.com/SouthAfrica/News/exclusive-zumas-free-education-adviser-was-a-spy-20171113

Mathale, Cassel

https://www.iol.co.za/news/south-africa/limpopo/limpopo-premiers-road-to-wealth-uncovered-1222475

Mathys, Leigh-Ann

http://www.702.co.za/articles/288018/eff-member-shares-inspirational-story-behind-being-young-and-politically-conscious

Mazibuye

https://www.news24.com/SouthAfrica/News/anti-cyril-lot-lying-20180531
http://ewn.co.za/2018/05/30/pro-zuma-group-confirms-new-political-party-on-horizon

Mchunu, Senzo

https://www.news24.com/SouthAfrica/Politics/snapshot-of-senzo-mchunus-20-year-political-career-20160523
https://citizen.co.za/news/south-africa/1834839/senzo-mchunu-gets-full-time-post-at-luthuli-house-not-part-of-cyrils-new-cabinet/

Mdluli, Richard

https://www.dailymaverick.co.za/article/2018-01-17-analysis-the-rise-and-fall-of-richard-mdluli-a-man-who-damaged-our-society/#.WysaIqczbIU
https://www.dailymaverick.co.za/article/2012-12-12-the-spy-wars-continued-crime-intelligence-in-mdluli-turmoil/#.Wyt5i6czbIU
http://amabhungane.co.za/article/2011-11-11-top-cop-failed-polygraph-test-twice
https://www.news24.com/SouthAfrica/News/mdluli-has-earned-a-full-salary-during-suspension-20170403
https://www.sjc.org.za/who-is-richard-mdluli-a-fact-sheet-about-the-suspended-head-of-saps-crime-intelligence

Mfeketo, Nomaindia

https://www.dailymaverick.co.za/opinionista/2012-11-01-mfeketo-and-zuma-you-scratch-my-back-ill-scratch-yours/#.WzZBNKczbIU

Mkhize, Zweli

https://www.timeslive.co.za/politics/2018-06-10-zweli-mkhize-denies-r45-million-kickback-allegation/

Mkhwebane, Busisiwe

https://www.fin24.com/Economy/court-to-review-bankorp-ciex-report-on-apartheid-bailout-money-20171205
https://www.news24.com/Columnists/Mpumelelo_Mkhabela/how-busisiwe-mkhwebane-is-hollowing-out-her-offices-moral-authority-20180419

Modise, Thandi

https://www.parliament.gov.za/person-details-fancy/1732
https://www.sowetanlive.co.za/news/2016-05-20-modise-loses-appeal-over-malemas-marikana-massacre-comments/

Moerane Commission

https://www.timeslive.co.za/politics/2018-02-26-kzn-political-violence-takes-it-toll-on-election-costs/

Mogajane, Dondo

http://www.destinyconnect.com/2017/06/08/new-treasury-dg-dondo-mogajane/

Mokgoro, Job

https://citizen.co.za/news/south-africa/1960559/eff-rejects-job-mokgoros-appointment-as-north-west-premier/
https://www.dailymaverick.co.za/article/2018-06-21-the-compromise-premier-candidate-is-walking-into-a-political-minefield/#.Wy4qPqczbIU

Montana, Lucky

https://www.news24.com/SouthAfrica/News/revealed-cash-for-lucky-montanas-r135m-property-traced-to-r4bn-prasa-contractor-20180430

Motshekga, Angie

https://www.iol.co.za/news/politics/motshekgas-new-bid-to-lower-pass-mark-in-public-schools-13506082

Motshekga, Mathole

http://ewn.co.za/2018/05/31/mps-raise-concerns-over-new-hate-speech-bill

Moyane, Tom

https://www.dailymaverick.co.za/article/2018-05-07-analysis-charges-against-tom-moyane-serious-detailed-devastating/#.WxEEg0iFPIU
https://www.dailymaverick.co.za/article/2018-04-10-scorpio-analysis-the-case-against-the-npas-case-against-pillay-van-loggerenberg-and-janse-van-rensburg/#.WxEPXEiFPIU

Msimanga, Solly

https://www.businesslive.co.za/bd/national/2018-05-18-it-is-no-secret-i-do-not-have-tertiary-education-solly-msimangas-former-chief-of-staff-says/

Mthethwa, Nathi

https://www.huffingtonpost.co.za/2017/06/12/nathi-mthethwa-some-have-betrayed-zuma-like-judas-betrayed-jesu_a_22137169/

Mushwana, Lawrence

https://mg.co.za/article/2009-10-30-shock-r7m-payout-for-mushwana

Muthambi, Faith

https://www.news24.com/SouthAfrica/News/anc-and-da-mps-agree-that-muthambi-must-go-to-prison-20180327
http://ewn.co.za/2017/08/30/mps-to-seek-legal-advice-on-muthambi-for-misleading-parliament

National Assembly

https://pmg.org.za/page/political-party-representation
https://www.parliament.gov.za/how-parliament-is-structured

National Council of Trade Unions (Nactu)

https://www.sahistory.org.za/article/national-council-trade-unions-nactu

National Development Plan

https://www.dailymaverick.co.za/opinionista/2014-07-30-ndp-doomed-from-the-outset/#.WxKJOkiFPIU

The National Economic Development and Labour Council (Nedlac)

http://blueapple.co.za/ndlc/wp-content/uploads/2017/10/Nedlac-Founding-Declaration.pdf
http://nedlac.org.za/founding-documents/

National Energy Regulator of South Africa (Nersa)

https://www.fin24.com/Economy/Eskom/eskom-gets-the-nod-for-r326bn-in-clawback-tariffs-20180614
https://www.iol.co.za/business-report/energy/eskom-to-push-nersa-for-clawback-of-r66-billion-14413064
http://www.nersa.org.za/Admin/Document/Editor/file/About%20Nersa/Part%20Time%20Regulator%20Members/Mr%20Jacob%20Rasethlake%20Daniel%20Modise.pdf
https://www.linkedin.com/in/maleho-nkomo-67b73453/

National Executive Committee (ANC)

http://www.anc.org.za/officials/national-executive-committee-0

National Union of Metalworkers of South Africa (Numsa)

http://aidc.org.za/numsa-crisis-cosatu-now-remembering-numsa-moment/
https://www.numsa.org.za/history/

National Union of Mineworkers (NUM)

https://www.timeslive.co.za/sunday-times/business/2017-06-11-num-is-digging-itself-into-a-dark-hole/
https://www.enca.com/south-africa/exclusive-num-denies-its-captured-by-guptas

National Working Committee (ANC NWC)

http://www.anc.org.za/officials/national-working-committee-0
https://mg.co.za/article/2018-01-20-anc-elects-new-national-working-committee

Nene, Nhlanhla

https://www.fin24.com/Economy/nhlanhla-nene-to-chair-board-of-governors-of-brics-bank-20180529

New Development Bank

https://mg.co.za/article/2018-06-22-00-brics-bank-fails-to-live-up-to-hype
https://businesstech.co.za/news/business/248015/new-development-bank-appoints-nhlanhla-nene-as-chairman/

New Growth Path

http://www.ilo.org/jobspact/news/WCMS_151955/lang--en/index.htm

Ngwenya, Gwen

https://www.iol.co.za/sunday-tribune/news/new-da-mp-gwen-ngwenya-is-a-polemicist-of-note-13585950

Ntombela, Sisi

Mhlabathi, H (2018), 'I am my own person', *City Press*, Johannesburg

Nxasana, Mxolisi

http://ewn.co.za/2017/11/21/high-court-says-mxolisi-nxasana-was-party-to-a-bribe

Organisation Undoing Tax Abuse (OUTA)

https://www.news24.com/SouthAfrica/News/i-am-not-a-dictator-outa-ceo-on-allegations-of-bad-governance-20180426

https://www.dailymaverick.co.za/article/2012-06-19-outas-wayne-duvenage-out-of-avis/#.WyeEGaczbIU

O'Sullivan, Paul

www.702.co.za/articles/322294/sunday-times-has-seven-days-to-confess-to-state-capture-role-warns-o-sullivan

https://www.timeslive.co.za/news/south-africa/2017-12-08-forensic-investigator-paul-osullivan-to-sue-state-for-r193-million/

Pan-Africanist Congress (PAC)

https://citizen.co.za/news/south-africa/1754612/narius-moloto-appointed-new-pac-president/

Passenger Rail Association of South Africa (PRASA)

https://www.businesslive.co.za/bd/companies/transport-and-tourism/2018-06-05-sibusiso-sithole-appointed-ceo-of-prasa/

https://mg.co.za/article/2018-06-06-prasa-chair-new-board-members-wont-stick-heads-in-sand

Patriotic Alliance

http://www.polity.org.za/article/patriotic-alliance-committed-to-nelson-mandela-bay-coalition-until-2021-2018-04-11

Phahlane, Khomotso

https://www.news24.com/SouthAfrica/News/phahlane-due-to-be-charged-with-corruption-20180207

https://citizen.co.za/news/south-africa/1402671/details-inside-the-phahlane-investigation/

https://www.news24.com/SouthAfrica/News/more-accused-could-be-added-to-phahlane-corruption-case-20180312

https://www.dailymaverick.co.za/article/2018-04-20-police-tech-head-lieutenant-general-adeline-shezi-allegedly-spent-saps-millions-on-house-construction/#.WxUWj0iFPIU

https://techcentral.co.za/eoh-was-caught-up-in-state-capture-war-asher-bohbot/80451/

Phiyega, Riah

https://www.news24.com/SouthAfrica/News/zuma-appoints-new-acting-police-boss-to-replace-phahlane-20170601

Premier League

https://www.huffingtonpost.co.za/2017/12/19/the-rise-of-the-premier-league-and-their-failed-bid-to-install-ndz_a_23310554/

Public Investment Corporation (PIC)

https://www.businesslive.co.za/bd/national/2018-06-08-pic-pays-it-executive-r7m-to-leave/
https://www.iol.co.za/business-report/companies/treasury-backs-dan-matjila-15237963
https://mg.co.za/article/2018-04-13-pic-will-not-invest-in-sagarmatha
https://www.businesslive.co.za/bd/national/2018-12-10-public-investment-corporation-inquiry-targets-steinhoff--bee-deal/
https://www.thesouthafrican.com/ramaphosa-commission-of-inquiry-public-investment-company/

Public Protector

https://constitutionallyspeaking.co.za/constitutional-court-nkandla-judgment-some-questions-answered/

Ramaphosa, Cyril

https://select.timeslive.co.za/ideas/2018-05-14-zumas-ghost-lingers-as-his-cronies-gun-for-ramaphosa/

Ramulifho, Khume

https://www.news24.com/SouthAfrica/News/da-must-take-the-mazzone-election-to-court-itself-da-mpl-20180416
http://da-gpl.co.za/team-page/khume-ramulifho/

Selfe, James

https://www.dailymaverick.co.za/article/2018-04-04-road-to-the-da-federal-congress-james-selfe-partys-enforcer-in-chief/#.WyoSFqczbIU

Ses'Khona

https://www.timeslive.co.za/politics/2018-06-14-cape-town-suspends-poo-thrower-after-it-hits-the-fan-on-facebook/

Shaik, Schabir

https://omalley.nelsonmandela.org/omalley/index.php/site/q/03lv03445/04lv04015/05lv04148/06lv04149.htm

South African Broadcasting Corporation (SABC)

https://www.businesslive.co.za/bd/national/2018-02-13-special-investigating-unit-delivers-r21m-blow-to-hlaudi-motsoeneng/

South African Human Rights Commission (SAHRC)

https://www.sahrc.org.za/index.php/sahrc-media/news/item/1014-cancer-patients-must-wait-until-march-2018-for-first-appointment
https://www.news24.com/SouthAfrica/News/go-home-eff-mp-tells-sahrc-candidate-20161014

https://mg.co.za/article/2012-09-11-mps-criticise-sahrc-for-marikana-investigation
https://www.sahrc.org.za/index.php/about-us/commissioners

South African Local Government Association (SALGA)

https://nationalgovernment.co.za/units/view/171/south-african-local-government-association-salga
http://ewn.co.za/2018/06/19/salga-facing-de-registration-for-breach-of-labour-act
https://www.pa.org.za/blog/who-are-salga-and-what-do-they-do
https://www.fin24.com/Economy/Labour/News/salga-smooths-municipal-wage-talks-after-dispute-20180628

South African National Civics Organisation (SANCO)

https://www.patrickheller.com/uploads/1/5/3/7/15377686/civics_rr84.pdf

Sisulu, Lindiwe

https://mg.co.za/article/2018-06-10-sisulu-un-security-council-tenure-will-be-dedicated-to-mandelas-legacy
https://www.groundup.org.za/article/sisulu-drafting-amendments-eviction-laws_2641/

Sitole, Khehla

https://www.news24.com/SouthAfrica/News/breaking-zuma-appoints-new-national-police-commissioner-20171122
https://www.businesslive.co.za/fm/fm-fox/2017-11-30-profile-meet-sas-new-police-chief-khehla-sitole/

South African Communist Party (SACP)

https://www.enca.com/south-africa/zuma-the-worst-leader-anc-has-ever-had-sacp
https://www.dailymaverick.co.za/article/2017-12-03-sacp-tests-the-waters-in-by-election-fires-warning-shot-to-anc/#.WuA5h4hubIU

South African Federation of Trade Unions (SAFTU)

http://saftu.org.za/the-federation/
http://saftu.org.za/affiliates/
http://theconversation.com/south-africas-strike-rate-isnt-as-bad-as-its-made-out-to-be-95470?utm_source=facebook&utm_medium=facebookbutton
https://citizen.co.za/news/south-africa/1905334/todays-strike-a-test-for-saftu-vs-cosatu/

South African Police Service (SAPS)

https://www.saps.gov.za/about/history.php

Survé, Dr Iqbal

Van Rensburg, D (2018), 'Iqbal Survé threatens to sue for "hundreds of millions, if not billions"', *City Press*, Johannesburg, https://city-press.news24.com/Business/iqbal-surve-threatens-to-sue-for-hundreds-of-millions-if-not-billions-20181218

Trade unions

https://www.timeslive.co.za/news/south-africa/2018-04-25-joburg-hit-by-multiple-protests-aside-from-strike/

Transnet

https://www.biznews.com/good-hope-project/2018/05/24/ramaphosa-transnet-popo-molefe-gets-busy/

Trillian

https://www.businesslive.co.za/fm/features/cover-story/2017-10-04-how-mckinsey-and-trillian-milked-billions-from-sa-inc/
https://www.fin24.com/Economy/npa-concludes-eskom-payments-to-mckinsey-and-trillian-were-criminal-20180117

VBS

https://www.businesslive.co.za/bd/companies/financial-services/2018-05-07-vbs-bank-saga-takes-another-turn-with-the-raid-on-vele-investments/
Van Rensburg, D (2018), 'VBS loans bonanza', *City Press*, Johannesburg

Yengeni, Tony

http://news.bbc.co.uk/2/hi/africa/1577682.stm

Zokwana, Senzeni

https://www.businesslive.co.za/bd/national/2017-07-12-agriculture-minister-senzeni-zokwana-suspends-his-director-general/
https://www.pa.org.za/person/senzeni-zokwana/
https://www.sowetanlive.co.za/news/south-africa/2018-03-27-senzeni-zokwana-denies-corruption-claim/
https://www.iol.co.za/business-report/economy/zokwana-may-be-liable-for-legal-costs-14638202

Zwane, Mosebenzi

https://www.sowetanlive.co.za/news/south-africa/2018-01-29-im-a-river-says-zwane-on-being-labelled-a-gupta-stooge/

Zuma, Jacob

https://mobile.nytimes.com/2018/04/16/world/africa/south-africa-corruption-jacob-zuma-african-national-congress.html?smid=fb-share
https://constitutionallyspeaking.co.za/constitutional-court-nkandla-judgment-some-questions-answered/
http://www.anc.org.za/officials/national-executive-committee-0
https://mobile.nytimes.com/2018/04/16/world/africa/south-africa-corruption-jacob-zuma-african-national-congress.html?smid=fb-share
https://select.timeslive.co.za/ideas/2018-06-25-zumas-fight-back-is-on-and-its-going-to-get-nasty/